raindance
producers' lab:
lo-to-no budget
filmmaking

To the person who

first showed me how to produce

– and get things done

Dorothy Helen Bechtel Grove

raindance producers' lab: lo-to-no budget filmmaking

ELLIOT GROVE

AMSTERDAM BOSTON HEIDELBERG LONDON NEW YORK OXFORD
PARIS SAN DIEGO SAN FRANCISCO SINGAPORE SYDNEY TOKYO
Focal Press is an imprint of Elsevier

Focal Press is an imprint of Elsevier
The Boulevard, Langford Lane, Kidlington, Oxford, OX5 1GB
30 Corporate Drive, Suite 400, Burlington, MA 01803, USA

First edition 2004
Reprinted 2004, 2005, 2006, 2008, 2009

British Library Cataloguing in Publication Data
A catalogue record for this book is available from the British Library

Library of Congress Cataloging-in-Publication Data
A catalog record for this book is available from the Library of Congress

ISBN: 978-0-240-51699-8

For information on all Focal Press publications
visit our website at www.elsevierdirect.com

Printed and bound in *Great Britain*

09 10 10 9 8 7 6

Working together to grow
libraries in developing countries

www.elsevier.com | www.bookaid.org | www.sabre.org

ELSEVIER   BOOK AID International   Sabre Foundation

Contents

Processing techniques – Process control – Force (push) processing – Cross-processing – Bleach bypass processing – Processing errors – Censorship – Printmaking – Black and white printing – Colour printing – Types of printers and their uses – Answer prints – Enlargement and reduction – Blowing up to 35mm – Internegatives and interpositives – Digital internegatives

movies – Bollywood – Exhibitors – Who buys films? – Attracting acquisitions executives – Career route of acquisitions executives – Choosing
your niche – Key artwork – Creating a one sheet – Trailers – In conversation with Graham Humphries

ments – Distribution deals – Anatomy of the box office – Why films are released in cinemas – Other release windows – Pay hotel or airline – Home video and pay cable – Terrestrial television – Ancillary – Alternative methods of distribution (in consultation with Claes Loberg) – Alternative buyers of your film – Branded entertainment – Self-distribution – Digital distribution – Distribution on the Internet – Censorship – In conversation with Simon Franks

Power tools for creating a business plan – 1: Pedigree – 2: Creating comparisons – 3: Creating a brand – 4: Running a business – Contents of a professional business plan for presenting to private investors – Presenting to the private investor – Business plan mistakes – 1: Unrealistic revenue projections – 2: Misleading foreign sales charts – 3: Hyping the audience – 4: The actor's influence – 5: Mentioning *The Blair Witch Project* – 6: The promise – Presenting to the industry: The package – Issues you must address – Legal advice – Blue sky rules

1: Measure success by more than a theatrical release – 2: Learn how to use agents – 3: Pre-sales – 4: New money vs old money – 5: Festivals besides Toronto, Cannes and Sundance – 6: Sales agents do not advance money – 7: Big sale vs big career – 8: Success is relative – 9: Get a sales agent early on – 10: If it ain't on the page it ain't on the stage

The development path – Securing story rights – 1: Public domain – 2: Copyright reports – 3: Chain of title – 4: Fact-based stories – Writer's contract – E and O – Copyright registration – Titles – Development financing – What is development money? – Typical development budget – How development finance deals are structured – Sources of development finance – The UK Film Council – Tools for raising development finance – The package – Making your project attractive – Pitfalls to raising development finance – In conversation with Tracey Scoffield

Private funding – Loans – Equity investment – Equity pitfalls – Family and friends – Pre-sales and foreign sales agents – Gap finance – Completion guarantee – Co-productions and European tax incentives – Bilateral treaties – General treaty restrictions – Finding a suitable co-producer – Structure of the co-production agreement – Application procedure – Sale and leaseback – In consultation with Dean Goldberg – The definition of a British film – Issues for British producers entering sale and leaseback – Other tax incentives – Deferrals – Other sources of funding – Strategies for raising finance – Seven essential steps: Step 7 – Talent

Preface

Just Do It

I started Raindance Film Festival in 1992 with a view to promoting independent filmmaking in London. At that time a pervasive gloom hung over the British film industry, with only six films being made that year. A once thriving British feature film industry had suffered a severe demise with the advent of TV. At the time, I was considered misguided, and Raindance was expected to collapse quickly.

But the notion of independent filmmaking, and indeed Raindance, has thrived to the extent that we are now one of the leading film festivals in Europe and together with British Independent Film Awards, are a force to be reckoned with. Independent film has become one of the buzz words of the cultural élite. Hollywood studios spend millions making films look like independent films – films like *Lost In Translation* and *The Good Girl* to name but two.

I have noticed that many people call themselves filmmakers, that many people threaten to make films, but few actually do. Why?

Partly because the barriers to making and successfully selling an independent film remain impossibly high and partly because many merely claim the title filmmaker with no real intention of making one. So many become discouraged by the rejection and the amount of work involved.

The only secret to my success at Raindance is that I have kept going against all odds and at 3.30am with torrential rain and storm clouds gathering, I endure. Never to quit. You do it too.

For those of you who seriously think of making a film, I have this advice: just do it.

Elliot Grove
London, January 2004

Acknowledgements

The film industry is a fiercely competitive industry and notorious for the hard work, low pay and broken dreams of filmmakers. It is an industry that is also full of inspiration, hope and incredible success stories. One of the best reasons for working at Raindance is the diverse range of talented and inpiring people one meets. No other job has as much to offer, no other industry full of such amazingly talented people.

This book is the result of my work at Raindance for nearly twelve years, and the meetings and associations I have had with hundreds of people. Three stand out – my editor, Christina Donaldson of Focal Press, whose energy and patience mentored this book; Dominic Thackray, visionary and therapist extraordinaire and Deena Manley, editor, typesetter and advisor.

It also goes without saying that I could not have done this without the love and support of my partner, Suzanne Ballantyne, who nurtured and supported me throughout.

I also thank the tireless staff at Raindance, past and present, whose suggestions and advice enrich this book, in particular Damjan Bogdanovic, Johanna von Fischer, Oli Harbottle, Chris Thomas, Emma Luckie, Emma Davis, Oscar Sharp, Rachael Castell and Tessa Collinson.

I also thank the thousands of filmmakers from all over the world who have submitted to Raindance Film Festival the products of their work, as well as the British filmmakers, actors, directors, writers, producers, actors, agents, and distributors who have supported the British Independent Film Awards. I also thank the members of Raindance who have seen us grow and who are my true audience.

To the hundreds of talented writers, directors, producers and actors who have crossed my path and offered friendship, assistance and inspiration over the years I thank you for the wisdom and experience you have shared that has made this book possible.

About the Author

Mesmerised by the moving image from a young age, but unable to watch TV or films until his early teens due to the constraints of his Amish background, Canadian-born Elliot Grove followed formal art school training with a series of behind-the-scene jobs in the industry.

He worked for nine years as a scenic artist and set designer on sixty-eight feature films and over seven hundred commercials in his native Toronto, where he developed a distaste for the wasted resources on set and union red tape that prevented filmmaker wannabes like himself from getting their own features off the ground.

Elliot moved to London in the late 1980s and nine years ago, when the British film industry was drowning in self-pity, launched the Raindance Film Festival devoted to independent filmmaking and emerging talent.

Initially, Raindance catered mainly to American independents who understood that the combination of a positive mental attitude and a pioneering spirit provides the essential foundation upon which to produce and distribute films successfully. Happily, that attitude has now filtered through to the UK; independent filmmaking, once a small organism, has become a global phenomenon. Elliot is proud of the fact that last year's Raindance line-up included over a hundred independent features from over thirty countries.

Upholding the ethos of Raindance, Elliot wrote, produced and directed the feature, *Table 5*, for just over £200. He also lectures on screenwriting and filmmaking throughout the UK and Europe, and in 1992 set up the training division of Raindance which now offers over two dozen evening and weekend masterclasses on writing, directing, producing and marketing a feature film. Elliot firmly believes that success in the moviemaking business is a simple matter of demystifying the process of breaking into the film industry and allowing individual talent to prosper. In 1998 Elliot founded the British Independent Film Awards to promote British talent.

This is Elliot's second book. His first, *Raindance Writers' Lab: Write and Sell the Hot Screenplay* was also published by Focal Press.

Elliot lives in London with his partner and two daughters.

1   Nobody Knows Anything

LET ME INTRODUCE MYSELF. I am an Amish farm boy with absolutely no training in film. In fact, as a child and teenager I was forbidden to watch movies. Then I got hooked. I snuck off to the cinema and saw *Lassie Comes Home*. I had absolutely no idea that a movie house existed, and no knowledge of the technology that made moving pictures possible. I could have landed on the moon, instead of that soiled, worn, red velvet seat with springs edging out of it. As soon as I could, I left the farm, and moved to London where I got a job sweeping floors and building sets at the BBC in its glory years: the final years of *Monty Python*, and *The Old Grey Whistle Test* were my playground – and an ideal playground it was. I suppose I saw every star of the time, from Mohammed Ali coming in for an interview, to British and American pop stars sneaking in the gates past the hordes of screaming fans, to politicians trying to bolster their ratings.

So what gives me any authority to talk about filmmaking? Nothing at all. Despite having acquired dozens of producer credits on shorts and features, having worked as a scenic artist and set designer on over seven hundred commercials and sixty-eight feature films, and running Europe's largest independent film festival for twelve years I have no formal film school training. Everything I have learned I have learned by watching and doing.

Hint No one can teach you how to make a film. You have to learn it by doing it. You might be better off putting this book down right now, grabbing a camera, any camera, and starting to shoot a film.

I am warning you right now that I don't know anything about filmmaking. But before you go back screaming to the bookshop to get a refund, or before you start thinking that I'm just another smart-talking Canuck trying to get a few coins out of your pocket, let me explain further what I mean when I say that I don't really know anything about filmmaking. To quote a Hollywood legend: 'nobody knows anything'.

The film industry is distinct from other manufacturing industries because of the way movies are made. Every film project is unique. Each film reaches its completed state via a different route. This distinguishes the film industry from, say, the automotive industry. In the automotive industry, if you have an idea for a car, first of all you draw it, build a prototype and test-drive it. Then you fix all the mechanical flaws. Once that stage is complete, you are then able to test-market the prototype. After the marketing men have their say, it's back to the drawing board to iron out any little wrinkles. Then voilà, a car is born, and born in the knowledge that it will perform to a certain pre-tested financial model.

However, in the film industry every project is a prototype. There is no chance to redesign a bad movie. You either make it a good film and sell it or you make a stinker. And unless you have had to face an investor in your movie asking you where their money went, you really don't know the true meaning of the word 'pain'.

Nobody knows anything.

Why Nobody Knows Anything

Banks

Do you believe that you could go to your local high street bank, walk into the manager's office and a few minutes later convince the bank manager to give you a loan for the entire budget of the film? A bank will give you the money if you have enough collateral. This is where my mother has always known more about independent filmmaking than me. She always says that you can tell the independent filmmakers in the crowd because they are the ones without a real job.

My friend Simon Onworah didn't let his lack of creditworthiness stop him. Needing to raise £50,000 ($75,000) for his first feature film, *Welcome to the Terrordome*, he got agreement in principle from Barclays Bank, Soho Square branch in London. This particular bank is a media bank and accustomed to servicing the financial requirements of film and television companies. The catch was that Simon needed to offer assets or other financial instruments to secure the loan. Perhaps the bank manager knew my mother.

In order to provide security for the loan, Simon decided to find fifty people agreeing to sign a loan agreement at Barclays for £1000 each. It was his 'Welcome to the Film Industry' plan and it went like this: 'If the film does well at the box office, you will get a percentage of the profits, if it performs poorly, you are on the hook to Barclays for forty months. Win or lose, at least you will get an opening title credit with your name down (along with 49 others) as producer.'

Unfortunately, the fifty producers had to plump for plan B after the film was unceremoniously trashed by the critics. The producers finished their 'Welcome to the Film Industry' plan about a year ago. But each of those producers has something you don't have: a credit as producer on a feature film that was released in cinemas. You might think that this is a bit superficial. Let's do a quick reality check here. Have you ever told someone that you accomplished, experienced or did something that you actually didn't do? At least these people have a movie with their name on it (and a wedge of bank paying-in slips).

The point is, nobody knows anything.

Channel 4

Channel 4 is one of the most successful film production companies in the world. Could you walk in as a director and producer team with little previous experience and walk out with over £2 million ($3 million) for your first feature? Do you think you could do that?

This is the story of producer Jeremy Bolt and writer/director Paul Anderson, who managed to get their entire film funded. Jeremy had some experience as a line producer on Ken Russell's pictures, and Paul had made some shorts. But neither had taken sole responsibility for a feature film. In order to get the money they had to convince the then Head of Development, Jack Lechner, that they had talent. They surrounded themselves with a veteran crew, all of whom were known to Channel 4. They made the movie *Shopping*. The movie was critically blasted and did virtually no box office. However, the film showed at Sundance, where Jeremy, a masterful salesman, managed to parley this commercial disaster into a directing job for Paul on *Mortal Kombat*. *Event Horizon* and *Soldier* quickly followed. Jeremy and Paul each command top fees for their services now. The lesson here is that even if the picture fails commercially, if the director has given it a 'look' it will still be good for the director's career. Terrible for the producer's career, however! Nobody knows anything.

Hint A commercial disaster may not affect a director's career at all. In fact, a film with a 'look' can enhance a director's career, although it can destroy a producer's.

Money

Do you think you could take a total of sixty cast and crew a hundred miles from London and plop them down in a hotel in the seaside resort of Blackpool, and shoot for six weeks without a penny?

Ask producer Lois Wolfe how she coped on her first shoot – *Seaview Knights* – without a penny.

She worked like a Trojan for a year and a half, raised the money, left with cast, crew and kit on a Sunday night for Blackpool only to be greeted by a telegram from her lawyer telling her that the financing had fallen through. Her lawyer begged her to stop and send everyone home. What to do? Lois decided not to tell anyone. After all, she had everything she needed to make a film. She had the 35mm camera kit, she had the film stock, and she had the crew and the cast. She started shooting, and used to call me collect from the payphone in the hotel whispering, 'I have no money!' Somehow she struggled on, until, with a few days to go, she was forced to stop. She went back to London, raised the finance and finished the film a few weeks later.

I am always fascinated by what causes disaster in improbable situations like this. Obviously the lack of cash was the problem. No, it wasn't the massive hotel and catering bill, or the grumpy technicians who had not been paid: it was the electricity bill at the hotel that the film's lights were plugged into that was the proverbial straw that broke the film's financial back. Nobody knows anything.

Scripts

Do you need a screenplay to make a film?

It is curious that the financial advisers to film companies know very little about scripts. Some even pride themselves in the fact that they never read a script.

The answer to this is yes. Unless you are Ken Loach, Mike Leigh or Jon Jost, all of whom have developed their careers as filmmakers over many years, you will need a script. Established filmmakers like Loach, Leigh and Jost have created a new approach to scripts. They may not work with a traditional screenplay, but they have scene outlines. Starting out, you will need a script if you intend to raise money for your project, even if that money is raised from relatives. Everyone will want to see a blueprint for your movie, and that script/blueprint had better be good enough to enable them to visualise the project through to completion.

In Mike Figgis' *Timecode*, the script was written on musical staves: one for each of the four cameras. The bar lines represented the minutes. The actors all synchronised their watches, and knew by looking at their scripts where their cues were: e.g. call at minute twelve to the actors at camera number two.

Lights

Have you heard the phrase 'Lights, camera, action'? Do you think you can make a film without lights?

Shooting with lights is good. Films shot with lights look very good. Remember that lights are expensive, and there can be another way to make a film without lights. Your film made without lights will look good, too – but different from a film shot with lights.

You can indeed. Eric Rohmer started the practice and developed what he termed shooting with available light. The practice is widely spread. To shoot with available light, you simply have to use a camera, or use film stock that is sensitive to a wide range of lighting conditions. If you are shooting indoors and need or want a bit of extra light to bump up an image, then you can insert Photoflood light bulbs – light bulbs that are corrected for the temperature of the film you are using. They are available in photo shops and hardware stores for about £1.25 ($2).

The advantage of working with available light is that you can work cheaply and quickly. A big advantage of shooting without lights is that you lose the lighting truck that needs an expensive parking bay, and expensive electricians. In the UK, an electrician's pay starts at £250

($375) for a nine-hour day. On top of that are travel and overtime. The other large expense is food. In the UK a film caterer will start at £10 ($15) per head per day, depending on the menu. The lighting truck itself contains up to ten thousand different items, large and small. It can cost upwards of £10,000 ($15,000) per day to rent a lighting truck.

The other disadvantage is the quality of work achievable in a limited time on a lo-to-no budget shoot. With a formal lighting crew, not only does it take up to an hour to light and re-light each angle on a location, there are at least another four people working on the set. If your scene is an intimate scene, for example, a director or assistant director screaming 'Quiet on the set' will also destroy the ambience.

By shooting with available light, it is possible to set up a shot in a matter of minutes. If the cinematographer or the director dislikes what they see through the viewfinder, the camera can easily be moved. In order to commence a take, the director works with the actors as well as the cinematographer and sound person without the encumbrance of an additional dozen lighting crew. The scenes will be done quicker and more efficiently. In addition, the director will have much more contact with the actors because of the absence of technology.

Nobody knows anything. When we shot *Table 5*, my cinematographer/director of photography, James L. Solan, lit scenes with a couple of practicals (Photofloods) screwed into gooseneck lamps. If there wasn't quite enough light, he simply put a white card on the wall or ground. Sometimes he would bounce an additional light off the ceiling.

A Photoflood or practical light bulb, available from any camera shop, is a light bulb colour corrected to tungsten light that produces more light than a normal bulb. A scene lit with a practical will look normal on the exposed film, and not bluish or greenish as it would if shot with normal light bulbs.

 To see an example of a scene lit by Jim using available light in a basement with no windows, view the CD.

Hint By using a 35mm or digital stills camera you will learn how different lighting situations affect image capture.

Camera

Who would think that a film could be made without a camera?

The American experimental filmmaker Stan Brakhage made films by scratching and drawing on old film stock. His films are enjoyed by experimental film fans around the world and do not use cameras.

What about Pixelvision? Pixelvision is the trade name for the PXL-2000 video camera made by Fisher-Price in the late 1980s. Its original marketing niche was aimed at yuppie parents of young children seeking to discover whether or not their progeny had what it took to become the next Mozart of the cinema. The marketing programme was a disaster, and the camera was discontinued. Independent filmmakers discovered Pixelvision cameras. Films made on Pixelvision started showing up at film festivals. Since then, the camera has developed a cult following. The PXL-2000 records audio and video on ordinary type audiocassette tapes, fitting about five minutes per side on a 90-minute tape. This limited bandwidth produces an image where the overall effect is grainy, with lots of dropout and a weird, almost slow motion appearance.

Whenever you see a movie, short or feature on TV or in a cinema, ask yourself three questions:

1. Does this show any talent?
2. How did they do that?
3. Could I do it?

Jack Lechner was Head of Development at Channel 4 in London and left to work as Head of Development at HBO. He was headhunted and became Head of Development at Miramax during the glory years of films like *Four Weddings and a Funeral*, *Good Will Hunting* and *Shakespeare in Love*. Jack didn't renew his three-year contract and wrote a fascinating book, *Can't Take My Eyes Off You* (2000), about his experiences behind and in front of the television screen. He is currently developing a series of television shows in the USA.

The first time I saw a Pixelvision movie was with Jack Lechner of Channel 4 at a London arts organisation. At that time, in addition to his production and development role, he was also able to suggest films to Channel 4 for purchase. He knew about my passion for independent film and video and invited me to see the work of an outrageously talented young New York filmmaker, Sadie Benning. As we watched the film, Jack kept commenting on the film's dramatic and witty dialogue, the incredibly hip musical score and the interesting camera movements. The film, a short, concerned the filmmaker's first sexual experience. Suddenly Jack went quiet, as the camera moved in on the actress's mouth and chin (played by Sadie Benning). While she was discussing her emotional sexual encounter, it appeared as if she was sucking a penis. Jack immediately commented that he didn't think that the British public was ready for such a scene. Suddenly the camera zoomed back and we could see that the girl was in fact sucking her thumb. The filmmaker had used the terrible image quality to her advantage. A few scenes later it appeared that a wrecked car was abandoned in the middle of what us non-New Yorkers would call a stereotypical New York park. Suddenly a giant hand shot into frame and moved the Dinky car out of shot.

Hint Make a film with what you have, not with what you want.

But even Pixelvision uses a camera. What about a 35mm feature film made with no camera at all?

This is the true story of a friend of mine from my hometown, Toronto. Lucy used to cycle through downtown Toronto on a Friday night, past the back doors of all the major film editing companies. Toronto is a major centre of film production. As she cycled by, she would look for the off-cuts and rejected reels from all the big budget commercials, pop-promos and features being shot and edited in Toronto. Friday nights seemed to be the nights that all this redundant material was discarded. When she got home, she would preview the material on a Steenbeck. She then assembled scenes cut from dozens of different productions, and wrote a script. Actor friends were drafted in to do the dialogue. Lucy recorded the soundtracks and did the final mix. When completed she had a narrative film with some of the best production values of anything you would ever see. Certainly the lip sync was a little off. One film I remember shows a female model leaping out of the latest luxury sedan as an Air Canada jet screams overhead. The woman's voice was camp, and very masculine. Lucy Byrne died an untimely death in 1994.

Hint The film industry has certain rules. Learn them, and then discard them. Remember that nobody knows anything.

Why do You Want to Make a Movie?

You are reading this book because you want to make a movie. You might not know exactly why you want to. As moviemaking is such an intense experience, before you actually embark on this journey, it would be useful if you could ask yourself, and answer, the following questions. Try and answer as honestly as you can.

1. Why, exactly, do you want to make a movie?

_____

Hint Realising the exact reasons why you want to make a movie will enable and empower you to position yourself in the marketplace.

_____

2. Do you have a unique message you want to get to an audience?

_____

Hint If it is a unique message, are you certain that a feature film is the best medium? Have you considered other media like television, radio, or the web?

_____

3. Do you want to make money with your film?

_____

Hint Making feature films for profit is an incredibly risky venture. If making money is your only goal, have you fully considered other forms of business?

_____

4. Do you crave celebrity status?

_____

Hint The movie industry is very glamorous and seductive. But it is also fiercely competitive. Are you sure you can handle the vast amount of rejection that can come your way?

_____

5. If you were trading on the stock market, you would be asked for your stop price, the point where you cut your losses and run. Do you have a fall back position, or a level where you might decide to abandon your project and start something else?

Summary

1. The whole point of this book is to make a film not with what you want to have, but with what you have.

2. Watch films and watch them again.

3. Successful filmmakers build their careers with resourcefulness.

Before we start the actual planning for your film, let me introduce you to some of the characters you will meet in the Hollywood Zoo.

2 The Hollywood Zoo

THE FILM INDUSTRY is populated by several stereotypical groups of people – animals even. Understanding who these are, and how they operate is one of the elementary tasks for anyone trying to break into the industry. With this information you can develop a survival strategy.

The Animals in the Film Industry Zoo

Bullies

Just like in school, there are many bullies in the film industry. They try bullying tactics to get their own way, and usually resort to humiliating and degrading tactics and comments to get their own way. Comments like 'only someone stupid would think/do that' are not uncommon.

Hint When dealing with a bully, remember that they are basically cowards, and operate out of insecurity. If you stand up to a bully, they will run away. Or just ignore and avoid them. Don't take what they say personally. They can't help themselves.

Screamers and Shouters

Something about the film industry attracts people who like to communicate at levels in excess of 90db. This is another form of bullying, also based on insecurity. Either avoid these people, or join them at the same decibel level. They may enjoy a mutually loud conversation for a change.

Snakes

Has someone ever stabbed you in the back? It is certainly one of the most painful and soul-destroying things that can happen to you. It is very easy to become known as a snake yourself. You become known as a snake by making negative comments about others. The film industry is a very small, compact group of people. Word spreads fast. Never say anything negative about anyone. Even if you have a justifiable excuse to criticise someone, don't do it.

Hint No matter how badly you have been treated, keep it to yourself, or confront the villain in person. If you don't then you run the risk of being labelled a snake yourself.

Crouching Tigers

Crouching tigers lie in wait for prey, camouflaged and well hidden. When an unsuspecting person comes along, usually a naive filmmaker spouting off ideas (which cannot be copyright protected) they spring and run off with the kill.

Hint Be wary of who you tell your ideas to until they are protected.

Casting Couch Lotharios

Every industry has its version of the casting couch. The threat of failure, or the chance of promotion linked to sexual favours is as old as the entertainment business itself, and it is simply not true. The casting couch scenario works like this: usually, the young intern, or lowest person in the art department, is coerced into a sexual relationship with the promise of a better job next time around. If they hesitate, then they are threatened with the phrase 'you'll never work in this town again'. If you are presented with this situation, you should remember that jobs on a film crew last three to four months. The likelihood of meeting and working with the same people again is remote. If this doesn't work for you, then seek the counsel of someone you can trust.

Men are equally at risk as women. The prevalence of women in top jobs has made this as likely to be a problem for men as for women.

A close friend of mine (male) married with two children was presented with the following dilemma. In order to get the dramatic television series he really wanted as a director, he was told by the head of the tele vision company that the job was his, if only he would sleep with her. He called me for advice. He reasoned that I was the one person to know how much his family meant to him, and how important his career aspirations as a director were. My advice was to talk it over with his wife. Needless to say, he lost the directing job, but he has often told me that it was the best decision he ever made.

Hint Never allow yourself to be forced into a position where you feel uncomfortable or used. If you are confronted with this situation, confide in someone you trust and seek their counsel.

Sharks

Sometimes you will be minding your own business, doing your job, when suddenly you hear a whooshing sound from behind, and before you can react, a shark rips part of your shoulder off and all you can hear as it rushes away is the sound 'sue me, sue me, sue me'.

This typically happens to first time writers. In the heat of the moment they forget that their first payment is due. Or they are too timid to mention the breached payment deadline as the sets are built and the actors arrive on location. The shark/producer tells them they have just been too busy to get to the bank. Suddenly the first day of principal photography arrives, and the money still hasn't come through. The writer is on the set, completely dazzled by the whirlwind of activity, and is too timid to confront the producer about the missing payment. Soon the picture has wrapped and the editor and director are secluded in the post-production process. The writer either can't find the producer (who's off on the next big deal) or is involved in the completion of the film. It is not uncommon for a shark/producer to enquire if the (unpaid) writer is available for the Cannes Film Festival at this juncture, using the argument that the film is 'just that damned good!'

Soon the picture is released and the box office receipts roll in, and the writer still hasn't been paid. Whenever the writer has the courage to breach the subject, the produce will use the phrase 'sue me'.

The shark/producer knows that the filmmaker has an air-tight case and will win in court. But s/he also knows that in order to be represented in court the filmmaker will need legal advice, which could easily run into tens of thousands, money which the filmmaker might not have. The litigation attorneys will need a retainer as well. And even if they do win it is likely that the filmmaker will be unable to collect because the shark/producer can easily hide behind a myriad shelf companies and UPVs (Unique Project Vehicles) which can easily be bankrupted by creditors and leave no legal liability for the owners to pay. Another tactic is for the shark to appeal the decision, thereby adding many more months to the process. At some point the writer will probably be offered a small percentage of the originally agreed price to 'walk' from the threatened litigation. And most filmmakers I know who have been in this position accept the derisory payment knowing that it is at least better than absolutely nothing.

Reservoir Dogs was swamped by litigation following its release. The four producers, Quentin Tarantino, his friend the actor Lawrence Bender, Harvey Keitel and Monte Hellman, all had shares in the profit of the film. Some four years after the film's release, a bank account in Los

Angeles contained $6 million of the film's profit, which was denied them by the sharks who distributed the film. At this point, Quentin Tarantino's career had taken off along with Harvey Keitel's. Lawrence Bender had become one of the most successful producers in Hollywood, with pictures like *Good Will Hunting* and *Pulp Fiction* to his credit. But Monte Hellman was desperate. Newly married to an acquaintance of mine from London, Emma Webster, Monte was waiting for another film of his, like his classic 1971 film, *Two Lane Blacktop* to hit. Meanwhile creditors were threatening his home. The offer on the table was for a mid five-figure sum. The sharks knew that Tarantino, Bender and Keitel were financially secure and likely to be willing (and able) to fight on and on. But they also knew that Monte was getting desperate. The shark hopes to save money by waiting for the other side to cave in.

Hint Check out the people you work with. Contact other filmmakers for references. Bad reputations travel fast in the film business.

Ruthless Climbers

Talking about ruthless climbers is very painful to me. I have been accused of this myself. A ruthless climber is concerned and obsessed about one thing only: their career. Any topic of conversation, no matter how emotionally charged for others, will be deemed as totally irrelevant if it has nothing to do with their career. This total selfishness has no place in the lives of successful people.

A simple test to ascertain whether or not you are with a ruthless climber or not is to ask the individual a question concerning the day's current events: the volcanic eruption in Africa, news of the famous personality's death – anything. As you ask the question, look into their eyes and see if they glaze over.

Hint In order to prevent yourself from becoming a ruthless climber, hope that you have someone in your circle of friends who is not afraid to kick you very hard in the shins and bring you back to earth.

Star Chasers

The film industry attracts a whole army of people who are easily impressed by a name. While not exactly groupies, as in the music business, star chasers rely on rubbing shoulders with the people who have already made it in order to justify their continued pursuit of their dreams. Often, star chasers put themselves in the unfortunate position of being used, and in extreme cases, suffer delusions that require the strong arm of the law to keep them away from their idols.

Hint Star chasing is really a form of lack of confidence. Remember that the only difference between you and the star is not talent or opportunity, it's just a moment in time when your box office gross (or lack of it) is being compared to theirs. Don't despair – your turn will come.

The Nice People

I have worked in property and the computer industry, I have friends in most of the arts – ballet, music, literature. I can truly say that the willingness to share information in the film industry is unparalleled by any other. The generosity of spirit and the readiness with which seasoned professionals spill their trade secrets constantly amazes me.

Saying Thank You

What you have to do, however, is learn how to say thank you. Taking from people without saying thank you can quickly earn you the reputation of being selfish, inconsiderate, or even worse, a ruthless climber.

At Raindance we are constantly bombarded with telephone calls from people starting out, asking us the most taxing questions. Often we are able to refer people, which reaffirms my belief that private companies like Raindance are usually better equipped to give advice than the overstaffed and overpaid publicly funded agencies. Equally amazing is the fact that so many people do not say thank you. They most usually mumble a 'thank you' into the telephone, but that doesn't really count at all. And it doesn't count because there is no thought or effort behind it.

How you say thank you is important. Be elegant and unambiguous.

The Greeting Card

A written thank you is best – and not by email. If you want to thank someone properly, purchase a greeting card and inside it write a simple thank you. It is a great way to tell the person who helped you that the information you received from them was worth all the effort it took you to go and get a card, sit down and write it, find a stamp and mail it.

Hint Saying a simple thank you will certainly get you noticed because so few others do it.

The Gift

Sending someone a small gift is another way to say thank you. Perhaps you are working on a movie and you have t-shirts made for the production. T-shirts and baseball caps make excellent gifts, although the recipient could decide that you are on ego overload and trying to dress them up in your branded gear. If someone does you a really super favour, nothing works as well as a bottle of champagne.

I like getting gifts of film magazines from other countries, sample script formats (I once got one from New Zealand), articles of interest from magazines and newspapers (cut out and photocopied).

The Postcard Theory

Part of the saying thank you exercise (along with good manners) is getting noticed. Developing a novel technique for saying thank you will get you noticed even more.

Richard Holmes' credits include *White Bhaji* (2004), *The Abduction Club* (2002), *Waking Ned* (1998) and *Shooting Fish* (1997). His first film *Soft Top Hard Shoulder* was made on a miniscule budget in 1993.

One of my favourite British producers is Richard Holmes. Hugely successful now, and with films that have done over $100 million international box office, Richard and I started out at the same time in London. One of Richard's traits was to always say thank you, and he did it with such panache. He was renowned for sending old 1950s black and white postcards that he found in various flea markets. Do Richard a favour, or even bump into him on the street, and a day or two later, one of these funky postcards would find its way into your letterbox with 'Thanks, Richard' scrawled on the back.

Hint The film industry is fiercely competitive and you must do anything possible to be noticed.

Developing a Personal Image

The film industry is all about entertainment. You can be certain that everyone you meet will be looking at you and sizing up how you look. Learn to use your attributes in a positive way, no matter what shape or size you are. Remember that the old adage – beauty is only skin deep – is true in all walks of life. The most important aspect of your personality is a clear, positive mental attitude. If you are able to couple that with passion for your project, you have developed your image terrifically.

Designing a distinctive wardrobe for yourself doesn't need to cost a lot of money, or make you look like a ridiculous fashion victim. An American filmmaker friend of mine wore earrings fashioned out of long pieces of silver. Although they looked like coat hangers, everyone she met would remember them, even if they forgot her name. Another, a

Canadian living in London, wore farm breeches and lumberjack boots – a rarity in London. Both of these filmmakers dressed in what they deemed to be comfortable yet distinctive clothes, and fortunately they both had real passion for their projects.

Needless to say, basic grooming is always essential. I have met many new filmmakers who are so pongy that meeting them in person is uncomfortable. Although this type of personal grooming makes you memorable, I don't think this us what you want to be remembered for.

Stephen Woolley, producer of many hit British films including *The Crying Game*, once appeared at a Raindance panel discussion and nonchalantly rode his bicycle up the centre aisle of the Electric Cinema in front of a hundred people and leapt on stage wearing baggy shorts and sandals.

Stephen Woolley is one of the producers I admire most. Although British, and based up the street from the Raindance office, he is equally at home in LA. As a chairman of BAFTA, he transformed the insipid BAFTA Awards into the British Oscars. Maybe I am jealous. Who wouldn't be proud to have his producing credits: *Borgia* (2003), *The Honest Thief* (2002), *Purely Belter* (2000), *The End of the Affair* (1999), *Little Voice* (1998), *24/7: Twenty Four Seven* (1997), *Fever Pitch* (1997), *Interview with the Vampire: The Vampire Chronicles* (1994), *The Crying Game* (1992), *Absolute Beginners* (1986).

The Three Reasons You Will Not Make a Movie

There are only three reasons that you will not make a movie. I base this on the hundreds of filmmakers from many countries I have met at Raindance, and have analysed what has contributed to their success and/or failure. The three most likely reasons you will not make a film are:

Lack of Confidence

You will simply not believe in yourself to the point where you will be crippled by lack of confidence. You must always remember that nobody knows anything in the film business. Some typical ways that new filmmakers destroy their confidence include:

- Using their inability to operate camera equipment (or other technical issues) as an excuse for not getting their film made
- Listening to the persistent questions from one's friends and neighbours, like 'Why don't you get a real job?' or 'Why are you wasting your life?' or even 'For what you spent making that short, we could have had Steven Spielberg come and give a lecture'
- Letting a lack of knowledge of how the industry operates create an apparently impenetrable mystique
- Being overwhelmed by financial pressure from family and landlords

Self Destruction

The less said about this the better, but the human species is unique on the animal planet in that each of us has an individual, 100% original method of self destruction, whether it is chronic lateness for meetings, irresponsibility to co-workers or your landlord, or diet and substance abuse. Common means of self destruction include:

- Tardiness
- Failure to say thank you
- Being a ruthless climber (see above)
- Financial irresponsibility
- Failure to keep verbal commitments

Procrastination

This seems to be a consistent favourite: 'I will read this book, and when I am finished reading this book, I will make my movie.' 'I will make my movie after I go to film school'. Common procrastinations begin 'I will start filming when...'

- The rest of the money is raised
- I have learned how to (insert: use a camera, edit etc.)
- Everything has calmed down
- Harrison Ford has committed

Hint How to avoid the three common reasons you will not make a film? Figure out how to put film into a camera and expose it to actors. After all, that is what filmmaking is really about.

Summary

1. Research the careers and reputations of those you meet and want to do business with.

2. Remember to say thank you in a creative way. It is, after all, the entertainment industry.

You will need some money. Find out how much in the next chapter.

Seven Essential Steps for Becoming Rich and Famous by Making a Low Budget Film

Step 1 Find An Excellent Screenplay

Producer Andrew Macdonald started off working as a film runner in Scotland. While there he met a wannabe screenwriter, John Hodge, who was a medical doctor. John had an idea for a movie that Andrew liked, and so he paid John to write the screenplay. The first stage was a treatment – which John delivered handwritten on the back of NHS hospital entry forms. Over the next eighteen months Andrew and John worked over the script. The finished film was *Shallow Grave*. The next project Andrew found was a published novel for which the screenplay rights were still available. All other film producers deemed the project to be unfilmable. Andrew loved the book, and purchased the screenplay rights and hired John to write another screenplay. The result was *Trainspotting*.

We are not going to have time in this book to discuss the elements of a great screenplay. Suffice to say, there are only two types of screenplay: the terrific and the terrible. There is no in between. By an excellent screenplay, the film industry means that the script is so good that everyone agrees there should be no changes. The shooting can start tomorrow. If the script is a comedy, it is so funny, that the first time you read the script, you set it down because you are laughing so loud, look for your telephone and call your best friend to tell them the joke. A comedy script that you sort of half smile at is not funny. Similarly, an excellent horror script is so creepy that you are afraid to turn the page. Screenplay and script are so important that I spent a lot of time thinking and writing about this in my first book: *Raindance Writers Lab: Write and Sell the Hot Script* (Focal Press 2001).

Your first task is to learn how to identify, find or create the great screenplay that will launch your career. A great screenplay may mean one of three things:

1. An original screenplay you have written, purchased or optioned

2. A novel, play or short story for which you have purchased the screenplay rights

3. The rights to a person's life story

Hint Film careers are launched with excellent scripts.

Financing Completed	Begin writing period
6th week	Research and treatment completed Begin first draft screenplay
14th week	First draft screenplay completed Begin second draft
18th week	Second draft completed Begin polish Begin casting Begin crew allocation Begin location scouting Lock production schedule Allocate equipment, props etc. Begin and/or ready sets
22nd week	Casting completed Locations secured Begin rehearsals Equipment, props, costumes secured
24th week	Begin shooting Begin editing
27th week	End shooting, start post production
29th week	First cut completed
37th week	Second cut completed
41st week	Fine cut completed Begin sound cutting Begin music composing
47th week	Score music
49th week	Sound editing completed Mix sound
50th week	Transfer to optical track Begin negative cutting
51st week	Negative cutting completed Time and begin first trial answer print
52nd week	Screen first trial composite

figure 3.1
Timetable for making a movie

3   Budgeting and Scheduling

BUDGETING IS THE OPERATION where each of the scenes of the script is broken down and analysed followed by a financial assessment of the total cost of each scene. The total financial requirements for the filming become the sum of the budgets of each scene. This budget is used to attract finance and is scrutinised by investors. During production, it is the yardstick whereby the producer, the crew and the investors can gauge the progress of the production and determine whether the shoot is being shot within or over the amount of money budgeted for the film.

Scheduling is the organisational process where goods, crew, equipment and actors are scheduled in the most cost-efficient way. The elephant may be required for a morning on page one of the script and a morning on page thirty of the script. If the script were shoot in numerical sequence at a rate of five pages per day, the elephant would need to be available on day one and day six of the shoot, incurring extra transportation and storage charges. If however, pages one and thirty can be shot on the same day, the elephant need only be on the set for one day, thus minimising storage and transportation charges. The schedule is also used to see if a production is being completed in the allocated amount of time or not.

During the shoot, the production company uses the information in the budget and schedule to determine whether or not the production is on budget and or on time. It is possible for a film to be on time (on schedule) but over budget. It is also possible for a film to be on budget, but behind schedule.

Choosing a Budget

The first task in filmmaking is choosing a budget. And choosing a budget suitable to your project will predetermine the route you take with your project, and to a large extent, will predetermine the success of your project. There is no point in trying to shoot a huge epic with thousands of cast and dozens of locations on a minimal budget. The result will most likely leave you dissatisfied. Neither should your very first film be structured to require a cast and crew in the dozens. You would run the risk of swamping yourself with technology and a series of organisational dilemmas which could threaten to swamp your creativity. A first feature script would probably be a slice-of-life drama set in an area near where you live that would lend itself to being shot with a small cast, minimal crew and readily available resources.

The Four Budgets

The Hollywood blockbuster budget started with movies like *Gone with the Wind*, and the first $1 million film: *Cleopatra* starring Richard Burton and Elizabeth Taylor.

Every film ever made falls into one of the following four budgets. A successful producer understands the different types of budget and what can be achieved with each one. With the demands of the script in mind, the astute producer chooses the budget appropriate to the project.

1 Hollywood blockbuster budget
Each summer the American film industry releases the most expensive film ever made. The budget is noted as a hyphenate: $185–$215 million. At no time is the precise budget mentioned, nor is the missing $30 million. It is always promoted as the most expensive film in cinematic history. By marketing this fact, the makers of the film hope that large numbers of people will flock to the cinema to see what a quarter of a billion dollars looks like on the screen.

It is improbable that anyone reading this book will have access to this budget.

2 The typical Hollywood budget
Each of the major Hollywood studios will make twenty to thirty films each year at budgets of $60 to $80 million.

This budget includes the cost of the actors and directors (above-the-line) the actual film production (making), and the marketing of the film. This cost has quadrupled over the past ten years because of increased costs for marketing, and the huge rise in actors' pay.

I would find it surprising if anyone reading this book had access to this budget.

3 The million dollar film
Million dollar films to see and study: *Blood Simple* (1984), *Reservoir Dogs* (1992), *Shallow Grave* (1994), *Broken Vessels* (1998), *The Corndog Man* (1999), *Sex, Lies and Videotape* (1989).

Until the mid 1980s, there were only three budgets, with the million dollar budget being the most typical entry-level budget for filmmakers. Some examples are *Shallow Grave* £1.2 million, *Blood Simple* £1.1 million, *Sex Lies and Videotape* £1.1 million and *Lock Stock and Two Smoking Barrels* £800,000. The producers of these films raised the budget through a variety of industry and private financing.

It is likely that one in ten people reading this book have access to or can raise $/£/€1 million.

4 The low budget
Low budget filmmaking has become a major force in the film industry since the making and international distribution of Robert Rodgriguez' *El*

Mariachi. While genre and B-movies have historically been produced on very low budgets, *El Mariachi* was at its time the cheapest film to receive international cinematic distribution.

Within Hollywood, a low budget is anything under $10 million. At Raindance, a hundred thousand pounds would be a huge budget. Accordingly, low budget has been further broken down:

1. Low budget – a budget of under $/£/€1 million
One in ten readers of this book will have access to a budget this size.

2. Microbudget – a budget of under $/£/€500,000
One in five readers of this book will have access to a budget of this size.

3. No budget – a budget of under $/£/€100,000
Everyone reading this book will have access to a budget between one and one hundred thousand dollars/pounds/euros.

Find the Right Budget for Your Script

Your immediate task, the first principle of filmmaking, is to take a realistic look at your script and decide which budget will do your script justice. You can pick any budget you want as long as it is a realistic budget for the script you want to shoot. The higher the budget, the longer it will take you to raise the money. There is no right or wrong decision at this point, but you must take a decision.

Remember that there has never been a film made in the history of cinema that has had enough money. If you want to finance the film through your own resources or private investors, then pick a budget that you can realistically raise within three months.

Hint You must be able to open a dedicated bank account for your project and deposit the money for your film. If you chose an overly ambitious budget, you will then procrastinate on the making of your film.

Describing Your Budget

The Budget Ladder.

If you want to raise a budget of $/£/€20 million for your film, go out and make a commercially successful film for $/£/€2 million. If you want to make a film for $/£/€2 million, go out and make a commercially successful film for $/£/€200,000. If you want to make a film for $/£/€200,000, go out and make a commercially successful film for the money you can put into a production account within sixty days of acquiring an excellent script.

Talking the Talk

Every industry including the film industry has its buzz words. Learn the buzz words and the correct way to use them, and you will look like a pro. Use buzz words with finesse and you will look like a producer who can gain the respect and admiration of talent, crew and investors.

The Nine Most Famous Words in Hollywood

My friend Dov S-S Simens recounts a truly hilarious version of TNMFWIH. for details of Dov, his work as a film instructor, visit www.webfilmschool.com

Do you remember a moment in the recent past where you announced to your friends and family that you wanted to make a movie? You would have received one of two responses: either 'Yes – you can make a really great movie', or 'Don't even think of giving up the day job'. For me, I remember a groundswell of euphoria that washed over me as friend after friend after relative thought that I could make a really great film. Then I made the mistake of making the same announcement that 'I want to make a movie' to the same person within a few days. Can you imagine their response? Actions do indeed speak louder than words.

But I was tied up in the feeling of being a filmmaker. All the glamour, the excitment of the opening night galas, the tension of viewing rushes, and the hard work seemed to me to be the perfect life-style occupation. My constant line of 'I really want to make a film' became so tedious to my friends after a year or two that I used to dread going to parties where I might be asked the dreaded question: 'What are you doing?' I never knew how to answer: either with my day job (I was working then as a computer software developer) or with my wannabe career in filmmaking. People who knew me really well would always sidle over to hear what answer I was going to give this time.

After one of these occasions, I arrived home late, totally dejected about a film career that was clearly going nowhere. I flicked on the TV and there, one of my idols, Steven Spielberg was sitting on a talk show and being asked: 'What are you doing now?' This was the same question I had been asked an hour earlier! To my amazement, Spielberg answered with what is now called The Nine Most Famous Words In Hollywood (TNMFWIH): 'I have numerous projects in various stages of development.' I had it! The answer to my dreams! I graduated from filmmaker (implying amateur or student) to 'an independent producer with numerous projects in various stages of development'. This did wonders for my confidence, and made me feel like I knew what I was talking about, even when I usually didn't. When those acquaintances of mine heard TNMFWIH, they gave me several weeks of peace and respect.

The Two Big Questions

You will find that The Nine Most Famous Words in Hollywood are insufficient to divert the attention and satisfy the interest of your friends and

Being a producer will always attract the attention of fascinated dilettantes and other frustrated artists. They will always want to know exactly what you are doing in order to discover the secret of your success, or find your weakest link in order to effectively destroy your ambitions.

relatives. They won't just leave it there and wish you luck, but will probe further, asking the two big questions that new producers dread.

1 What is it about?

Most new producers are instantly reduced to a nervous wreck by this question. They are afraid, because they are concerned that someone will ask them details about their script, and they haven't even got an idea for a movie yet. In Hollywood, this question is deflected and diverted with the phrase: 'It's a character driven drama'.

2 What is the budget?

Astute industry professionals who want to discover whether you are a serious filmmaker or a wannabe with absolutely nothing will ask far more detailed questions. You will often be asked the budget of your film by investors and by friends as well. Financial sense dictates that you must never mention the budget for your film to anyone except your accountant or the taxman. Here are some ways that you can tactfully answer this question without actually stating a financial total.

i Feature length

Ninety feet of film stock passes through the projector or camera every minute, making a 35mm feature film 8,100 feet or ninety feet times ninety minutes.

'I'm shooting an 8,100 foot feature'. What you have stated is the fact that you are shooting a 35mm feature and the length is ninety minutes.

I'm shooting a 50,000 foot feature. This does not mean that you are shooting a nine-hour epic. What it says to an industry person is that you have raised enough money to buy a total of 50,000 feet of 35mm film stock on which to shoot all the scenes that will eventually be edited down to an 8,100 foot feature.

Everyone in the industry knows what the cost of film stock and lab processing is, so they can deduce the amount of money you have for your feature.

ii Shooting ratio

At a ratio of 6:1, presuming that it's a 90 minute feature, they know that you will shoot 540 (90 x 6) minutes of footage, or 50,000ft of film (540 x 90ft of stock through the camera per minute).

Another way of describing your budget to potential investors is to tell them what your shooting ratio is. The shooting ratio for a 50,000 foot feature, shooting a ninety-page script, is approximately 6:1 (you will shoot six minutes of stock for every minute of screen time). They will do the maths themselves and so will be able to guess at your budget.

Hint Walk like a duck, talk like a duck, get treated like a duck. Walk and talk like a big time producer and you will get treated like a big time producer. Remember that a 50,000 foot feature film is a larger job to the lab than any of the big pop promos and commercials. You are a big job. You are important. Never forget it or underestimate yourself.

---

iii Describing the schedule

You can also describe your budget by telling an investor how long the schedule for your shoot is.

Guerrilla Filmmaking:
Return the camera on
Monday lunchtime. Call the
camera rental facility with an
excuse of how your van has
broken down and lie about
your location, and continue
shooting. It's likely that the
rental facility won't charge
you for the additional hire, but
you will probably be unable
to use them again.

Three-week shoot

This is a very common length of time for a low budget shoot. Another way to describe it is as an eighteen-day shoot: six days a week for three weeks. An advantage of this schedule is the additional leeway the three Sundays offer should you fall behind.

Two-week shoot

Industry personnel will find this very uncommon, although DoP John Ward shot Ray Winstone's *Love, Honour and Obey* in two weeks with 40,000 feet of film stock. Another way to describe a two-week shoot is to call it a sixteen-day shoot. Pick up the camera on a Friday and shoot every day for two weeks, ending on the second Sunday night.

One-week shoot

A one-week shoot is fun and if planned and scheduled properly, simple. It can also be described as a nine-day shoot:

figure 3.2
A one-week shoot

Fri	Sat	Sun	Mon	Tue	Wed	Thu	Fri	Sat	Sun	Mon
Pick up camera			S	H	O	O	T			Return camera

Advantages of a one-week shoot

A one-week shoot has many financial benefits. It is much easier to hire cast and crew for little or no money if you are asking them to commit to just one week. People with regular jobs can fit your shoot into a week of holidays. Successful freelancers are very reluctant to give up three weeks for little or no money: after all that is approaching a month's fees. But a one-week shoot is more accessible. And everyone in the industry knows that the one-week shoot is the fun week.

It is true that the more time you have, the better looking a film you can make. However, time is money, and you may not be able to afford the time required to achieve everything you want in your film.

In a previous career, I worked as a scenic artist and crew member on sixty-eight feature films and over seven hundred commercials. I worked on many of the three-week shoots that came to my hometown, Toronto. They were usually American movies-of-the-week that were shot quickly and cheaply in Toronto so American production companies could profit from the beneficial Canadian dollar exchange rate.

On a three-week shoot, I found that each week had a specific rhythm: The first week was the fun week, the family week. One was reunited with old acquaintances and everyone swapped tales during the coffee breaks. The pervading atmosphere was: 'Hey! We're making a movie!' The second week was the zombie week. Fatigue definitely kicks in on day two or three of week two following a string of sixteen-hour days. If you had a Sunday off, you usually had just enough energy to get the stains out of your clothes. Week three is the hostility week. Tempers flare. Arguments break out and you are constantly threatened with 'You'll never ever work in this town again'.

On a one-week shoot, guess which two weeks you miss? You miss Zombie and Hostility, leaving Fun. I have only ever worked on two one-week shoots, both of which I produced, including the one I wrote and directed as well. They were both an incredible amount of fun, although a few zombies do sneak in on about day six.

Elements of a Budget

A budget is divided into two parts: above the line and below the line. The above the line items summarise the cost of the talent: producer, writer, director and actors. The below the line items list everything else.

The top sheet summarises the entire budget (see figure 3.3), and the rest of the budget breaks out the detail of the top sheet, as in figure 3.4, which shows the breakdown of budget Line 700, Talent.

How to Choose Your Budget

Whatever your position, your first task as a producer, assuming you have a great script, is to choose a budget that will provide enough time and money to bring the story in the screenplay to the screen. Through the rest of this book, we will be analysing the different line items in detail, and giving advice on how the budget should be allocated.

How I Chose a £10,000 Budget

Making a feature film on 35mm for under £10,000 is considered ridiculously impossible in the industry. But we are marketing the cash budget. The fact that it was to be shot at such a ridiculously low price was one of the most newsworthy assets we had. If you factor in all the hundreds of hours of labour – over the script, the storyboards, the editing and the acting, you essentially have increased your budget by several hundred thousand pounds, if not more. But it is not cash spent – it is goods and services in kind. The major film companies know that you are much more cost-effective and efficient than they are. Your overheads are small, and you are able to negotiate payment to staff, crew and talent for a fraction of what they pay.

I developed the £10,000 budget when an acquaintance called me up and asked if I would like to see a new version of the stage play *Othello*. He then told me that his new job was head of tourism for Hackney Council in London's East End. For those unfamiliar with Hackney, or East London, suffice to say that a tour of the Third World could start from Hackney Town Hall where I met the tourism officer. He informed me that in order to attract the arty types to this impoverished London borough, the Council had hired him to attract tourists. With his modest budget, he had decided to fund the arts – more specifically, theatre and film. The theory being that if the artists came, the yuppies and property developers would not be far behind.

Based on the assumption that £10,000 would be available I started on a budget using reverse budgeting techniques. I then fell victim to procrastination – one of the great reasons you will not make a film, and why I didn't make this film.

Raindance Film			Dr Psychedelia
Producer: Elliot Grove			35mm
			18 day shoot
			6:1 shoot ratio
			Director: Elisar Kennedy

Account	Description	Page	Total
500	script	1	3,000
600	producer/director	1	14,000
700	talent	1-2	22,460
800	fringes	2	2,246
Total above the line			**41,706**
900	production staff	2	10,025
1000	camera dept	3	6,200
1100	camera	3	6,000
1200	art department	3-4	9,300
1300	art/props	4	7,640
1400	electrical department	4	3,400
1500	grip department	4	1,950
1600	grip electrical package	4	12,340
1700	production sound	5	1,670
1800	stunts/SFX	5	6,715
1900	police/fire/safety	5	0
2000	craft service/catering	6	7,530
2100	wardrobe/make-up	6	7,350
2200	location manager/scouts	6	2,700
2300	locations	7	10,350
2400	transportation	7	7,950
2500	picture vehicles	7	200
2600	accommodation	7-8	3,000
2700	general office	8	9,735
2800	raw stock/developing	8	24,970
2900	insurance	9	7,500
3000	legal	9	7,100
Total production			**156,675**
3100	editing	9	20,900
3200	music	9	3,175
3300	post production sound	9-10	35,235
3400	answer print	10	9,140
3500	titles and opticals	10	10,575
Misc			0
Total above the line			41,706
Total below the line			235,650
Above and below the line			277,356
Total VAT within budget			15,765
Contingency			27,735
Total (UK sterling)			**305,091**

figure 3.3
Budget top sheet from horror pic
Dr Psychedelia

RAINDANCE PRODUCERS' LAB: LO-TO-NO BUDGET FILMMAKING

Line 700: Talent

Line	Act	Amt	Unit	Quant	Rate	Total
	Principal Cast					
701	Janey	3	wks	1	1,200	3,600
702	Dr Psychedelia	3	wks	1	1,200	3,600
703	Babs Boyer	3	wks	1	1,200	3,600
704	Guy Hendrix	3	wks	1	800	2,400
705	Vincent	2	wks	1	800	1,600
706	Santana	1	week	1	800	800
707	Dr Stalker	2	days	1	250	500
708	Bridget	3	days	1	250	750
709	Iris	2	days	1	250	500
	Day Players					
710	Gordon Grump	1	day	1	250	250
711	Madame Doe	1	day	1	250	250
712	Trixie	1	day	1	250	250
713	Nun	1	day	1	250	250
714	Psychedelia 22	1	day	1	250	250
715	Candy	1	day	1	250	250
716	Psychedelia 35	1	day	1	250	250
717	Doctor 1	1	day	1	250	250
718	Doctor 2	1	day	1	250	250
719	Drunk	1	day	1	250	250
720	John 2	1	day	1	250	250
	Extras					
721	Sailors	1	day	3	30	90
722	Slave girls	1	day	7	30	210
723	Hookers	1	day	2	30	60

figure 3.4
Budget break out for Line 700: Talent

Through my contacts in the UK, word of this project found its way to Lloyd Kaufman of New York's Troma Studios. He called me up out of the blue and asked me what I could tell him about this Shakespeare project that I was working on. I asked him to get a pencil and paper and write down the title of the film: *Othello*. I then asked him to underline the word hell in the title: *Ot<u>hell</u>o*

He instantly got an idea of how the stage play was going to be translated to the screen. I then told him that I had changed the title and asked him to put a period after the O and the T and to turn the T into a J: this made 'OJ. Hello'.

I told him that *OJ. Hello* was the story of a black man beating up a white woman and was a tale of domestic violence and sexual jealousy. He was really excited and asked me what the budget was. When he heard that we were planning to shoot the film on a budget of £10,000, he told me he could get a million. I waited and waited and then Lloyd made *Tromeo and Juliet* instead. Had I made the film then (at the time when the OJ Simpson trial was in full swing) I would have made a film that was both timeless and timely. I missed my window and I have regretted it ever since.

Hint Procrastination is one of the three reasons that you will not make your film.

How I Chose a Zero Budget

Out of frustration, I then decided to shoot a feature film with a budget of absolutely zero. I developed a script that could be shot in and around the Raindance office and drew up a budget or a list of everything we would need on the shoot and then put a zero beside it. I knew I could write that cheque immediately. I then sat down with my producer, Jamie Greco, and devised a plan to get everything on the list and come in under the budget.

Hint A budget should always be done in pencil. The reverse end of a pencil has an eraser.

Item	Budgeted	Actual	
Producer	0	0	
Script	0	48.72	photocopying
Actors	0	0	
Writer	0	0	
Camera	0	65.00	delivery and collection fees
Film Stock	0	0	got free recans and ends
Lab	0	0	contra deal for deliveries / collections
Make-up	0	15.00	cigars x 3
Wardrobe	0	12.00	dry cleaning
Location Fees	0	0	
Insurance	0	0	under Raindance insurance
Crew	0	0	
Art Department	0	43.52	paint
Transportation	0	0	
Telecine	0	0	
Tape Stock	0	94.14	
Edit	0	0	
Titles	0	0	
Answer Print	0	0	not done
Legals	0	0	
Misc	0	0	
Contingency	0	0	
Total	**0**	**278.38**	

figure 3.5
Budget for zero budget feature Table Five

Refrigerator Theory of Budgeting

If you really want to make a film, consider the refrigerator theory of budgeting. It works as follows.

As soon as possible, go and buy as much film stock as you can afford without compromising your landlord or diet. It can be a simple roll or two of 16mm, or a large box of 35mm film stock. Store it in your refrigerator.

When you have announced to the world that you are going to make a film, have enjoyed the wash of euphoria, have struggled to get a screenplay and started to raise money, time passes. You also attract unwanted criticism from those you love, and from competing individuals. Usually these people will call you late in the evening, either to convince you to get a proper job, or to prick your confidence. After a call like this, you will find your resolve has taken a beating, exposing you to the first reason you will not make a film – lack of confidence. In order to bolster your ego, you will then go to the kitchen to get something to eat. You open the door, and there is no food. The entire refrigerator is filled with film stock.

If you follow the refrigerator theory of budgeting, within six months you will figure out how to expose actors to film stock. After all, that's what filmmaking really is.

Preparing the Schedule

All scheduling means is taking account of the different variables and figuring out the best combination for the film. One line producer I know likens it in a way to arranging the seating at a dinner party.

The industry method is to take the script and break it down into the parts which are pertinent to budget requirements and to use these parameters to decide which scenes will be shot when. Once you've done this, you'll have a clear plan of what has to be done, how much it will cost and will be able to plan the shoot to be as efficient as possible.

Script Breakdown

In order to get to this point, you have to discover and annotate the elements of the film to work out how much each scene will cost. The script has to be broken down into its parts. All of the elements of the film: the actors, props, locations, sound effects, music, special effects, wardrobe, vehicles and animals needed during the shoot need to be identified, organised in a useful manner and costed.

The first step is to eighth the script out. See figure 3.5 overleaf. Eighthing a script is subjective. When you look at the script, you need to evaluate the action and dialogue content of each scene, and the elements relevant to the scene.

In this example, it could appear that the first two scenes are roughly the same length. You will notice that the second scene contains action,

```
7    INT. HOSPITAL OFFICE -DAY                              7
     A typical hospital office, cold and univiting. A receptionist
     is tapping at an official looking form.

                         NICK
          You mean, to get her in surgery I need to
          go private and that costs £10,000? What
          if I pay cash?

                                              CUT TO:
```

Scene 8 is 2/8ths of a page

```
8    INT. HOSPITAL OUTSIDE ELEVATOR. - DAY                  8

     Nick is standing with the flowers

                         NICK
             It just wasn't meant to be, darling.

     He goes to give the flowers to a CHILD going by in a
     wheelchair. Her MOTHER is pushing.He thinks better and turns
     and leaves.

                                              CUT TO:
```

Scene 9 is 5/8ths of a page

```
9    EXT. SOHO STREET - NIGHT                               9

     Nick is working out furiously doing puships on the back of
     the car.  The flowers lie on the back seat.

     He is flipping through a stack of file folders and legal
     papers.

                         NICK
             Shit.

     He winces as he moves his shoulder. He quickly strips of his
     shirt, and we see the blood soaked bandage over his shoulder.
     He reachs into the glove compartment and pulls out a couple
     of squeezy bottles full of fluid. He strips off the bandage
     and the angry gash is plain to see - held together with
     crude stitches.

     Nick runs some water over the wound and pats it dry. He then
     swallows a couple of capsules and wraps the wound up with a
     freah bandage.

     He puts his shirt on and swithches off the dome light of the
     car.

     We see Nick sleeping in the car, covered in an old blanket.
     Frost is caking on the windscreen.

                                              CUT TO:
```

figure 3.6
Sample script page 'eighthed'

where the first scene contains a single dialogue. Accordingly, it would be prudent to allow more time to shoot the second scene.

The third scene really is a half page (4/8) but given that each page must add up to 8/8, and this section includes a lot of complicated action, it is given in this example 5/8ths.

Once you have eighthed the script, you then transfer the information about each scene onto a strip of card in preparation for creating the production scheduling board. Each strip of card needs to contain information about the location of the scene, the actors involved, and any special requirements for props, stunts, animals, or special effects. Once this material is prepared, the schedule can be started.

There are fourteen parameters which you need to take into account when scheduling. Each eighthed section of script needs to be analysed to see which of these fourteen elements it contains.

i Locations

Locations present a whole series of special problems in addition to the actual structural construction of the buildings, or geography of the land. Mundane issues like parking, transport facilities, toilets, proximity to police and fire stations as well as hospitals need to be thought out.

If the location requires pre-build, then adequate preparation time needs to be built into the pre-production schedule.

Scheduling a shoot on a public holiday requires special attention. Not only are the neighbours at home, but public transport may not be available for your cast and crew, leaving the production stranded.

ii Cast members

Actors may not be available when you need them due to other commitments. If you are trying to schedule several different actors together for a series of a few days, your schedule will fall apart if one of them has a must-do commercial on the second day. Try to negotiate with the actors and get them to commit to a spread of days even if you don't need them for the entire time.

Actors dislike arriving on set only to find that, due to a scheduling error, they are not going to be needed for many hours. Try to make sure they arrive with just enough time for make-up and wardrobe.

iii Day/night shooting

Your script will contain references to DAY or NIGHT. If you have a series of day shoots, with just a single night shoot, try to schedule the night shoot before a day off, in order to allow the crew time to recover.

Scripts sometimes call for dawn or dusk – a very difficult period to shoot as the so-called magic hour often lasts for much less. Usually dawn scenes are shot in the evening, as it is easier to get crew out late than early.

iv Exteriors and interiors

Along with DAY/NIGHT, INT/EXT are the second pair of common variables in a script. When you are scheduling an exterior shot, you should always have a back up scene to shoot under cover should the weather turn unfavourable.

v Shooting in sequence

Sometimes, for creative reasons, a director will want to shoot a series of scenes in their chronological order. This can strain the schedule depending on which actors are needed. It would not be uncommon for an actor to appear in a scene shot on a Monday, and not then be needed for another ten days.

vi Child actors

Child actors are subject to a wide range of regulations including number of hours worked per day, special tutors, and an accompanying adult. If you fall foul of these regulations you will find yourself facing civil and possible criminal actions.

vii Changes in time periods

Sometimes a set will change from, say, the present day, to Victorian times. The schedule has to allow enough time for the set to be redressed. It is also important in the schedule for the different time zones to be clearly marked.

viii Time of year filming

You must consider how the changes in the season will affect your film, and what impact that will have on special effects for creating weather hazards like snow and ice if you are shooting on location. Be aware that daylight hours are much shorter in winter.

ix Weather conditions

When you are shooting out-of-doors, you must also be aware how adverse weather will affect your shoot and make alternative arrangements where possible. If you want to shoot in torrential rain, then make sure that your cameraman and spark are informed in plenty of time so that they are prepared with the right kit to keep all your equipment safe.

x Special effects and stunts

Any special effects or stunts must be scheduled to allow for enough preparation time, and then, most importantly, enough time to film them in the best and safest way possible. Accidents on set usually happen when the director and producer are rushing everyone like mad to get finished on time.

xi Second camera and/or second unit

Second unit work, i.e.: work with no actors, can be scheduled and almost treated like a separate shoot.

xii Special equipment

Pages of the script that need special equipment like cranes, dollies or other grip equipment need to be noted. Shoot them in one day where possible to keep expensive rental and operator fees to a minimum.

xiii Geography of locations

An astute producer will try and keep all of the locations within a short distance of each other. When locations are changed during the day, remember to allow adequate time to move from location to location. See figure 3.8 and the section on low budget screenwriting below.

xiv Miscellaneous factors

You have scheduled all of your actors for the shoot with much cajoling and pleading. You have that special helicopter rented for the shot of your actors jogging up Piccadilly through near-deserted streets. Your camera crew and actors arrive promptly on location at 7am and suddenly you realise that the throngs of crowds around you are there for the Gay Pride Parade, and nothing is going to happen.

A good producer thinks quick, and comes up with an alternative plan.

An inexperienced producer who worked with me in London saw two locations in London: one east and one west, and saw they were just four miles apart. Allowing for traffic at twenty miles per hour, she calculated fifteen minutes in travel time, based on looking at the map. Unfortunately, she scheduled the move during the mid-day rush hour, failed to realise that her preferred route was closed for road works resulting in a nearly two-hour crawl around London!

Production Board

When you have analysed all of the variables that appear in each section of the broken down script, you need to create a production board. The board will enable you to quickly see which is the most efficient order for filming the movie. Do this by going back to the broken down script, and taking each scene and create a 'strip' for it. Each of the variables listed above will need to be marked on the production board, as below.

SHOOTING DAY	DAY 1				DAY 2			DAY 3		
DAY / NIGHT	D	D	D	D	D	D	D	D	D	D
INT / EXT	INT	INT	EXT	INT	EXT	EXT	INT	EXT	INT	INT
LOCATION / STUDIO	L	L	L	L	L	L	L	S	S	S
PAGE COUNT	3/8	9/8	11/8	1/8	9/8	9/8	6/8	3/8	11/8	11/8
TITLE _____ DIR _____ PROD CO _____	Sally's bedroom	Sally's kitchen	Sally's garden	Sally's bathroom	School grounds	High Street	Tobacconist	Spaceship	Spaceship	Spaceship
SCENE NUMBER	60	83	15	03	32	34	36	41	110	111
CAST:										
ACTOR 1 BOB					1	1	1			
ACTOR 2 SALLY	2	2	2	2	2		2	2	2	2
ACTOR 3 BILL	3	3		3						
ACTOR 4 FRED									4	4
ACTOR 5 JO										5
ACTOR 6 FERGUS					6	6	6			
ACTOR 7 SAM						7	7			
ACTOR 8 EXTRAS					8					
ACTOR 9 FIREFIGHTER		9	9	9						
ACTOR 10 FIRE CHIEF		10	10	10						
PROPS:										
SWORD (SW)					SW	SW	SW			
FIRE TRUCK / HOSE (FT)		FT	FT	FT						
PISTOL (PL)									PL	PL
CAMERA EQUIPMENT:										
DOLLY (DO)								DO	DO	DO
CRANE (CR)								CR	CR	CR
GRIP (GR)	GR									
SPECIAL EFFECTS:										
FAKE BLOOD (FB)						FB	FB		FB	FB
WOUNDS (WD)	WD		WD	WD		WD	WD			WD
WATER (WT)		WT	WT	WT						
FIRE (FR)		FR	FR	FR						
ANIMALS:										
DOG (DG)	DG	DG	DG	DG						
SPIDER (SP)									SP	SP

figure 3.7
Sample production board

Writing for Lo-To-No Budget Films

On the CD you will find lo-to-no budget story tools. These are printable templates to help you to write a script for a lo-to-no budget movie.

Before looking for a screenplay that you can produce, it is an excellent idea to explore the possibilities you have, as a producer, to minimise costs on any items that affect the story. Special consideration should be given to locations, actors, animals, props and wardrobe. Obviously, items that you can get for free, or very cheaply, must be able to add to the screen production values of your film. Once you have these items in place, then you can see what story can be built up around them.

The traditional approach is back-to-front. For example, if you have a screenplay that absolutely requires you to shoot a film on an aircraft carrier, then as a producer you must prioritise gaining free or cheap access to a suitable ship. The lo-budget approach is to write the script if and when you have free access to the aircraft carrier.

The first task in writing a lo-budget script is to list everything that you might have access to for nothing or next to nothing. If you take the traditional budget one sheet, simply list all of the available items that you know you don't need to pay for.

Producer	0

This is you. Whatever you do, make sure that your living expenses are covered for at least four months.

Script	0

You will be partnering with a writer, will you not? And most probably sharing the financial risk too. Perhaps you will write the script yourself.

Actors	0

List all the actors you know who would work for you if there was a suitable part. Pay special attention to any child actors or animals that might be available. Common advice is to limit the cast to four or five parts, and although this could hamper your creativity. You also have to balance this against the extra cost involved: the more actors, the more expensive transportation and catering will be. Try to keep it as simple as you can without limiting your creativity.

Camera	0

Whatever originating format you choose, make certain that it will deliver the images you need in order to sell your film.

What sort of camera can you blag? What format is it? 16mm, 35mm, or DV? Is the camera available for a stretch of several weeks, or is the great deal only available on the weekends, which would affect your shooting schedule. Do you know anyone who belongs to a college film club, or film school where they might have access to free equipment? These limitations could affect the story that you will be able to tell.

Make-up	0

Are there any special make-up effects that will help to tell your story? Fake blood, prosthetics, wounds and wigs can add to your budget unless you can convince a talented newcomer to work for free.

Wardrobe	0

Guerrilla filmmakers would return the already cheap costumes to the clothes store after filming to keep the budget at zero.

Are there any unique wardrobe items that you have access to that would increase your production values without increasing the budget? Used clothing stores can often provide useful costumes and props.

Location Fees	0

Which properties can you shoot in for free? What about your own home or someone else's, your college, your children's school or a local church.

Insurance	0

You'll need insurance to guarantee to the owner of the camera that you can replace it if it is lost, damaged or stolen. Your insurance broker may let you add the kit to your home contents insurance during the shoot.

Crew	0

You are making a feature film that will further the careers of everyone involved, and they want you to pay them? Learn how to say the word 'next'.

Art Department	0

Props, prosthetics, special effects. Whoever the hapless art director is on your shoot will constantly be nagging you for money to buy more paint. If you can't afford to give them any, make sure you hire an art director who has lots of contacts and favours to pull in. Search for unusual and expensive-looking items that could add to the look of the film. I once worked on a shoot near a quarry; we shot the sound, smoke and debris of the blasting and it enhanced our low-budget war feature.

Transport	0

What transport do you have available? Robert Rodriguez had a school bus. Do you know someone with a prison truck, a delivery van, a Second World War vehicle – anything that can either facilitate the making of your movie, or can be used as a prop in the movie. Or both?

Grand Total	**0**

Now, armed with your list of freebies, you are ready to write a script that you have the budget and the resources to actually make.

Moving the Budget Down

Screenwriter William C. Martell is an expert at gaining free access to military bases and ships for his producers. As a writer, he sources naval installations, for example, and then researches the storylines that could be set in a nuclear submarine. He makes sure that the story meets government standards (i.e. no dirty dealings by US Marines) and then approaches a producer knowing that his script has a free, big budget location like an aircraft carrier or nuclear submarine. His feature film, *Crash Dive* with Gary Busey, was created in this manner.

Suppose you have just £3,000 ($5,000) to make a feature film, using 35mm film stock. This is not the impossible dream that everyone inside the industry will tell you. In order for a film of this budget to succeed, you must develop a clear strategy.

Budget in reverse: work up the budget sheet, first putting the grand total in – this is the amount that you know can get your hands on. Then work up the budget sheet, and figure how much you can spend on each element, consider what you can get for free and what is on your doorstep and then you can work out what kind of film you can make with what you have, not what you want.

Strategy for Producing a Zero Budget Film

There are several areas of concern when developing a no-budget film. Each area must be considered in advance, and potential problems solved with fresh ideas.

The more you can bend and twist the traditional film professionals' notions of what can and cannot be done, the more likely you are to earn their respect and the chance of a proper job.

The more you are able to surprise and entertain audiences with the story, the sooner the audience and the film buyers will forget the miniscule budget and offer you a handsome reward for your film.

Hint The astute producer with a no-budget film seeks either notoriety or celebrity status.

Script Strategy

A movie with no budget is about how much cable you can afford to rent and how many power points are available for you to tap into. The most successful movies for this budget will typically take place in one or two locations which are geographically close to each other.

The locations are few so that the film can be shot relatively quickly; they are close together because a 35mm camera kit is heavy and expensive to move.

Hint The most successful careers in America are launched with the same script: take a gang of kids to a house and chop them up. *Reservoir Dogs, Clerks, The Blair Witch Project, Night of the Living Dead.*

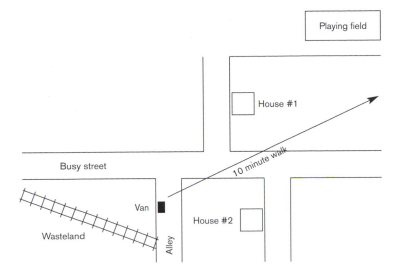

figure 3.8
Location map to show how a low budget story is filmed

Locations Strategy

Locations can make or break your film. A great location can add thousands to your art department budget – literally for nothing. The trick is to find the right location for you and your story.

The most important element an astute producer looks for is a location that they can have complete control of during the time the cast and crew are on location. Then, a good location is one that can safely accommodate the needs of the script, the crew and the performers. A good location will also be close to first aid, police and fire stations, and public transportation. Of course it will be photogenic. Lastly, a good location must be cheap or free.

Naturally, this is an extremely difficult combination to source. Often, a more lateral approach to locations can be used. If you are to shoot in an area of a town or city try to choose different locations within a ten-minute walk of a central location. This location should be one where you can park a van or two, and will be the area where your catering truck will sit. A second van can double as a mobile camera and sound equipment store. From this central location you can then walk with your equipment to each location, minimising costs and maximising time on location.

Writer director David Baer used a useful technique when working on his first feature, *Broken Vessels* and then while in pre-production on a current project, *Mattress Man*. He found several different alleyways where a catering van could park. He then set off in ten minute walks in each direction, scouting for possible locations: a park, a school yard, a strip mall, a house and some wasteland beside a disused railroad siding. It took several attempts to find the right location for the catering van. He then researched the locations, and discovered that each location has two very different exteriors: the front and the back. By some clever and cheap art direction, he was able to use each location as if it were two, thereby adding scope to the story, and production values to the film. A particular stroke of luck was his discovery that the owner of one of the locations had three geese for watchdogs, and was willing to allow his pets to serve as stunt animals in the film, creating an entirely new element to the story.

David already had an idea of the story he wanted to tell, and also had some pretty good ideas of how he wanted it to look. With these elements in mind, he wrote an extremely good first draft in two weeks, and pre-production commenced while he wrote the second draft. The search for locations also impacts on the story, with key elements of the scripts modified to fit in with new opportunities.

Talent Strategy

Raindance is always falling foul of guilds and unions who think we preach that you should never pay cast or crew. Of course that is nonsense. We think that everyone working on a film should be paid, and paid well. But, what if the film won't get made unless a whole lot of talented people donate their time for free? How good is the screenplay? How good is the producer? And what payment deferral programme will you have in place?

Attracting big name actors to a project like this is fraught with difficulty. Usually they will be unconvinced that you can make them 'look good' with no money, and especially with no time.

A strategy here would be to allow the actor to direct. Tell them it is an experiment, and only if it works out will you try to sell it. Or give a bit player a leading role, and dazzle them with some special effect you are able to pull off with no money. Then see if they want to see themselves killed in a new way. You are essentially improving their showreel.

Another increasingly popular strategy is to use non-professional or semi-professional actors. Depending on your skill as a director this is also a valid way to find cast, but you may need to include extra rehearsal time to accommodate the less experienced performers.

Hint Named actors will help you to sell your film. Also, try to get a cast that is as varied and physically striking as possible.

Special Effects Strategy

Stay clear of gunshots and swordplay unless you have a licensed professional on set. If you don't, you could end up in prison.

Try to find a novice special effects supervisor, and/or a fight/stunt director by trawling through art, drama and film schools. Simple punches, slaps and falls look far better when a fight director is involved. A good fight director can also create a good brawl scene.

A well choreographed fight scene or a convincing special effect will enhance the visual impact of your film dramatically and give you whole new story possibilities.

Shooting Schedule Strategy

Keep the shoot as simple as possible. Perhaps you can shoot the film in chronological order. This allows the performers closer contact with the script, and creates more of a 'stage play' feel to the shoot.

Sample £3000 35mm Shoot

This is a plan to shoot a 35mm feature film in a week for less than £3000 ($5000).

A producer discovers that he is able to book his local church hall basement for free most days of the week. He decides to take advantage of this, follows the strategies listed above and gets an excellent script written by a professional writer in exchange for partnership in the profits of the film.

It is a one-location shoot set in a church hall basement. The story is the wedding banquet after the wedding and the relationships between the bride, the groom, and the bride's three ex-boyfriends who are all guests at the wedding. The script has been professionally written and rehearsed through a series of workshops and rehearsals, during which the writer has carefully rewritten the script to create a dozen characters.

Day 1 Monday

Food	25.00

The cast meet at a rehearsal room (which could be the location) and rehearse. The working day is light. It could be from 4pm to 10pm to allow for day work, or from 10am to 4pm to allow for evening work. In either event, the day is professional and well run. Tea and coffee are available. Sandwiches are prepared by the director's assistant.

Day 2 Tuesday

Food	25.00

As above. Rehearse.

Day 3 Wednesday

Food	25.00

More rehearsal, as above. The actors are realising that they are getting professional on-set rehearsal time, which there is rarely time for in a more traditional kind of production.

Today you may not be able to use the church basement as you had planned due to a Boy Scout meeting. Move to another location.

Day 4 Thursday

Food	25.00

Additional rehearsal, but this time with the director of photography and the sound recordist. They watch the rehearsal and make notes. The costume designer also attends and takes measurements. The men will be wearing tuxedos (provided by the local tailor in exchange for publicity) and the women will be wearing formal gowns (supplied by the actresses). Notes are made regarding hair and make-up.

Day 5 Friday

Food	25.00
Delivery charge for camera	60.00
Transport for assistants	10.00
Insurance	400.00
Sound equipment	200.00

An assistant is sent to the film stock company to pick up nine 1000 foot rolls of free film stock supplied in exchange for promotion. The camera package is delivered. The camera package is free because the week-end used for shooting is off-peak, and the camera rental facility has several unused cameras. They are assisting in exchange for promotion.

The sound man arrives with the recording equipment. It is difficult to arrange for free hire of sound equipment, and this particular sound recordist is just starting out and has not yet got his own equipment.

Do not burn out your cast. Keep everyone well rested and motivated.

Actors, make-up and wardrobe arrive late morning for one last run through, followed by a technical rehearsal with camera and sound. Make sure that everyone leaves in good time for a sound night's sleep and that the equipment and props are well secured.

Day 6 Saturday

Food	25.00
Wedding cake	60.00
Prop food	100.00
Prop drinks	60.00

The film must be shot today. The church basement is not available on Sunday due to commitments to the local churchgoers.

Crew arrive at 8am to set up. Actors arrive at 9am for make-up and wardrobe. Dress rehearsal begins at 10am. At 1pm, cast and crew break for at least an hour for lunch and at 2pm the shoot begins.

The story revolves around the head table at the wedding reception. Since the production has just nine rolls of 1000 foot film, which run at around eleven minutes each, the actors only have one take. The point of the rehearsals was to make them totally comfortable with the script and the dynamics of the shoot. If they stumble during a take there is no possibility of a retake. They must be able to recover, as in a stage play.

The DoP is using a wide-angle lens, which means that the entire room is in focus. By moving in close to an actor, that actor will appear cloe up with the rest of the actors in frame and in focus. Handheld or with a dolly, the camera will move in and out of each actor's face, under the table and around the room in a fluid medium master shot.

At the end of each roll, the director will whisper 'cut', and the actors will keep on talking. The sound will keep rolling, and the magazine will be quickly changed (this should take no longer than a minute). On 'action' the camera will roll, and after about a hundred minutes, the film will be shot. The sound is left running to allow for the possibilities of overlapping, or to allow for an edit whereby the picture cuts, and the sound is played over leader tape until the camera rolls again.

When the film is finished, the equipment is packed away ready for collection, and the cast and crew can party on the prop food!

Post-production

Develop negative at 6p per foot x 9000	540.00
Telecine at £100 per hour x 4 hours	400.00
Tape stock	200.00

Editing should be elementary on this project, but the key note here is to spend as much time as possible on sound: using ADR and foley as necessary in order to give the film playability.

Marketing Strategy

One sheet	100.00
VHS preview cassette	300.00
Press kits	300.00

Robert Rodriguez made *El Mariachi* for $7500. We made our film for $5000.

Robert Rodriguez shot his on 16mm. We shot ours on 35mm!

Hint In Hollywood, they say if you can make a stage play look like cinema, then you have talent. You essentially have a stage play. If you have Hollywood talent, you will earn a sinful amount of money.

Summary

1. Choose a budget that is realistic for your project.

2. Choose a project that is realistic for your budget.

3. Make the most of what you can get for free.

The first thing you need when you are making a film is film stock.

Seven Essential Steps for Becoming Rich and Famous by Making a Low Budget Film

Step 2 Find Some Money

Making a movie need not be expensive. One of the goals of this book is to demonstrate that you will not need as much money as you think you might. Filmmakers have welcomed the advent of digital video. While it is true that digital video and desktop editing systems have democratised the filmmaking process by making certain elements of the process cheaper, money is still needed.

How much is up to you. Some filmmakers shoot and record their own sound on a digital video camera. Others, like Steven Spielberg, require crews of hundreds. Is Spielberg's film more valid because more people worked on it? Hardly so – it just looks different.

The main consideration when deciding how much money you need is to be realistic. It is fine and good to say you have a £20 million budget, but the chances of that happening on your first film are very remote. Why not choose a simple project for your first film: one that takes place in a limited number of locations, and is easy to shoot.

The bottom line is that many wannabe filmmakers use the fact that their budget is 60% raised as a way to procrastinate, one of the three reasons you will not make your film. These same filmmakers are the ones who believe that filmmaking is hanging around the set with Cameron Diaz. If you are ever in a position where you have 60% of your budget raised, why not reduce your budget by 40% and shoot with the money you already have. You will quickly learn that the 60% has been pledged with so many strings as to not really to have existed in the first place.

The important thing to do is to find a project that fits with the amount of money you think you can raise in a specific period of time: for example 'I need £50,000 in ninety days'. That way you will have a start date built into your schedule from the outset, which will help to build the immediacy of your project into every pitch.

Hint You cannot raise money until you have an excellent script (see step one). Do not proceed further until you have found or written a superb script.

---

4   **Originating Formats**

IN THIS CHAPTER we discuss all the different picture originating formats, and learn how to negotiate maximum value for the budget.

Traditionally, movies have been shot on costly film stock using expensive cameras and developed and processed at a lab, where money evaporates quicker than it could be raised.

Today there are a host of cheap and inexpensive ways to record pictures, in both of the two main originating formats: film and tape.

A great deal of debate centres on the value of celluloid at this stage in the 21st century. In London, the major tape camera manufacturers hold seminar after workshop after demonstration on how wonderful tape formats really are. Yet most feature films are still shot on film.

I have worked on both formats, and love them both. Each format has its own characteristics and virtues. The danger for filmmakers is trying to make a tape format look like film by using one of the so-called 'film-effect' software programmes. In so doing they neglect to use the attributes of digital video, something a sculptor would call 'truth to materials'.

I studied sculpture at art school and was taught the concept of 'truth to materials'. That phrase means that if you were carving, you should choose the material (marble, granite, sandstone, pine, oak, beech) that would best express the shape you were trying make. A truly great sculptor would use the truth of the material to enhance the shape. So too a filmmaker should use the medium (the material) that best suits the images and the story they tell.

Hint   Choose the originating format that suits your story, the look of the film you want to make and the budget.

About 45% of the 2000 short films submitted to Raindance Film Festival in 2003 were shot on film.

Choosing the best format is a complicated issue, especially if you are converting to film. Before making a final decision, you have to consider the following variables: price, availability, quality, flexibility, artistic qualities and reliability.

Originating on Digital

Digital video can be confusing. There is DV, MiniDV, DVCAM, Digital Betacam (DigiBeta), DVPRO and HDTV. Everyone in the industry lets these words, or acronyms slide off their tongue, and many people don't even know what they mean.

DV is an international standard created by a consortium of eleven companies for a consumer digital video format.

Here's the techie stuff.

DV, originally known as DVC (Digital Video Cassette), uses a 1/4 inch metal evaporate tape to record very high quality digital video. The video is sampled at the same rate – 720 pixels per scanline – although the colour information is sampled at half the D-1 rate: 4:2:0 in 625-line (PAL) formats. Video is compressed using a Discrete Cosine Transform (DCT), the same sort of compression used in motion-JPEG. However, DV's DCT allows for more local optimisation (of quantising tables) within the frame than do JPEG compressors, allowing for higher quality at the nominal 5:1 compression factor than a JPEG frame would show.

DV uses intraframe compression: each compressed frame depends entirely on itself, and not on any data from preceding or following frames. However, it also uses adaptive interfield compression; if the compressor detects little difference between the two interlaced fields of a frame, it will compress them together, freeing up some of the 'bit budget' to allow for higher overall quality. In theory, this means that static areas of images will be more accurately represented than areas with a lot of motion; in practice, this can sometimes be observed as a slight degree of 'blockiness' in the immediate vicinity of moving objects DV video information is carried in a nominal 25 megabit per second (Mbps) data stream. Once you add in audio, subcode (including timecode), Insert and Track Information (ITI), and error correction, the total data stream come to about 36Mbps.

The irony of DV is that the signal recorded on a cheap high street camera is the same as one recorded on an expensive professional machine. The real difference in quality lies in the camera and lens sections of the individual cameras available.

There are approximately a dozen different digital formats, geared to specific types of cameras, each with different advantages and disadvantages. These formats are divided into three main groups by cost.

Cheap – Consumer/Prosumer

Remember that the image signals recorded are the same, regardless of the DV camera.

If you are looking for a DV camera and have a limited budget, MiniDV and DVCAM are your first options. The technology used by manufacturers of these cameras is very similar and the picture quality is fundamentally the same regardless of the manufacturer or type of camera. These cameras are Standard Definition digital formats (SDTV).

Advantages

Consumer format cameras will give you the same image quality as Betacam SP, but with all the advantages of digital and at a fraction of the price. They can produce broadcast-quality images. You can also do high-quality 'online' editing on consumer-grade, home computers.

Limitations

The true test of a MiniDV and DVCAM system is to see how they handle wide angle and panorama shots – which have a huge amount of information to record. Doing a camera test on these sorts of shots will tell you instantly whether or not the camera is up to the task you require.

MiniDV and DVCAM cameras are not equipped to handle the amount of visual information in wide shots or rapid pans. The chip size that generates the picture is about a third of an inch across. While these shots may look good on a TV monitor, they can look soft or fuzzy when blown up onto a screen (either from a film print or by a digital projector). They are very good in medium shots and close-ups.

Having said that, movies like *The Intended*, *Timecode* and *Tadpole* all screened at Raindance Film Festival and were shot on prosumer cameras like the Sony PD100, which have either looked fantastic when screened, or the fuzzy and grainy image qualities did not matter because of the quality of the script.

These formats also lack many of the higher-end professional 'bells-and-whistles' features in the camcorders themselves which can limit some of the artier shots which you might require.

Hint These formats are able to produce broadcast quality images and sound at incredibly cheap prices. Picture quality is the same regardless of the camera used. Buy the camera with the best lenses and picture capture card you can afford. Creative control of the precise look of the actual images is best left to post-production.

Medium – Broadcast Professional

Analogue post-production picture edit utilised on/off-line tape decks. Brand new they cost tens of thousands. I found one in perfectly good order last week abandoned on the sidewalk. They have been made obsolete by Digital Betacam and Final Cut Pro/Avid editing software.

There are three formats. In order of quality: DVCPRO from Panasonic and D-9 from JVC are similar technologically and produce similar quality pictures and sound. Higher quality cameras come from Sony with their Digital Betacam cameras – the Betacam SX and the higher quality Sony Digital Betacam. These cameras were originally created for TV news programmes and to update analogue formats in order to make the cameras compatible with advances in digital post-production. These formats are often found in semi-professional environments like universities.

Advantages

Cameras are usually supplied with a wide range of lenses and other accessories making in-camera effects more possible than in consumer cameras.

Hint Digital Betacam is the highest quality in the SDTV digital formats (4:3 ratio). If you are shooting for a 35mm blow-up, professional opinion dictates that Digital Betacam is really the lowest quality you should use.

Limitations

These cameras are not recommended for shooting at unusual speeds: either slow or fast motion.

High Definition (HD)

HD has four times the resolution of DigiBeta. The HD formats all have an aspect ratio of 16:9, whereas all the Standard Definition formats are usually 4:3 (with a function to switch to 16:9). High Definition rivals the quality of 35mm on a big screen making it the most logical format to consider for a theatrical release (on film or large-screen digital projection).

A relatively new camera, called the Viper, records directly onto a hard disk. This is the camera used on *The Russian Ark* – a one-take feature film, which is a tour de force of blocking and staging. It requires the use of large batteries of monitors, hard drives and cables making it less flexible for location shooting than a tape-fed camera.

For a full exploration and explanation of HD and its associated costs and implications see Appendix 1.

Advantages

There are five basic advantages to High Definition (HD) versus Standard Definition (SD).

– enhanced picture quality
– better contrast capability
– progressive scan mode (film look)
– a new interface for transferring signals called HD SDI
– the picture size is three times the size of DigiBeta

Features shot on HD include: *Star Wars 1 & 2*, *Matrix 2: The Matrix Reloaded*, *Ghosts of the Abyss*, *Shadowlands*, *Spy Kids 2*, and *Bowling for Columbine*.

The great advantage of shooting on HD is cost. A BBC study states that shooting on HD saves 30% over Super16 film.

Limitations

HD Cameras are the most expensive tape formats to rent and in some cases approach and even exceed the rental rates of 35mm. However, with the differential in film stock purchase and lab costs, production costs can be significantly lower.

HD lenses also have a greater depth of field than their 35mm cousins, and it takes a great deal of careful lighting and shot set up to make sure the audience is focused on the part of the picture they are meant to be looking at.

Hint Whichever format and camera you choose, your crew costs will be the same.

Summary of Digital Options

The more money you spend to rent or buy, the more operational features exist on the camera to assist you in exploiting the medium. The

Do not forget that all digital cameras record the same kind of information. It is the lens and features that vary from camera to camera.

more expensive the camera, the better the lens quality. Certain cameras are better suited to certain kinds of filmmaking; for example for a documentary you may need the portability of a small camera that can be used handheld. When you consider the type of project you are making, then you can decide how important the 4:3 or 16:9 format really is, and whether or not you need a quick-release plate on the camera mount.

Digital Q&A

Native 16:9

The term 'native 16:9' or '16x9' refers to a CCD sensor which is constructed to the 'widescreen' shape in the first place. CCD sensors made to the original 4x3 television format (i.e. an aspect ratio of 1.33:1), which appear to be switchable to 'widescreen' do this simply by cutting off the top and bottom of the frame. By doing this, they use fewer pixels to stretch and cover the same area, and therefore must be delivering a less 'concentrated' picture quality when compared with true 16x9 CCD sensors.

All this will change as Standard Definition Television (SDTV) slowly disappears from the general landscape.

What are the picture quality differences between MiniDV and HD?
There is a huge difference in quality between MiniDV and HD. Image quality is dictated by the size of the chip. Chip size determines the number of pixels per frame that can be recorded.

MiniDV cameras use a quarter or third inch chip, HD cameras use a 2/3rds inch chip, and as a result, the amount of image information that HD can capture is physically greater, and so the quality is higher.

What other physical items affect image quality?
Lenses and lighting. Cheap cameras have cheap lenses. Cheap cinematographers give you cheap lighting.

What is an artifact?
When digital compression technology is pushed to the limit (tries to store more information than it is designed to) we see something called an artifact mixed in with the images as they get softer.

What do I need to be aware of when shooting on digital, and doing post-production on a non-linear editing system?
Some formats are not well supported in post. Make certain you choose a format that is supported in post-production so that you avoid any costly and time consuming delays.

Where are the big jumps in cost, and what are the advantages?
There is not that big a difference in the actual shoot, money wise. Tapes will range between £5 and £60. But there is a huge jump in image quality between MiniDV and HDCAM.

The main price differential is in camera hire. In London a good prosumer camera like the Sony PD150 rents for about £50 per day, while a complete High Definition kit rents for about £5000 per week or £1000 per day.

I am planning to convert my digital movie to a 35mm film print. What are the cost differences between shooting on MiniDV or on HD?
There is no cost difference to converting MiniDV to 35mm or HD to film as the processes are almost identical.

Originating on Film

Video uses 'white balance' to electronically achieve the same result.

There are two types of film stock: indoors (tungsten) and daylight. Tungsten is balanced to a colour value, or colour temperature of 3200°K (Kelvin). If you have ever used indoor film stock outside, you will notice that it can look very orange. Conversely, daylight film stock is balanced to 5500°K. If you use daylight film stock inside, it can look very blue. You can use any type of film stock you wish, as long as it is colour corrected using the correct photographic filter on either the lens or the lamps. Be wary too if you use mixture of light sources – daylight and tungsten together. Different film stocks also come with different sensitivities to light, or 'speeds' measured by an 'ASA' or 'ISO' rating.

I went to art school where I studied oil painting. Despite all of the technical advances with acrylic paints, many artists still prefer to use oil paints. The oil paints they use are little changed from those used by Rembrandt.

Film still remains the format of choice for a vast number of filmmakers. Motion picture film stock is categorised by its width in millimetres. The most common widths (formats) are 8mm (amateur film), 16mm, 35mm (standard movie theatre film), and 70mm (IMAX). Super8 and 16mm are entry level film formats. 16mm is traditionally used in film schools.

Super8

In May 1965 a new film format – Super8 film – was introduced by the Eastman Kodak Company. The original standard 8mm film had been derived by dividing 16mm film in half. Sprocket holes were punched in both sides of the film, so that the gears in the camera could move the film along. Then, engineers discovered how the film could be advanced using just a single set of sprocket holes down one side of the film, leaving the extra margin for picture. So Super8 film has a larger picture area than standard 8mm, which is hardly ever used any more. Today a filmmaker can acquire a sophisticated array of Super8 cameras and lenses for a very modest outlay.

Advantages

The Straight 8 Film Festival in London operates a clever entry policy: They only take single rolls of film, undeveloped. All entries are accepted. The festival develops the films and spools them together, and screens them, sight unseen at the festival!

The cameras are cheap and light. It is possible to get a wide range of camera accessories. Filmmakers can exploit its grainy quality.

Limitations

Developing film stock is difficult in Europe. There is now an outlet of Pro8mm, an American company, in Soho, but otherwise, film has to be sent to the US to be developed. The grainy quality of the pictures is not suitable for some work.

16mm/Super16

16mm became the film stock of choice for UK TV. It was shot at 25fps to match the European frame rate.

16mm and its sister Super16 are attractive formats because of the cheapness of camera equipment hire (at least 75% cheaper than 35mm, and the film stock and lab costs are reduced too). In addition,

Film is made of two parts: a carrier material called celluloid and a light sensitive coating called emulsion. The celluloid has holes punched into it down either one or both sides – depending on the gauge or format. The holes, called sprocket holes, allow a gear mechanism in either a camera or projector to advance it past the aperture in the camera in stages. Each time the film stops, the aperture is opened and the film is exposed to light; then the aperture is closed again and the next frame is advanced into place. This happens 24 times every second in a motion picture camera. The light hits the light sensitive coating on the celluloid, and depending on the strength of the light, the emulsion will respond proportionally. When the film is developed, a series of baths wash away the unexposed emulsion creating the image.

the cameras are a great deal lighter than 35mm. As with Super8, Super16 has holes down just one side of the film, allowing for a greater image capture area.

Advantages
Cheaper, lightweight cameras, with an acceptable image size to support a 35mm blow-up.

Limitations
The disadvantage is that finished 16mm film cannot be shown in any commercial theatre, although it can be played in art houses and certain private screening rooms. If you shoot Super16, it becomes virtually impossible to screen the film on film in a screening room, as few projectors are able to accommodate Super16 projection. Some also claim that it does not look good blown up as the graininess is increased. Also, because 'picture' now occupies the space where sound normally goes, a 'sound Super16 print' does not exist.

Some schools like the New York Film Academy use old 16mm news cameras which also have a magnetic stripe for audio, allowing for picture and sound to be recorded on one pass through the camera. When developed, the audio track is already synchronised with the picture.

35mm/Super35

35mm film stock is the industry standard. Despite the advances of HD, if you tell any industry executive you are shooting a 35mm film, they instantly assume you are a professional filmmaker. Again, Super35 has only one side with sprocket holes, allowing for greater image area on the negative.

Advantages
The film comes in a vast variety of film types and is supported by an impressive list of cameras and accessories. The image size produces excellent results, and your finished film can play in every commercial cinema in the world.

Limitations
A basic 35mm kit is heavy and big. It is also extremely expensive at £200,000 upwards. Insurance, crew and transport costs rise enormously from 16mm.

16mm vs 35mm

Mike Figgis' *Leaving Las Vegas* (1995) was shot on Super16. It was hard to believe it had not been shot on 35mm due to the quality of the blow-up

When shooting with film stock, 16mm is at least 60% cheaper. If you decide to shoot on film, 16mm is an option, but the finished film will need to be blown up to 35mm if the film is to be shown in cinemas. A blow-up can be very expensive, costing upwards of £30,000 ($50,000). Some filmmakers find that using this money allows them to shoot on 35mm.

But if cash is tight, the film can be shot on 16mm and then blown up at the end of the post-production stage if you raise more funds.

If the film is to be shown solely on television, or a DVD or video format, then no blow-up is necessary and the cost advantages of shooting on 16mm are obvious.

However, if you are shooting for cinematic release where the end result is a 35mm print, then the options become more interesting.

You can originate on tape, 16mm or 35mm. 35mm is the most expensive format to shoot on. But when it is finished, it is in the correct and, as some would argue, the professional format. If you shoot on tape, then you have to pay for a very expensive tape-to-film transfer which could cost £75,000 ($115,000) or more.

And if you shoot on 16mm, then you have to pay for a blow-up to 35mm, which can cost from £15–25,000 ($25–40,000).

Some would argue that it is better to put the blow-up costs into paying for the more expensive film stock and to shoot on 35mm in the first place.

Others argue that shooting on 35mm is so expensive and such a risky thing to do (especially without the guarantee of a cinematic release) that is smarter to shoot on 16mm or tape, wait for the film buyers to see and love it – and then get them to blow it up to 35mm.

I had to say this. It will make me very unpopular, but I have done it!

There is something about a 35mm shoot that is professional. It reflects in the energy levels and commitment of the crew. Shoot 16mm and you look like a student film. Shoot DV and you run the danger of looking amateur.

Time	35mm@24 fps	35mm@25 fps	16mm@24 fps	16mm@25 fps
1 min	90ft	93ft 9in	36ft	37ft 6in
5 mins	450ft	468ft 9in	180ft	187ft 6in
10 mins	900ft	937ft 9in	360ft	375ft

figure 4.1
16mm and 35mm length chart

16 frames of 35mm = 1 foot

40 frames of 16mm = 1 foot

Three Types of Film Stock

Film stock is sold by the foot and in cans of 100ft (16mm only) 400ft, 1000ft (35mm only). Since 16mm pictures are smaller than 35mm pictures, the overall length of the film is shorter.

The three types of film stock are described by the manner in which they are sold: retail, resale market and black market.

Buying retail

Making a film is not just about writing cheques. As a producer it's down to you to find the great idea and then to find the money. Once you have the money, then you can start writing cheques to bring the great idea you have to the screen.

There are many differences between individual producers, but one quality all good producers have is the ability to negotiate.

When buying retail film stock, negotiating skills can save you a huge percentage of your film stock budget.

Negotiation tactics

The secret to successful negotiating is to always try to get the person on the other side of the negotiating table to mention the number that they are after. The first person who mentions the amount of money they want concedes the negotiations to the other side.

Real estate agents are trained to get new clients to mention their budget. The first question you are asked when you walk into an estate agency is: how much can you afford, or what is your budget. I moved recently in London and when I spoke to my first agent I answered the budget question with a hyphenate: £150 to £175 per week. The agent never even heard the £150 per week number and I was soon looking at properties in the £200 per week price range. I lost the argument. I learned from the exercise to mention one number, i.e. £175 per week, and stick to it.

If you don't ask, you don't get. In Robert Rodriguez' excellent book, *Rebel Without a Crew*, he relates the story of one shoot for which he paid retail prices for the film stock. When he found out that the film company had a student rate, he asked why he wasn't given it. 'Because you didn't ask' was the response. If you don't ask, you don't get.

Film stock negotiation techniques

Negotiating over the retail price of film stock is not complicated. The first fact to consider is only two companies manufacturer motion picture film stock: Kodak and Fuji. These two companies directly compete with each other, and dislike each other immensely.

Kodak controls approximately 85% of the market. Up until twenty years ago, the quality of Fuji's film had a somewhat dodgy reputation – the precision of the perforations punched into the sides of the film stock could vary minutely. That problem was corrected in the 1980s and camerapersons agree that Fuji is now an excellent film stock. Kodak has a larger market share because it has an aggressive advertising and marketing programme in schools. As a result most new camerapersons have only trained on Kodak.

When you are negotiating film stock prices, you use the telephone. There is no warehouse or showroom that you go to and view samples. You call up both Kodak and Fuji and tell them that you want to buy some film stock. Your cameraperson will already have told you the amount of indoor and outdoor stock they need, as well as the number of 400ft and 1000ft rolls. If you ask them for the price list, they will fax or email you the list immediately, with the film stock priced per foot. They have lost the first round of the negotiating battle.

If you compare the two company's price lists you will notice that Kodak is fractionally more expensive. The only physical difference is that each company uses a different type of plastic carrier for the film.

Here is how you can call up Kodak and instantly save 30% on your film stock budget.

You: I am an independent producer with numerous projects in various stages of development.
Kodak: Mmmm
You: The first project I am shooting is a fifty thousand foot feature and I have your price list.
Kodak: How much is your film stock budget (they will have a rough guess, given that your shooting ratio is 6:1).
You: Seems like your prices are a little higher than my budget can stretch to.
Kodak: We will work with you. (For some reason, salesmen always say that they will work with you.)
You: (Here you use one word.) Fuji.

The Kodak price should instantly drop about 30% at this point.

Hint God invented first time filmmakers to pay retail. Don't pay retail. Ever!

Basically, since Fuji is a smaller company, it should be possible to drive a better deal with them. After all, their office overheads are much smaller. In the UK there are only two Fuji sales reps, whereas Kodak has a dozen.

Resale market

Out of date film stock is officially unavailable from either Kodak or Fuji for two reasons. Firstly, they are supposed to return the unsold film stock to Japan or the USA in order to reclaim the silver, and secondly they are afraid that if they sell you unused film stock that is past the sell-by date and it malfunctions, you will publicise the fact that this Kodak or Fuji film stock was substandard. However, if you develop a good rapport with the sales rep, you should be able to acquire out-of-date film stock at a substantial (up to 90%) discount.

Occasionally film stock is left over on a shoot, and it is not possible to return it to Kodak or Fuji. This film stock is then sold to a film stock reseller, who then markets the film stock to filmmakers at a discount from its retail list price.

Resellers offer three different types of film stock.

Brand new unopened film stock

Left over from a shoot (which is pretty much the same asking price as the manufacturers, but in smaller quantities).

Recans

These are full rolls of film stock that have been loaded into a film magazine, not used then unloaded and replaced in their original cans for resale. There is a slight chance of light damage, so they sell for up to 40% less than unopened stock. Generally, because the clapper loader was on a professional shoot, the film stock will have been looked after.

Ends

Portions of rolls that were unused during the shoot. The filmmaker sends the exposed part of the roll to the lab, and puts the unexposed part of the film stock back into the can in order to preserve it for later use. Sometimes the filmmaker then sells these ends to a film reseller at a massive discount. They will then sell it to filmmakers at anything up to a 90% discount on the list price, depending on the length of the stock.

figure 4.2
35mm ends chart

Long End	Mid End	Short End
Greater than 750 feet	450–750 feet	Under 450 feet

Black market

My reason for telling you about the black market is because I don't want you to supply the black market yourself. It works like this.

In my position at Raindance, I get a call every few weeks from a 'number withheld'. It's someone I don't really know saying that if I meet them down at the corner, they have five thousand-foot rolls of brand new unopened Kodak or Fuji film stock for as little as £50 ($75) per roll. I know immediately that this film stock is stolen. A brand new unopened thousand footer is worth £300 to £400, plus sales tax.

One of the unwritten rules of engagement for camera crew working on big budget pop promos or commercials is that they get to steal film stock. It's not right. I don't believe in it. But you have to understand that it is part of the perceived industry. Don't let your production supply film stock to the black market.

On the first day of the shoot, the cameraperson will want you to give them all the film stock. Don't do it! Ask them how many feet they have budgeted for that day, and give them that amount. Politely let them know that if they need any more you will need sufficient notice, but you can get it. And then keep the balance under lock and key. That way you won't end up supplying the black market with your film stock.

Getting Film Stock for Free

Film stock is very expensive. Even when using Super8, your film stock budget will soar to thousands of pounds when you start shooting over a 5:1 ratio. Here are some ways to get all the expensive film stock you need for free.

Hire the right director

Directors working on big budget pop promos and commercials often get to take home the left over ends, recans and even brand new unopened film stock at the end of the shoot. While they are supposed to re-enter this film stock into the production company's inventory, or take it to a reseller for resale, the paperwork involved is often too time consuming and the films stock spends a few days after the shoot in the trunk of the director's car, and then in their house for safe-keeping. Before long, another shoot and another four or five thousand feet of film stock accumulate in the director's home.

Many directors of pop promos and commercials have 50,000 feet of 35mm film stock (or more). And these directors, although making an extremely good living as commercial directors, really want to make a feature film. You come along with that terrific script (golden rule number one) and bingo! They get to direct your film, and they bring along the entire film stock required for the feature.

Hint If you choose this route remember that these directors are not used to shooting low budget, and although you will get the film stock free, you could end up with a host of other big-budget equipment and crew that could easily undo the advantage of free film stock.

Do a camera test

Phone up the sales rep at Kodak or Fuji and tell them that you are an independent producer with numerous projects in various stages of development. Tell them that your first project, a 35mm 50,000 ft feature is due to start shooting in sixty days' time and you would like to test their new film stock.

You will get a few thousand feet from Kodak, and a few more thousand feet from Fuji. Then, if you are really ambitious, get a friend who lives out of town to call up and use the same line and get a few more thousand feet.

Hint If you use this route, the batch numbers and brand numbers may not match; you may have some Kodak indoor film and some Fuji outdoor film. Try to use one type of film stock per scene to maintain the same 'look'. If you aren't going to have enough of one type of film stock to cover the whole of a scene, try to use the same type for each element of the scene – use one type for all the wide shots and one for all the close-ups.

Getting film stock from a lab

Labs often have offcuts they recan as ends. They use a portion of these ends when they print trailers, or when they print short optical effects, such as CGI scenes or animations for special effects houses. Go to your lab with a copy of the script and see if you can convince them to give you ends for your shoot. In effect they are becoming your financial partner. Of course, you will then give them the processing work as well.

Hint When a lab gives you free film stock, they will be looking for one of two possible recoupment positions. Either they want you to come back in a few months' time with a proper job and a proper budget for processing or they are looking to become a financial partner in your film with the same benefits as your other investors. Either way, you will need to impress them with the quality of your script.

Redundant film stock

Film production companies always have redundant film stock left over from other shoots. Unopened cans, recans and ends. The difficulty is discovering who in a production company makes the decision about whether or not you can have this redundant film stock.

The quickest and easiest source of the names of film production companies is the *Yellow Pages*. Scroll through the listings and call up. Some companies simply shoot for television on tape, and will not have any 35mm film stock. Other companies, if they are shooting documentaries for European television, will probably shoot only on 16mm, or on tape and will not have any 35mm film stock.

But companies that shoot features, that shoot commercials and pop promos will have redundant film stock.

When I met Matthew Vaughn and Guy Ritchie, they were working as runners for competing advertisement production companies. They didn't know each other at that time, and I am certain that neither of their companies had any redundant film stock!

In larger companies, the person responsible for the storage and safe keeping of redundant film stock is the head runner. In smaller companies, in one to three man bands, it is likely to be the person who answers the telephone who is in charge of this.

Simply call up and ask for the head runner, or the person in charge of redundant film stock. When they are on the line, pitch them and ask them if you can have their redundant film stock for your project.

They will ask you some details, like the subject matter. No one likes to be supplying politically incorrect projects. Sometimes, the head runner will tell you to fax or email a short letter outlining the main points of your project. And sometimes this person will tell you that they can't let you have any of the film stock. In this case, you have just found a budding producer or director. All head runners really want to make their own film. Ask them if they have found a script yet (golden rule number one).

Using vs utilising
At Raindance we have found that calling up and asking for redundant film stock that we could use usually meant that we were turned down. Somehow, the head runners didn't like to give away valuable film stock.

But when we called up and asked them if they had any redundant film stock that we could utilise, we had a near 100% success rate. This always seemed odd, especially when you consider the fact that film stock, like a cigarette or cup of coffee, is pretty much used up when it is utilised. In fact, how can you re-utilise a utilised roll of film stock?

Saying thank you
Saying thank you begins the moment you find out that you have what you want. Make sure you show up at the right time to collect the film stock. Maybe bring a card with you and give it to the person. If not then, make sure a thank you card gets dropped in the mailbox as soon as you get home.

Emailing contacts on a short circular that keeps everyone up to date with the progress of the film is another idea, along with sending them a ticket to the cast and crew screening. These early favour-givers can form the nucleus of your marketing and focus groups, and ultimately, if you are successful, your fan club!

Choosing a Format

Ask yourself the following questions before choosing a format:

1. What sort of production you are undertaking? Is it a mockumentary with a large number of handheld shots that would suit a lightweight camera? Or is it a drama to be shot in a secure location or studio in which a large format film or tape camera would work best? Are there a lot of panoramic and pan shots which would be difficult to capture on a cheap MiniDV camera?

2. What sort of distribution are you planning (tape, DVD, broadcast, theatrical)? Remember that film buyers are still resistant to buying features shot on tape.

3. Does your finished film need to play in a cinema? This alone might dictate whether you should shoot on 35mm.

4. What physical aesthetics of the camera appeal to you? Does it feel

right when you are using it? Do you know your camera and are you familiar with its capabilities and limitations?

5. Can your budget afford the camera you have chosen? If not, are you using lack of money as a way of procrastinating and not making a movie? Get a cheaper format, and shoot!

6. Have you considered how the format you have chosen will impact your post-production budget? Have you considered the costs of transferring film to tape, and when finished editing – of transferring tape to film?

7. Don't let anyone dictate which format you use. Make sure you understand the reasons why you have chosen the particular format, and be prepared to defend your choice to everyone.

8. DVC does not mean Do it Very Cheap.

Summary

1. Choose the format that suits you and your project.

2. Make sure you consult with the other members of the team: cinematographer and editor.

3. If you are not sure about something – ask!

If you thought that was complicated, try talking to a lab!

In Conversation with Carl Schönfeld

Carl Schönfeld has been managing production companies for ten years, producing award-winning documentary and drama for TV as well as theatrical release, working with industry financiers, completion bonds, sales agents and has been invited to panels, masterclasses and film festivals around the world. His digital feature, *My Brother Tom* screened theatrically in seven countries and won over a dozen major awards.

What are the advantages of working in digital?

There is a great feeling of liberation that grips everybody working on the film: the camera department can shoot and move much faster, the director can concentrate more on the acting, the actors love to shoot scenes all the way through – for them it's closer to the theatre experience. It enables them to stay in character and they have to put up with fewer of the long waits that are associated with traditional filmmaking.

Digital filmmaking provides new opportunities for fresh voices, that's what keeps the art of cinema alive. Thomas Vinterberg, would not be the festival-travelling, star-directing, household name he is today without *Festen*, and Lars von Trier would find it much more difficult to reinvent himself without the possibilities of digital technology. Across Europe filmmakers take advantage of creative possibilities and lower cost, like the German films *Halbe Treppe* and *Halbe Miete* or 2002's Raindance winner from France, *Strass*.

What are the disadvantages of working in digital?

As in any liberation there are traps that you only discover when you are out there. You can compare it to non-linear editing, when directors got lost in all the possibilities. Here you can change the set-up in minutes. With *My Brother Tom* all our camera equipment including back-up fitted into a gym bag so we sometimes moved very fast, sending the art department into a panic. More than ever, you need to keep an eye on set preparation. Technology changes all the time, not all gizmos that came out are good at all or appropriate for your project. I recommend early collaboration with a good facilities house who knows what you want to achieve and has an eye on digital developments.

Does the digital medium make your job as a producer easier or harder? Why?

As producer you just want the right look hence the right equipment for the project. For the detail you have to rely on the people you have chosen to work with. Of course if you try to know everything and do everything yourself, you go mad. There is more choice of various directing approaches and looks now, which is a good thing.

Do you agree with those who say digital will never 'look as good as film'?

I don't really care about these para-religious discussions. It's like arguing about the relative merits of PC or Mac. The digital developments allow much better control of the look of a film for an affordable price, and that control may mean to make it look like *The Last Tango in Paris* or Super8 Kodachrome. 35 mm film has a certain texture that nobody wants to lose, but it becomes one tool in a big toolbox; in acquisition it becomes a creative choice rather than industry standard.

Distribution is different. There, 35mm will remain the gauge that can be shown in cinemas all over the world and be converted to all media, unless a huge shift in attitudes to digital distribution occurs.

Digital cameras and tapes are obviously cheaper than film cameras and stock, but are there any other financial benefits of working in digital?
Depending on how you use it, you can move your crew quicker between sets and set-ups, the shooting schedule becomes faster, and that means fewer shooting days, lower costs for wages, location hire, catering, fringes, insurance etc.

Does digital increase or decrease your creative options?
Digitally there are a lot of different ways to shoot a film, faster, slower, HD or DV etc.

Will digital always be on a lower rung than film or will it eventually become just as artistically and commercially accepted?
With *Star Wars* and *Dogville* being done digitally we are past that question. Quality control, the way broadcast technicians used to approach it, is now much more difficult to ensure and that is a good thing. I remember when Hi8 came out we made a documentary for Channel 4 in Sarajevo, some scenes were shot during the regular power cuts in candle light. The technical quality was terrible, but what the people had to say was very moving so it was worth showing.

How would working in digital film aid a beginning film producer in breaking into the industry?
Lower cost helps to lower the risks for investors. But that depends on the project. If the script happens all in a hotel room, like Richard Linklater's *Tape*, the trapped atmosphere and good acting shot in close up works well and DV can make a lot of difference to the budget. If it's a period piece with a huge art department, you won't see much of the design work in low resolution and the saving in camera hire is negligible compared to the budget total. When we decided to shoot *My Brother Tom* in digital it was mostly to get closer to the actors and achieve an intimate atmosphere that would bring out the story better, but it made the finance plan work, too.

Do you think digital will create any sort of shift in the film industry? If so, what kind?
The next exciting step is a kind of punk rock revolution that will happen in post-production; teenagers with Macs in their bedrooms giving a story a more exciting finish than the facility houses in Soho provide for a few hundred pounds per hour.

More films are produced, but fewer make it into the cinemas. As a whole variety of worthwhile films are made that don't get into theatrical distribution or onto terrestrial TV, both smaller festivals like Raindance and DVD sales become more important to audiences who feel over-saturated by Hollywood's blockbusters and standard telly fare.

5   Labs

IF YOU ARE SHOOTING on a tape format, and finishing to a high quality tape, then this chapter will not be particularly relevant, as it deals with the celluloid side of filmmaking. However, understanding what a lab can and cannot do is a vital part of the filmmaking process. New filmmakers are fascinated by the workings of a camera, somewhat bewildered by the choices of tape and film stock, but totally mystified by what actually happens in a lab.

Basically, a lab takes your exposed negative and develops the film in a series of chemical baths. The lab then prepares the negative for post-production, either by making a positive copy on inexpensive film stock (known as the one-light or the work print) if it is to be edited on film, or, if the film is to be edited on computer, cleans and prepares the negative for telecine. When your film has finished post-production (editing) the lab will take the edit points decided on by your editor (edit decision list, or EDL) and cut the negative in exactly the same places as the edit list, and then make another positive copy against which all the edit points are double checked, to produce the answer print.

If you have shot on tape and want to screen on film in a cinema, then at some point the lab will be involved in a transfer to film. During that process there are still the possibilities of changing the look of your movie at the answer print stage.

Telecine is the mechanical process whereby film is transferred to videotape. During this process the film (usually a negative) passes over a bright light and a video camera, and the images are then recorded onto the tape format of your choice. Before the film is transferred it is previewed by an operator, called a colourist, who can change the types of light, i.e. colour and intensity, in order to manipulate the image on tape to the directions of the director.

Visiting The Lab

When you drop off your film negative at the lab, they will need several pieces of information:

- Your name, contact address and telephone number
- The camera report, which details the shots exposed onto the film, completed by your cinematographer or their assistant
- Any special instructions i.e.: if sections of the film were over-exposed, then they would like to know whether or not you would like them to compensate on that roll. It is important to indicate where there might be possible perforation damage, so that they can watch for problems
- When and where you need it returned

- Payment method
- Job title and number, and purchase order number
- The number of rolls, roll numbers, length and type of film
- Instructions for operations to be performed
- Complete shipping instructions, including destination, carrier and insurance requirements
- The disposition of original material: hold or return?

Here is a sample of how your order may be written:

To: The Lab
Street address
City

From: your address
and phone number

With this order:

0-100' rolls colour negative type _____

(Rolls 1-10)
Please process and make one light dailies Y/N
Print through latent image edge numbers Y/N
Return dailies on cores via (carrier) Y/N
Hold original Y/N
Insure for £/$_____

Contact:

---

figure 5.1
Sample lab order

People who work in labs are very nice and polite. But they cannot bear lack of basic information, which may delay the completion of your job (and make the lab look bad as a result).

Getting Credit

It is sometimes possible to get a lab to give you credit, but only if you have involved them in the project, and negotiated the terms under which they will be repaid. In essence, the lab owner becomes one of your financial partners, and is entitled to the same treatment as any other investor with money in the film. Since they represent a key cost in the production budget, expect them to drive a tough deal.

The first step in getting a good deal is to understand how the lab operates.

How labs operate

Labs are located near the airport where rent for industrial buildings is cheaper. They are usually located in industrial space that has a good sized parking lot, a main entrance/reception area, a few offices, a staff room, a screening room, the lab room and a large storage area of several tens of thousands of feet.

The owner of the lab has to purchase chemicals for the developing tanks. These tanks need replenishing every week. This is usually done on a Saturday, meaning that labs are closed on a Saturday. Labs reopen on Sunday night.

The employees who actually do the lab work are semi-skilled. The owner has to have them come in shifts, in order to accommodate the workload.

When your job arrives, and if you are looking for a cheap deal, the first thing the lab owner will want to know is whether or not you need daily rushes. If the answer is yes, your job will have to be scheduled alongside the high-priced feature films and advertisements going through at the same time.

Hint You are more likely to get a really cheap deal at a lab if you do not require dailies.

The next detail the lab owner will want to know is whether or not you need a work print. If the answer is yes, they have to purchase the actual film stock in order to make this, and suffer a financial cost. If the answer is no, and if you do not need the rushes urgently, then you stand a much better chance of getting a cheap deal on developing the film negative.

Hint You are basically utilising spare capacity. The lab owner has already paid the rent, paid for the chemicals and paid for the labour. Doing your non-rush, develop-only job means that they might see some return, however small, for their investment.

The Basic Deal

Film stock processing is priced in pence per foot.

There are three types of deals that are used with laboratories: The first is the rate card price, which also means that you must pay within thirty days. It also assumes that you are credit worthy.

The second deal is the cash on delivery deal. If you are sending 1,490 feet to the lab and the rate card price is 10p per foot, then your COD price might fall to as low as 5p per foot – a saving of 50%.

The third deal is the deferred or pay-you-later-out-of-profits deal. This price could be as much as double the first deal. It all depends at your negotiating skill.

Hint On a deferred deal the lab is essentially becoming one of your financial partners.

Processing Techniques

Never underestimate the processing requirements for a given film and the printing needs for the whole production. There are essentially two times that you will require a lab's services: if you are shooting on film, you will need them to develop the negative and prepare it for telecine transfer. When you have finished editing, you will need the lab to create the final print which then goes out to play in cinemas. To help you appreciate the role of the lab, we will look at the different processes and machinery used in the lab.

When your roll of film arrives at the lab, contact details and processing instructions are checked and double checked. The cans are then opened in a light proof room, and fed into a machine called a continuous processor especially equipped to handle the long lengths of film. This machine moves the film stock through a series of developers, fixers, stop baths, washes and dryer at a controlled speed. As the film moves from tank to tank, squeegees remove the liquid from one tank before submersing it in liquid of the next. The machine is designed to move the film either by engaging the sprocket holes, or by moving it along rollers by its edges.

Normal processing refers to the speed and time a negative moves through the tanks. The only major change from normal processing is to accommodate different camera speeds.

Process Control

The continuous processor is a machine which can be speed controlled. The actual chemicals in the various baths can also be controlled through their temperature and the chemical composition of the developing agents. This is referred to as process control.

The degree of development in the first development stage is the most important factor in determining the final image quality. Careful control is critical at this point. Development is affected by the time of contact between the film and the solution, and the degree of agitation. The other processing steps are also affected by the same factors.

Force (Push) Processing

I once had film stock overexposed by five f-stops that came back with picture and detail after being 'pushed'.

Sometimes you may wish to instruct the lab to ignore normal processing procedure and 'push' the film through the processing process. A camera operator may elect to shoot film at a higher exposure index (EI) than the film's rating, thus underexposing the film, to obtain usable footage under low-light conditions.

The film turned into the lab for force processing is usually underexposed by a known degree. This underexposure can be compensated for in the first developer stage by keeping the film for longer in the development phase of the process. As processing is a continuous process, and the machinery will need to be slowed down to let force processing happen, this can only be done when the lab is not processing any other film.

Hint Make certain your cinematographer understands what will happen if your negative is pushed. Unless you are trying to rescue an accident, experiment. Labs also have showreels of their own work for other filmmakers and will show you other examples of their work in much the same way as a printer can show you several different styles of wedding invitations.

Cross-processing

One option is to use one type of film stock and have it processed as if it were another type. The most common is to use colour reversal films (Kodak VNF-1) which forms dyes in processing using the same Kodak developing agent as colour negative films use to produce a positive image. However, it is possible to process this film stock as if it were negative to create an unusual image. Red and green gain contrast while blue contrast decreases, and a subjectively different look is created. The Spike Lee film, *Clockers*, used Kodak 7239 (in 35mm) cross-processed as negative. You should experiment with some test footage.

Hint Colour negative products have their characteristic long dye life built in at the manufacturing stage. Colour reversal films are different and require additional treatment in processing for long-lived colour dyes. Without this processing step, reversal colour dyes will begin fading immediately and will have lost significant density in a few months unless they are properly fixed.

Bleach Bypass Processing

Bleach bypass processing is also known as skip bleach or silver retention. These are all terms for the same process.

In black and white negative processing, the exposed latent silver image is developed to metallic silver, then the fixer solution removes the remaining silver, which is unexposed and undeveloped, leaving the black, silver negative image.

The same reactions occur in colour negative processing with a couple of extras. During developing, used (oxidized) developer helps form the dye image as the silver image is formed. Once the dye image is in place, there is normally no further need for the silver, so it is converted back to the undeveloped form and then removed by the fixer along with the unexposed silver, leaving only the dye image.

The bleach is the solution that converts developed silver to the undeveloped form. By eliminating the bleach step the developed silver remains in the film and the processed negative will contain both dye and silver images. One might think of the result as a colour image and a black and white image sandwiched together.

When the bleach is bypassed in the negative processing stage, the additional density from retained silver is greatest in the highlights. Conversely, skip bleach positive print process leaves the greatest density in the shadows. Each has its own distinctive look.

The appearance is one of muted colours and somewhat higher contrast. Spielberg's *Saving Private Ryan* used bleach bypass processing to very good effect.

Hint Visualise the final image you want, and then do a series of controlled tests until you get the desired result.

A normal colour image can be re-acquired by simply re-processing the negative (or print), thus removing the retained silver.

Processing Errors

Things can go wrong at the lab. Here are some of the basic processing errors that you should be aware of.

Forced development

Forced processing is most simply defined as over-developing the original in an attempt to compensate for underexposure in the shooting. Side effects include increased grain and higher contrast. Often the resulting pictures are unsatisfactory and the film is unusable

If you are choosing forced development for its artistic merits, then it is usually wise to shoot each scene twice: once for normal developing, and once for forced, on separate rolls, of course.

Scratches

Sometimes a scratch will develop. Scratches can be caused by a particle of dirt (called a hair) on the inside of the camera, the magazine, or a malfunction at the lab. When a scratch develops, the lab and camera operator typically blame each other. If the scratch is on the emulsion side of the film, there is little the lab can do. If the scratch is on the carrier side of the film, then there are certain steps the lab can do to correct or minimise the damage.

Censorship

Labs are bound to report material which they deem to be offensive or immoral. Returning from Iraq, a young British soldier found himself in prison after the local photo lab found still pictures of the war showing severe breaches of the Geneva Convention. The eighteen-year old soldier was court-martialled and awaits trial!

Printmaking

Labs use several techniques to create the positive copies of your film.

Black and White Printing

Black and white printing practices are essentially the same as colour printing practices. However, the lack of such considerations as colour balance, saturation, etc., make black and white printing a less complex operation than colour printing.

Colour Printing

A contact printer, which allows for scene-to-scene density and colour-balance changes, is required for colour printing. It is possible to enlarge or reduce images using an optical printer. If it is necessary to create separation negatives or positives for extended keeping purposes, a step-contact printer is required to provide precision in positioning each successive frame of film. Certain kinds of special effects, like monchrome cross fades, or title inserts may also require a step-optical printer.

Types of Printers and Their Uses

Continuous-contact printer

Film printing is when the lab makes a positive copy of your negative using a light source to produce the exposure. When the image size of the print is the same as that of the original (i.e. 35mm to 35mm, 16mm to 16mm), the printing is usually done in a continuous-contact printer.

The large printing sprocket advances both the original and the print film at a constant rate past the light source. The original and print films are positioned emulsion-to-emulsion with the light passing through the original and exposing the stock to be printed. It's amazing to go to a lab and see thousands of feet of stock fly through the machines every minute.

Step-optical printer

The step-optical printer combines the precision of a step-contact printer with optical flexibility. Like the step-contact, the step-optical printer finds its main use in the production of intermediates and special effects. Whenever the image size of the print is different from that of the original or certain special effects are desired, an optical printer is used. The optical printer can be thought of as a projector on one side and a camera on the other. The image produced by the projector is focused at the plane of the film in the camera gate. Optical printers can be quite complex, providing a range of effects including blow-ups, reductions, skip frames, anamorphic compression, zooms, mattes, etc.

Wet-gate printing

A scratch (digs, abrasions, cinch marks, etc.) are a filmmaker's worst nightmare and can run through all the stages of the printmaking process through to the final print. In order to minimalise this, the film is printed with a wet-gate.

The negative is surrounded by liquid in the hope that the light diffused by the scratch will be absorbed by the liquid thereby minimalising the effects of the scratch. If you are lucky, it works.

Answer Prints

The first time I saw an answer print, I nearly died. Somehow, the print was screened in black and white, even though the film was intended to be in colour. A prime example of poor communication.

The answer print is the first moment of truth. It is called the answer print because it answers all the questions of the director and editor. Each time it screens is called a trial i.e. first trial answer print. The print is screened at trial after trial until the questions are answered and the print is accepted. After all the editing of pictures and sound is done, a trial screening of the answer print is held with the producer, director, editor, cinematographer and lab technician. At the first screening or first trial, each expert notes errors and passes them to the lab for correction in the second trial.

Enlargement and Reduction

When an image on the negative needs to be reduced or enlarged into another negative an optical printer must be used. Because this is a delicate and expensive process, it is usually left until as close to the end of production as possible.

figure 5.2
Aspect ratios
a: 1.33:1 – Television/16mm film/
   35mm Academy aperture
b: 1.66:1 – Widescreen
c: 1.85:1 – Widescreen
d: 2.2:1 – 70mm film
e: 2.35:1 – 35mm film anamorphic
   projection

Blowing up to 35mm

The traditional advice has been to shoot on 16mm or tape and then get the distributor to pay for the blow-up. While fine in theory, most distributors will charge you cost plus a handling fee to facilitate this. Only consider this option if your budget is so tight that it might otherwise not be possible to make the film.

Whether for creative or financial reasons, if you have shot on a film format other than 35mm, you will need to transfer the film to 35mm in order for it to play in a commercial cinema. The process is very expensive, and could also be a deciding factor in whether or not you decide to use 35mm as an originating format or not.

Particular care must be taken when shooting for blow-ups to 35mm. The 16mm frame is enlarged considerably when blown up to 35mm, resulting in a larger apparent grain size. To maintain the finest grain structure on the 16mm original, careful selection of film stock, proper exposure and normal processing is essential. Flashing or forced processing should be avoided, as both processes tend to increase grain size. Camera lenses and magazines should be thoroughly checked and tested.

A properly composed 16mm negative can be blown up to 35mm at a 1.33:1 aspect ratio. This print can be used for television and projected theatrically in the United States, Europe and elsewhere. For a 16mm or Super16 negative shot as 1.66:1 or 1.85:1 to be blown up to 35mm, four techniques can be used

1 Panning and scanning
Where an operator moves each frame into a viewfinder and selects the best portion of the frame to blow up to 35mm. This is a very labour intensive process.

2 Masking aperture of camera
Certain cameras allow a plate to be inserted in front of the gate. This allows a certain area of the film to be exposed to light. In this way, a 16mm frame with a 1:1.33 aspect ratio can be reduced to 1:1.66 or 1:1.85 which makes a 35mm blow-up simpler, not requiring panning and scanning.

3 Masking viewfinder
The filmmaker can mask the viewfinder knowing that only the images

within the frame are 'safe' for the blow-up. This means that the transfer becomes predictable and mechanical, unlike panning and scanning.

4 Projection

Play the film on a high quality studio monitor and film the images using a 35mm camera. This is the quickest and the cheapest alternative, but you will suffer some image loss. Don't use this method if the look isn't right for your project.

Internegatives and Interpositives

Because the threat of scratches on the negative is very real throughout the filmmaking process, most producers elect to make a positive copy of the negative (interpositive) from which a duplicate copy of the negative is made (internegative). Successive positives are made from the internegative, thus protecting the original negative.

Digital Internegatives

In 2002, technology was introduced allowing filmmakers to make a digital copy of the negative by scanning the negative to create a digital file. From this digital file, positive copies can be made either by scanning back onto film, or by printing the images directly onto celluloid using a printer similar to a laser printer you might use in your office.

The main advantage of digital internegatives is the protection they afford the original negative. Also, a further benefit is the ease with which digital masters can be shipped around the world.

Summary

1. Make sure you understand the procedures you need from the lab.

2. Be as professional as possible when dealing with the lab. If you are not sure of technical details, ask your cinematographer to attend.

3. Remember, labs are there to help you, and want to help you. Learn how to communicate with them.

We've really jumped ahead talking about labs. What about cameras?

6   The Camera Package

THE BASIS OF MOTION picture camera technology was invented in 65 BC. The Roman poet Lucretius proposed a theory called persistence of vision that basically states that when the human eye views an object under bright light, the image remains for one tenth of a second after the light source is turned off. Ptolemy of Alexandria proved the theory two hundred years later.

A movie is made of a sequence of many individual pictures or frames, each slightly different from the previous one. In each second of a movie, there are twenty-four frames. Because of persistence of vision, our eye does not interpret each single frame, but rather a fluid continuous motion. In reality, the screen is black for about sixty percent of the time as film is advanced between frames.

A movie is captured on film using a motion picture camera. The camera is loaded with film made of a material called celluloid coated with light sensitive material. The celluloid has holes punched into it either down both sides or just one side – depending on the gauge or format. The holes, called sprocket holes, allow a gear mechanism in either a camera or projector to advance it.

Like a stills camera, a movie camera takes separate still images but is constructed to take twenty-four stills every second. In order to separate the images from each other, the film must stop behind the lens each frame. The image is then recorded, and a shutter closes to allow the film to be advanced to the next frame. A device known as the claw inserts itself in the film holes in order to advance it. It stops for each frame to allow the shutter to open. This series of operations happens at the very fast rate of twenty-four times per second.

Camera Movement

Sitting as director of Raindance Film Festival in London, I have had the privilege of seeing several thousand films from over forty countries. One of my favourite cinema experiences is watching camera movement.

One of the primary differences between American and European cinema is camera movement. European directors (until very recently) tend to place the camera on a tripod and use pans, zooms and tilts (see below) whereas American filmmakers tend to keep the camera moving, even if it is barely perceptible.

Camera movement can be the result of physically moving the camera or an apparent movement when using the zoom control. Camera motion should only be used with a purpose and in a manner that is not visually disturbing. Walking around the room with a camera or frequent panning between speakers can distract the viewer from the intended message. While it is not unusual to see professionals use camera movement, they have access to equipment beyond the consumer grade camcorder and tripod. Camera movement should be a rarely used method when using consumer grade equipment. The three primary camera movements are the zoom, pan/tilt, and track.

Equipment for moving cameras is called grip equipment.

Independent cinema has been awash with poor camera movement giving it a tainted nickname of 'shaky camera' movies in some circles.

Hint Camera movement is vital to cinema because in our own life, our eyes (our cameras) are mounted on our necks and are continuously moving.

Zoom

Professional cinematographers use the zoom very sparingly and generally prefer to move the camera. Amateurs love the zoom and can create some very nauseating motion by combining zooms and rapid pans. A zoom changes the angle of display so spatial relationships also change.

A zoom refers to using your camera controls to change the focal length, resulting in a telescope-like magnification of the view. On film cameras operators can choose between motor driven or manual driven zooms. Some filmmakers use camcorders with a smooth-slow zoom, but most produce a more jerky result. The recommendation is to zoom only for a specific purpose such as to emphasise size or to indicate entry. Zooming can be distracting unless it is done for a purpose. Cutting between a series of closer and closer shots (called jump cuts) will be easier to watch and achieves the same effect.

Hint Zooming makes the image flatten onto the screen and reduces audience involvement. A more effective way to enlarge an object is to track in (see below).

Pan and Tilt

Panning refers to sweeping your camera lens across the scene horizontally, tilting is the same movement vertically. Panning and tilting can be a distracting or even disorienting technique. Pan or tilt only for a specific purpose such as to show size. For example, while a speaker describes a classroom set-up, a cut-away to a slow pan across the room might be appropriate. Never pan or tilt just to change the framing unless you will be able to edit out the pan. Attempting to pan or tilt with a handheld camera or low cost tripod head will lead to a jerky movement which betrays you as a rank amateur. A good tripod head provides an adjustable and constant resistance to movement preventing jerky changes in motion in a horizontal pan or vertical tilt. Even with a good tripod it takes experience to pan and tilt correctly.

Hint A fast, blurred pan from actor to actor is called a whip-pan and is used to emphasise speed or highly charged emotion.

Track

Tracking refers to following moving objects within the scene by actually moving the camera at the same rate. This gives the viewer a feeling of walking or riding along beside the camera's subject. While this is common in professional video, the professional has equipment that you may not. The typical process for tracking involves building something similar to a small railroad track upon which the camera and tripod roll. You can use just about any wheeled object to support your camera for a tracking shot. The best no-budget alternative is to use a porter's dolly with pneumatic wheels that can be softened to absorb bumps. Another alternative if you are shooting outside, is to use the back of a car which is then pushed by a few camera assistants.

Dolly

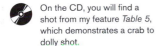

On the CD, you will find a shot from my feature *Table 5*, which demonstrates a crab to dolly shot.

A dolly shot is a shot that either moves the camera closer to your subject (tracking in, or dolly in shot) or moves across the face of your subject (crab shot).

Professional grip equipment contains a wheeled dolly and track upon which the dolly sits and is pushed. (See grip equipment below.)

The Camera

Certain functions of the camera can also be controlled in order to manipulate the image.

Film Drive and Transport Mechanisms (Film Cameras)

Film drives transport the film to the film gate and operate the shutter and take up the film from the supply reel. Cameras require energy to operate, and these energy sources are called film drives. Film drives are designed to eliminate any drive roller contact with the film emulsion surfaces, thereby reducing the risk of scratching and damaging the films. Precise film tracking is ensured through use of individual 16mm and 35mm exposure rollers, which have the added benefit of ensuring proper resolution by maintaining the film at exactly the correct distance from the lens.

Tachometer

A tachometer is a gauge on a camera measuring the film speed when the camera is running.

Shutter speed

During the infamous Squidgy tape affair in the UK (the Princess Diana and James Hewitt telephone conversations), Jon Jost, the American cult filmmaker and I hatched a plan for a short film. The idea was to find a scientific camera capable of shooting 1,000 frames per second (they are used for filming controlled car accidents, and bullets leaving guns) with a ten thousand foot magazine (again, created for scientific experiments). We were going to place a Prince Charles lookalike actor in front of Buckingham Palace, have the camera arrive in front of the actor in a van. The back doors would fling open, and I was going to throw a cream pie at the Prince. The entire scene would then be filmed at 1,000 frames per second. Played back at 24fps, the pie would edge slowly across the screen toward Prince Charles, while the soundtrack would play the voice of his wife and her lover. The film was timed to last six and a half minutes – the length of the tape.

A shutter is a light-blocking device that controls the duration of light exposure to the film negative. A shutter's primary function is to establish a consistent exposure – the film has to be stationary to receive an unblurred image (move the film during an exposure and you've got a blurred image), so the shutter is timed to unblock the negative in the film gate only when the film has momentarily paused and receives the light of the image transmitted through the lens; following the exposure, the shutter blocks the film gate and the film is advanced behind the shutter to the next unexposed section of film. Once an image is burned in the film gate, it becomes a frame. The second function performed by the shutter is found only in a variable-type shutter. Just like the shutter speed of a 35SLR still camera, a variable shutter provides the means to reduce the duration of exposure, independent of the frame rate (frames or exposures per second). Since motion picture film exposes at a rate of 24 frames per second, a motion picture camera's theoretical shutter speed is 1/48 of a second – at best. In fact, most shutters run slightly faster. If you've shot stills at a shutter speed under 1/100th of a second, you know that shooting a moving object will blur. You also know that to kill that motion blur, you'll have to speed the exposure up (which also means you'll have to go to a wider f-stop to maintain the same overall exposure). In a motion picture camera, the exposure can be sped up, not by spinning the shutter faster, but by reducing the angle of the shutter. That's why shutter speed on a motion picture camera is graduated in degrees.

The camera's shutter speed can also be varied to be slower (to create a speeded up look) or faster (to create a slow motion look). Regardless of the speed it was shot at, wherever the film is shown in the world, the projector will run at twenty-four frames per second.

While in South America filming, a British cinematographer realised that he was running out of film stock. As there was no possibility of getting him fresh supplies of film stock, he simply looked at his shooting schedule and shot the balance of the film, nearly a third of the script, at ten and twelve frames per second. For that, he has been called a genius of style.

Lenses

Lenses are glass or plastic filters put in front of the shutter to distort the image that enters the camera. A cinematographer will use a series of lenses, to 'paint' the scene.

The field of view (FOV) is the angle described by a cone with the vertex at the camera's position. It is determined by the camera's focal length, with the shorter the focal length the wider the FOV. For example, for a 35mm lens the FOV is 63° (wide-angle), for a 50mm lens it is 46° (normal), and for a 135mm lens it is 18° (telephoto). A wide-angle lens exaggerates depth while a telephoto lens minimizes depth differences.

Each lens has a different field of view, also know as anglefield or angle of view. Sometimes in a movie you will see a close up where the actor's face is in focus, but everything behind their ears is out of focus. Field of view is determined by the type of lens on the camera. A sensible camera package will contain a selection of several lenses. The smaller the number on the lens, the wider the angle. A 10mm lens is fish eye, a 50mm lens approximates human sight, and a 200mm lens focused on an actor would clearly define a nostril, with the rest of the face out of focus.

Lens Sharpness and Contrast

Lens sharpness is the lens's ability to render and reproduce very fine details onto film. It is desirable that a subject should render on film the equivalent contrast as the scene in reality – this is the quality known as lens contrast. A successful black and white or colour scene should have a pure white highlight area and a pure black shadow area as well as the ability to render and reproduce subtle tones in colour.

Camera Rental

The main manufacturers of 35mm camera equipment are: Panavision, Arri, Moviecam, Aaton and Mitchel.

When the awards for best cinematographer are announced at the Oscars™, one never hears the name of a manufacturer in the acceptance speech. There are five main manufacturers of camera equipment, all of whom make very good equipment, which any professional cameraperson can operate with a few minutes of training. The main consideration when asking for a camera is to ensure that you are given a sync sound camera, i.e. one that operates so quietly that a microphone placed nearby will not pick up motor noise (which would render the sound useless).

Below are the component parts that you would expect to receive when renting 35mm camera kits.

Camera body
This is the basic camera unit to which all of the other accessories and attachments are fitted.

Magazine
A magazine is a removeable, light-proof case into which a camera assistant (called the clapper/loader) loads the film stock. Several mag-

azines are required during the shoot. A 400 foot magazine loaded with 35mm film stock runs just over four minutes.

Lenses
A typical lens kit will consist of a set of 10mm, 25mm, 50mm, 85mm and 125mm lenses.

Sometimes a zoom lens is used, allowing for focal lengths from 10–200mm to be used on a single lens without having to change. The disadvantage of this lens is that the extra panes of glass require much more light, and may rule out certain types of lighting scenarios.

Matt box
A device which fixes to the camera body to prevent stray light from entering the camera.

Batteries
A charger and batteries are supplied with the camera body. They must be recharged and kept ready for the camera.

Intervalometer
Used to control the shutter speed and used for time lapse photography.

Aperture control
Used to control the aperture electronically. Used during complex shots.

Speed control
A device which allows for the speed of the camera to be altered during a take. Used for slow motion effects.

Follow focus
Device which allows the focus of a lens to be altered during a shot, such as when an actor is moving.

Zoom control
Device which controls the rate of a zoom smoothly.

Light meter
Device used to measure the amount of light in a scene. A spot meter measures the amount of light reflected from a selected area. An incident light meter is used to measure the light falling around a subject.

Filters
Used to convert between tungsten and daylight.

Phase adjuster
Matches the frame rate of a camera so it can be used to film TV sets.

Changing bag
Used to load and unload magazines.

Video assist
Device that connects to the camera allowing the shot to be played on a television monitor.

Head
The device that attaches the camera to the tripod.

Legs
A tripod. Long and short legs refer to the height of the tripod.

Barney
A rubber jacket that is draped over the camera body to help deaden the mechanical noise.

Negotiation Techniques

Most camera rental facilities will rent a camera to you at much less than their normal rate if you negotiate with them professionally and consider the special needs that they have in order to run their business.

How camera rentals are negotiated

Camera rentals are priced by the day. If you need a camera for a week, you in fact pay for five days and keep the camera for nine: pick up on Friday and return on the following Monday. You can negotiate a four-day week, a three day week, a two day week, or even a one day week where you pay for one day but keep the camera for nine days (See figure 3.2, page 24). Other filmmakers will pay a one-day weekend rental and rent the camera on a Friday, and return it on Monday morning – getting nearly three days' use for the price of one.

How successful you are at getting a cheap deal will depend on your ability to negotiate with the rental company, your passion for your project and the availability of equipment.

Requirements of a Cheap Camera Rental Deal

1. Demonstrate that you know how to use and care for the equipment. If you don't know how to use the equipment, send your camera operator to the hire facility for a training session, which will last about a day.

2. Present them with a valid insurance certificate. No one will let an expensive piece of 35mm kit out of their warehouse without insurance. Your insurance will need to cover not just replacement if the kit is damaged or stolen, but also the rental company's loss of revenue through having no kit to hire out until a replacement can be sourced.

3. You must understand their other clients. It is no good to try and expect a camera in the summer months when they are busy. Perhaps you should schedule your shoot over Christmas or Easter when they are nearly closed.

4. Make the camera rental call your last. Facilities managers are very busy. If they agree to rent you a camera cheaply, and then you postpone, it is unlikely you will get them to agree to another cheap deal.

5. Don't expect the best camera in the place. All rental facilities will have brand new kit which they rent out at full list price to large production companies. If you learn to know what their inventory is, you have a far better chance of getting their older cameras (which are just as good technically) at a cheap price.

Summary

1. Choose the package that suits your story and your budget.

2. Understand the possibilities and limitations of the camera that you intend to use.

3. Keep the camera moving.

4. Look after the kit, and it will look after you.

Collecting images is just part of the filmmaking process. Next we discuss sound recording.

In Conversation with Sally Inman

Sally Inman is one of the unsung heroines of the British film industry. At Arri Media she is able to provide advice and low cost camera rentals to filmmakers new to the industry.

How did you get started in this career?

After university, I went to work for a post-production company in London. When I was there, I was offered a job at a production company. Then someone said that I should go into cameras as I am a technical person. I wrote my letter to Arri Media, and luckily a position as a receptionist came up and then I moved to the hire desk.

Are you working on any specific projects right now?

Yes we have projects happening all the time. Graduation films, dramas or students wanting to get more material for their showreel.

What is your policy for student and low-budget filmmakers?

At Arri we have a very good policy on helping out students and independent filmmakers. We like to see a bit about the production beforehand. What we ask to see is pre-production paperwork; synopsis, treatment, script, a full list of the crew and their CVs to see who's working with our equipment and what they've done before and an outline of the budget. And of course a camera wish list. Once I've received all that information and the script, I go through it all. I never feel that it's really down to me to say if it's a good script or not. But if I see that all the paperwork is there and they are really keen on doing this project and have a lot of enthusiasm, that is enough for me to be able to say, 'Yep, I'll help you out'.

Are there set camera packages that you offer?

This is the thing, we don't have a student packages as such because every shoot is different. They might want to shoot for one day or two weeks. The kit they need may vary from a handheld kit to a full production kit, so that is why we ask for a wish list. Then we tailor the package to what the student or low budget filmmaker wants. It's very individualised and we give students or independent filmmakers the same treatment and equipment we give any paying client. Our equipment is serviced regularly and it is kept to the very best quality.

What would be the best approach for a filmmaker to take if they needed a little help?

I actually have here a list of terms and little hints and stuff [this is included at the end of this interview]. The first thing that you'll need to do is send me pre-production paperwork and you can either send it to me by post, email or fax. If you like the personal touch, you can come in and pitch it to me. I have an equipment rota with two 16mm SR2s that I can allow out to students. Once they've done a few 16mm shoots with us and we've got a good relationship with each other, then if a graduation piece came up and they wanted to shoot on 35mm, I would allow them, but it's not something that we give out to just somebody off the street. We are about building relationships.

Let's say a past client has no budget at all. If you had a good working relationship with the client in the past, would you be more inclined to help them out?

Oh yes, exactly! We have a book price of about £1,000 a day for a standard 16mm kit. If a filmmaker is honest and tells us exactly what their budget is, we will try to accommodate them. We do require a little bit, just for the prep fee. We always do scratch tests in the camera and use up a roll of stock for that. So a little bit of money just to sort of cover our costs is normally advisable.

What type of camera is requested most often?

A lot of students and low budget filmmakers do request an SR3, but they are used by paying clients all the time, so we can only provide them with an SR2. The SR2 can run from 5fps to 75 fps (frames per second). When you book an SR2 with us it automatically comes with three 400ft magazines, 4 inch bellows, mattebox and support MB17, extension viewfinder, variable speed unit, four 12V on-board batteries, battery charger, film changing bag and an 85 combination filter set (85, 85B, 85N3, 85N6, 85N9, 81EF). These cameras can be booked up to two months in advance so it's best to get in touch as soon as possible.

But you do occasionally loan out 35mm cameras as well?

That's a special thing. It's very expensive equipment and the majority of our professional shoots are on 35mm. We like to build up a relationship and know that we can trust them with the equipment. After a few shoots then we can maybe do a 35mm shoot with them, all depending on availability. Giving a £200,000 kit out to someone we don't know can be very scary at times. I do hold everyone's CVs and keep a list of all the crew that's worked with our equipment before, so if they have looked after the kit in the past then I will try to help them in the future.

At Arri what are the most common projects that filmmakers come to you with?

I think short films are the majority. We do a few pop promos for up and coming singers and stuff and have had some good responses back from them. Also a few commercials, but it's mainly short films and dramas.

In general, where does Arri receive its best turnover?

It changes from month to month. In general, it's split between Commercials, Features and Dramas. Commercials are busy between March and September and features and drama normally starts in April and runs to September. It's very seasonal.

Recommendations for Hiring Equipment from Arri Media

Pre-production paperwork must be submitted before any consideration will be given. This can be supplied via email, fax or post and must include: synopsis, treatment, script, budget, camera wish list, crew list and CVs. Any other information that might help get your story across should be included as well.

Arri Media does not have a standard student or low budget package. We prefer to try and supply everything you need, where possible, or at least offer good alternatives, rather than impose restrictions due to budget. For this reason supply your equipment wish list and be honest in terms of budget, Arri Media will try to do everything possible to help.

It is also important to advise Arri Media of the project as soon as possible in order to avoid disappointment as bookings are made up to two months in advance and equipment may not be available for the required dates. To do this:

- Simply call and ask for the client contact responsible for student and low budget work. Give a rough outline of your project and advise when you will be able to supply the required paperwork or send in the required paperwork before calling to allow the opportunity for the project to be assessed.

- Make an appointment with the relevant Client Contact to pitch your project face to face.

Arri Media will then pencil-book equipment for you and advise which items we can help with, but availability cannot be guaranteed until a couple of weeks before the shoot due to the nature of the rental business.

If you are an independent production company and do not have an account with Arri Media, a cash account will have to be set up. In order to do this you will be sent a customer information sheet, which you will need to complete and return as soon as possible. This will mean that you will have to pay cash upfront and that we will need to see your insurance cover before equipment will be allowed to leave the building.

Arri Media will advise the insurance value of equipment. This will include the full replacement cost of the equipment and the cost for thirteen weeks loss of hire. Your insurance must cover both values and cover the day of collection and return.

When hiring equipment the following must be remembered:

- Arri Media must have payment and insurance details before kit will be allowed to leave the building.

- Crew will be asked to come in to test the day they are collecting equipment. This is to ensure crew are happy with the equipment and that any questions have been answered.

- Whilst shooting, if you do have problems with any piece of equipment please call Arri Media straight away, do not try to fix it yourself. Arri Media will replace the item as long as it is available, but you must collect it yourself. This is why it is important to check equipment before it leaves the building.

Arri Media's opening times are: Monday to Friday 6am to 10pm and Saturday 9am to midday. Equipment must be collected and returned between these hours and agreed with your client contact.

Once the shoot is completed and equipment returned to Arri Media it will be checked over. If there are any missing or damaged items you will be informed of the missing items and/or advised the cost of damages.

7 Sound

IF THERE IS ANYTHING I have learned about filmmaking, it is that a sound track can make or break a movie. A sound track is often as complicated as the image on the screen. The entire sound track is composed of three essential ingredients: the dialogue, the sound effects and the music. These three ingredients must be mixed and balanced together to create the effect of real sound.

Three Sound Ingredients

Dialogue

When the dialogue is recorded so the voice texture suits the character the audience witnesses a very real person on the screen. If the sound is improperly recorded, the audience sees an actor struggling with their craft. Recorded properly, the audience sees a character struggling with life.

Sound Effects

Sound effects are those sounds matched to what is viewed on the screen. For example, if an actor is walking across a marble floor, his/her footsteps are recorded and matched to the picture in order to enhance realism in the movie.

Sometimes the audience does not need to be aware of the sound and so it is not recorded or added to the soundtrack, for example, the sound of a window sliding open. In other circumstances, for example, during a scene showing a cat burglar entering a bedroom, the sound of the window opening might be exaggerated in order to create suspense.

Asynchronous sound effects are not matched with a visible source of the sound on screen. Such sounds are included so as to provide an appropriate emotional nuance, and they may also add to the realism of the film.

Music

Often Hollywood will use loud music to try to disguise a bad scene or sequence.
Mike Figgis, the director, writer, composer and editor calls this 'shagging the movie'.

Film music is used to add emotion and rhythm to a film. It often provides a tone or an emotional attitude toward the story and/or the characters depicted. Music often foreshadows a change in mood. Music can also be used to link scenes. This is most often used to associate certain characters or locations with themes. Modern film sound tracks are brilliantly conceived pieces in which the composers and sound editors play on the subconscious of the audience.

Recording Location Sound

Good sound recording is the keystone to a good film. Location sound recording is a vital element in the post-production process. Poor location sound recording can be costly and time-consuming to correct.

Sound Crew

The adage of hiring the best crew and equipment you can afford has extra weight in sound recording. A small increase in expenditure on sound recording can save thousands in post-production. A good sound recordist will attack sound on the set and solve problems before they arise.

One-person sound crew

A one-person crew has a very limited capability. The microphone is physically tied into the tape recorder or into the camera via cables, thereby restricting the movement of the microphones and the sound recordist, and the quality of sound that they can record.

Two-person sound crew

A two-person crew is more versatile, and, should your investors turn up, more impressive. A truly theatrical quality soundtrack can be achieved. Usually one person operates a mixer from near the camera, and the other operates a boom in a strategic position near the talent.

Sound Consistency

There are three aspects of consistency that the sound recordist must be attentive to:

1. Consistency within the shot.

2. Consistency between shots within the scene.

3. Consistency between scenes.

Sound levels should remain relatively constant between actors and also between background ambience in each shot. Actors are not expected to match each other in terms of recording level; variations are normal. But their own level should remain consistent throughout. As they banter, the actors' audio should appear somewhat constant. There should be no unwarranted sudden changes in volume, except when justified by dramatic intent.

If you were to close your eyes, the changes in audio from shot to shot should not be unnatural or unexpected. This is not to say that if an actor walks distantly away from camera that his voice level should not diminish. Of course it should, as it would in real life. But a variation in camera angle (as opposed to a change in actor location within the set, visual or implied) does not warrant a major change in audio levels. However, a major change in camera location may justify a change in relative audio, particularly the background sound levels.

For example: if the first scene in a sequence is in an office, the second is in the emergency stairwell, and the third is inside an ambulance, or on the street, it is clear that each scene will have to be adjusted to account for the very different levels of ambient noise in the locations.

Changes in audio levels are inevitable. Recording sound is an art form, and the nature of production is such that certain variables like ambient noise and mic placement are often beyond the control of the sound person. The principle of location sound recording is to try to keep the sound level changes to a minimum. Any flaws are then fixed in post-production.

Microphones

Getting sounds onto tape requires a microphone input of some kind. Getting good sound onto tape requires some understanding of how a microphone works.

How a Microphone Works

Popping and smacking refer to the different aspirant noises made by actors when speaking. Each actor will have a different popping and smacking range, depending on their pronunciation and accent.

A microphone is an electromagnetic device that has an element that acts as a reed, which vibrates when hit by sound. The 'reed' causes a flux in a surrounding electromagnetic field that generates a signal. The weak signal flux is relayed down a cable to the input jack on the recorder where it is amplified and charged onto the recording tape. The electromagnetic field surrounding the 'reed' (which is a very sensitive paper and carbon element) can be vibrated by the wind or interfered with by extraneous electromagnetic fields. A foam or athletic sock over a microphone will eliminate wind racket and moderate 'popping' and 'smacking' from the actors' lips. All wires are surrounded (over their entire length) from external electromagnetic fields by a sheath of metallic braid.

Types of Microphone

On-camera microphone

As a rule, try to avoid using any on-camera microphones. Not only are they usually poor quality mics, but on-camera is a very poor position from which to record high quality sound. A sensitive mic will pick up all the humming of the camera, plus ambient noise, and any noise the cameraman makes, rendering dialogue recording nearly worthless.

You can use a high quality boom mic and plug it into the camera if you have an XLR balance box.

Lavalier microphone

Tie-clip microphones are called Lavalier. Some are wireless and much more susceptible to electromagnetic interference. There are good affordable, wireless models but these may complicate your shots (it's just one more thing that can go wrong). These are great microphones for interviews and can be well hidden while filming an action scene that includes dialogue. Each of the wireless microphones has its own radio frequency, so that the sound is received separately from each actor before being mixed together.

Cardioid microphone

These have patterns that cover a spherical zone like your ears do. These are good for some work but act like on-camera microphones at a distance, picking up everything you don't want to hear.

Shotgun microphone

For wide shots where the microphone must not enter the frame, a shotgun microphone is very useful for isolating the actors' voices because it is unidirectional. It only picks up sound in a very narrow pattern that cancels peripheral or ambient sounds while getting clean reception of the sounds within its narrow reception pattern.

Boom microphone

A microphone attached to the end of a boom or rod enables you to extend a microphone over an actor's head without the need for the operator to enter the frame. This is especially helpful during wide shots. You'll notice that a professional mike boom has a rubber band-like suspension cage at the far end that isolates the mic from the vibrations from the operator's hands. If a mic was taped to the end of a broom stick without this insulation, every finger movement would send that sound straight through the stick and right into the microphone. That sound would drown out any dialogue.

It's All Just a Chain

The easiest way to discuss location sound is to think of the entire audio path as a chain. In the case of location sound, the 'links' are:

- The sound itself
- The microphone(s) that capture the sound
- The cables and connectors that carry the signal from the microphone to the mixing or routing device and from the mixing or routing device to the recording device
- The mixing or routing device that carries the signal from the microphone to the recording device
- The recording device itself (Camcorder, VTR, Hard Disc Recorder, MiniDisc or DAT recorder)
- The monitoring circuit of the recording device

Just as in an actual chain, the audio path is only as strong as the weakest link. This means that a high-quality, accurate recording device paired with a low-quality microphone will not be able to record anything better than what the microphone is capable of picking up. It means that a great microphone and audio mixer paired with a substandard recording device will only be able to record to the limitations of the device's recording circuit.

Hint Five sound principles

1. The principles of location sound are the same for almost everyone shooting anything.
2. No matter who the audience is, at the very least, they expect 'transparent' sound.
3. Sound conveys emotion – picture conveys information.
4. The better your soundtrack, the less it is consciously noticed.
5. The closer the microphone is to the sound source, the better you will record what you want your audience to hear.

Sound as Picture

The immense popularity of digital video, combined with sophisticated editing tools means that the average person now has the means to produce work of quality. The one area that most new filmmakers ignore is sound; many independent, lo-to-no budget projects seem doomed to suffer with sound that ranges from merely average to barely usable. Audiences today expect 'transparent' sound on your soundtrack.

It is a surprising truth that almost all of the emotional impact of a film comes from the sound track. Test this out be watching a favourite scene from a movie with the volume turned off. Typically, the moving images on their own have little emotional impact. What may be less obvious to you if you are new to film and video is that audiences of all kinds now expect to be entertained while you are conveying your message. Emotional involvement from your audience is what defines good entertainment. Your sound is largely what will determine whether your project is entertaining to your audience. Unless you want to conceive your project as a 'silent film', you have to be concerned ('obsessed' might be a better term) with your project's sound.

One of the toughest concepts for many newer filmmakers to grasp is that the better job you do with your project's sound, the less it will be noticed. This concept is one of the reasons why most projects don't end up with very high quality soundtracks. We are very used to spending time, effort and money on a better camera, lens, bigger and better lighting, crew and visual effects and seeing an immediate payoff when our images are viewed. It's instantly recognisable if a scene is lit effectively or if a visual effect is done well. We feel justified in shooting on a higher quality, more expensive format or with a bigger crew because the end result is usually easily identifiable on-screen. Most of us can immediately recognise if a project was shot on 35mm film versus DV or if a project's motion graphics or visual effects were well executed. If we notice a sound mix though, it is usually because the sound was done incompetently. This is the central concept of 'transparent' sound. If your location sound is recorded correctly, the easier it will be to work with the basic audio during the post-production process.

Another surprising fact of sound is that a poor soundtrack will make the picture look dim. If you have ever witnessed a cinema screening when the volume is too low, the act of straining to hear the dialogue makes the picture dim.

Hint The better job you do with the sound during video and audio editing, the less the audience will notice it. The only sound that is noticed in a visual medium is poorly executed. Great sound works on a subconscious level with the viewer by drawing them into what they are viewing. Great sound supports and enhances the stories you are trying to tell.

Recording Sound for DV

In addition to great video, DV can also record a pair of audio tracks that rival that of CDs and digital audio tape (DAT). With a hardly noticeable reduction in sound quality, you can record two pairs of stereo soundtracks; perhaps an audio track recorded at the time of taping and a music or narrative track added later. Best of all, you can add, erase or edit the audio without affecting the video and vice versa. DV camcorders record superb sound using a process called Pulse Code Modulation (PCM). The process is very complex, but what's most important is what it allows you to do; it has two recording modes.

1. Two channel, or 16-bit stereo is used for the highest quality sound.

2. Four channel, or two 12-bit stereo, has a little less quality, but it allows you use two stereo channels instead of one. You can use one channel when doing the initial recording and then use the other to add music or narration later.

Both modes offer dramatic sound improvements over previous video formats. However, both modes are not always available on a given camcorder, so be sure to check before buying.

The Meaning of 16-bit and 12-bit

When sound is captured by the camcorder's microphone, it is converted into a digital signal. This process includes both sampling and quantisation. The higher the sampling and quantization rates, the better the data represents the original sound.

The analogue signal is like a wave, with peaks and valleys. Sampling measures this wave at specified intervals so the wave can be reassembled when it is played back. The more frequently the wave is sampled, the more accurately it can be reconstructed later. In DV, the audio can be sampled 48,000 times per second (48kHz), 44,000 times per second (44.1kHz) or 32,000 times per second (32kHz). 12-bit sound is sampled at 32kHz. The choice is up to the manufacturer of the DV camcorder or VCR. (For comparison purposes, DAT uses 48kHz sampling and CDs use 44.1kHz sampling.)

Quantization converts the measured value into a digital number. In digital video, the value is stored at its highest quality using 16 bits, or at a slightly lower quality using 12 bits. The more bits used to store the audio, the more accurately it can be played back, but the larger the size of the file. 16-bit can use 65,536 different numbers to represent any sample while 12-bit can use only 4,096 numbers.

DV: Camera or DAT Sound?

As Raindance is about to start the filming of its first DV feature, this sound issue has yet to be decided! As the producer, I have yet to convince the director, the sound recordist and the editor that recording directly into the camera is as good as recording the sound separately. I calculate that recording the camera via a good microphone and connection into the camera could save three man-weeks of synching sound to picture, and at least a week in the editing process.

When working on a DV production of some significance (e.g., a feature), the question of how to record sound invariably comes up. Specifically, do you record sound directly into the camera or use a separate audio recorder? A typical sound recordist's response is to use a separate audio recorder because the quality is better. But consider the additional work of recording sound and picture separately, and then combining them in the editing process. By recording directly into the camera, no synching is required.

Sweetening the Soundtrack

It is a fact that most of the sound we hear from a Hollywood movie is sweetened in post-production using ADR and foley. Although sound is recorded on set and on location, it is considered to be of inferior quality when compared to studio sound and is usually discarded in its entirety. Plenty of studio time is always budgeted and scheduled for the talent to come back in to do ADR.

ADR

ADR is Automatic Dialogue Replacement. An actor's contract will stipulate that some weeks after the shoot they are contractually bound to return to a post-production sound facility to do ADR, which is also sometimes called looping.

They stand in a sound booth with a good microphone and watch the edited scenes play on a screen. They listen to the original sound on headphones (called the guide track) and on cue re-do the dialogue.

At this point the director is still able to alter the performance. They can say louder or softer, but not quicker or slower. Often the actor will be asked to say the line many times, in different ways, to give the editor and the director dramatic options in the final mix.

It is also possible to re-record dialogue in a homemade ADR facility. All you need is a quiet room, a television, the original soundtrack, and a good microphone.

Foley

Foley is the recreation of sound effects. A foley studio consists of a screen and in front of the screen a series of floor coverings or foley pits with several different surfaces: gravel, sand, wood, marble, grass, shag carpet and regular carpet. The foley artist (also sometimes called a 'walker') looks at the screen and sees what sort of surface the character is walking on, and what sort of shoes the actor is wearing: high heels, boots or trainers. He (and they are, for some reason, most often male) selects the appropriate footwear and walks with the same rhythm as the actor. When the feet are not visible, as in a medium shot, the artist will be able to guess the type of footwear from the way the actor is walking. The sound of his footsteps are then recorded and added to the final soundtrack.

Foley sound is often tweaked in the mix so that it is much louder than the sound that would normally be heard.

The foley artists also do sound effects for things like handshakes, breathing, and rustling clothes (body noise). Foley also refers to other sound effects like running water, door slams, gunshots.

Three top foley noises:
- footsteps
- paper
- body noise

Hint If you listen carefully to the soundtrack of any film on television or in the cinema, you will hear loud footsteps and other atmospheric or incidental noises amplified out of proportion to their actual or natural sound. We, the audience, have come to accept this and don't notice how exaggerated it can be.

Sound Design

On the CD-Rom is an example of sound design: the 2003 Raindance Film Festival trailer.

The importance of sound tracks has led to an entirely new breed of professional called a sound designer. A sound designer recreates the emotional impact of everyday sounds using unrelated noise and music to create the emotion of the sound.

One of the first movies to recognise and do this was the Coen brothers movie, *Barton Fink*. In the boxing scene, what we hear when the middle aged boxer hits the deck is not the sound of flab on canvas, but the sound of wood splintering.

Summary

1. Get the best chain of sound equipment you can.

2. Make recording excellent location sound a priority.

3. Allow for a proper ADR and foley budget to sweeten the soundtrack.

4. Consider the editing process and choose a sound system that your editing system can support.

5. Remember to consider the emotional impact of sound.

You have hired a sound recordist. Now let's consider the pictures you want to capture, and the role of the person in charge of capturing them.

In Conversation with Ernie Warwick

Ernie Warwick is one of the last of the analogue sound specialists left in the UK and is the only engineer able to create an optical sound track. He is highly regarded as a sound advisor for cinematic sound.

How did you get started in this career?

I've been involved with cinema since 1958. I started working whilst I was still in school with an employment card after school hours. I was running film cans between two cinemas that shared the Pathé News. I went to agricultural college, passed out with a degree, but my first love was cinema, I had a fall out with my parents and walked out of the house and went to London and got a job in the cinema. A few years later I had the opportunity to work in the West End as a projectionist in a studio and that was in 1966. Since then I just sort of built myself up.

What are some of the best ways to edit and cut sound?

No one will ever persuade me to use anything other than film. Everyday of the week we have someone walk in who wants to know what speed their film should be. They know what it should be, but its been jumbled up in digital this and non-linear that and everything is a major problem. I am a firm believer in the fact you don't save that much money using non-linear editing. It's nice to be able to rearrange your shots without damaging or affecting things, but you've got the old time synchronising problem when you cut the film and then cut the sound. You know exactly where you are if you post on film. I've got a non-linear set-up on a computer at home and I get involved with little documentaries and things, but there's no way I'd use non-linear editing for anything serious.

What are some specific problems you encounter editing sound?

None the old way, but with non-linear editing there are lots of problems with synching and it takes a lot longer to do. In the old days you had a soundtrack, a piece of magnetic film which had a sound effect on it, you just find the picture, you drop it into it. Nowadays you've got to place it and if you're not working with a time code which is similar, you've got to take it, you've got to place it, then you've got to move it and shift it.

With modern technology, we've got a 24 channel radar workstation, and organic work station, it's nice to be able put all the tracks together and have them all running next to each other. In the old days that would be up to 24 different pieces of film. Until someone designs something which is an idiot's way of editing, it its very difficult. I haven't come across a system yet which uses two pointers at the same time, so you can click the front of something, you can click the end of it then you can shift it immediately to the point. In both of our machines, you pick the front up, but you can't pick up front and end at the same time. You find your source you then pick the front of it up, and you then find its target and place it on its target point and then there lots of jiggling backwards and forwards. One day the ideal system will be made and a five year old child will be able to edit a feature film.

What projects are you currently working on?

We are doing optical soundtracks on features and commercials. We get some quite big pictures through here for their final optical sound track transfers because we do Dolby digital and DTS, we do features like *Dog Soldiers* all the time. I've also got a thing, shot on MiniDV, a TV feature type, an erotic thriller it's claiming to be. We're doing that in a few weeks. Any mixing we have to do on the weekends because the optical transfer works through the week. We can only get involved with big things like that at the weekends. We've also got commentary and foley facilities all on the site, and in the not too distant future this room is going to be converted from an office to a telecine facility.

What does sound add to a picture that makes it so important?

Well you'd never sell a silent picture these days. The main problem is that sound is always looked upon as the poor relation to the picture and as the sound is done at the last minute, as the final part of the whole process, when invariably the money is running out, especially on low budget productions, and a lot of low budget productions don't even think about sound to start with.

It's amazing the way directors and producers come in and they want work done for free. I refuse to do things for free because invariably if you do something for free there will be a cock up somewhere in the system and you'll end up having to do it again, This happens in the West End of London regularly. It's just quite amazing how you do someone a favour and invariably you end up paying for it.

Do you have any advice for sound recordists on the shoot?

It depends what they're shooting on. If they're shooting on a Nagra, because it's analogue you don't have too many problems. The most dangerous thing you can use is a gun mic. Most schools teach people to use that for sound because it's very directional, but actually if you play with a gun mic, and have various close-ups and mid shots, you've only got to get the gun mic at a slightly different angle and, if you're using a motion picture camera, the camera noise changes between shots. You've only got to move it slightly and you'll be amazed the difference in the camera noise. That is the main problem with the Nagras.

With DAT people don't realise that the dynamic range (the difference between the peak and the bottom) is upwards of 100dbs. When the recordist is listening to the sound he can hear the very lows and highs on his headphones; but when you come to the final optical soundtrack of the film it's fine if it's digital because the digital will retain the dynamic range, but analogue won't. On analogue, when you're using noise reduction, you're lucky to get 60dbs. You can lose some of the lower level stuff, that's why if you have the choice of recording on Nagra or DAT, I would always use Nagra because the sound recordist hears the hiss, the noise which isn't there on a digital recording.

And 16mm, of course a lot of young filmmakers use 16mm, there you've got a terrible problem if you use optical sound because the dynamic range is, if you're lucky, 35dbs. So as far as sound is concerned it's the dynamic range which is the problem. The old filmmakers of course were brought up with it and understood it, young filmmakers, they don't. There are even studios in the West End of London that do commercials and the mixers, they just don't know what they're doing.

What's the best way to record ADR and foley so it's easy for you to work with?

We have the facilities here to do it. I would have thought that unless it's a period piece and if microphones are used properly, you shouldn't have to do ADR or foley for more than one or two per cent of the film. In my experience, and I've done many, many, many ADR sessions with big directors, you'll find that they do not improve the performance by doing ADR. In fact because the majority of actors the moment they see a microphone in a studio think they are doing a commercial, they'll go right close to the mic and drop their voices. I could name stars and bits in films you could listen to that I could tell you was ADR.

Any examples?

You get a roundness in the sound, which comes from close micing. I worked with Klaus Kinski on *Nosferatu* with Werner Hertzog. Klaus, it was rumoured, slept in a coffin in his hotel room. He mumbled. He was a European version of Marlon Brando, and no matter what I did I could not get him to speak up. When you're doing ADR, you play the original sound for the actor in the headphones, they see a visual cue on the screen and at that cue they speak following their original dialogue. In the end with Klaus, we had to blast high level traffic noise through the headphones so it was so deafening that he had to project. It was the only way to get him to give a performance. He would struggle closer to the mic. No matter how nice you were to him, he wouldn't speak up. There are a lot of actors like that. It's the Cadbury's flake phenomenon.

Cadbury's flake phenomenon?

Well Cadbury's Flake is a flakey chocolate bar, and it's always a women who does the voice over on it and it's always sensual and sexy, and the only way you can get sensual and sexy is to get right close to the mic and whisper.

Film Sound Glossary

Acoustics
The individual characteristics of reflection and absorption that give a space such as a living room, concert hall, or cinema an identifiable sonic 'signature'.

Ambience
Low-level sounds (including sound reflections) that set a mood or suggest the character of a particular place. The 'natural' sound of a space. Often sound designers will add ambient sound, which has not been recorded on location but mixed, to create an emotion.

Analogue vs digital soundtrack
The width of an analogue soundtrack varies in a way that is directly analogous to the varying soundwaves of the original sound. When played back, the varying width of the track is translated to a varying electrical voltage which causes the theatre's loudspeaker cones to move back and forth to recreate the original sound.

With a digital soundtrack, points along the soundwaves of the original sound are assigned a numeric (or digital) value, consisting of ones and zeros represented as tiny dots on the track. When a digital track is played back, the numeric values are converted to the varying electrical voltage needed to drive the speakers. (See also 'optical soundtrack'.)

Atmospheres
Low level background sounds, such as wind or traffic noise, on a film's soundtrack which add to the reality of a scene. These sounds are sometimes recorded separately at a shooting location, creating what is called a wild track for mixing into the soundtrack later.

Dolby digital
The most widely used multichannel digital sound format in the world. This is used for everything from 35mm films in the cinema to HDTV broadcasts and DVD discs in the home. Dolby Digital provides up to 5.1 channels (left, centre, right, left surround, right surround, and low-frequency effects). The original function was to inhibit system 'noise'.

Dubbing theatre
A theatre equipped for and dedicated to mixing film soundtracks.

The sound systems in dubbing theatres where soundtracks are mixed and those in cinemas equipped for playback are calibrated to the same standards. This helps makes it possible for audiences to hear the sound the director heard – and intended – when the soundtrack was mixed in post-production.

Dynamic range
The range between the loudest and softest sounds a soundtrack and/or sound system can reproduce properly.

Effects
Sound effects, i.e., the non-musical elements other than dialogue.

Foley
The art of recreating and re-recording incidental sound effects, such as footsteps or rustling clothes, in sync with the picture. Named after one of its first practitioners.

LFE
The LFE, or low-frequency effects, channel on soundtracks carries the powerful low bass frequencies (explosions, rumbles, etc.) that are felt more than heard.

Magnetic soundtrack
Narrow stripes of oxide material (similar to the coating on recording tape) added to a developed release print, then recorded in real time with the film's sound. Introduced in the 1950s to provide the first stereo sound in the cinema, magnetic soundtracks have been superseded today by advanced analogue and digital optical soundtracks, which are more practical and durable.

Mix
The blend of dialogue, music, and effects, recorded both during the shoot and in ADR and foley, which comprises a film's soundtrack.

Also, when used as a verb, the process of assembling and balancing these elements electronically, thereby creating the final soundtrack.

Optical recorder
The machine that transforms a completed mix on magnetic tape or disc into an optical soundtrack. It creates a photographic negative of the

optical track, which is combined ('married') with a negative of the picture to create a unified release print. (See also 'printer'.)

Optical soundtrack

Photographic strips on movie prints that vary in some way with the variations in sound. Analogue optical soundtracks vary in width, while digital optical soundtracks have patterns of dots (see also 'analogue vs digital' and 'variable area'). As the film is pulled through the projector's soundhead, a narrow light beam passes through the moving soundtrack, which causes the intensity of the beam to vary. The varying light falls on a sensor, creating electrical signals, which the theatre's loudspeakers convert back to sound.

Printer

A machine that exposes raw film stock to negatives of the movie's soundtrack and picture, at speeds up to twenty times faster than film is projected, to create a release print.

The rapid, simultaneous printing of sound and picture contributes significantly to the relatively low cost of 35mm optical release prints (see 'optical soundtrack').

Release print

The actual film played in the cinema. A release print consists of reels approximately twenty minutes long which are played consecutively without interruption either by alternating between two projectors, or by splicing the individual reels together into one large reel called a platter.

Stereo

Sound recording and reproduction onto more than one (mono) channel. In the film industry, 'stereo' is understood to include surround and centre channels in addition to left and right. To avoid confusion, multichannel stereo is often referred to as 'surround sound'.

Subwoofer

A loudspeaker dedicated to reproducing very low bass.

Surround sound

The reproduction of ambience, atmospheres, and occasional special effects that are recorded on one or more dedicated channels, and played through speakers placed along the sides and rear of the auditorium to surround the audience.

Variable area

The technical term for the analogue optical soundtrack whose width varies with the sound. An analogue optical soundtrack sometimes is referred to as an SVA track, for 'stereo variable area'. An earlier type of optical track, variable density, varied the track's photographic shading (rather than its width) with the sound.

8 Cinematography

THE DIRECTOR OF PHOTOGRAPHY (DoP) is the person responsible for the images the director wishes to capture. The DoP will also have their own creative input based on their interpretation of the scene to be filmed. The partnership between DoP and director is one of the most exciting and dynamic in the making of a movie, as it will directly influence the nature of the final images on the screen.

Part scientist, part mathematician and part artist, the DoP has to have a thorough understanding of emulsions (if shooting on film) or the sensitivities of different tape formats. The DoP must also be able to calculate the appropriate amount of light for each shot and make the adjustments to the camera, lens and equipment. The DoP also must have a creative eye for the best angle or movement for each shot, the best lighting, the best lens, as well as the most suitable framing. A good DoP will also understand the drama of a scene and be able to alter or adapt the shot in order to heighten the action or drama suggested by the script.

These elements make the job of DoP so interesting and exciting. Nothing can prepare you for the immediacy and thrill of viewing rushes for the first time and experiencing the visual elements of the movie.

The Production Process

As stated elsewhere, the production process is divided into three parts: pre-production, production and post-production. Although the DoP is mainly involved in the production process, they have responsibilities in the other parts of the process as well.

1 Pre-production

The DoP must first understand every aspect of the film that s/he is about to shoot before they embark on the shoot.

The first job is to read and reread the script carefully and decide if the film is something that interests them. The DoP should determine whether they can respond to the point of view of the story. Next, the

DoP must decide whether or not the script suits their style of lighting and camerawork.

The first meeting with the director is probably the most important. How one will interact with the director – someone with whom one will be working for several intense months – will determine whether or not one will get the job (or accept it). Having accepted the job, the director and DoP will then decide how to shoot the film to give it the look that the director envisages.

If the film is a period film, the DoP will research the architecture and costumes of the period in order to gain a comprehensive understanding for the detail. Libraries, museums, books and magazines can provide useful information. Sometimes other films, especially documentaries, shot in the period provide useful background information.

The study of the architecture of the period is especially valuable when considering interiors, because the light fittings and windows suggest the amount and type of natural light available for interior scenes.

As the start date approaches, the DoP will need to commit to the job completely. This period can be from a few weeks to several months, depending on the complexity of the shoot. The DoP will also liaise with the production designer and art director to discuss how props, wardrobe and sets can be altered to make the shoot easier. Of particular interest will be the colour choices. Certain colours and certain fabrics do not photograph as well as others.

The working relationship between the DoP and the art director is an important one, which will exert a powerful influence over the look of the finished piece.

On low budget shoots, the DoP will usually complete preparations at home in the evenings and start full time work a day or two before the shoot.

DoP and director James L. Solan spends every spare minute either at the National Gallery in London, where he researches lighting and composition used by the old masters, or watching and studying classic films.

Location scouting

The producer and director may have chosen a location for a particular scene based on visual appeal and budget. The DoP has to work out how best to light it and shoot there.

The most important aspect of pre-production is going to look at the various locations and sets that will be used in the film. This will probably involve a number of visits to see what the place looks like at different times of day or to talk about any problems that may be encountered when filming.

The final visit is known as the technical recce and will involve the director, first assistant director, sound-recordist and the DoP. Other members of the camera and lighting crew will also attend including camera operator, key grip, and the gaffer or spark. As well as photographing the film the DoP is also regarded as head of the camera department and will choose his operator and focus puller etc.

The camera crew

Choosing a good crew is of course essential but choosing a crew that will get on well together, and with the director, is equally important. A traditional film camera crew consists of four people.

Director of photography

The DoP is the person responsible for making sure the director's vision of the film is captured on the camera. The DoP does not handle the camera. The DoP makes creative suggestions to the director regarding the lighting of the set and the angles used during the shoot. The DoP has responsibility for the way the light and photography capture the director's vision of the film. A DoP will usually get an opening title credit at the start of the film, and brings considerable creative expertise to the production.

Camera operator (Cinematographer)

Whilst the camera operator's main task is to operate the camera during the shoot, s/he must also act as a second pair of eyes for the DoP as well as a sounding board for the director when setting up shots. When shooting begins s/he may work more closely with the director when choosing lenses and camera angles.

Focus puller

Hairs are not actual hairs, but refer to any piece of dirt inside the camera mechanism or the film gate.

The main responsibility of the focus puller is to make certain that the image in the frame is fully focused. A focus puller will use measuring tapes to measure the precise distance of the subject to the camera, and then calculate the depth of focus by consulting mathematical charts which determine the focal length of each lens and the f-stop the lens requires for the lighting conditions of each shot. The focus puller is not just responsible for keeping the shot sharp but must make sure that the camera equipment is fully operational. Keeping the equipment clean and setting up the camera with the correct lens and film stock, checking for scratches or hairs in the gate.

Clapper loader

The clapper loader is the busiest person on the camera crew.

The clapper loader will also act as an extra camera assistant as well as loading the magazines with film. S/he must also put the clapperboard on each take and write up the camera sheets for the lab. The clapper loader will also unload the magazines and make note of all exposed film stock sent to the lab. Often on larger feature films a camera trainee will work with the crew as an extra assistant under the supervision of the clapper loader.

Additional crew in the camera department

The DoP, operator, focus puller and clapper loader look after the actual camera and film stock. Additional crew is required to manipulate the lights and construct camera rigs, dolly, track and specialist equipment like car mounts.

Grip

Grips are responsible for any equipment that the camera is 'gripped' to. The grip is not just responsible for the dolly work. He will supervise the laying of tracks, setting up cranes, building camera platforms, car attachments and all aspects of the camera support equipment.

Gaffer

A DoP will have to choose a good 'gaffer' to handle lighting. He is the head of the electrical department and will supervise every aspect of the technical side of the lighting. He has an assistant known as the 'best boy' who may take over when the gaffer has to leave the set maybe to pre-light another set or location. If the camera operator is a second pair of eyes for the DoP then the gaffer is an extra pair of hands and eyes. He will ensure that the lamps are correctly and safely set up, often referring to the notes he made on the technical recces. He is also responsible for the stores that may be needed such as spare bulbs, filter and diffusion gel and the making up of gel frames. A large feature film may involve 20 or 30 electricians as well as trucks and generators; all of this must be organised by the gaffer. Due to the complex nature of some films special riggers may be brought in to build scaffold towers for lamps and camera platforms. Many DoPs will work with the same gaffer and camera crew for many years going from one film to another together. This continuity enables the crew to work smoothly, understanding what is required for a particular shot with a minimum of instructions.

Crane operators and riggers

The use of specialist equipment will necessitate the employment of additional temporary crew members: crane operators and riggers. All of these people come under the responsibility of the DoP, but are managed by the head gaffer.

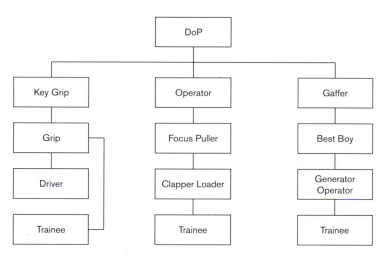

figure 8.1
Camera & lighting crew

Hint With all the complexities involved in modern filmmaking it is essential to plan every detail in advance. It is often said that filmmaking is 5% inspiration and 95% perspiration. A successful pre-production process ensures that most of the perspiration happens before filming commences.

2 The Shoot: the Life of a DoP

This is an account of the shoot by veteran cinematographer John Ward, who is also an instructor for Raindance.

John Ward has been a camera operator and DoP for many years, gaining opening title credits on *The Firm* (1988), *To Die For* (1994), *1977* (1996), *Final Cut* (1998) and *Love Honour and Obey* (2000) amongst many others.

Finally the first day of production arrives and it is time for the DoP to put all his experience and research to work.

Although there are many similarities between different films there are no hard and fast rules as to how a particular shot will be lit. The director, production designer and DoP will all have had their creative input about the scene. Some scenes may require small detailed lighting while others need big broad sweeps of light. This may require different types of lamps or placing them in more unusual positions. Although the key light is often a directional fresnel spot some scenes require a softer look and so a soft light, normally used for the fill, can be used instead. This can give the effect of the daylight coming from a large window and produces softer shadows. The DoP has to be ready to deal with technical problems caused by so-called unconventional lighting.

For example: one of the problems caused by bouncing the light or shining it through large frames covered in a diffusing material is that it requires much more light to achieve the required aperture for exposure. However this style of large soft lights has become much more popular since the introduction of faster film stocks and more efficient light sources. Another reason is that soft lighting can often give a much more natural look to the scene. Alternatively in a thriller or horror movie the use of a low angle key light and hard deep shadows gives the scene a menacing feel especially if there is little fill light and the contrast ratio is high.

Of course lighting the foreground subject isn't the only problem the DoP encounters. A good DoP pays as much attention to lighting the background. A well-lit background gives the shot a sense of depth and balance. Sometimes this will occupy as much if not more time than lighting the foreground action and this may involve using more than one lamp to do the same job.

For example if the key light's direction is coming from the left of frame, then another lamp will be set up to light the background from the same direction. Another example of the use of multiple lamps is when lighting a large foreground area and where one key light would not cover the whole area. Another problem is light fall off when an object nearest the lamp will be much brighter than one further away. This effect can also cause problems when actors move around the set and change their relative distance to the key light. And of course unlike a still photograph, the film camera can also move through the set. The DoP must be aware of the different areas that will be seen during the track or pan. All of this can lead to a complicated rig of lights and is a good reason for shooting on studio sets so that lamps can be positioned without the restriction of ceilings and fixed walls. Location shoots are usually restrictive for lamp placement. Each lamp on a set will produce a shadow; much time is spent eliminating these shadows. Reflection or shine is another lighting problem that must be overcome.

Once the lamps are set, the DoP's next job is to get out the meter and establish the exposure for that particular set-up. Many DoPs will use an incident meter to measure the amount of light at various points around the set. Incident meters are preferred over reflected light meters as they will give an exact measurement of the amount of light at a particular point without being affected by an overly bright or dark subject. Another advantage of incident meters is that the DoP can walk around the set and measure the light themselves, without using an actor. Some DoPs use spot meters to compare the amount of light in different areas of the set by measuring reflected light from a very small spot on a wall or on the actor's skin. Skin tone is usually the most important tone to expose for correctly. Spot meters can also be of use when using telephoto lenses and the subject is some distance away from the camera. However the light is measured, ultimately the decision on the amount of exposure is down to the DoP's interpretation of the information from the meter. How the DoP decides to interpret the information required for the exposure can greatly affect the final image on the film and is down to experience, judgement and sometimes pre-production tests. Here, the DoP's choice of film stock, lenses and filters can be crucial and will contribute to the overall look of the film. Finally, at the beginning of each set-up, the DoP will shoot a grey scale to enable the laboratory to grade the shot and match the colour balance when printing the rushes.

After the final rehearsals, and make-up, hair and costume checks, the time has come to commit the shot to film. At this point on most feature films the DoP will stand back behind the camera and watch as the shot progresses looking for any problems that may arise. An actor may miss their mark and stand in a shadow or the sun might go behind a cloud, any little thing that may detract from the photographic quality of the shot. Very often the DoP will need to make specific comments on a particular shot and will give the clapper loader notes to write on the sheets that are sent to the labs with the rushes. These notes will detail how the shot has worked, and will give any changes that may have happened such as a particular change in a lighting effect. This might mean that the shot starts in darkness and the light is switched on part way through. The lab will need to know how to grade the print to get the best effect and so the instructions from the DoP are essential. Some DoPs may operate the camera as well as lighting the film but most feel it is better to have an operator who can concentrate on the framing while they are free to observe the lighting.

During the shooting of the film much of the DoP's time is concentrated on the lighting, but there are still a great deal of other duties to be performed. Keeping a check on the number of rolls of the various film stocks that might be being used on the film, for example checking that there is enough fast film for the night shots or that there are 400ft rolls for Steadicam shots. A DoP will make sure that all additional items of equipment are ordered in time for the shots that will require them, such as high speed cameras or specialist cranes. The DoP will be constantly checking with the laboratories that the exposure levels are consistent with the required look of the film. This is done by checking the printer light levels reported on the returning lab sheets that are sent with the rushes and will be filed by the camera assistant for future reference.

Visiting the sets and locations that are yet to be shot or are still under construction is time consuming but very necessary if the DoP and gaffer are to be ready in time for the actual day of shooting. It may be that another lighting crew can be brought in to pre light that set or lay out long cable runs and for the riggers to set up lighting towers etc. Throughout all this mass of paperwork and practical on set activity, the DoP will have to deal with the constant pressure of a schedule that is usually too tight or director who makes numerous changes to the script, plus a producer who will always want it done quicker and cheaper. There are two well-known sayings in the film industry which always get quoted when producers try to cut financial corners:

'The cheapest deal is never the best deal, it is only the cheapest.'

'If you pay peanuts you get monkeys.'

3 Post-production

This is an account of the post-production process by veteran cinematographer John Ward, who is also an instructor for Raindance.

Throughout the pre-production and shooting of the film the DoP will be in frequent contact with the laboratory. The lab will provide one person who will act as the contact and will view the rushes prior to them being sent out to the editor, who will prepare them for screening by the director and DoP. The lab contact will give the DoP a report each morning after viewing the rushes and point out any problems with exposure, focus, scratching or light flares. The lab will also supply a set of sheets with a list of the printer lights, which tells the DoP exactly how much exposure the film has received. All this information will help the DoP keep track of the exposure and ensure a consistent look throughout the film. It will also be of use at the post-production grading stage.

The rush prints will then be used by the editor as a cutting copy to bring together the various shots and cut them to the required length to form the film as it will eventually be seen. This final cut of the film will then be used to enable the DoP and the laboratory grader to grade or time the film. Here the DoP will attend a screening of the final cut film and make notes and give instructions to the grader as to how light or dark a scene should be and if any colour adjustment may be necessary.

From this screening the grader will take his notes and instruction and make the changes to the printer lights and produce a first graded answer print. Another screening will then take place and again a number of changes may have to be made so leading to a second answer print. This process could then be repeated until the DoP and the director are both happy with the final look of the film and a show print is eventually produced. If the film is to be widely released many prints or copies may be needed and in this case, in order to protect the original negative, an intermediate negative will be produced. At this point, the DoP may well wish to judge the interneg grading to ensure consistency with the original show print. Finally when the film is transferred to tape to produce the video version the DoP will probably attend the telecine session to oversee the video grade. Nowadays much of the post-production work is done digitally and as a result some producers are reluctant to spend the money making expensive rush prints. Instead the camera negative may be scanned directly to tape and conformed onto one or other of the electronic editing systems. However most DoPs will argue for at least some proportion of the rushes to be printed onto film to enable them to make more accurate judgements of the photographic look of the film. There are also other reasons for printing rushes on film such as judging focus, contrast and colour matching which cannot accurately be done from a video tape.

And finally, after all the trials and tribulations, months of painstaking work and much sweat (but hopefully not too much blood or too many tears) the DoP will have achieved a minor miracle. A fabulous looking film that will excite, enthral and dazzle the audience, and yet 99.9% of them will not even notice the lighting. But with any luck a few other DoPs might just think the film good enough and the long awaited nomination for an Oscar™ or BAFTA may eventually arrive. Not that any DoP can rest on their laurels; another film is waiting and the whole process is about to start all over again.

Film Lighting Crash Course

Our eyes are set a few inches apart and bring in information to the brain which we blend in order to create the impression of three dimensions. A camera only has one lens, and in order to recreate the illusion of three dimensions, we use lights. The three basic lights are: key, back, fill.

If you look at anyone standing in a room, you will notice large pockets of shadow under their eyes. This is unflattering and unattractive. In order to get rid of these shadows, a key light is shone into the actor's face. The shadows disappear. But now the face has absolutely no modelling.

All good cinematographers go to art galleries to study the old masters, looking in particular at how they interpreted light and shadow on their subjects. In order to bring back some modelling to the face and give the portrait shape and modelling, the DoP will use a side light, called a fill light. This lamp will put gentle shadows back into the face.

Key and fill lights make the face look 3D. But because the light on the face is now so intense, the actor's face looks as if it has been pushed back into the background of the set. To compensate for this, the DoP places a light behind the actor and points it to the back of the actor's head. This is the back light, which creates a halo around the actor's head, pushing it away from the background and creating depth.

The Low Budget Shoot

In the low budget world, it is impossible to use the same number of people as on a full-blown production as described above. Accordingly, the roles of the camera personnel tend to blur and overlap. For exam-

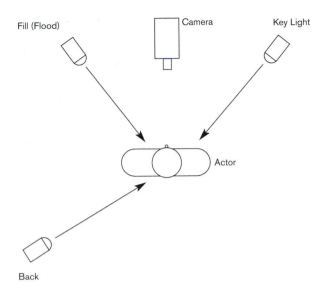

Fill (Flood)   Camera   Key Light

Actor

figure 8.2
Lighting a person in a room

Back

Jon Jost, the American experimental filmmaker, shot many features with a single sound assistant. He created a career by shooting 35mm features and shorts on shooting ratios of less than 3:1. His filmography is vastly overlooked, and is well worth a look. *Muri romani* (2000), *London Brief* (1997), *Albrechts Flügel* (1994), *The Bed You Sleep In* (1993),*Uno a me, uno a te e uno a Raffaele* (1994), *Frame Up* (1993), *All the Vermeers in New York* (1990), *Sure Fire* (1990), *Rembrandt Laughing* (1988), *Bell Diamond* (1985), *Slow Moves* (1983), *Plain Talk & Common Sense* (1987), *Psalm* (1982), *Stagefright* (1981), *Godard* (1980), *Chameleon* (1978), *Last Chants for a Slow Dance* (1977), *Angel City* (1976), *Speaking Directly* (1973).

Mike Figgis developed a unique steering wheel device to mount a DV camera and a high performance mike to. By placing zoom and focus controls on the wheel, he is able to shoot and sound record his own movies with a crew of one.

ple, the DoP may also operate and focus pull (although it is technically impossible for a DoP/operator to also focus pull on complicated tracking and dolly shots). There is no reason why one person cannot operate, focus pull and load a 35mm camera shoot, although the constant pauses for loading/unloading would certainly justify the expense of another camera assistant.

From an economic point of view, the greatest saving in the camera department on a shoot is to avoid or exclude lights, thereby saving not only the expense of hiring the lights, but the salary of the lighting truck driver and the expense of the gaffers and the sparks. Add to this the saving you make on catering, and it is easy to save £15,000 ($22,500) per week on a shoot by working without lights.

Shooting Without Lights

When shooting without lights, it is still possible to recreate the elements of key, back and fill lights by using available light. Sometimes the available light can be enhanced by using reflectors. Reflectors can be fashioned from a sheet of white (or coloured, if desired) cardboard.

Some DoPs will carefully consider the placement of their subjects before shooting, thus creating natural key, back and fill lighting. Others will place their subject immediately in front of a bright light to create a burn and silhouette effect, which, although technically considered wrong or incorrect, has a certain beauty and power within the parameters of shooting with available light. The financial and logistical advantages of this method are:

1. Fewer crew, vehicles and rentals make the shoot more cost effective.

2. Smaller crew makes for a more intimate set.

3. Lighter equipment and fewer crew mean quicker set-ups.

Hiring a DoP

When hiring a DoP one needs to consider their artistic ability, their technical ability and their ability to work with the director. When choosing a DoP you will solicit showreels from prospective DoPs either by contacting labs, agents, or on recommendation from other filmmakers.

Once you have reviewed and shortlisted the showreels, you send the prospective DoPs a script, and then set up a meeting.

You are looking for someone who understands the look of the film you want to shoot. You also need to make certain that the person you hire is a true collaborator, and not someone who will take over the job of directing as well.

Career Route of a DoP

DoPs go to film school where they learn the basics of celluloid and tape response to imaging, as well as the mechanics of operating cameras. They also try and shoot as much film as possible – working as loaders, operators and DoPs on student shorts. When they graduate, they usually have two business cards printed: one of which says Clapper Loader, and the other says Director of Photography. If they meet you in a bar, which card do you think you are going to get? The DoP card, of course. If they meet an established focus puller, operator or DoP they will hand them the clapper loader card in the hope of paid work.

When you discuss payment, you will probably start with their weekly rate. By mentioning a number, they just lost the negotiation arguments. You now know where they sit on the pay scale.

If you want them to work at a reduced rate, or even for free, ask them whether or not they have an opening title credit as DoP on a feature film. At this point you will get an amazing amount of humming and hawing, and answers that refer to some second assistant to the assistant to the clapper loader on a Stanley Kubrick film some decades ago!

At this point you have got them. Now the decision is all theirs, and they will decide whether or not to take this job based on the elements that will promote their careers as well.

Hint The elusive opening title credit is your first step up the career ladder. With it, you can get listed on IMDB, an online movie database, and use it on your CV. As a producer, you are handing out opening title credits. Never undersell or underestimate the value of your credits.

Summary

1. A feature film is a huge opportunity for a cinematographer to become a director of photography.

2. Make certain the DoP you hire is compatible with the director.

3. Look for a DoP that can solve problems, not create them.

We have everything ready to go: lights, camera, sound. But before we roll, what about the set?

In Conversation With Jim Solan

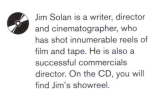

Jim Solan is a writer, director and cinematographer, who has shot innumerable reels of film and tape. He is also a successful commercials director. On the CD, you will find Jim's showreel.

What is it that makes you decide to do a film?

The script first and foremost. And you always have to look at the director involved and what they are going to be bringing to the piece. But predominately it's the script. You have to give it a good read – you know that you are going to have to work within that story. You consider what visual opportunities it presents to you as a cameraman, and if it touches you in any way.

What about working on a project for less than your normal rate?

Again, it's the script. You ask yourself what you can do that's within the budget. You look at a script and you look at how ambitious it is, look at the director and how ambitious they are, and you talk with the director and producer and figure what format you're going to shoot it on. And then you make an assessment of what you can add to your repertoire from doing that film. You judge whether you think that the director will go on to bigger and better stuff. You've really got to consider how much you love the project, how much you rate this director and production team and the other members of the crew, and decide for yourself if you think it's going to be a worthwhile project. It's got to be worthwhile.

The potential of the rest of the people working on the project is important to you?

Yeah, it's the potential that the people have, and also the potential of the whole project. What potential does the film have to work, what potential do the people have who are working on the film to create a good result. You can be the best cinematographer in the world, but if the actors are rubbish, it's pointless. You can't light your way out of a bad production design. You can't light your way out of bad acting, and you certainly can't light your way out of a bad script. You can do everything you can, and when all the elements of all the departments are pushing in the right direction, hopefully you get something good. But if you feel that a low budget script is overly ambitious and too much money is going on one thing, or something is going to be forgotten about, then you have to question it. Particularly important is the acting. Is this going to be a load of rubbish because of the performance levels? I mean, ultimately that's what it's all about – performance. If the people in front of the camera don't perform, it doesn't matter what the rest of us do, it's going to be poor.

What do you like to have in a 35mm kit or a digital video kit?
I want the right camera for the job. If it's digital, it can be DV but it's got to be the right DV camera. A lot is said about the Canon XL1 and that particular family of cameras, but I personally think the DSL500 is the only good DV camera out there to shoot a digital film on. Of course, there's HD and DigiBeta. Again, you want the right camera for the job. And with 35mm or 16mm, you need the right camera. It's got to be a sync camera. Obviously with 35mm you need a decent set of lenses.

Lighting wise, it all depends on the script. Often you're going to be putting in certain bits of kit for certain days, and the hire company may be delivering specific kit for each day. If you're doing night shoots, you're going to need bigger lights – 6 KHMIs, 12 KHMIs. And you don't want to be carrying them around with you for a whole shoot. You can be restricted with a truckload of camera and lighting. Again, it depends. Do you have a generator? What sort of on location lighting facilities are you going to have? Are you going to be able to plug in somewhere? There are so many different scenarios that you're going to be in, you should just make a list of the facilities and requirements of each location and set-up.

It also depends on the style that you've discussed with the director. Say we're going to shoot this entire bit on a long lens, so we don't need a wide lens. Or we're going to shoot a lot of wide-angle shots so we don't need a long lens.

Are there differences between lighting for 35mm and for DV?
No. I think you have to approach both exactly the same, and that will come from your treatment of the script.

Yes, DV doesn't have the exposure latitude of film, but when you're lighting, you don't say 'Well, I'm shooting for DV so I'm going to light it massively differently'. Instead, you employ backlights, key lights, maybe an eye light. It will always come from the script not from the format you're shooting on. I think that's a big mistake that many people make with DV. They forget that you can light it, and you can make it look very, very good. It's no different from lighting film. The only difference is you have an exposure meter when you're lighting for film.

Fundamentally you have to approach them the same. There is that slight contrast issue with DV. The highlights will bleach out more easily than film, and dark areas will have no information more readily than in film. The only other thing is in exposing DV and tape generally: you should slightly underexpose than overexpose. That way the camera will always be able to capture information. It works differently from that of the 35mm where, if you overexpose, you get more information on your negative, and when you make a print in the lab that will also get increased saturation – deeper blacks. I'm not going to say you can underexpose and use that as a tool on film, but there is a rule of thumb that if you overexpose, you're going to get more information. It might not be right for your look, but that's for you and the director to decide. On DV, I tend to underexpose a third to a half a stop.

Lighting Terms Glossary

Accent light
A light which brings the eye to an area or object.

Ambient light
Natural light available in a shot.

ASA (ISO)
Sensitivity rating of film emulsions.

Attributes of light
The factors affecting the quality of light are: hard or soft (or in between), intensity or brightness, direction, colour and beam pattern. All but colour are affected by the light's size and distance from the object it is lighting.

Available light
Existing light on an interior or exterior set.

Backlight
A light or lights angled onto the background to reveal the character of the background, which helps to separate the main subject from the background. Often used with smoke, gels, steam and filters.

Barndoor
A device of several panels or doors which can be attached to the front of a stage light in order to shape and shade the scene or protect the camera lens from a beam of light.

Base light
Bland, diffuse set illumination.

Bounce light
Soft light effect created by bouncing light off a colour-neutral surface.

Butterfly
Large frame with fabric diffuser or net to soften or reduce harsh light.

Camera-top light
The flat-light look of on-board lights for news-type shoots.

Cinema lighting

The process where artificial lighting is used to create mood and drama, divide the space of the shot into planes, artificially suggesting depth, enhancing character.

Colouring light

Gels correct the colour of light sources relative to each other or the film. Coloured gels distort light for dramatic or artistic purposes.

Colour temperature (Degrees kelvin or °K)

Briefly: how red or blue, the 'white' light is. Films are 'white-balanced' by choosing the correct colour temperature source (daylight, about 5600°K, tungsten usually about 3200°K) or by filtering.

Continuity of light (Matching)

The process whereby the director of photography records the lighting levels of scenes shot out of sequence in order to be able to match them in post-production. Beware of camerapersons who dodge this one by saying that you can fix it in post. You can but it is expensive.

Contrast ratio (Brightness ratio)

Compare two reflected-light readings: compare the lightest significant area of the subject or scene with the darkest. Also see Lighting ratio.

Cookaloris (Cucoloris, cookie, kook)

A device with patterns placed in front of a hard-light which throws shadows or dappled light on bland areas. Also known as gobo or flag. A good cookie can change the look of a scene.

Cool light

Gels or subjects in the blue-green region of the colour spectrum.

Cut

To remove light from the scene.

Cyc (cyclorama, cove)

A background where floor and walls are joined in a gradual curve.

Dichroic

Vapour-deposited coating that reflects unwanted portions of the light spectrum, or a coated filter. For daylight correction of tungsten light.

Diffusion

Translucent materials that soften highlights and shadows, reduce contrast and increase beam-angle.

Distance (Throw)

The light to subject distance not only controls fall-off, but also sharpness, and (effective) size of the light, relative to subject size.

Dominance

If several sources are needed, one of them (or one direction of light) should dominate.

Fall-off

Light, from a point source, falls-off inversely to the square of the distance. Move the light from ten feet away to twenty feet away and you have 1/4 of the intensity; forty feet, 1/16th. Diffused lights appear to fall-off even faster.

Fill light

Fill lightens shadows and controls contrast and lighting ratios.

Finesse (Light control)

The art of refining white light by using focusing knobs, barndoors, fancy-scrims, gels and anything handy that won't melt instantly.

Flag (Cutter, gobo)

An opaque panel, used to block light and shadow the subject, background or camera lens. It can also hide lights in the dark recesses of a scene. Which term you use depends on the device's size.

Flare

Flare occurs in the optical system of cameras. Keep bright lights and strong reflections out of the lens to avoid it.

Flat Light

All light is characterless, textureless and shallow-shadowed when the source is close to the camera.

Flood

To increase the angle of beam-size of a focusing light, which decreases its intensity.

Focus

To vary a spotlight's beam-size and intensity.

Footcandle (fc)

A unit of incident illumination, largely unaffected by the subject's luminosity (brightness).

Foregrounds

Dark foregrounds help hold the eye within the frame and increase the illusion of depth. Bright foreground objects, especially out-of-focus or moving ones, can be distracting.

Fresnel

A thinner, lighter, 'stepped' version of a plano-convex lens. Also, a spotlight with such a lens.

Gel (Gelatin, media)
As used with photographic lights, a strong flexible, fire-proof and fade-resistant material used to change the colour, amount or quality of light.

Glare
Light reflected off of shiny surfaces. In moderation, it is one of the most useful ways to add life to drab subjects.

Glare angle (Angle of reflection)
The law-of-the-light states: the angle of incidence equals the angle of reflection. Simply: light is reflected at the same angle it came from, but in the opposite direction. See Plane lighting.

Good eye
To help develop sensitivity to light and composition: study good films, photographs and paintings; keep an image file; observe the subtleties of light and shadow all around you, even when not shooting. Good DoPs often carry sketchbooks with them.

Hard light
A relatively small, direct, usually focusable source, with or without lens, that produces strong highlights and dark shadows. The quality is more dramatic and controllable, but generally less flattering than soft-light; often improved with diffusion.

High-key
Lighting which results in predominantly middle-grey to white tones.

Incident-light meter
Tool which measures the strength of the light that reaches the scene.

Intensity (Light output)
The 'strength' of the incident-light source.

Key light
The key, or main light, tends to set the character of the lighting. It may suggest a source, like the sun, or a window.

Kicker
A low-angle side-backlight that adds glare to the side of faces.

Kicks (Hotspots)
Bright light reflections that add sparkle.

Kill
To turn-off one or more of your lights.

Lamp
Trade name for light bulbs.

Lamp-life
The number of hours at which half the test lamps fail.

Light (Fixture, head, luminaire, instrument)
The contraption, regardless of name and shape, that surrounds the lamp.

Lighting director
The person responsible for lighting video productions.

Lighting grid
An overhead pipe-like structure in a studio to support lights and electrical connectors.

Lighting ratio
The ratio of key-light plus fill, vs fill-light only, using an incident-light meter. (If the first is 200 foot candles and the second 50, the ratio is 4:1.) Optimum and maximum lighting ratios depend upon subject matter, mood, media, and type of reproduction as well as personal taste. In television, a timid ratio is 2:1, a dramatic one, 8:1; a maximum one, about 16:1. Film and slides can handle higher ratios than video and printed photos. See also 'brightness ratio'.

Limbo
A photographic background that appears to disappear.

Location
An area used for shooting, or considered for use, other than a studio.

Low-angle light
The ideal key for villains and monsters and nymphs. See Motivated lighting.

Low-key
Lighting which results in predominantly grey to middle-black tones.

Lux
A unit of measure of incident light (not reflected from the scene). The US equivalent is footcandles. To convert: fc x 10.8 = lux.

Matte
A non-reflective, dull subject or surface. Also, a technique originally used to create special effects within the camera.

Magic hour
The time of day (dusk) when everyone would shoot almost everything, if only it lasted longer, because the sun is low and strong and golden.

Motivated lighting
Where photographic lights appear to come from actual sources.

Moving sources (video/film)
Effective when justified by the action, baffling at most other times. There are a few exceptions: diffused sources moving with the cast and camera, outdoors or where background shadows are not a problem, or when used symbolically.

Moving subjects
It is challenging to light moving talent correctly. Rehearse the action, do it before you light and note where people pause. Don't attempt to light large areas evenly; movement is enhanced by intensity changes. If movement is not predictable, set the lights far away, and high.

Multiple shadows
Few things expose the novice and the artifice of cinematography faster than multiple shadows, unless they are motivated or done with real style.

Night vs 'Night'
Film is illusion: it doesn't have to be night, it only has to look like it. Try shooting late in the day, with the low sun as your back light and with a little fill. If you want to see street lights or the sky, shoot during late dusk or real night.

Opaque
An object or material that does not transmit light.

Plane lighting
Visualise your subject, or the entire scene, as a series of planes at various angles to the lens. Position lights to reveal those planes effectively. Light planes to different levels of brightness, usually the closer or larger ones should be darker. See 'glare angle'.

Polarising filters
Polarising camera filters can be set to reduce most glare as well as darken blue skies. They work by admitting light only from a selected direction.

Practical light
A prop light seen in shot that can be operated by the cast; sometimes doctored to control brightness, colour or coverage; usually positioned to motivate or justify the key or other source.

Reflected light
The light reflected from a surface, after losses due to absorption and scattering. See Glare, Bounce and Spill for further reflections.

Reflected light meter
Meters that read the intensity of light reflected off the subject or scene.

Reflections
The rules that affect reflections are the same as those for glare.

Reflectors

Curved contraptions that concentrate the lamp's beam, and flat devices that recycle light from lights, sun and, at close range, even overcast sky.

Rigs

Assemblies designed, or adapted, to support lights, backgrounds etc.

Scrims

Metal screen, put in front of lights to reduce intensity without diffusion.

Set light

The video equivalent of background light.

Shade

Consider all the subtle shades of shade: wide-open, dappled, flat, side, kicker and back-lit varieties. Keep your eyes and your options open, and your reflector handy.

Shadows

Backlights and low-angle lights can exaggerate shadows for impact.

Sharp

As applied to shadows, a hard, clean edge. The farther away subjects are from a light, and the closer they are to backgrounds, the sharper their shadows will be. The edge of a spot beam produces sharper shadows than the centre.

Side-light

This half-key-half-kicker hits subjects at an angle of 90°. It is doubly mis-used, at times, in matched-pairs, from opposite sides. See 'dominance'.

Silhouettes

Dark shapes and figures against light backgrounds can have impact, even on small screens.

Size and distance

The larger the light, the softer its quality, but the effective size of a source also depends upon subject size and distance. A large, distant source is, in effect, small and hard (e.g. the sun). A four square-foot softlight backed off to cover a car is small, but lighting a watch, enormous.

Snoot

Snoots are front-of-the-light 'tubes' that project a circle of light on a sub-ject or background and refine the area that light falls onto. See 'sharp'.

Softlight

Soft-shadows and subtle highlights are produced by large, indirect, heavily diffused or bounced light. The largest, cheapest soft source is an overcast sky.

Spill

Light that falls outside of the intended area, but which can be useful in reducing contrast.

Spot

To adjust a focusing light toward maximum intensity and minimum beam angle. Also, a hard light.

Spot meter

Light meter which reads a narrow angle of light reflected from the subject.

Strobe light (flash)

Electronic source that produces a burst of light which can freeze motion.

Top-light angle

Directly over the subject. If you want to light eyes, not nose-tops, save this for non-human subjects. Soft, top-front-light is ideal for some faces.

Translucent

An object, material or vapour that transmits and diffuses both light and images, such as frost gel and dense smoke.

Transparent

An object or material that transmits both light and undiffused images.

Two-D preview

One way to anticipate what will happen to our three-dimensional world when it becomes a two-dimensional image is to view the shot with one eye, or to light and compose through the lens.

Volts

On the CD, you will find a breakdown of the different voltages used in every country in the world.

A measure of electrical 'pressure'. Formula: volts = watts divided by amps; better to say A x V = W. To save bucks and save face, check lamp voltages before plugging in, and overseas voltages before grabbing your passport. Common voltages: 12V, 30V, 120V, 220V, 240V and in Japan, 100V.

Warm light

Gels or subjects in the red-orange-yellow range of the colour spectrum.

Watts

An expression of electrical power.

Wild wall

An easily removable section of a set, to facilitate camera positioning and lighting.

9   Production Values

THE COMBINED EFFECT of the look of the film, and the quality of the 'look' is the production values. If you shoot a scene that looks like it cost a million dollars to film, when you actually did it for ten thousand – well, that is giving your film high production values at a bargain price.

The look of the set, make-up and wardrobe translates directly to the screen, creating production values that will enhance your film. Knowing where to spend additional funds at this stage will predetermine the final look of your film. Understanding how production design and art department work will enable you to maximise the art department budget which will translate directly to screen production values.

Role of the Production Designer

Where the director is responsible for the look on the screen, and the DoP responsible for what is recorded by the camera, the production designer is responsible for how the set and wardrobe look. S/he reports directly to the director, and consults with the cinematographer. The production designer will also talk to the performers to make sure that special effects, costume and make-up are properly designed to allow for performances.

The production designer will meet initially with the director, having read the script, and will offer suggestions for the designs. Once commissioned, the production designer will have a list of sets, props and wardrobe requirements for each actor in each scene, along with a budget for the creation of the sets and wardrobe (art department budget). Once the drawings and location scouting is complete, the production designer heads up a small army of assistants, and brings the sets, make-up and wardrobe in on time and on budget.

Art Department

In a commercial feature film production, the production designer gives the drawings and specifications to the art director, who executes the drawings and delivers props, wardrobe and sets under the direct supervision of the production designer. Wardrobe assistants, prop builders, scenic painters and set carpenters all work in the art department.

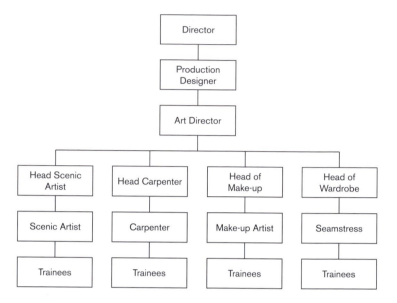

figure 9.1
Structure of production design crew
roles

Low Budget Art Department

The first sacrifice you make when working on a low budget film is people. Thus, the production designer doubles as the art director, and very often the set carpenter, scenic artist and wardrobe mistress as well. While this is an excellent way to learn valuable techniques it can also be frustrating because you rarely meet people with more experience than yourself, which hinders your development.

However, the low budget art department has certain advantages over a fully-fledged industry standard art department – and that is creativity. Often the effects achieved with little or no money have greater impact than the really big budget productions.

One just has to look for the dirt in a Hollywood movie to realise that somewhere a production designer yelled 'dirt' and then an art director yelled 'dirt' and then some scenic assistant scurried back to the goods desk and yelled 'dirt' until a sleepy clerk shuffled over and put a couple of dirt cans on the counter.

Hint Isn't your first film going to be a gritty slice of life drama shot in and around where you live, work or go to school? Get a talented production designer to make the dirt look better! Simply arranging the dirt can sometimes make it look more photogenic.

Low Budget Special Effects

When Roger Corman spent ten days at Raindance, I asked him what the secret to a successful low budget movie was. He replied in his lovely gravelly voice, that a successful movie had to have sex and violence in it. Then he said: 'Let's just call it action!'

The quickest way to get production values into your script is to create action. Here are a few basic tips, but remember, they are just tips. I am sure you can come up with better, more creative ways.

Fake Blood

Independent films often have to rely on a certain amount of violence or nudity to sell – just ask Roger Corman – he's made an entire career and no small empire based on violence. Filmmakers are always finding new ways of creating realistic looking blood on screen. In order to give you the latest in screen blood, I talked to Jake West, whose cult hit *Razor Blade Smile* created a furore usually reserved for big budgeted Hollywood films. Here are two of Jake's simple formulas for making movie blood.

1 Syrup-based blood

Alfred Hitchcock famously used Bosco chocolate syrup in his film *Psycho*.

Get a bottle of light corn-syrup, add in red food colouring, a little blue, and just a touch of green. Obviously, most of the food colouring you use should be red. By experimenting with the amount of blue and green, you should be able to come up with some very realistic looking blood. This will not run freely from a wound, but it will do well for blood-stains, zombies, gunshot victims, etc. Remember to adjust for the lights and the film/tape stock you are using. It could well be that the actual blood is nearly blue or purple to the eye, but will give a sickening 'blood' look on screen.

2 MB2-based blood

This blood formula is more realistic. As there's no sugar and very little food in the formula it's less attractive to insects (an important consideration if you are shooting outside). [Conversion: 7.5cc = half a level tablespoon, 10cc = two level teaspoons]

Flour base:
Decide how much you want in total then mix 7.5cc to 10cc plain all purpose flour per cup (250cc) of water. Mix the flour into the water completely (no lumps) before heating. Bring it to the boil and then let it simmer for half an hour. Stir frequently. Allow it to cool before adding food colouring. This makes a good base for stage blood.
One cup batch of MB2:
1oz (29cc) Red food colouring
1/8 teaspoon (0.6cc) green food colouring
This quantity is enough to colour one cup of the base (250cc).

The shelf life of the MB2 formula blood is just a few days at room temperature. The blood does not go rank but ferments a bit and loses viscosity with time. This formula will temporarily stain skin but will wash out of cotton clothes.

All you need now is to make certain you have a superb stills photographer around when you shoot the blood. You'd be amazed how useful a bloody still is when you go to sell the movie.

Wounds

The key to convincing low budget effects are simple festering sores, the all-important, classic wound, which can be easy and cheap. After all, the indie filmmaker needs realism, diversity of options, and recognition of the proverbial empty wallet. Also handy is a blood bag which will burst on contact with a fake knife.

1 Stab wound

You will need:

A retractable knife

A solid piece of plastic or metal

A latex glove or a condom

1. Strap the piece of plastic onto the victim, placing it where he/she will be stabbed.
2. Attach a baggie of fake blood (in the finger of a glove or the condom) over top of it.
3. Cover it with their shirt (duh). Thenwhen tehy are attacked on camers, the bag should burst. If you have a retractable knife, this will be easy – just stab the knife onto the blood bag.

Use extreme caution when dealing with knives, retractable or otherwise.

2 Cuts

1. Roll two long, thin pieces of tissue and connect them at the ends, leaving the middle part separated.
2. Using liquid latex, apply the tissue to your skin.
3. Make the outer edge rise from the skin, and the inner edge (the 'cut') rise sharply.
4. Apply more than one layer of liquid latex and cover with make-up (and blend).
5. Squeeze fake blood into the centre of the cut and let it run down.

Special effects make-up artists are more than dedicated – they are creative and they are thorough, and they post their instructions on the web.

Stunts

Health and safety is a serious issue. If cast and crew are hurt, it will also affect your schedule and the producer could end up in prison. Use an expert – a stunt coordinator or fight director.

Any physical action that may endanger the cast or crew, or any physical action that an actor is not willing to do should be considered a stunt. This can include nude or sex scenes.

No matter how simple a stunt may look in the script, for the stunt to work safely it will require much more time to shoot than a regular scene. If the stunt is something like a fight scene, the production will also – for that scene – require more editing and shooting time, which will impact on the production and post-production schedule. A typical page of dialogue may take only one day to rough-cut and a few hours to film, but a good fight scene could take a week to edit and two or three days to film. This will impact on your budget, as will the health and safety considerations; whenever there is a stunt, you may be required to also hire a stunt coordinator in addition to the stunt person.

Sex Scenes

In one of my first directing roles, I hired an actress who would not appear nude. However, wearing a g-string and skimpy bra was not considered by her to be nude. The lesson learned was to make sure your talent understands what is expected of them before they are signed to your shoot.

Sex scenes should be regarded in the same way: you can't assume that any actor you might have in mind for a certain role will get involved with sex scenes or nudity. Your producer will have to negotiate with the agent for permission, and it will usually cost more. Scenes involving nudity also take longer to shoot, especially if you've written in lots of close-ups of fingers clutching bed-sheets. During production it will be a 'closed set', and only a fraction of the crew will be working on the scenes, so things may take longer to shoot. In some cases, body doubles may have to be used, which is just another body on set that the producer has to feed, transport, pay and apply make-up to (and lots of it).

Firearms

For scenes involving guns or rifles, your have to make sure that a licensed gun handler is on set at all times. This could be a special effects coordinator, or it could be one of the art department crew. A special effects artist will have to be hired for any 'hits' you want your firearms to make. If the gun or rifle is fired, a pay-duty policeman or armourer will have to be hired. The fees for such police are higher than regular pay-duty police.

If you've written scenes with explosions, the complications can be daunting. A special effects coordinator will have to be hired; the local fire department will have to be notified, and in some cases may have to be hired as well, along with a truck. As with stunts and other special effects, it will be cost-effective to cover the scene with multiple cameras, thus using more film stock, the hiring of extra operators and assistants, etc. The area the explosion takes place in will need to be secured by additional pay-duty police. There are only slim distinctions which govern who is responsible for certain effects. Sometimes the props person can handle it, sometimes you'll need a professional special effects artist. It is best to seek advice from a certified stunt coordinator, who will be able to help you with risk assessment.

Screen Combat and Fight Directing

Violence on a stage or set is managed and choreographed by a fight director. On film and television, the fight director will work under the direct supervision of the stunt coordinator or action designer.

A stunt coordinator is very similar in job description to a fight director, however, the role covers a broader spectrum of action scenes such as wire work, fire, cars – things that often don't take place on the stage (the role of fight director evolved from the same job in the theatre).

While there is no legal obligation to hire a fight director, it is advisable to use a fight director on a production for two very good reasons:

1 To make the fight safe
Safety is the primary reason for using a fight director. The fight director's main role is making the fight safer for all those involved.

2 To make the fight good
Making a fight that serves the production. The FD will install a sense of security in the actors that will allow them to perform without fear of accident. S/he will tailor the fight not just to the production, but a good FD will also tailor the fight to the needs and abilities of the actors.

Working with a Fight Director

There is an interview with fight director Tim Klotz on the CD, where you will also find a glossary of fight direction.

A fight director needs to be informed about several technical aspects in order to assist the actors in creating the right fight for the scene. They need to make sure that the fight is safe and that it looks as good as it can on screen.

Designer or design department
The FD needs to know what surfaces the fight will be on, and what other elements, such as props, need to be brought into the scene.

The props department
The FD needs to see what weapons have been designed for the scene. If there are firearms, then an armourer will have to be hired.

Wardrobe
Wardrobe should be informed of the necessary safety requirements. They may be required to hide back padding or knee braces etc. under the costume. They may have to provide specific safety gear such as gloves and they may also be required to have stand-in costumes for fights which involve potentially getting dirty or bloody. The FD will have to discuss footwear with them also.

Lighting
The FD will want to make sure that cross lighting will not blind the performers. Also, the director of photography and the FD may wish to discuss the elements of the fight in order that it can be shot in the best and most effective way possible.

Director
The FD needs to make sure that the director's vision is being followed. A good FD helps bring the director's vision to life.

The producers, first AD or other production personnel
It is a good idea to introduce the FD to the rest of the production team.

Summary

1. Always seek the elements that will enhance the visuals of your film.

2. Make absolutely certain that you adhere to health and safety issues.

3. Be inventive. Learn to use the budget limitations of your project to advantage.

If you are shooting on public or private property, you will need to make legal arrangements. The next chapter tells you how.

Low Budget CGI

Keys to the Special Effects Kingdom on a Lo-to-No Budget by Floyd Webb

Floyd Webb is one of the pioneers of CGI graphics and an expert in low budget CGI. Floyd is currently in Los Angeles, although he travels frequently to London and Paris where he designs motion for websites (to make a buck) and works on feature films with a host of the most respected indie filmmakers in America.

CGI effects for independent films can be achieved these days for very little money. That is, little money relative to what you hear about being paid for big budget feature effects. Right now it is about access to hardware, software and the people who know how to use it.

Whether you shot on film or digital, you are always going to be posting non-linear in Final Cut Pro, Avid, Razor, etc. That is unless you are some cinema Luddite still obsessed with the smell of film cement and the clickety-click of a Steenbeck and navigating jungles of film strips hanging from a clothesline (ahh, those were the days). With Adobe After Effects, Electric Image, Maya, 3D Studio Max and a number of other software packages you can accomplish some amazing things.

As filmmakers we should remain aware that this is a collaborative art. One of the first things I try to do is find out who my possible collaborative partners might be. As a director, writer or producer we should concentrate on those skills we have chosen to pursue. While we may want to and even be able to do it all, we should not. Sure, you can try to learn every job, but take it from one who knows, it is better to have a pool of people to coalesce with and be able to delegate duties, especially with CGI. Have you got 400 hours to learn to use the software? If you do – great – if not, then you need another solution.

Do some research on what it is you require for your script. Try to gain some familiarity with how 3D animation works, and the various software packages. This will keep you ahead of the game and allow you to identify people who are more then posers. Time is of the essence and no one has any to waste.

'Social engineering' is a hacker term that describes how to get something you need out of a person. While somewhat manipulative and devious as a practice, the core technique is sound. As filmmakers we are in a social business and we lead with charisma, passion and dedication to our ideas. There are people who can help you with whatever you need. All you need do is look for them, sell them on your idea, ask nicely, pay them a token fee and always feed them well. Take your people to lunch. Listen to their ideas about what you are doing and always be ready to compromise. Those forty-seven light sabre fights in the first ten pages may actually might not be a good idea after all. Listen and learn.

If you get someone who is really skilled at CGI, has the hardware and software, believes in what you are doing, and needs the working credit, then you are in. Show them some respect, compensate them based on your ability to pay or not (never promise what you don't have) and take them to meals, invite them to screenings, parties, introduce them around (after you get done with your project).

You can try to search for people who work at post production houses to get a deal – see if there are any talented people who are looking to make a name for themselves working for the next George Lucas. They may not be able to do the work at the post house. It is most likely that someone who has their own software and equipment at home will be most helpful to you. But these guys are working nine to five for big money. They will give you top flight work, and they may give you the hard sell, but if you have a small budget to pay them for their out of hours time (they work really fast) this could work for you.

If you have absolutely no money, the first place to locate people is art schools. Find out what colleges and training facilities have advanced students on the verge of entering the workforce (but are not stuck in exams two weeks after you get started). Put up a flyer promising fame and credit on a new hip indie film in production. Look at a few portfolios and take note of each person's strengths and weaknesses. Talk to department heads and teachers to find out who they think the most gifted students are. And by the way, you have a legitimate film project. What you lack is money. Say so at the beginning. You're a producer – you should have the patter down before you start talking to people.

Some students might be good at character animation, others at 3D environments, and still others at visual effects. You need all three and it rarely comes in one person. If you find that special one – great – if not, build a small team. One of these people should become your point person, someone who might have management ability and can liaise with you smoothly. You now have your very own visual effects supervisor and this could save you a lot of headaches down the line if you locate a bright kid with a good work ethic. The best advice I ever got from someone was in LA, of all places. He told me that 'the key to being a successful independent filmmaker is surrounding yourself with people of like mind and superior work ethics.' Works for me.

Try to attend conferences of 3D animators or professional associations like SIGGRAPH. Again check the Internet to see where they are or ask around. Go with that charm and sophistication you exude so well and sell your idea to whoever you find that is skilled at 3D animation. Go to booths touting the newest 3D animation software and talk to the sales guys. They always know people.

Another good place to find people is on-line. Communities and discussion boards exist for all of the major animation and 3D softwares. On these sites work is placed for review, problems are solved, issues clarified and yes, you can recruit someone to help work on your film. People post samples of their work online on these forums. It does not matter if they are in Slovakia or Katmandu: if they have a connection and can receive storyboards and images, you can work with them online. Contact user groups: search online or ask around. There is a local user group for software in most urban areas. A few online user forums that may be useful are:

– Maya Community http://www.alias.com/eng/community/index.jhtml
– Lightwave Community http://vbulletin.newtek.com/
– 3D Studio Max http://support.discreet.com/
– Adobe AfterEffects http://www.adobe.com/support/forums/main.html

Set up a paypal account online. It is free. Go to www.paypal.com. You can use this site to set up an online account to pay for any possible shipping or supplies expenses. Or surprise someone who has done a great job for you on zero dollars with a few bob/dollars/euros.

Never require someone doing free work for you to leave themselves out of pocket for your project unless you discuss that first. Even if they offer, try to cover any expenses required for the job. Before you talk to them try to have as much information as you can on what you need, and always have a strict schedule. Storyboards are always appropriate. CGI effects must be pre-visualised and hopefully you will have talked to your CGI people before you have shot any scenes. Nothing beats good planning. Make it easy as possible for the CGI artist. Get them extra RAM or an additional 120gig hard drive if needed. Little things mean a lot when you are dominating someone else's time.

Build effects around content. Don't make the mistake that so many films do and forget the story in exchange for scintillating effects. Be judicious and respectful of the effects artist's or animator's time. Be critical of work produced in an affirming way. You are not paying anyone to take abuse. Be ready to accept criticism as well and understand that visualisation is what the effects person does. All relationships are balancing acts, especially in film production.

In Conversation with Simon Hughes

How did you break into the business?

Simon Hughes is based in Winnipeg and is one of Canada's brightest young designers. The feature he designed, *Hey! Happy!*, did for Winnipeg what John Waters did for Baltimore.

I am an artist by training and still am a painter, film and video maker. When I was finishing my degree in visual arts I couldn't imagine that you could make a living from being an artist (although in fact you can) – and that's why I embarked on this strategy of trying to get into film. In the end it has worked out that I alternate my years working on films with doing my own work as well.

I was lucky in that this move coincided with the rise in offshore

American film production in Canada; American companies shoot in Canada to save money. So I started volunteering on little no budget shorts for film as part of a co-op called the Winnipeg Film Group. Gradually I worked to get union membership and was doing scenic painting and set dressing and miscellaneous props calls. Then I started to be more visually oriented; I got into helping out with design and art direction on low budget movies. So I had this dual career where on bigger money things I could go work as a painter and make a proper wage and then be the boss of the entire department on a low budget feature and make less money than I was making painting sets for American TV movies of the week. It was a trade off because although you get to build your reputation and CV as designer or art director, you don't make that much money. It was nice to have a foot in the legitimate movie world too because you learn so much even if you are low down on the ladder. It's better to see how it happens at the lowest end of the art department; you actually see everything being built and you learn how the designs can end up being completely changed in practice. You learn about the nature of shooting and how you flexible you have to be. You learn that it's not like building a house where you just design and then build it according to the plans. Everything can change from day to day; the DoP will decide that he wants a different look and the entire set has to change; the actor's blocking can totally dictate how the sets are built; the colours have to go with the costumes and whatever else. It was nice to have been on both ends.

To date my credits would be designer on *Hey! Happy!*, which was an ultra low budget Canadian feature which played at Raindance and Sundance and bunch of other grungy festivals in the New York underground. I was art director on *Inertia* which won best Canadian feature at Toronto last year and is not doing too badly. I have been a general producer/director/art director on a couple of music videos for Canadian bands. Art direction on a historical documentary and scenic artist – well, I'm a jack-of-all-trades!

Is there a certain project that you're very proud of or that you found particularly rewarding?
Well in *Hey! Happy!*, the art direction is largely invisible. I was just proud that I survived making because that budget was so low and that we could even pull it off was an achievement. Otherwise the first music video that I did and designed and produced with a friend was a proud moment. The first time I saw it on Much Music (the MTV of Canada) it was a really weird sensation. To have watched that channel your whole life and then to see your video on it – it's like you entered the matrix! Any low budget thing I've done I am proud of.

How closely do you work with directors and cinematographers?
Very, very closely. The designer has equal credits with the DoP and all the key people, but on the shoot it's the director and the DoP who run it. You really have to pay attention to what they want. At this point in my career most of the things that I have learned are from mistakes.

At the earliest stage try and get hold of the director's storyboards even if they are crude little sketches, because when you read the script you have an idea of what it's supposed to look like but the director will have his own vision and will know how he's placing everybody and it's super important to know. I learned that on the last feature that I worked on (*Inertia*). It matters so much: you could spend two weeks preparing a set and then look at the storyboard and find that all it is is a close-up of a hand picking up a teapot off a counter and you were building a whole apartment. You've got to work really closely with them when you are on a budget. In a budgeted film, you just build everything. Then you have complete safety; you can turn the camera 360 degrees and there's always a set there, but when you're on a budget you can save money by keeping things to a minimum.

Working with the DoP is really important too because lighting is part of the set and if you can combine the two you can get really interesting effects. Also on a practical level you have to know where they're looking so you know where to put walls. They might need a wall to go away suddenly and you need to know that so the construction of the set allows it to move around. The first sessions of working with the director and DoP are conceptual, like 'This is what we are trying to do and this is what it all means and these are the colours and this colour means that the character is sad'. When it comes down to it, though, it's all the practical stuff that you have to know about.

You have worked on a few low budget films – how do you cope with the restraints?

It's frustrating when you have done proper industry work – it would almost be better if you came from nowhere and had nothing to compare it to. On the other hand it can be good as well because you have a structure in your mind and you work towards that even though you know you can't quite pull it off. The biggest lesson I learned about coping with a low budget is to try to make your life as comfortable as possible. The first thing you should do with your budget, no matter how small it is, is to figure out how many people you can get – volunteers or kids out of film school who want something for their CV. Even if you can't imagine what you could possibly use fifteen people for, you will need them for something and in low budgets there are always people who are happy to come out and help because they want experience. Gather as many bodies as you can even if some of them end up being bodies and are kind of useless – there's always a few people who will rise to the challenge and do better than any union Joe on $500 a day.

The other super important thing is transportation, something that I didn't think about on the first couple of projects that I did – it's crucial. It might seem to you or the production manager that it's a big expense to get a proper truck or van for the art department. The truth is that the art department is the ghetto of the production. The camera department gets all the gravy and we get the rotten chicken bone left overs. It's very important in the early stages to fight it out with the production manager for vehicles because you can always find stuff cheap or almost free to make sets out of but what if a guy says to you 'I have got a load of lumber you can have for free – just come get it' and all you've got is an old Ford Pinto and a rusty bicycle because there's no budget. What seems like spending money will end up saving money. Transport is the most important thing to the art department along with bodies and people, because there's always tons of stuff to carry and move.

It's so unfair. The camera guys just get to show up and point their camera at the set. Obviously they have to carry a lot of heavy stuff too but they just don't realise that for them to change something it's just a move of the camera or a change of lens and for us it's taking down a wall or redressing an entire sofa – not that I'm complaining. Vehicles and people are the two most important things when you are dealing with a low budget.

At what point do you like to get involved in a project?

You get told about it in the very early stages but generally the designer starts working at the same time as the production manager. The general protocol is that the designer starts several weeks ahead of the rest of his department because that's the time of research and drawing out plans. Then ideally an art director comes on a little later and then the key props master, set decoration, construction coordinator – but if you are dealing with a tiny budget obviously all those people might be you. The earlier you can start thinking about it the better.

When I say low budget this is an extreme example. A feature that I did had a total budget of $90,000 Canadian which is about $60,000 US and the art department budget was under $9,000 Canadian so that's quite drastic. The beauty of it was that the director was very helpful because he just made this call that all the sets he'd planned as interiors were now all going to be outside. For the DoP and me it completely saved our bacon. It was a good example of how an aesthetic decision can come about from money because it just saved so much. I didn't have to build any walls. The DoP didn't have to bring in tons of lights. You should read John Water's book, *Shock Value*, about his early productions which is all about making low budget movies.

Any words of wisdom for up and coming production designers?

I probably did it the wrong way because I didn't get a design degree or architecture which apparently is important. There is a great production designer book, it's one of the *Screen Craft* series. There is one on cinematography, production design, editing, costume design. It's a big nice coffee table book on design and they interview all these big designers. The great thing about it is that you see how not all of them come from the same background, there's a few classically trained architects who switched over into film but there's some people who, like me, just started out painting or doing little jobs in the art department, just observing, keeping quiet and watching how it's done and then eventually making your mark. There are some really good points in there. One of the designers says that the main thing is curiosity. You see something and you're just curious about how it stands up or how it works.

Locations And Permits

OFTEN A PRODUCER will decide that it is cheaper to shoot on private or public property than to hire a studio or sound stage and build expensive sets. In order to find appropriate locations, a film company usually employs a location scout who will recce possible locations, and present them to the director and production designer. The location scout may consult databases of properties compiled by a private location hire firm, or from the files of a local film commission. A film commission is a publicly funded organisation designed to smooth the red tape of shooting in a city, area, state or country. A good film commission will also assist filmmakers in finding crew and locations.

The London Film Commission, now a part of Film London, has worked miracles at reducing the amount of red tape a filmmaker needs to complete to shoot in London.

Film London, 20 Euston Centre, Regent's Place, London NW1 3JH

T: 020 7387 8787
F: 020 7387 8788

E: info@filmlondon.org.uk
W: www.london-film.co.uk

Either way, the production designer and the director will decide on a suitable location which will allow the scenes to be filmed in a manner where the production can manage the sound, light and passing traffic to a degree sufficient to allow the filming to be completed. An agreement with the owner is entered into, and a rental price agreed. The rental price is usually based on the number of days of the shoot, insurance of the property, on the cost of restoring the property after the shoot and the cost (if public) of providing additional security and policing, along with lost revenue from parking meters.

Some cities, like Toronto and New York, are known for being very hospitable to filmmakers. Others, like London, have a reputation of being difficult and bureaucratically complex.

Location Scout

During the pre-production period, the director and producer may engage a location scout to hunt for suitable properties, to attend and photograph them, and then negotiate for their use with the owner or managing agent. A good location scout needs a flair for property, and must have a good sense of direction while travelling country lanes.

Location Manager

A location manager takes charge and control of a location from the moment the first members of the crew arrive. S/he is responsible for making sure that the interests of the film company, and those of the property owner are both met, and that everything stipulated in the contract between the parties is adhered to.

If an electrician needs to screw an eight inch hook into a period ceiling in order to suspend a crucial light, the location manager is the person who liaises with the owners, and seeks permission. The location manager is also the person who is responsible for health and safety on a location, although it is the producer who takes the ultimate risk on health and safety.

The location manager will recce the location prior to the shoot and make notes on mundane items like parking, the location of portable toilets, electricity supply, and security. The location manager will also need to know where the nearest police and fire stations are, the quickest route to a hospital and the shortest route to a working photocopier. If the shoot is to last more than a few days, then s/he will arrange for a portable or temporary office, most often shared with the assistant directors.

Shooting on Private Property

When shooting on private property, the producer looks for a secure location in which the filming can be contained, and where there is adequate electricity, water and local amenities like shops, police station, fire station, photocopy shop, hospitals and ample parking. It is also a bonus if the location is near good public transportation, which means the production does not need to rely on expensive private transport.

Additional Budget When Shooting on Location

Even if you are shooting in your best friend's house in the leafy suburbs and not paying a location fee, you will still need some money.

It works like this.

On the first morning when you arrive, the husband of the house is making you tea, and the lady of the house is running around with muffins. Everyone is oh-so-happy that you are using their place for a movie. On the second day you are greeted with a stony silence. You, the producer, are scratching your head trying to figure out what went wrong. Then you realise that someone in your crew dropped not one but two cigarette butts on the rare hand-me-down carpet in the hallway, and the entire crew trampled through the prize orchids in the front garden. Somehow you make it up to them and you move on.

'We are N.G. sound!' is what the recordist will shout to let everyone know that the take has been interrupted and the sound he has recorded is no good.

And on the third day it is outright hostility. They may even ask you to leave. What now you sob. It is of course not your location hosts, but their neighbours. What no one realised was that thirty vehicles are turning up every morning and staying there on the street until late at night – which means that the neighbours have nowhere to park when they get back from work. You will probably figure this out yourself on the third morning, when the director yells 'Action!' and at that precise moment, the neighbour three doors down decides to chainsaw their oak tree, and you are N.G. sound. What works really well in situations like this is taking £50/$100 notes door to door. 'Hello Mrs. X. Here's a small token of our appreciation for your continued cooperation'. If you don't have cash, then bottles of champagne, steaks, or frozen turkeys work wonders in community relations.

Of course, if you are shooting with a minimal crew, problems like this don't arise. It is quite likely that a minimal crew can get better results than a so-called proper crew with dozens of techies loitering around waiting for their call to action.

Shooting on Public Property

Whenever you shoot on public property, you are required to have a permit. The permit will state the length of time you have to shoot, as well as limit the number of vehicles you are allowed to park.

Guerrilla Filmmaking

I produced a 35mm short in which the director insisted on a shot of a lingerie section inside a department store. Even if we had the budget to build a set, we didn't have the time, and no amount of persuasion would make him change his mind.
We agreed to attempt a shot at a major department store a few minutes walk from the Raindance office on a Sunday morning. The store opened at noon and at 12:05 the DoP, the director, the actor and myself did a recce of the store. We noticed that there was an elevator that took you to the lingerie department. We regrouped in the office, and the DoP decided on a lens and the assistant loaded up a 400ft roll. As we approached the store, the camera started running, and we all calmly walked to the elevator. Meanwhile the actor was in place 'browsing' upstairs. We got out of the lift, and the shot was done in about a minute. The DoP even had time for some close-ups. We got back in the lift and we were done! In the end, the director had the nerve to cut the scene!

One of the many filmmaking practices referred to as guerrilla filmmaking has to do with shooting on the street without a permit. The authorities in most urban areas have decreed that it is against local laws to use a tripod which rests on public property without first obtaining a permit.

If you are ever in front of Big Ben in London when the tourist buses pull up, I wager that you will see dozens of guerrilla filmmaker tourists.

The authorities are worried about two things: health and safety. They do not want you to impede or redirect the flow of traffic, and they do not want you to put anyone at the risk of injury. Accordingly, you must not ever ask a car or pedestrian to stop or wait until you get a shot – as that is disrupting the flow of traffic.

But what if you could not or did not get a permit?

I was once working as a producer's assistant on a shoot in Trafalgar Square on Easter Monday morning at 8am. The shot involved a set of three stunt cars coming around the bend together and disappearing off camera. Unfortunately on this occasion, the location manger had failed to procure the necessary permit. Sure enough, about half way through the early morning work, a policeman, probably two weeks away from retirement, decided that he had nothing better to do than bust some filmmakers. He asked for the permit. I was fainting. The producer asked him politely to wait and proceeded to go through his pockets. After several minutes, the producer told the policeman that the permit was in the office. By now I was really getting worried, as I knew there was no permit, and that our office was just around the corner. Imagine my amazement when the producer then said that our office was in Brighton – some ninety minutes away. Off the producer went, and the policeman settled down to wait. About an hour later I got a call from the producer who was shocked to hear that our legal friend was still in attendance.

After about three hours, as we were starting to pack up, the producer returns and brandishes a permit, duly completed. He thrust it under the policeman's nose, only to be told that the permit was invalid because there was no official receipt on it. Cursing, the producer slapped his forehead and disappeared again, only this time it was for a well-deserved lunch around the corner at which we all joined him some half hour later.

Shooting on the Street

Even if you have a signed letter from the Chief of Police giving you permission to shoot on the street, on the day, the lowliest bobby on the beat has the final say – only he can tell if your presence is disrupting public order. Policemen are able to confiscate your equipment if they want, and it takes five or six weeks to get it back, during which time you are on the hook to the rental facility for the rental payments.

Shooting on the street does require a permit. The value of the permit varies from locality to locality, but it is generally calculated on the amount of money lost to parking meters, and for the wages of any policeman that might be needed to redirect traffic.

Many policemen and permit-approving-officials do not understand that the low-budget filmmaker might be able to snatch a shot of a couple of actors wired with radio mics wandering through a busy city square in a few minutes, and that they will be able to do it without a dozen vans and catering trucks taking up the side of a city block.

At Raindance we shoot 35mm and HD on the street all the time, but without permits. We do however, follow a few simple rules.

– We always telephone the local police station and tell them that we are about to do a student test demonstration between these hours and make certain the police station supervisor has our cell phone to call in case of any complaints. We find that the police are more accommodating for a 'student' film than a professional film.

– If a policeman, with nothing better to do (like stop bank robbers or solve murders) confronts us, we immediately pack up and leave, no matter what. The confrontation is never ever worth it.

– We try not to use a boom mic with a sock. Even when we have been carrying a huge 35mm kit with barn doors through a busy city street, we find that the most attention is created by the sound man and the sock. People think that a boom mic equals a movie.

– If anyone asks what you are making, always tell them you are making a student video with no one in it – even if it's untrue.

– Keep the amount of film equipment to a minimum. If you, the cameraperson and the sound person cannot carry everything you need between you, then you are probably attempting too much.

Permissions

Opposite is a simple location release form that you can use to confirm your arrangements to shoot on someone else's property. Even when you are using a friend's or relative's space, it can be a good idea to make the agreement formal and so protect the production in case anything should go wrong.

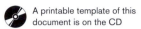
A printable template of this document is on the CD

LOCATION RELEASE FORM

Mr Bigshot
Film Producer
Address

To: [Name of owner of premises and their address]

Dated: [dd/mm/yyyy]

Dear [Name of owner of premises]

Name of film _____ (the 'Film')

This letter is to confirm that you have agreed that we may film at your property known as _____ (the 'Property') from _____(start time) to _____(finish time) on _____(date) together with a setting up period of _____ hours and a striking period of _____ hours.

It is therefore agreed as follows:

1. That you will allow the equipment, props, artists, personnel, vehicles (can be limited, if necessary) employed on our production onto the Property for the purpose of setting up, filming and striking on the dates and for the periods agreed.

2. You agree that you have read the script of the scenes to be filmed at your property and you confirm and agree that these scenes can be filmed at your property.

3. You hereby agree that we may use all films, photographs and recordings made in or around your property in the Film as we decide and without any need for further consent from you.

You may wish to take a simple video 'hosepipe' record of the condition of the premises when you first do a recce. This will prevent property owners making false claims of damage caused to the property during filming.

4. Structural or decorative changes to your property cannot be made without your prior consent, and in any event, we agree to reinstate your property to the state it was in before our alterations, or to a better state.

5. Should we be unable to complete filming on the dates agreed, you agree to a further day(s) at a mutually agreeable time for a fee of _____ per day.

6. In consideration of the rights granted in this letter we will pay you the sum of £_____ (amount) on _____ (date).

7. You agree to indemnify us and to keep us fully indemnified from and against all actions, proceedings, costs, claims, damages and demands however arising in respect of any actual or alleged breach or non-performance by you of any or all of your undertakings, warranties and obligations under this agreement.

8. This agreement shall be governed by and construed in accordance with the law of England and Wales and subject to the jurisdiction of the English Courts.

Please signify your acceptance of the above terms by signing and returning to us the enclosed copy.

Yours sincerely,

_____ (signed)

figure 10.1
Location release

Risk Assessment Forms

To complete the table opposite, you must rate the severity of each risk that is present in your location. First assess each risk's severity on this scale and enter it into the table under 'Severity'. If it is a negligible risk, mark 'N', for slight risk mark 'SL', for moderate risk mark 'M', severe risks are listed as 'S' and a very severe risk is denoted 'V'.

Then assess the likelihood of each risk on this scale and enter it into the table under 'Likelihood'. If it is very unlikely that the risk will actually cause a problem, mark 'VU', if it is unlikely mark 'U', if it is possible write 'P', if it is likely mark 'L' and if it is very likely mark 'VL'.

Then determine the risk factor using the matrix below and enter this final factor into the assessment table opposite.

	Very unlikely	Unlikely	Possible	Likely	Very likely
Very severe	3	4	4	5	5
Severe	2	3	3	3	5
Moderate	2	2	3	3	3
Slight	1	2	2	3	3
Negligible	1	1	2	2	3

figure 10.2
Calculate the risk factor

You then need to decide what action to take. The table below should help you to assess and prioritise the risks.

Risk factor 5	Very severe	Take immediate action
Risk factor 4	Severe	High priority
Risk factor 3	Moderate risk	Programme for action
Risk factor 2	Low risk	Action may be required
Risk factor 1	Negligible risk	Probably acceptable

figure 10.3
Decide the action to take

The form on the facing page is part-completed as an example. There is a template for this document on the CD.

Next you need to complete a hazard form for each risk identified. Copy and paste the table below beneath the hazard list (as opposite). Then sign the completed risk assessment.

Hazard Number		**Risk Factor (1-5)**	
Description			
Person(s) exposed [Detail if cast/crew (C), outside company (O) or public (P)]			
Action to take [include date to be completed]			
Person/company responsible for action			
To be completed on date set above:			
Exposed person(s) informed? Yes ☐ No ☐	Agreed action taken? Yes ☐ No ☐	Risk removed? Yes ☐ No ☐	

figure 10.4
List each risk identified

figure 10.5

Risk assessment form

This low-budget, limited crew shoot will take place in an atmospheric, disused warehouse. Its shell is secure, but not all of the interior is. The scenes to be shot involve a fist fight including falls and require the actors to smoke on set.

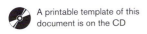

A printable template of this document is on the CD

Complete a hazard form for every risk that you have identified as present in your location.

If the producer has not completed the risk assessment themselves, then they should countersign it.

Risk Assessment: Kill Phil		Emma Luckie (Prod. Manager): 0755599966			
020 55 7287 (Production Office)		Oscar Sharp (1st AD): 0755500099			
Shooting 25 to 30 June		Elliot Grove (Producer): 0755599900			
Disused warehouse		Disused warehouse			

	Hazard	Present?	Severity	Likelihood	Risk factor
1	Alcohol/drugs	No			
2	Animals/insects	No			
3	Audiences	No			
4	Camera cable/grip equipment	Yes	SL	L	3
5	Confined spaces	No			
6	Derelict buildings/dangerous structures	Yes	S	P	3
7	Electricity/gas (other than normal supplies)	No			
8	Fatigue/long hours	No			
9	Fire/flammable materials	No			
10	Hazardous substances	No			
11	Heat/cold/extreme weather	Yes	SL	L	3
12	Laser/strobe effects	No			
13	Machinery: industrial crane/hoist	No			
14	Materials: glass, non-fire retardant	Yes	M	P	3
15	Night operation	No			
16	Noise: high sound levels	No			
17	Non-standard manual handling	No			
18	Public/crowds	No			
19	Radiation	No			
20	Scaffold/rostra	No			
21	Smoking on set	Yes	M	VL	3
22	Special effects/explosives	No			
23	Special needs: elderly, disabled etc	No			
24	Specialised rescue/first aid	No			
25	Stunts, dangerous activities	No			
26	Tall scenery/suspended ceilings	Yes	S	VL	5
27	Vehicles/speed/traffic	No			
28	Water/proximity to water	No			
29	Weapons	No			
30	Working at heights	Yes	S	VL	5
31	Working overseas	No			
32	Food and drink: on set/prop food and drink	No			
33	Other risks	No			

Hazard Number	4	Risk Factor (1-5)	3
Description		Trip hazards – lights/camera cabling	
Person(s) exposed		C – all those involved in scene	
Action to take		Secure and mark all cabling by 25/06/04	
Person/company responsible for action		Gaffer	

To be completed on date set above:

Exposed person(s) informed? Yes ☑ No ☐   Agreed action taken? Yes ☑ No ☐   Risk removed? Yes ☑ No ☐

Completed by	Position:
Signature	Date:

Health and Safety

Failure to ensure the safety of your cast and crew could leave you exposed to a charge of criminal negligence which could lead to a fine, imprisonment or both. Often, a new producer will ignore the necessary steps to prevent an accident on the basis of cost. However the extra costs incurred by spending more time rigging, issuing hard hats and ensuring that a set or location is safe for use by all cast in crew will be far less than the possible medical bills and legal fees you might get landed with if you don't do these things. Your insurance policy may also stipulate certain provisions that you must take in order for the policy to take force.

As the producer , you must accept ultimate responsibility for health and safety on a set. A good producer will delegate this responsibility in part to a crew member trained in health and safety, usually the first AD, the line producer or the location manager.

As soon as possible, in pre-production, a good producer will examine the production for possible risks, in order to take responsible action to downsize or minimise the risks. Factors a producer considers are:

- What is the likelihood of an accident occurring?
- What are the possible consequences?
- How can the danger be eliminated, reduced or controlled?
- What protection is available against the danger?
- Which experts, procedures or guidelines are available to assist in the process?
- Who specifically is at risk?

As a producer, it is your call as to which risks you will bear, and which you will not. Certain precautions seem like common sense, and are very cheap: taping down cables, wearing hard hats, surge protectors. Other risks may prove too expensive to make safe, or too dangerous. Only by doing a proper risk assessment can a producer judge each situation.

Skillset has devised industry guidelines on the standard levels of health and safety that should be expected from different crew members. www.skillset.org

It is good practice to keep a record of all your workings over health and safety and risk assessment. In the worst case scenario, you could demonstrate in court a clear and responsible approach to health and safety, which has far more weight then 'Oh, but we thought about it'.

Hint Make sure that adequate time and money is budgeted to allow for safe working practices. Make sure that there is money to pay for proper safety specialists and equipment, and that the production is crewed in relation to the type of activity taking place.

Health and safety training is broken into three units:

UNIT X2 Ensure your own actions reduce risks to health and safety. For everyone at work regardless of position or number of hours worked.

This unit is about making sure that risks to health and safety are not created or ignored.

UNIT X3 Conduct and assessment of risks in the workplace.
For those undertaking risk assessments.

UNIT X4 Develop procedures to control risks to health and safety.
For people who write health and safety procedures and review their implementation.

Skillset has set out that everyone involved in production – from carpenters to accountants should have Unit X2 level qualification. Most heads of department should be at least at Unit X3, and the producer and construction manager, and sometimes line producer and first AD should be at Unit X4. For further information see www.skillset.org.uk.

Basic Principles of Health and Safety

1 Be safer than you need to be – you have far less to lose
Remember to consider both your cast and crew, and members of the public at all times. If you're filming on a street remember that your crew may be aware of a cable, track or tripod, but a passer-by may not. If you cannot ensure obstructions are securely out of the way, employ a runner to direct the public around it.

2 Develop pre-set arrangements for emergencies
During shooting, the producer would usually assign safety responsibility to the production manager and first AD. Details of their responsibilities are contained in the PACT Health and Safety Policy Document. There should always be someone on set with authority to take charge in emergency situations. Key crew should know details of the nearest hospital, as well as the mobile number of production manager and first AD. Even if you don't have a first AD or production manager, make sure someone takes responsibility for this role on set – otherwise it is the job of the producer.

3 Ask the cast and crew if they have any medical conditions they should tell you about.
Always do this in confidence and privately. Find out from anyone with a condition what you should do in an emergency – such as a nut allergy sufferer accidentally swallowing a peanut – and ensure that your on-set health and safety designates are aware of this.

4 Complete a risk assessment of your shoot
Work from a checklist of potential risks. Of those that exist, estimate both the severity of the hazard (from negligible to very severe), and the likelihood of it occurring (from very unlikely to very likely). Then decide the action to take. Keep a written record of this process.

5 Make sure equipment on set is safe

Kit such as hoists, cherry pickers and vehicles must be supplied with the relevant test certificates. Manufacturers' instructions should be supplied and followed with appropriate training and instruction where necessary. When equipment is supplied with an operator (e.g. a Steadicam), checks should be made into the competence and track record of the operator. If you are in any doubt over the safety of a piece of equipment it must not be used until it has been checked by a relevant expert.

6 Have first aid

A recognised studio will have a first aid department, and make sure your key crew know where it is upon arrival at the studio. If you work late, the studio first aid centre is likely to be closed, so you will have to make alternative arrangements.

On location, you must take a first aid kit and nominate a first aider or, budget willing, a unit nurse. Advise all crew members who the first-aider is, so if there is an accident, they will know who to go to for help.

7 Develop a fire policy

Well, firstly you should have taken every reasonable measure to prevent one from happening in the first place. You should also ensure that there is adequate fire fighting equipment at each location and studio, and that all cast and crew are aware of a pre-nominated safe area where they will assemble in the event of a fire. If a fire occurs you should follow a pre-determined process similar to the one outlined below. You should use these in conjunction with any local fire regulations of studios or locations that you are using.

When a fire is found, the first AD must be informed immediately (either in person or via radio/talkback). S/he will be responsible for informing the director/producer and production manager/supervisor and instructing a member of the crew to alert security (if available) and activate the nearest fire alarm or dial 999. Crew members should be instructed to immediately switch off all equipment and move equipment away from sets and fire exits.

The first AD will order the floor/location to be cleared and escort the artists and crew to a pre-nominated safe area. If, in their opinion, the fire is dangerous s/he may order the immediate evacuation of the studio/location and inform the producer of the decision. Once all crew and cast members are assembled in the pre-nominated assembly points it should be checked that they are all present and the absence of a unit member must be reported immediately to the producer or appro-priate nominee or fire chief if in attendance.

If you are filming in a studio with an audience, then there are fur-ther regulations you need to observe – see the PACT guidelines for more information: www.pact.co.uk.

8 Personal protective equipment

Personal protective equipment (PPE) covers all equipment that is worn or held to protect against risks to health and safety – this may include

Question: anyone figured out how the sound recordist can wear both headphones and a hard hat?

flame-resistant clothing, goggles and respirators, gloves and hard hats. PPE regulations lay down the type and standard of PPE to be used when risks cannot be avoided, and the regulations state the PPE should only be used after all other attempts to reduce the risk have been removed. The following should apply:

- PPE should be provided to employees at no charge where a risk requires its use and the risk cannot be controlled by other means.
- PPE must be kept in good condition and working order.
- You should carry out a risk assessment regarding the suitable use of PPE.
- Make sure when using more than one type of PPE that it is compatible with other PPE in use.
- Arrangements must be made to ensure that any necessary safety equipment is available to those who require it.

9 Shooting at night

When your cast and crew are tired, night shoots can demand extra safety precautions. Ensure that adequate work lights are installed. Budget for more of everything: more time, more food, more heating, more clothes and fluorescent jackets.

10 Handling dangerous substances or equipment

Before you bring something hazardous into a studio or location, specialist advice should be sought at the earliest possible opportunity. Items that you should use with expert advice include (not exhaustive):

- Any substance hazardous to health.
- Any substance or equipment that may cause a fire or an explosion.
- Any radioactive substance.
- Any bacteria, viruses, or other infectious material.
- Any drugs normally requiring a prescription.
- Any high risk equipment, e.g. lasers, thermal lances or any similar scientific devices.
- Any compressed gas.
- Equipment with exposed, dangerous moving parts.
- Equipment capable of producing very high or low frequency sound levels.
- Equipment with exposed dangerous voltages.
- Prop food, which may be on set under hot lights for several days.

11 Dealing with noise

Hearing can be permanently damaged by loud noise, the risk being a function of both volume and exposure. High sound levels produced by loudspeakers and headphones without distortion can be particularly hazardous because the effect is not always unpleasant or even thought of as noise. Noise At Work regulations were introduced to protect the hearing of industrial workers. Special care should be taken on locations such as airports, motor racing events, and pop concerts. A safety conscious producer will post warning notices and give ear defenders to those working in areas of high noise.

12 Animal safety

All animals – regardless how small or tame – should be considered potentially dangerous and therefore handled in the correct manner.

There are a number of regulations which control the keeping and movement of certain animals. If the script calls for an animal to be used in a way which creates an illusion of cruelty, a vet should be informed in advance. It is an offence under the Protection of Animals Act to cause, procure or assist in the fighting of any animal. The suppliers of all performing animals should comply with the Performing Animals (Regulation) Act in regard to the training of animals. For lions, tigers, etc., in order to comply with the provisions of the Dangerous Wild Animals Act it is necessary for the keeper to hold the appropriate licence. This should be checked before any animal covered by the act is allowed in a studio, set or location.

13 Explosions and pyrotechnics

PACT and Bectu have an approved list of special effects technicians.

To create an explosive or pyrotechnic effect legally you need to use an expert. Make sure that the provisions of the Bectu Code of Practice are referred to. Your crew and cast must be fully briefed before participating in any rehearsal, including a practical demonstration of the effect whenever possible. If you can't rehearse, than increase the safety precautions accordingly. Make sure that the fire brigade and police are informed before any outdoor or location explosive or pyrotechnic effects are carried out. If there are a lot of people involved, it may be necessary to have a nurse present at the time of the effect.

14 Using and handling firearms

Using a firearm on set, even a gun firing blanks, without an official handler (or armourer) is a criminal offence, and the producer responsible can be charged with attempted murder. Every firearm must be considered a lethal weapon – loaded, unloaded or lying on a table.

Weapons, including replicas or dummy firearms should only be used with the authority of the producer, and then only with an armourer.

15 Working with heights

Make sure that any risks of people or objects falling is controlled – be it through harnesses, safety barriers or toe boards (rims at the base of platforms). Remember that no-one should be asked to work at height against their will, and to get specialist advice where needed.

If you're building scaffolding, make sure it's erected by a professional – the Screen Industry Training Advisory Committee (SITAC) issues a PACT and Bectu approved list of recognised riggers and scaffolders and this is available through the Producers Industrial Relations Services (PIRS) offices – 020 7380 6680.

16 Working with water

Water requires preparation. Find out which of your cast and crew can and cannot swim. Ensure that buoyancy aids and lifelines are available. If you need divers and power boats, always ask for professional help.

When shooting on a coastline or at sea make sure you plan fully around tidal times. Monitor the weather right up to the shoot, and have contingency plans for adverse conditions. If you're shooting at sea always consult life-boat coxswain, coastguards, harbourmasters or other recognised local authorities for advice. When shooting on rivers, canals or lakes, you must consult local authorities in order to assess the degree of pollution and the accompanying risk of infection. Many rivers carry nasty industrial and agricultural pollutants: immersion may require a hospital check-up. When using a boat, then ensure that it is manned by a competent skipper. When in doubt, always seek professional advice.

You must inform police if you plan any of the following:

- The firing of maroons, firearms or other explosive substances.
- The simulations of accidents, disasters, invasions, sinkings, drownings or other events which might in any way be mistaken for genuine events either by the authorities or members of the public.

17 Filming on a roadside

Crews should wear reflective high visibility waistcoats when filming on or near public roads. Make it very clear policy that your crew knows not to stand on the road. If you have to shoot in the road itself, you need to notify the police and place appropriate cone and diversion signs around your shoot. If you need to control traffic, you will need to get the police to assist you. This must be arranged ahead of time; it is usually organised when you are getting the location permits.

18 Using stunt artists

No member of the public may participate in a stunt or be put at serious risk of injury by the performance of one. When artists, contributors and crew are involved in stunts you should make an assessment of their fitness to do so. Stunt artists are responsible for taking measures to ensure their own and the safety of others who may be affected by their activities while they are performing the stunt specified in their contract. This responsibility extends to the selection of equipment or materials used. You must inform the actors and producers guild of any stunts to be performed.

19 Filming underwater

For more information contact the Association of Media Divers on 020 8567 4213.

No artist or crew member may use underwater equipment on a production unless previously examined and authorised by an approved medical authority in addition to being qualified under the terms of the Diving Regulations.

The producer should advise the unions and PACT on the production notification sheets whenever underwater filming is to take place.

20 Filming underground

Underground, the slightest spark can ignite flammable gases and cause explosions. Special 'sparkless' equipment may need to be used.

21 Filming with children

There are very strict laws to protect children at work. A specific licence must be obtained from the local authority based on your detailed schedule and shooting proposals. Work hours and welfare arrangements will be specifically and rigorously enforced.

22 Drivers

Goods-carrying vehicles with a maximum permitted weight (vehicle and load) exceeding 3.5 tonnes need to be fitted with a tachograph and the driver has to comply with EU Drivers' Hours Regulations (1968 Transport Act) and subsequent amendments. These state:

- Drivers cannot work more than 4.5 hours without taking a break
- Breaks must be at least fifteen minutes, and a minimum of 45 minutes during or immediately after a period of 4.5 hours driving
- A working day is nine hours maximum
- A rest period must be taken after six consecutive driving days
- Drivers cannot work more than 90 hours in a two-week period. The weekly maximum is 56 hours
- If the driver is also doing other work, they must have at least eleven hours daily rest period (which can be reduced to nine hours on up to three occasions in any one week). Any reductions in the daily rest period must be compensated for before the end of the following week
- The minimum weekly rest period is 45 hours. This can be reduced to 36 hours (24 hours if the vehicle and driver are away from base) provided always that the reduced rest periods are fully compensated within the succeeding three weeks.
- Driving off road or away from public roads does not count as driving, but is regarded as other work.

23 Local rules

Skillset provide a list of all UK health and safety training providers as well as offering funding for freelancers looking to extend their health and safety knowledge – www.skillset.org.uk

Many locations – factories, industrial sites, large buildings and so on will have in place 'local rules'. These rules are specific to the site and cover health and safety as well as issues like evacuation procedures, working practice and handling. Adherence to local rules will be a condition of entering the site – you must follow these rules.

Summary

1. Simplicity is a real virtue on a location.

2. Keep equipment to a minimum.

3. Make certain you have proper permits, and follow health and safety regulations to a 't'.

You're going to need somewhere to do all this stuff.

11   Office and Essential Paperwork

The Office

Finding a location that will enable you to conduct your business in an efficient and safe manner is one of the challenges facing a filmmaker whether you live in a major city, town or village. Getting this element of your career or project right is a major step towards success. It is not a good idea to try and use your second bedroom at home. Firstly, it is unprofessional. Secondly, the volume of traffic to and from your front door will most likely irritate anyone you share the space or common entrance with. Thirdly, there is something uplifting and motivating about saying to yourself every morning 'Time to go to the office', even if it means walking through your garden to a converted garage.

Location and Equipment

A good office is between 500 and 1000 square feet, is centrally located and convenient for public transport and has access for deliveries.

Hint   The three essentials of property are location, location, location.

A well equipped office should have comfortable workstations for each person, with appropriate computer terminals. As the cost of computer equipment comes down, aim for a computer that allows you to write your own CDs and DVDs. These features allow you to send movies and large graphic and text files by post, and look slick. If your budget won't allow this, maybe do what I did for the first three years that I started out: I shared with a graphic designer who not only had the equipment, but did design work for me much cheaper than I could have found commercially.

A great temptation is to 'borrow' software from friends in order to reduce your set-up costs. This is theft, and creates bad karma in your workspace. It also exposes you to potential criminal action if you are caught.

The minimum software requirements are: a word processing package, an accounting spreadsheet package, a graphic design package and an email and Internet browser programme. This basic combination allows you to send faxes from your computer, keep company records, write business plans, and design professional quality print materials like posters, catalogues and leaflets. Depending on your budget, editing software would allow you to cut your own trailers in your office. Programmes like Photoshop and Illustrator allow you to manipulate and create images. You may also want to design your own website using a programme like Dreamweaver. With the cost of software and hardware plummeting, these programmes and a powerful computer to run them can be acquired for around £5000 or even less. Five years ago, the computing cost for similar functions would have been ten times that.

Your telephone must contain an excellent answering machine and a fax machine with a separate line. Do not use a single telephone line for telephone and fax messages: it looks amateur to have a tel/fax line.

If possible, try to invest in a high speed or broadband line for your Internet access. The added cost will be offset against the savings in time and money waiting to collect email or log onto websites with huge files. This investment will also enable you to use the Internet as a research tool more efficiently.

As you are a film company, it is a good idea to have a television, a DVD player and a VCR so you can watch show tapes and trailers. Try and get a multi standard VCR and DVD so you can watch tapes and discs from every country in the world, regardless of whether they are NTSC, PAL or SECAM. A supply of cool drinking water, and a clean corner to make tea or coffee are worthwhile additions.

Make sure that you have adequate storage, both shelving and filing cabinets. Remember that as you delve into production, you will need to house dozens of cassettes, hundreds of photographs (of actors and locations) plus all the miscellaneous paperwork.

Finally, remember your fire, safety and security responsibilities. A well-protected office has a strong lock, and is a safe place to work. It has safe wiring, adequate ventilation, good lighting, a first aid kit and fire and smoke detectors and extinguishers.

How Your Office Works

Your office houses your business records, and is the place from which you conduct your business. You make telephone calls from your office, prepare business documents, and receive mail and visitors.

A well-designed letterhead with a good logo will immediately make your company look professional. The registered name of the company (if there is one) along with the VAT number (if registered) must appear on the letterhead. The logo should appear fresh and exciting, while looking clean and simple. Sometimes, you will have a partner of significant standing in the industry, or several people who are well known who will allow you to use their names as patrons. These names should be incorporated into your letterhead as well.

Remember that the design of your logo must work well in black and white (for faxes) and on your website in low resolution.

You can also design business cards and compliments slips. A simple business card is a mini advert for your company, and everyone who works with you should be encouraged to give out as many as they can.

Another useful tool is a rubber stamp with your address on it. This can be used to stamp envelopes, and for temporary letterhead and receipts. Cannes requires an 'official' company stamp for accreditation.

Answering the Telephone

First impressions are always the strongest. The first impression that anyone will get from your company is on the telephone. How your telephone is answered is going to create a lasting impression on your potential clients, investors, and talent. Try to promote a clear-cut impression of who your company is. Sometimes I call a production company and I get a mumbled 'Hrumphted film company, eeer, limited'. Get used to answering the telephone in a positive, clear way, giving the entire name of your company. It might sound a little strange at first, but you will get used to it, and hopefully, proud of it. After all, if you are not proud of your company, its name and what it is trying to do, how are you going to get anyone else interested enough to invest their time or money into your business? A further benefit is that a clear, strong, positive telephone answering voice will cheer you up on those days when everything is looking bleak.

Staff

As your business expands you will need to hire additional people to work with you. Before you take on anyone, make certain that you are fully conversant with the financial risks attached to employing staff. Make sure you can afford to pay not only the wages, but the fringe benefits of holiday pay, national insurance contributions, pension plan contribution and maternity/paternity leave and pay that are required by law.

The secret to maintaining good people working for you is to maintain an open, friendly work environment. Part of this environment should be a clear set of expectations for each employee, and a manageable procedure for voicing complaints and grievances.

Hint Make sure that anyone you work with is in tune with and excited by your vision.

Sweat equity
Sometimes, in order to preserve cash flow, you will offer an equity position to an employee in exchange, or in part exchange for work. If you are

interested in operating this sort of arrangement, make certain that you take the time to draft the necessary paperwork so both sides know exactly what the parameters of the deal are.

Employment contracts

Each time you enter into an employment arrangement with a new person, you should prepare a contract outlining your company's policies on items as diverse as dress code, place and hours of employment.

If you are developing a sensitive database, or working on a screenplay, it is highly advisable to get each new employee to sign a non-disclosure contract as well.

Self-employed

It is possible that you will be able to survive as a self-employed person – at least until your company grows. Self-employment has certain advantages. It can be a more tax efficient way to expand your business, as certain expenses are tax deductable if they are genuine business expenses.

Hint Take the advice of an accountant. The money spent at this stage will be well worth the investment.

Interns

Should you manage to create a stable working environment in a decent location, you might be able to attract interns or those seeking work experience.

Interns are not simple dogsbodies. They are highly intelligent, if inexperienced people, interested in the same sorts of things that you are. They differ from you in that they are presently in higher education, and may know more about the film industry than you do!

If you do agree to an internship, remember to keep it challenging, and allow enough time to direct and guide your charges.

Other Uses for Your Office

A well located and functional office will also become the ideal location for casting calls, saving you the expense of hiring an audition space. Try to ensure that the furniture can be rolled to the sides in order to make a working area for actors.

A secure office can also become a great place to store camera equipment, and, space permitting, props. You might even want to use your office as a location – this is one of the things I did to keep the budget down on my ultra low budget feature, *Table 5*.

After the shoot, the office can double as a post-production editing facility. All you need to do is carry in the computer, make sure that there's a couple of comfortable chairs, drag in a radio for some mood music, and voilà – an editing suite.

Essential Paperwork

Everything you always wanted to know about incorporating a company but were afraid to ask

Philip Alberstat, entertainment attorney Raindance tutor has provided this section. On the CD and in Chapter 14, you will find more from Phil, including all the information you will need about contracts and paperwork for above the line talent – the producer, director, writer and actors.

There is also a version of Filmmaker Software on the CD, which is a database and organisational system offering a means of controlling budgets, creating forms and letters - everything you need to run your production from start to finish.

There are various ways in which to run a business. However the most common way is to incorporate a private company. The main reason for incorporation is limited liability. A private company is a legal 'person' which must not be confused with the people who formed the company and are its members.

Limited liability means that the members are not personally liable for the debts of the company and that if the company goes bankrupt, the most the members risk to lose is the amount they invested in the shares of the company.

There are also disadvantages to incorporation. There are a lot of administrative requirements, form filing, certain information must be disclosed to Companies House for the public record, i.e. the changes in the company's circumstances and particulars, and the company name and certain information must be displayed on the company stationery.

Before incorporating

In order to be able to incorporate a company there are a number of issues to consider and of documents to prepare:

– The type of company
– The memorandum of association
– The articles of association
– The company agents

1 Type of company

There are four main types of company:

– Private company limited by shares – the members' liability is limited to the amount they have invested in the company's shares
– Private company limited by guarantee – there are no shares in such companies and the members' liability is limited to the amount they have contributed to the company's assets
– Private unlimited company – the members' liability is not limited and they can be held personally liable for the company's debts
– Public limited company (PLC) – the company's shares may be offered for sale to the general public via the stock exchange. Liability is limited to the amount invested in shares

2 Memorandum of association

This contains the following information realting to the company:

i The company name

The choice of name is limited. It must not be already used by another company, it must not be offensive and its use must not be a criminal offence. Some words and expressions should also be avoided:

- If they imply national or international pre-eminence ie British, English, Scottish, Welsh etc.
- If they imply pre-eminence or representative status ie association, authority, institution etc.
- If they imply specific objects or functions ie assurance, fund, chartered, charity etc.

ii The company's registered office
This can be anywhere in England or Wales. It is the address of the company and appears as such on the register.

iii The company's authorised share capital
The memorandum must state the authorised share capital, the number of shares and their nominal value and whether there are different classes of shares.

iv The company's object
This is just to give an idea of what the company does.

3 The articles of association
The articles of association rule how the company is run internally and how the powers are divided between the members and the directors. The Company's Act 1985 provides precedent articles of association called 'Table A'. When writing the articles of association of a company there are three options.

- The articles can be especially drafted for a company
- Table can be adopted as the company's articles without any changes
- The articles can be partly drafted and comprise part of Table A

4 The company's agents
The company must have at least one director and one company secretary. Anyone can be a director or company secretary – there are no qualifications needed. However, you cannot be a director if you are an undischarged bankrupt or have been disqualified by a court.

Incorporating the company
Once all of the above information has been gathered, incorporation can take place. The following documents need to be sent to the Registrar of companies:

- Memorandum of association signed by at least one subscriber
- Articles of association signed by the subscribers to the memorandum
- Form 10. This document details the registered office and the company agents. It must be signed by the subscribers to the memorandum
- Form 12. This document is a declaration that all the requirements of the

- Companies Act relating to the incorporation of companies have been complied with. This document can be signed by anyone named on
- Form 10 (or by their solicitors) and must be sworn before a solicitor or commissioner for oaths
- Registration fee of £20 or £80 for same day registration

  Once the company is incorporated, the Registrar of companies sends out a certificate of incorporation.

Shelf companies

Another way to set up a company, which saves having to go through incorporation, is to 'buy' a shelf company.

Shelf companies are ready-made companies, which are available from company formation agents, accountants and solicitors.

They are already incorporated and all that is needed is to adapt it to specific requirements.

The following would need to be changed:

- The name of the company – there is a fee of £10 for this or £80 for a
- same day change of name
- Its agents: directors and company secretary (Form 288a for appointing new agents and Form 288b for removing current agents)
- Its registered office (Form 287)
- Its authorised share capital (not always necessary) (Form 123)
- Its object (not always necessary)

These changes can be effected by holding a board meeting and a members meeting.

After incorporation

After incorporation of a company, Companies House must be kept informed of:

- The appointment or retirement of company agents or their change of personal details (Forms 288a, 288b or 288c)
- The details of new shares being allotted (Form 88(2))
- Certain resolution of members meetings
- Details of any charges created by the company (Form 395)
- The change of the registered office (Form 287)

In addition every company must deliver an annual return (Form 363) to Companies House at least once every twelve months. There are automatic penalties for the late filing of returns.

The above information is a short synopsis of what is needed to form a company. Companies House staff can advise you on matters generally but when you start a company it is important to get things right. Everyone has different circumstances and therefore it may be sensible to consult a solicitor, company formation agent or an accountant when appropriate.

See www.companies-house.gov.uk

In Consultation With Sean Faughnan

Structuring Success

By Sean Faughnan, who worked for 11 years as an investment banker. He and I have recently set up a film production company that is putting together a slate of multi-genre movies, from low to high budget.

As a relative newcomer to the film industry, I was immediately struck by two things. First, by the enormous energy and enthusiasm of almost all of the people I have met. You just don't see it in most other industries. Second, and more negatively, I was also struck by the look of blind panic that comes over so many people's faces when you ask them how they plan to transform all of this energy and enthusiasm into real projects with real money. The film industry may be different from other industries in many ways, but in one vital respect it is exactly the same: it is a business.

Here's the good news: it's easy to become a producer. All you have to do is go down to your local print shop and get yourself 100 business cards that have your name, a logo, and the word producer on it. Hey presto, you are a producer!

Here's the bad news: You have probably just wasted your money.

I have a very simple, even simplistic, view of life. In my world a Producer produces. And in order to do that he's going to need a great many things, the least of which is a business card. He's going to need money, great scripts, creative people around him, access to distribution, etc. In other words, he's going to need to set up a company. And that is what I would like to focus upon; structuring your production company correctly.

At this point, I can almost hear the groans and see the yawns. Structure – yuk. But before you turn the page to something more interesting, read the next sentence. I guarantee that without the right company structure you will either fail or be much less successful than you should be. Put it another way: If you decide to ignore the question of company structure, the chances are that success will decide to ignore you.

So what do I mean by structure? The question can be answered in one word: control! When I ask how is a company structured, what I am really asking is how is it controlled? How are the decisions made? Get this aspect of the business wrong, and it will be hard for anything else to work right. For the most part (though not always), the shareholding structure of a company dictates who has control and how decisions are made. The more shares you have the bigger your potential say.

In the text below I have looked at four different shareholding structures for a new production company, and their relative advantages and disadvantages. The list is certainly not exhaustive and even within the four cases I examine, there are numerous possible permutations. Moreover, the scenarios I have established are a bit simplistic. But I hope the examples will, at the very least, identify some of the issues that need to be addressed when starting a new venture. In particular, I would highlight two right now. Firstly, the more money someone puts in, the bigger the stake of the company and its profits they will require.

Secondly, the shareholding structures evolve over time, as new investors come in and older investors cash out. The structure should, right from the start, take this into account.

Shareholding structure 1: Going it alone

Aspiring Producer wants to set up his own production company, to be called Beginners Film Production, Ltd (BFP). From the start, he takes 100% of BFP's equity.

The advantages of this are that Aspiring Producer has complete control of BFP and that Aspiring Producer gets to keep 100% of BFP's profits. But there are disadvantages. Aspiring Producer has complete responsibility. If something goes wrong, it's all down to him, also Aspiring Producer has to put in 100% of BFP's costs. He'd better have deep pockets and/or a friendly bank manager. On top of this, Aspiring Producer must bear 100% of any losses incurred by BFP.

Shareholding structure 2: Half and half

If a third investor is brought in and given even 1% of the company, both of the original partners lose their negative control, since they are now below 50% (49.5%). The third investor is now pivotal: He can break any deadlock between the two original partners because his 1% is enough to give either side a victory (49.5% + 1% = 50.5% = victory). In a very real sense you could say that control of the company has just been handed over to him.

Aspiring Producer decides to bring in a partner, who has great industry contacts and will put some money into the company. He gives him 50% of the company's stock.

The advantage is that BFP is now a genuine partnership, with a sharing of the costs and other burdens. The company has additional money and the second partner may be able to strengthen the company through his industry contracts.

The disadvantage is that Aspiring Producer will now only ever have 50% of the profits. Also, the 50/50 structure is a recipe for deadlock. Each of the partners has what is called 'negative control': they can stop something happening by voting against it, but they do not have enough shares to make something happen without the agreement of the other.

Shareholding structure 3: Major and minor

Aspiring Producer decides to bring in a partner, but only gives him 30% of the company's stock in exchange for some money.

The advantages of this structure are that the Aspiring Producer has found someone to share the load. There is also additional money in the company, although less than there would have been had Aspiring Producer given away more of the company. With this structure, there is no confusion over control: Aspiring Producer has 70% of the company.

On the other hand, Aspiring Producer has to share the profits. The partner may, over time, become dissatisfied with his minority position, particularly if he thinks Aspiring Producer is not running things properly.

Shareholding structure 4: The three musketeers

Aspiring Producer decides to bring in two partners and give each of them one-third of the company in return for them working for the company for little or nothing.

BFP is now a genuine partnership, with each having an equal stake Running costs have been brought down since the new partners are working for very little money (also called 'sweat equity'). If a decision has to be made, there will always be an automatic majority unlike in the 50/50 example, i.e. they will either all agree to something or there will be a two to one majority. Deadlock is not possible.

However: Aspiring Producer has to share the profits three ways Since the other two partners have more than 50% of the company between them, they could in theory collude together and completely ignore Aspiring Producer.

No one, including myself, likes to spend a great deal of time thinking about structure. It's the boring side of business. However, if you don't get structure right from the start, it will at some time make your life very 'interesting' indeed. As in horribly interesting as your company becomes a battleground between discontented owners and your dreams are ripped apart. Believe me, you just don't want to go there.

Insurance

My background taught me to distrust the concept of insurance and insurance agents and brokers. The theory was that buying insurance against a disaster tempted fate, and would wreak havoc on your life. Accordingly, my Amish forbears and relatives scorned insurance and refused to buy it. In that community, however, there was a natural order of insurance. Should someone's barn burn down, then all the neighbours would show up for a barn raising, and bring with them a calf, pig or chicken. Presto! The farmer would have a new barn and new herd, and the community as a whole saves more money than the cost of insurance premiums, which is still my philosophy.

A combination of common sense and good security systems will ultimately be cheaper than paying for certain insurances. In the filmmaking world however, it is unlikely that fellow filmmakers would be willing to fork out the cash for lost or stolen computer and film equipment.

There are two types of insurance that you must have to operate legally in the United Kingdom.

i Public liability insurance
This protects the public should they suffer an accident caused by you, your employees or your company's activities (on a shoot, for example).

ii Employers liability insurance
This protects you and your staff.

There are other types of insurance that you may require. Make certain that the cover you obtain is sufficient to cover the risks that you and your investors are taking on during production and post-production.

i Equipment insurance
Covers the costs of damage or theft of the camera and sound equip-

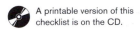

A printable version of this checklist is on the CD.

Office Checklist		Production	
The Set Up		All actors and day player deals	☐
Establish office space	☐	Crew deals:	
Establish production company and complete all legal paperwork	☐	director of photography	☐
		editor	☐
Register for local/national tax and employer compensation schemes	☐	assistant directors	☐
		miscellaneous crew	☐
Acquire public liability insurance	☐	Location agreements	☐
Hire accountant	☐	Releases	☐
Hire legal counsel	☐	Equipment agreements	☐
		Facilities agreements	☐
Screenplay rights		**Post-production**	
Review chain of title with legal counsel	☐	Title clearance	☐
Assign rights to production company	☐	Lab agreements	☐
Register assigments at UK/US copyright office	☐	Composer agreements	☐
		Music package	☐
Get copyright to any underlying work	☐	Other music clearance	☐
Get clearance report and revise if necessary	☐		
		Delivery	
Register copyright of screenplay with UK/US copyright office	☐	Register copyright with UK/US copyright office	☐
Financing		Errors and omissions certificates	☐
Negotiate finance agreements	☐	Laboratory access letters	☐
Negotiate sales agent and distribution agreements	☐	Credit requirements lists for adverts	☐
		Delivery of video and sound masters	☐
Negotiate completion bond	☐	Key production and music contracts	☐
Pre-production		Chain of title documents	☐
Obtain production insurance	☐	Copyright/title reports and opinions	☐
Obtain errors and omissions insurance	☐	Stills	☐
Hire casting director	☐	Trailer	☐
Negotiate key deals for:		Key art	☐
principal cast	☐	Music cue sheets	☐
director	☐	Certificate of origin	☐
heads of department	☐		
producer	☐	Rights transfer instrument	☐

figure 11.1
Office checklist

ment – and the loss of revenue that the hire company might suffer while the equipment is being repaired (usually twelve weeks).

ii Negative insurance
This covers the cost of reshooting a scene should the film be damaged within the camera or at the lab. Labs do not provide insurance, and since this cover is very expensive to procure, it is used mainly on higher budget films. On a low or no budget shoot with a small crew and cast, it is usually cheaper to reshoot the scene.

iii Cast insurance
This covers the risk to your production should an actor be unable to complete your film due to death or illness to themselves or to a member of their immediate family. The director can also be covered by this insurance. Anyone covered will have to submit to a full medical examination before the coverage will go into effect.

iv Props, set and wardrobe
Covers against loss, damage or theft. Usually this insurance has a cap on the amount to be paid out for the loss or damage to specific items i.e. jewellery, furs, specialist props.

v Automobiles, airplanes, boats
This covers the property damage risk for any moving vehicle used in the production of the film. Should you have a van, for example, that is used as a prop in the film, then it is almost always cheaper to use private motor insurance in the way one would cover one's own van than engaging the services of a specialised film vehicle insurance specialist.

Summary

1. Make a functioning office a priority.

2. Design the image for your company.

3. Take care of the nitty gritty legal and financial details.

Now we are ready for the shoot.

Seven Essential Steps for Becoming Rich and Famous by Making a Low Budget Film

Step 3 Telephone

When I travel around Europe talking to new filmmakers, I always ask them what the most important piece of filmmaking equipment is they will ever need. The script goes like this:

Elliot: What is the most important piece of filmmaking equipment you will ever need?
Filmmaker: Camera
Elliot: What do you need to get the camera?
Filmmaker: Actors.
Elliot: What do you need to get the actors?
Filmmaker: Crew.
Elliot: What do you use to get the crew and actors together?
Filmmaker: Money! (See Step 2)
Elliot: But what do you need to get the money?
Filmmaker: The telephone.

A telephone is easily the most important piece of film equipment you will ever need. And by telephone I mean that in order to get a film made you need to acquire excellent interpersonal communication skills.

Each industry has its own unique buzz words. I have worked in computers, theatre, and for an ill-fated few years, property. And in the film industry there are also some unique buzz words, which I would like to share with you.

To illustrate how to use the telephone, let me tell you a story.

When I was in high school, I had a bad haircut and dressed in odd clothes. I was the geek, the nerd, the guy who could barely speak. I was hated and despised by most of the other students. To compensate, I studied really hard, and was always first or second in my class – which made my fellow students hate me even more. I was always being accused of being teacher's pet – except the teachers probably hated me too.

In my last year of high school I spied a beautiful girl – also in my year. I suppose it would be easiest if you could imagine the head cheerleader of the school. I fantasised about dating her, but because of my nerdish looks was too embarrassed to ask. I took elaborate measures to avoid her – even going to the extent of changing my timetable so I wouldn't have to sit in English class with her. During the last term of that last year, fate struck, and we were assigned adjacent lockers. This added even more stress to my daily avoidance routine. Sure, we nodded hello in the halls, and said the odd word in the cafeteria. But nothing more. Then in the last week of school, fate struck once more, and I was suddenly getting out my Biology books while she was trying to find her German or Latin books. In a moment of sheer bravado, I turned to her and said: 'What would you like to be when you grow up?' And she smiled and said: 'I want to be an actress. What do you want to be?' What would you say if you were me? I took the only career option of a guy desperate for a date and said: 'I am going to make a movie.'

Well, she bought that hook, line and sinker and we have been together ever since. And because of her, I now have a half decent haircut, although it took me years before I actually made a movie, and then she wasn't in it! But I really really hated going to parties with her, because people would walk up to me and say: 'What are you doing?' And I never knew whether to answer my day job, or 'filmmaker'. And every time someone asked me that question, my gorgeous partner would sidle up to hear what I was going to say because it was different every week.

I was starting to lose confidence. Then one night I was channel surfing and feeling sorry for myself when I stumbled across an interview with Steven Spielberg. The interviewer was asking him questions like: 'What are you doing next?' or 'What are you doing now?'. This really caught my attention because it was all too familiar. Steven said: 'I have numerous projects in various stages of development'. A few weeks later I caught George Lucas saying the same thing. In fact, it seemed to me like everyone in the entire industry was saying it.

Suddenly it hit me: If you talk like you know what you are doing, then it seems to others that you know what you are doing, and everyone starts to believe in you and better yet, you start to believe in yourself.

My friend Dov Simens bases his Two-Day Film School around this phrase and calls it the Nine Most Famous Words In Hollywood.

So, for a start, when you are using the telephone, or networking, introduce yourself as an independent filmmaker with numerous projects in various stages of development.

Hint Never claim to be a filmmaker. Within the industry, filmmaker smacks of student films and art house. If you want to make a movie, you are a producer. If you want to direct movies, you are a film director, if you want to write for film, you are a screenwriter.

Well, I used that phrase for a good many weeks, and was starting to bask in the glow of success, when at a party one night someone responded with 'What's it about?' Back to channel hopping, until I heard a celebrity filmmaker say: 'It's a character driven drama'. I was back in business, even if it was a fantasy business.

12 The Shoot

THE SHOOT IS THE period of time when a skilled crew and actors set out to record the audio and visual information demanded by the script.

The days and weeks leading up to the shoot are stressful. The actual shoot is not only stressful but is physically demanding as well. The actual shoot, if organised properly, can be an enjoyable experience. If the shoot descends into chaos, it is a nightmare.

The Seven Steps to a Successful Shoot

Step 1 Get Organised

Having dozens of cast and crew arriving at different times and locations and working with different combinations of people is an organisational nightmare. The key to getting a shoot together is by creating a clear and concise schedule. A good schedule should let you know at a glance what part of the script is being filmed, who is needed (both cast and crew) and what props, wardrobe and other special equipment are required. A good schedule will also help determine the order of the filming so that people and resources can be combined in the most cost-effective manner. Chapter 3 deals fully with planning the schedule.

Shoot planning paperwork

These pieces of paper will help you to run an efficient, on-budget shoot. Prepare these well in advance in consultation with the relevant members of the production crew.

Script breakdown sheet

Analyse what you need for the shoot by breaking down the script. Analyse each scene individually and list the actors, props and special effects involved.

The information you produce will become an essential resource when you prepare the production board. This is a straightforward process which is explained in detail in Chapter 3. The production board will, in turn, form the basis of your call sheets.

Production board

Next you need to create a production board. This is the foundation of the production. Again Chapter 3 contains full details of how to do this.

Call sheets

Call sheets for the next day are usually completed by the third assistant director and given to the location or studio manager for distribution to the cast and crew before they leave at the end of the day's filming. Cast or crew not on the set will be contacted by telephone, email or fax.

The call sheet is a summary of the work to be completed the following day, along with specific directions to the location, or, if transport is being arranged by the producer, detailed instructions. Often the call sheet will include emergency telephone numbers of the cast and crew in order for last minute changes, or travel emergencies to be coordinated. See figure 12.1 opposite for a breakdown of a call sheet.

Movement order

A movement order is a sheet of paper that clearly lists all the practical considerations that cast, crew or anyone else travelling to a location will need to know in order to arrive on time. Include a map of the location and alternative travel plans as well as the locations of the nearest emergency services and hospitals. It is vital that a cell phone number is included for the line producer and location manager in case of travel problems. See figure 12.2 opposite for a sample movement order.

Step 2 Hire a Line Producer

In television a line producer is called the production manager.

A line producer is the person who makes sure that you finish the film on time and on budget. They are the most anal people you will ever meet – the person going absolutely berserk if you are three minutes late from lunch. I have never understood why anyone would like a job like line producing – because you seem to be permanently on the telephone nagging or pleading. The right line producer will assist you in completing your production board, and will also be able to help you with crew contacts. A good line producer can also help to negotiate any rental or lab deals you may be trying to do.

Step 3 Hire the Right Crew

If you are trying to break in as crew, make sure you keep in touch with the producer of anything you have worked on – as they will be the ones to refer you on to other shoots.

Choosing the right people for the right job is the real skill of a producer, and to a certain degree, the director. In many cases, the below-the-line staff will be chosen, or recommended by the line producer, whom you will have hired, in part, for access to their black book of contacts.

In the film industry, the production crews are organised military style around heads of department, with the assistants lined up in descending order of importance (and usually, the further they are removed from the head of department, the more work they have to do).

<table>
<tr><td colspan="2">Production title / Director's name

Producer / Telephone

Line producer / Telephone

1st assistant director / Telephone

2nd assistant director / Telephone

3rd assistant director / Telephone</td><td>Date _____

Start time _____

Wrap time _____</td></tr>
</table>

Include the address, directions by car and by public transport and any information that will help cast and crew get to the set on time e.g. train timetables, road maps.

Location information

Listing the story day/time helps the actor to keep their character consistent: they need to know if the scene comes before or after their character discovers her partner's adultery.

Scene no.	Script page	Int / Ext	Description	Day / Night	Story day	Eighths (pages)	Cast

The actor number and eighths of a page relate to the production board.

Pick up time is when a car will arrive to collect the actor from home.

Turnover is the time when the camera will start rolling.

Give details of any special effects or stunts to be done today.

Actor no.	Artist name		Character name	Pick up time	On set to rehearse	Make-up / costume	Turnover

Additional information

Advance call for next day:

Scene no.	Script page	Int / Ext	Description	Day / Night	Story day	Eighths (pages)	Cast

figure 12.1
Sample call sheet

Going to	**Going on** (Date) _____
Address	**Map** to the location
Contact Details Include name / mobile telephone for: Production company Film Title Producer Line producer Director Location manager	
Additional Information Directions by car Parking instructions Facilities Emergency facilities – police, hospital, fire	

figure 12.2
Sample movement order

The Crew

Director
The supreme commander, and in charge of everything that affects what you see or hear on the screen. The director is also the only one allowed to talk directly to the actors while they are on the set.

Assistant directors
The first assistant director is in charge of making sure that the director is aware of scheduling problems on the set, the 1st AD also sets up the shot by calling: 'Quiet please. Roll Sound. Roll Camera…'. It is the director who calls action. And cut. The second assistant director makes sure that all the accessories (props) for the shoot are in place and that the actors arrive at the set when they are needed. The third assistant director works on organising the shoot and preparing call sheets. They make sure that the film is collected for the lab, and are the main point of contact to the director while the director is on the set. Also part of this team is the script supervisor, who records the lines of dialogue as shot, along with action sequences. These notes are recorded as an assist to the editing process.

Camera department
The director of photography (head of department) is the head of the camera department. They are responsible for making sure that everything the director wants is set up, plus, they add their own creative input as to how the shots will look.

The camera operator makes sure that everything the DoP and the director wants is in the frame. The focus puller makes sure that everything in the frame is in focus. The clapper loader keeps the camera clean, reloads the camera, does the camera reports, and marks the slate with the scene and take numbers.

A gaffer is an electrician. The term refers to anyone who has anything to do with lights and electricity. The gaffer works under the DoP. The gaffer's assistant is called the best boy.

A grip is anyone who works with anything that 'grips' or attaches to the camera. Tripods, dollies, wedges and track are all operated by a grip. The head grip is called the key grip. A dolly/crane grip works the dolly. Grips also work under the DoP.

Art department
The production designer is the head of the art department and is the person who creates all the drawings for the sets and locations. S/he is directly responsible to the director. The designs are given to the art director, who oversees their execution.

Sets are built by the scenic carpenter and painted by the scenic artist. Any assistant to the art department is considered part of the swing gang.

The heads of make-up and wardrobe and their assistants deal, unsurprisingly, with make-up, hair and wardrobe. Sometimes they also

```
CORE TEAM
Writer / Producer / Director

HEADS OF DEPARTMENT
Art / Sound / Camera / Script / Craft

CREW FOR A FILM WITH A BUDGET OF UNDER £50,000
Make-up Artist / Scenic Artist & Props & Runner / Sound Recordist / Director of
Photography / Camera Assistant / Catering & Runner / Stills Photographer

CREW FOR A FILM WITH A BUDGET OF UNDER £100,000
All of the above plus:
Costume / Art Director / Sound Assistant / Production Assistant / Focus Puller / Key Grip
/ Gaffer / 1st Assistant Director / Continuity & Script Supervisor

CREW FOR A FILM WITH A BUDGET OF £100,000 TO £300,000
All of the above plus:
Scenic Artist(s) / Scenic Carpenter(s) / Stunt Co-ordinator / Stunt Performer / Sound
Editor / Musician & Composer / 3-5 Production Assistants / Line Producer / Executive
Producer / Production Accountant / Camera Operator / 1-5 Gaffers / 2nd Assistant
Director / Storyboard Artist / Special Effects Co-ordinator / Casting Director / Unit Driver
```

figure 12.3
Outline of a crew

create the costumes. Make-up and wardrobe work under the production designer and art director. See Chapter 9 on production values for more detail.

Sound crew
The sound recordist manages the sound department. The head sound recordist takes the responsibility for recording the sound and is assisted by a boom operator.

Craftsperson
Food and catering services are supplied by the craftsperson. On set or location they usually report to the third AD who will tell them when to expect meal breaks.

Gofers
General production assistants are called gofers and can work for any department.

Hiring and firing
When you hire someone, make certain they are completely aware of what is expected with them and what they are to be paid. Make clear which responsibilities are a priority.

If you face the unpleasant task of firing someone, it is my advice to be very direct, explain to them precisely what the circumstances are for their dismissal, and pay them any money outstanding. Unless there has been a criminal offence, such as theft, then wish the person well, and apologise for the fact that it hasn't worked out. If you are firing the person because of a personal flaw, such as tardiness, make sure the person knows what the production tolerances are: i.e. three times and you are out. Should you fire a person caught stealing, you will have to decide what other action you will take. You may decide to allow the person to come clean, and return the goods, or, you may decide to take the step of involving the police. Either way, I believe that a clear decision is better than no decision at all, and the rest of the crew will probably support a strong decision maker – even if the decision you made was wrong.

Integrity and trust are vital qualities of an effective production crew.

Interview process

Interviews should be short and direct. People who have travelled to meet you are not impressed by half an hour of idle chit chat. Be polite, and make sure to ask them questions about what they expect out of the job. This is most important when you hiring people for little or no pay.

Advertising

Local film schools and theatre groups are excellent places to look for crew. The most difficult people to find are gaffers – electricians. Gaffers will most usually be union men or women, and will be the most expensive crew members. Word of mouth is the next most effective way to find people – either from your new line producer, or from other producers who have just finished a shoot.

Deferrals

Producers like to hear the sound of large numbers whooshing past their lips. When the DoP names their price (several thousand a week), an inexperienced producer will say something like: 'What if I give you a third in cash, and the rest (of your overly inflated fee) as a deferral?'

Deferrals hardly ever get paid. It is just one of the facts of life that there are so many hands in the gravy of the profit of a film at the distribution end, that hardly anything trickles down to the producer. This can destroy personal relationships: if your friendly DoP reads the newspaper to see that your film took a million, he'll wonder why you've screwed him out of his two grand deferral if he doesn't realise that you, the hard-working producer, have yet to see a dime yourself.

Avoid deferrals if at all possible. If you defer, try a universal deferral scheme where everyone is paid on deferral in accordance to the length of time they have spent on the set. This democratises your payroll, putting a lowly gofer on the same level as the crusty DoP.

Payment

Whatever arrangement you make with your crew, make certain that you follow local laws regarding tax deductions, National Health or Workmen's Compensation deductions, and any union or association payments that you must make. As far as possible, pay people on time; this is not just good practice, but it shows respect for the job your crew have done, and may also mean that your crew will want to work with you again or will recommend you to their colleagues.

Union crews

For the latest information on union crew wages contact Bectu, 373–377 Clapham Road, London SW9 9BT, T: 020 7346 0900, F: 020 7346 0901, E: info@bectu.org.uk, W: www.bectu.org.uk

Step 4 Make Sure Everyone Knows Who's Boss

As a producer or director, keeping control of a set is vital. As the numbers of people on the set increase, so do the chances that your authority might be undermined. Here is my tip list for keeping in control.

1. Don't be the nice guy. Nice guys get walked all over. Remember that Margaret Thatcher was hated by everyone. I don't mean that you can't have a laugh, but you just can't be nice all the time.

2. If you hear mutiny, stamp it out. Unfortunately there are certain types of people who mutter and complain behind your back and who will criticise everything you do – from the location to the menu for lunch. You cannot and must not work with people like this. Get rid of them.

3. Have rules given to each crew member on their first day, which clearly states company policy on things like tardiness, dishonesty and drugs. People will get the idea that you don't fool around, and are more likely to take you seriously.

4. Never rebuke someone in front of the rest of the crew. It will only make you feel and look like an idiot and you will have broken your relationship with that person past mending point.

5. A little praise goes a long way. A few words of thanks will help the crew learn what turns you on, as well as what turns you off.

Step 5 Be Professional

Make sure all of your company paperwork is in order and that you have carefully considered health and safety issues and taken all appropriate measures to minimalise the risks. See Chapters 10 and 11.

Step 6 Food

The prevailing theory of film production management states that whatever else you do you need to feed your crew well. The history of this theory goes back to the Hollywood of the 1920s when the studios were a good three-quarters of an hour drive outside of the city. It then became cost effective for the studio to bring food into the set in order to keep cast and crew together. Since then a whole tradition of film food has sprung up, where filmmakers demand and expect food on the set. Several of my friends have in fact given up other jobs to work in movies simply because they get a free lunch. Are there any other industries where lunch is provided?

Some simple rules for food: make it fuel. Don't serve food. I once had the unenviable task of organising catering for the crew of a Dennis Potter-directed movie starring Alan Bates. Since I had worked on many sets as a scenic artist, I thoughta that rather than give the crew bangers and mash, I would cook up some French food, maybe a few Thai dishes – in short make picturesque meals that you might have mistaken as coming from a well-reviewed restaurant in the centre of London.

On the second day of the shoot, a giant, burly gaffer grabbed me by the scruff of the neck and lifted me up off the ground, and said 'Fuel, not food'. I had to admit then and there that if you are working long hours, then carbohydrates are what does it for you. Out went the canapés and in came the mashed potatoes. Everyone was happy.

What if you have no money for catering? What do you serve then? Maybe you can get a relative to cook up some curry. Or go to the local supermarket and get some day-old sandwiches and fruit. I've done that. I once worked on a shoot where the only food was white rice. After a few days on that, you certainly see your energy drop to near zero.

The people I hire in the better positions: the camera department, the actors, either all have some money of their own, or if they are working for me they are so convinced that the project will elevate their careers (which it has in many cases) that they are quite happy to work for free and buy their own lunch. The people on the set that I really worry about, food-wise, are the crew. These are students who genuinely are broke. To each of them I pay a fee of between £100–150 out of which I expect them to pay for public transport to get themselves to and from the set, and to buy a substantial lunch.

At Raindance, when I am producing, I serve reality burgers. When it's lunch time, I say that the reality is that they are serving burgers in any one of the myriad cafés and burger shops within a walk from the set.

Step 7 Learn to Say No

See below, the fourth essential step for becoming rich and famous by making a lo-to-no budget film.

Being a Runner in Soho by Oscar Sharp

Oscar Sharp is a producer at Raindance who, like everyone, started out as a lowly runner in Soho.

If you think of the film and television industry as having 'career ladders', the runner is not so much on the bottom rung, as in the small, greasy puddle in which the ladder is standing. Still, running is often trumpeted as 'the way in'. It can certainly allow you to meet a lot of interesting people, and see exactly how the business works.

Beyond this, I'm afraid, I can't tell you much about what a Soho runner actually does. This is because 'runner' is a borrowed term, which used only to refer to an on-set job – the assistant director's assistant's assistant's assistant (seriously). This kind of runner works long and hard for very little pay, but is rewarded instead with on-the-job training from the entire crew. This sort of apprenticeship is so desirable that the rest of the industry, soon realised that just by labelling their lowliest position 'runner' they could offer the worst of conditions and still get hundreds of willing applicants. Because of this, there are as many different kinds of runner as there are film and TV companies.

One thing I can say; runners don't actually run. At least, not unless they're asked to. If they are asked to run, they hurtle about as if in mortal danger, scattering tourists and old ladies without a second glance. The word 'no' simply is not in the runner's vocabulary. When runners do experiment with 'no', they rarely make it to the '-o' part before being fired, replaced, and completely forgotten. If, despite all this, you still want to join Soho's legions of runners here's how.

First of all, try to fix on some semblance of a plan, justifying to yourself why you want to be a runner at all. You'll need to hang on to this when times get hard, so make it good. 'To learn about producing', or 'to become an editor' is good, because it gives you a clear direction. Something like 'to get an insight into...' is fine, but remember, once you have gained that insight, to move on. 'I just want to break into the industry' is risky; if you want to find out what interests you, then fine. If you just have a notion that 'The Industry' is somehow 'cool' or 'glam', then you will either end up sorely disappointed or a soulless git.

Secondly, shed your pride. Try visualising yourself in a prison, emptying out somebody else's filthy slop bucket for the eighth time that day, whilst they sip on champagne and giggle to their friends about how crap you are. Now imagine smiling benignly back and offering to top up their champagne. Now imagine doing this every day for weeks on end, during nonsensical hours, being begrudged a minimum wage for your trouble. Imagine not minding much. You have now shed your pride.

Prideless, you are ready for the third stage – a job in post-production running. The notion that running work is hard to get is a myth. The big post-production houses employ lots of runners on a very high turnover. Log on to www.theknowledgeonline.com, gather some numbers and phone around. You'll have a job in a week or two. The going rate is £4 per hour. You will probably be employed on a freelance basis, with no rights and a notice period of thirty seconds.

Stage four: you are now a Soho runner, but of the lowest kind (yes, there are even tiers within runnership). Your days are spent serving refreshment to whichever twenty or so clients are currently utilising your employer's facilities. If you're lucky, they will occasionally acknowledge your existence. Occasionally, you will get to take packages to other companies in and around Soho. This is a key qualification – you will learn the layout of industry Soho, and therefore become considerably more employable as a fully fledged runner by a production company, agency, distributor or suchlike.

Five: keep in mind your plan from stage one. If post-production is your thing, stick at it. If not, fire off CVs and phone-calls constantly. You will often be told 'We're not looking for anyone just now, but please send us a CV and we'll keep it on file'. Unfortunately, 'on file' is usually either a dustbin or, if your covering letter is really pitiful, the bottom of a box marked 'light relief'. To stand a chance, your CV needs to land on the right person's desk just as, or slightly before, they are recruiting runners. Keep an ear to the ground – if you aren't worried too much about keeping your post-production job, gently pester appropriate clients (those you have managed to impress) about running work. From here, you're on your own. Before long, you'll be running the world.

Summary

1. Plan, plan and plan some more.

2. Let everyone know who is the boss.

3. Learn to say no.

You've shot your movie. Let's get it edited and ready for the cinema.

Seven Essential Steps for Becoming Rich and Famous by Making a Low Budget Film

Step 4 Saying No

One of the most difficult things to do in the film business is learning how to say no. No one in the industry ever says it; instead they say 'Yes!' or a 'That's a really great idea'. The theory for this is if an executive turns you down and then you go on to be discovered by a rival, they do not want to be known as the one that turned you down in the first place. The loose and vague comments are designed to leave you hanging in limbo without a real decision. If in doubt, remember that the only true yes in the film industry is a contract and cheque made out to you.

Film schools teach the theory that in order to succeed you must build strong personal relationships with the cast and crew. This theory will lead to your downfall as a producer, especially if you suffer from any personal insecurities or are trying too hard to be nice. The film school theory will teach you to be transparent and show everyone in your cast and crew the budget of the film. The first person who will run out of money will be the art director/production designer. They run out of money first because they start first. If you use the film school approach, the conversation between the art director and the skinflint producer plays out like this:

AD: I need more money.
SP: What for this time?
AD: I need to turn that big long wall green.
SP: How much is that going to cost?
AD: A hundred.
SP: Shall I show you the budget so you can see that there's no money?
AD: I don't care where you get the money, as long as I get a hundred.
SP: (Shows AD the budget) Would you like me to buy less film stock?
AD: Yes.
SP: Or maybe shoot mute? Think what we'd save on sound equipment!

And if you decide to continue this polite approach, then you will probably get a lecture similar to the one that I got from the art director on my first shoot:

AD: If you don't get me a hundred now, no matter what, if I don't get a hundred, then (stabbing at Elliot's nose with a finger) no matter if the actors give the performance of their lifetime and the cinematographer takes pictures that are the best ever in the history of cinematography, when the scene is cut you will have well acted, well lit, well photographed shit. So give me a hundred now or I'll know that you know nothing about filmmaking.

The best way to say no is to use the Hollywood no: 'Thank you for sharing that with me'. As soon as you use the Hollywood no, you have to leave the set.

Learn when to listen, learn when and how to say no and your career will start to zoom.

13   Thirteen Steps of Post-production

THERE ARE THREE stages to filmmaking: pre-production, production and post-production. Pre-production is most likely the stage you are at while you are reading this book. The stage where you are researching various filmmaking techniques, and toying with different ideas for a film, getting a script together and starting to raise finance.

Professional pre-production is the stage where you are actually spending money – on script development casting location scouting and securing crew. The second stage, production, is right after you get financing. You get everyone together and spend nine to eighteen days of fourteen to eighteen hours each shooting. Pre-production is physically easy but mentally draining. Production is both physically and mentally draining. During production everything happens at once. The actors, the crew, the technical problems and the creative concerns all descend at the same time. Production, although typically presented as being fun and joyous, will probably be the most tiring and draining two or three weeks of your life. Finally your film is in the can. You bring out the flat beer and celebrate. Everyone hugs everyone (except you, the skinflint producer) and goes home. You pass out and wake up approximately two days later. On waking you find 50,000 feet of film or twenty hours of tape at the foot of your bed. You're all alone. What do you do now? The answer, of course, is simple. You begin post-production.

Post-production, somehow, is the process that intimidates people most. Remember, it is not difficult. Production is massively difficult. Post-production is not, as long as you take it step by step. Your first phone call will probably be to your DoP who, although s/he probably hates you by now, will be able to introduce you to several good editors.

The Thirteen Steps

As a producer, all you need to know about post-production; finishing your film is a matter of following the thirteen steps listed below. Just take them one step at a time, in the order they appear. Unlike production, there will be no eighteen hour days. Your function will be to hire people and oversee them by dropping in for half an hour here and there.

1 Pick an Editing Format

There are two ways of doing post-production. One is the old way, the film way. Shoot film and edit or splice film on film editing equipment. Although I personally admire classic film editing on film, we will not be discussing it in this book.

Second is the new way, the electronic way. Shoot film, but don't get a print at the lab, just develop a negative, then transfer the developed negative to a tape medium (see telecine below) or digitise it to a non-linear format and edit electronically. This chapter is not about the pros and cons of film vs non-linear editing, so just pick a format. The steps are pretty much the same in either format.

2 Hire a Picture Editor

After you have selected a format for post, your cinematographer will probably be able to introduce you to two or three editors with demo reels. Select one, and allow him/her to pick an assistant and tell them to give you a rough cut with numerous versions of key scenes within eight to ten weeks. When they have finished, your 50,000 feet or twenty hours of tape will be cut down to 8,100 feet or ninety minutes of storytelling.

What makes a good editor?

Many excellent directors have started out as film editors – David Lean for example. When Roger Corman attended Raindance as a guest in 1996 he told me that new employees were given the following jobs to do if they wanted to direct. Only by satisfactorily completing these tasks were they allowed to progress to the next level.

1. Clean the garage (to demonstrate good manual and organisational skills).

2. Work as an assistant editor logging rushes on 3–5 features (learn discipline).

3. Work as an assistant editor on 3–5 features (learn how to do a rough cut).

4. Work as an assistant director or editor on 3–5 features (learn how to look for unusual shots).

5. Direct (prove your talent and ability).

A good film editor must be a natural storyteller, possess the ability to negotiate the various business and political minefields when dealing with a director, and producer.

The entire outcome of the film, and the investment by financiers largely rests in the hands of the editor. A skilful editor can mask poor performances and technical blemishes, and assemble a final cut where these imperfections are concealed from the audience. Scenes may have been photographed poorly and performances might have been less than inspired, but a skilled and creative editor can assemble the film so that the audience will never see these imperfections.

Hint Involve your editor at the earliest possible stage of the production – preferably at script development level.

What is editing?

Suppose you are at a cinema, the lights dim. Titles appear, and we see the skyline of a major city. We zoom in a little closer and see that it is London. Buckingham Palace. A figure shrouded in a cloak leaves a brown package next to the Palace gates. The guards chase him, and he flees. The sounds of his shoes on the cobblestones fade into horse's hooves cantering down Pall Mall past a hobo with a banjo. He sings a rustic song.

The screenwriter, director, cinematographer, actors, lighting designer, sound designer, and, finally, the film editor all created this scene. The film editor works with the director and shapes its final form. S/he views countless hours of rushes, considers the use of stock footage for the skyline, and from this material edits a sixty-second scene.

The scene appears to take place in Central London, near and around Buckingham Palace on a summer morning. In fact, little of what the audience sees was filmed in Central London at all.

The opening shot of London has come from a stock library picture shot which the producer felt was cheaper and better looking than anything they would be able to film. The shot of the man placing the package under the Buckingham Palace Gate had to be done in a studio, with either a photographic backdrop of the palace, or by cutting between close-ups of the package, the man's hands and an establishing shot of the Palace. It certainly wasn't all filmed in the same morning.

The sounds of the man's feet, the horse's hooves and the hobo's song were all recorded separately in a studio, and then mixed together. The finished piece flows as if taken at one place at one time and this is down to the editor, who ensures that the pictures, sound and music all work together despite the fact that the multitude of sound and pictures were recorded at different times and places.

The six stages of film editing

The methodology of classical film editing is very similar in every country around the world.

Editors need discipline so they are not overwhelmed by the multitude of variables. Classical film editing has developed a methodology which structures the work process into precise stages. Each stage has its own procedure and order.

Hint Editors need to 'get the material in their head'. An editor needs time to take a break from reviewing the material, even though it can be reviewed at the speed of light at the flick of a switch.

---

i Logging

The dailies or rushes are sorted and labelled in 'bins'. Each take may be accompanied by extra notes from the director or the cinematographer. This is the first time the editor sees the film, and since it is shot out of sequence, it is out of context of the story. A good editor views the rushes and looks for fluidity of movement and nuances that will later be incorporated into the film.

ii First assembly

The editor considers all the visual and audio material collected on the shoot and then re-orders it in the way to tell the story best. In the scene described above, the editor may decide to open with an aerial shot of Central London and then track in to Buckingham Palace. The next shot might be a close up of the hands of the bomber followed by a dissolve to the hands of the hobo playing the banjo. There are dozens of possible combinations the editor can use for this simple sequence, each of which create a different mood and tell the story differently.

Editing on a large budget feature usually commences as soon as the film starts shooting. An editor will work on the rushes and assemble scenes for the director and producer to view. Often at this point the editor and director will decide that additional footage of key moments is necessary in order to make more editing choices available during the edit.

Hint First assembly is like a sketch of the finished scene. It is a good idea to save these sketches for reference, should the editor get stuck.

iii Rough cut and variations

The rough cut can take up to three months to complete. Each editor works differently. Sometimes the editor works alone and shows the day's or week's work to the director and producer. Sometimes the editor and director work together, discussing every nuance.

In the rough cut, the scenes are placed in order and checked for continuity. This all-important step in the editing process allows for revisions and new ideas to be tried and tested.

Hint Make the edit points between the scenes very obvious in order to emphasise the 'roughness'. Failure to do so may result in the editor committing to an edit before it is ready.

iv First cut

The first cut is the rough cut that is accepted by the editor, the director and the producer. This is sometimes known as a rough fine cut. Selection and sequence are basically fixed, although changes can still be made. The later film is visible. Detailed fine cut starts out from its proportions, structures, rhythms and emphasises them.

Hint Never be afraid to let the first cut 'rest' for a few days so everyone involved can see it with fresh eyes.

v Fine cut

The fine cut no longer focuses on the entire film, but on the details of each and every edit point in the movie. The fine cut emphasises and strengthens the rhythms and structures identified in the first cut.

vi Final cut

When a fine cut has been agreed with the editor, director and producer, the sound designer, music composer and title designer join the editor (for more detail on the process from this point onwards, see Step 3). Sound effects and music are created and added to the final cut.

When everyone has agreed with the final cut, the edit decision list is sent to the lab where a negative cutter 'conforms' the negative to the EDL in order to create a negative that is an exact copy of the final cut. The EDL is a list of the exact frame numbers which comprise each shot, and the length and the order in which each follows the last.

Editing functions

The huge range of professional computerised editing machines has created a bewildering array of functions that can overwhelm editors, especially beginners. There are literally hundreds of options.

A drawback to this huge technological advance is that an editor's attention can be drawn from the pictures and sounds to the demands of the machine. The technical skills needed to operate an editing computer are fairly easy to acquire. An editor could do their work with just two buttons: one for separating and one for combining. What about the other hundreds of functions? Defining the basics of editing brings us to seven elementary functions which combine to produce all the others:

- Separating (segmenting, make subclip)
- Linking (sequencing, adding)
- Selecting (select, activate, mark in/mark out)
- Inserting (substitute, splice in)
- Removing (eliminate, extract)
- Replacing (permutations, replace, overwrite)
- Making longer or shorter (expand and compress, trim, slip, slide)

3 Hire a Sound Editor

About two months after the picture editor has started, the film is tight but you need to enhance the look with sound. Hire a sound editor and assistant for five to six weeks to cut dialogue tracks, to recreate and place sound effects, and to get cue sheets ready for Steps 7 and 13.

4 Do ADR

This is automatic dialogue replacement, which takes place in a large hollow room with a projector that plays the work print (from Step 2). The actors come back and lip sync, re-record and loop any dialogue that wasn't sharp and clear in the original. Chapter 7 has full details.

5 Do Foley

Go to a room that looks like (or could very well be) the ADR room and this time, without actors, have sound people called foley artists – or 'walkers' – re-record the noise of footsteps and certain other sound effects into your film. This is covered in greater detail in Chapter 7.

6 Secure Music

It is a common misconception that you can have an actor walking past a radio on a set with a Beatles song playing out of it and not have to pay. This is simply not true. A sound clip of any Beatles song of less than eight seconds can cost as much as $150,000. Here is the story of Tarantino's *Reservoir Dogs*. Tarantino had the script, and had sent it to all the major studios who had used the typical Hollywood 'no' and told him that they loved it, but thought it was too violent. He then raised about $30,000 and was preparing for a 16mm shoot when his friend, Lawrence Bender pleaded for the option, knowing that the script deserved a better budget than the one Quentin had planned. Tarantino agreed, and for $10 Lawrence had an option for a month. He sent it everywhere, and had no luck. Then he discovered that his ex-girlfriend had moved to New York and was taking acting classes at the Actors Studio where she had met and was now sleeping with Harvey Keitel. At that time, Keitel's career was nearing rock bottom. Through the personal connection of Keitel's lover, Tarantino and Lawrence Bender were able to get the script to Keitel. Keitel instantly agreed to play in the film. If you think about it, Tarantino is an expert in assessing and accessing talent. Think of Travolta in *Pulp Fiction*, and Pam Grier in *Jackie Brown*. But time was running out, and Lawrence needed to get some money to the table. With about a week left in his option (Tarantino had already told him that he was a loser, and shouldn't have wasted his time), Lawrence went back to Keitel and asked him if he would be interested in producing.

In his naïveté, Bender assumed that this meant he could get money based on Keitel's commitment. But Keitel did not express commitment, only interest. The only real commitment is when an actor agrees to appear at your set or location for a specific period of time (the window). That is meaningful.

Hint If you ask someone to produce, are you not really asking them to write cheques?

Keitel agreed, got some money from a home video distribution company, Live Entertainment, got a bit of private investment from the amazing filmmaker, Monte Hellman, and together with Tarantino agreeing to waive his fees, got a total of $800,000 together. The film was shot with a below-the-line production budget of around $250,000.

They cut and edited the film and used the Stealers Wheel song, 'Stuck in the Middle With You'. In their naïveté, they forgot to clear the music rights. When the film was delivered, the distributor was horrified, because they had financed a movie that could play absolutely nowhere except film festivals. Sensing that they could have financed a turkey, they decided to test the film at some film festivals, starting with Sundance. The response was overwhelming.

Now the discussion with Stealers Wheel needs to start. Had they approached this band of aging (well, very aged) rock stars before the movie was shot, they could have expected to pay in the region of a few thousand dollars. But because the newspapers and film magazines were now full of Tarantino's triumph, the band was able to negotiate a mid six figure deal, rumoured to be $600,000 – almost the entire budget of the film! And, in addition, when released, the film promoted their back catalogue and they benefited from a huge increase in their sales.

Tarantino I am sure has never made this mistake again. And if you look at his filmography, it always contains a vast amount of music from the forgotten artistes of the '70s and '80s whom he resurrects by putting them in his movies.

Don't use any popular old song that you haven't purchased the rights to. Although you can use public domain music, remember that you still have to purchase performance rights if the recording is less than seventy years old. But a recording done more than seventy years ago is unlikely to be of good enough quality for your soundtrack.

If you want to use Beethoven's Fifth, remember that the score is public domain, but the recording of the London Symphony Orchestra playing in 1985 is not, and to use that you will have to buy it out. Another alternative would be to hire session musicians and a studio – which adds up.

I was re-editing my first feature in a valiant and brave attempt to turn a shambolic screenplay into a movie I could sell when my new editor suggested that I use a Chris Christoferson song recorded in 1974 as he was crossing over from gospel to country. I called the MCPS and filled in a form with my budget and sent it off for a quote for a universal all media buyout. I was astonished when the price of $2000 came back. I thought it was a bargain.

Film music from pop stars need not be expensive. We had a panel at the Raindance Film Festival which included Damon Albarn, one of the Cocteau Twins and Stephen Tin Duffy – all big stars in the 1990s. In the open Q&A at the end of the session, I was astonished to hear them all say that several of their songs, released to top forty acclaim seven to ten years ago, had had their copyright revert back to them from the record company. As they had already realised profit and critical acclaim from these songs, they were all willing to consider a no-money fee for these songs in a movie if they liked the script. The reason they were willing to do this was because they wanted their older music, music that they now had control over, music that they were proud of, to reach a new audience (by plugging the back catalogue). And they confided that if this music was placed properly in a film, then they all hoped that they might be able to use it as a calling card to get real paid work as a film score composer, and thereby add a possible revenue stream to their 'business'.

My good friend and confidante Phil Alberstat was the executive producer on a movie which featured the music of Dave Stewart of the Eurythmics, including eight original songs. I was astonished to find out that Stewart's fee was just £34,000 for the entire soundtrack – although the album rights went to his record company. This enabled the

When the Russo Brothers first attended Raindance with their first feature film, Pieces, they included the song 'The Girl From Ipanema'. The song was not an essential element to the film, unlike 'Stuck in the Middle With You' in Reservoir Dogs. Because they had failed to clear the music rights before they attempted to sell it, they had to pass on several lucrative offers, and this excellent film became unreleasable. Even so, their film was good enough to get George Clooney and Steven Soderbergh interested in producing their next feature. Welcome to Collinwood cleared all its music rights before release and did exceptionally well in sales, despite lukewarm reviews.

To find out who owns the copyright to a song or performance that you would like to use, contact the Mechanical Copyright Protection Society, Elgar House, 41 Streatham High Road, London SW16 1ER
T: 020 8378 7744
F: 020 8378 7740
W: www.mcps.co.uk

If you want to watch and listen to my personal favourite sound track of the last ten years, get your hands on a copy of Six String Samurai. I simply cannot believe that this film didn't do more business. The soundtrack by the Pink Elvises – an émigré Russian street band from Santa Monica is nothing short of brilliant.

producer to use the phrase 'Original Soundtrack by Dave Stewart' to market the movie.

It can pay to find out from a major record company which bands they handle and who they are about to spend money on promoting. If the timing coincides, you might be able to get not only the music for free, but some cash for the production budget as well (see Chapter 24).

Hint As a producer it is your job to discover talent. How many demo tapes have you listened to? How many clubs have you gone too looking for new sounds, new ideas and new bands. Don't be lazy. Find and hire a musician with his or her own studio to compose brand new original songs and tunes that you have the rights to. The UK is the home of new music, and the USA is the largest market. Hundreds of new musicians hit the market place every week. And what about Europe? Have you heard the new music coming out of France, Germany, Italy and Serbia? It is absolutely terrific.

The Blair Witch Project also has an exceptional soundtrack. Exceptional, because the noises and 'music' in the soundtrack are bordering on subliminal, and use human noises like heart beats and respiratory noises to great effect.

Hint Uncleared music is a major reason why a sales agent or film buyer will pass on your film. They will always ask about music rights.

7 Re-recording or the Mix

At this stage you will have twenty to forty tracks of sound (dialogue, ADR, foley, music). You must layer them on top of each other to artificially create a feeling of sound with depth. This is called re-recording or the mix. In the mix session, a sound engineer will mix the sound in time to a projection of the picture. Depending on the nuances of the scene, a good sound mixer will mix the sounds, dialogue and music to maximise the dramatic effect of the scene.

8 Get an M&E Track

Movie sound mixes are reduced to three tracks: music, effects and dialogue. Somewhere in the not-too-distant future you will be selling the rights to your film to foreign nations. The distributor/buyer in that nation wants a sound track without English dialogue in it to facilitate dubbing the film with the voices of actors in their own language. M&E stands for only music and effects tracks, and excludes the dialogue tracks.

Hint You will debase the value of your film in certain foreign territories by up to ninety per cent if you do not have an M&E track.

9 Get Titles

Your editing is now done. What is now left is to get the final pieces needed for the answer print and give them to the lab to finish. Your six to eight opening title cards and then the rear title crawl can be created on any graphic format, but need to be transferred to film or to the same tape format as your finished the picture and sound are on. This is done at an optical transfer facility.

Keep the opening titles swift and sweet. There is nothing wrong with opening with the title of the movie, and then putting all the 'opening title credits' at the end of the film as was done in *Terminator 2*. Remember, no one watching your first film will have heard of anyone in it!

Hint Keep your opening titles brief. The most common opening title credits for a film submitted to the Raindance Film Festival that we do not accept has a sequence such as: title of film, written by, directed by etc, and then special thanks to Uncle Norman and Aunt Emma (without whom this film would not have been made) and go on and on and on, until we are left screaming 'Who are these people?' and getting bored before the film even starts.

Two Types of Title

In camera titles

The titles are filmed as part of the narration (as in Bob Dylan's *Don't Look Now)* or handwritten signs are filmed and become part of the actual show.

Optical titles

Where a graphic designer with a good software programme like Quark, Illustrator or Photoshop creates a title and exports it as a jpeg for printing on the final film, be it actual film stock or high quality tape.

10 Get an Optical Track

From the mix you have a magnetic or digital sound tape that is incompatible with the 35mm picture frames. This sound tape must be converted from magnetic sound to an optical track that the lab can place on the film in between the sprocket holes and the picture frames.

11 Cut the Negative

If you are cutting the negative, you will send the entire negative from the shoot, plus any optical effects created in the lab to the negative cutter. The negative will then be cut according to the EDL. This is also called conforming the negative. If you have originated on tape, the masters will be sent to an on-line editor who will select the scenes by referring to the EDL. A new master is then created which conforms to the EDL.

12 Colour the Print

With a negative and an optical sound track, you can now have the lab give you an excellent colour print. This is sometimes called the 'timing'. The only artist at the lab is the 'timer' or colour corrector and s/he will colour your film frame by frame with a computer. It will end up looking prettier and more unified than the original work print you've been working with. All the settings will be saved on a computer for future use.

13 Strike an Answer Print

The lab now has the following: your cut negative; a correct colouring code; the optical soundtrack; the list of fades and dissolves; and the opening and closing titles.

The lab puts this all together and gives you a 'composite print' or a 'first trial' at your answer print which is screened at a screening room at the lab. Attending will be the lab technician, the director, the producer, the editor and DoP. They will be taking notes and deciding what is right and what has been forgotten. This information is then collated, and the lab puts together a second trial print. This process is repeated until all parties are satisfied, but normally the 'second attempt' is your finished film ready to be shown to festivals, critics and film buyers.

Summary

1. The editor is a key creative. Meet them as early as possible.

2. Make certain you and your editor agree the editing formats.

3. Lack of cleared music rights will prevent you from selling your film.

The rest of this book relates to dealing with the creative people in your project, and the marketing and distribution of your film.

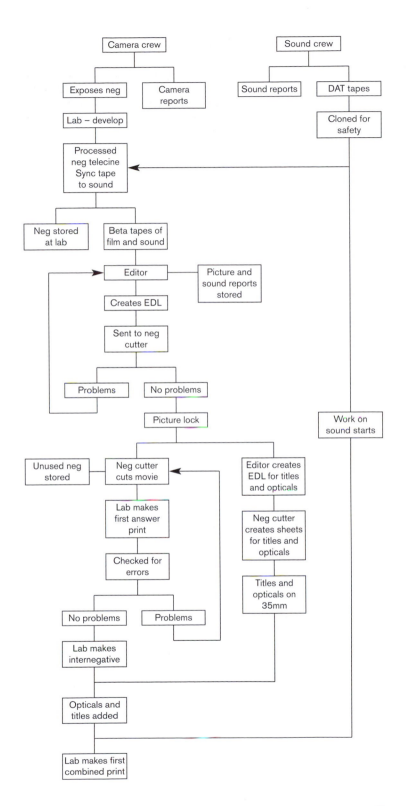

Camera crew

Exposes neg — Camera reports

Lab – develop

Processed neg telecine Sync tape to sound

Neg stored at lab

Beta tapes of film and sound

Editor — Picture and sound reports stored

Creates EDL

Sent to neg cutter

Problems — No problems

Picture lock

Unused neg stored — Neg cutter cuts movie — Editor creates EDL for titles and opticals

Lab makes first answer print

Neg cutter creates sheets for titles and opticals

Checked for errors

Titles and opticals on 35mm

No problems — Problems

Lab makes internegative

Opticals and titles added

Lab makes first combined print

Sound crew

Sound reports — DAT tapes

Cloned for safety

Work on sound starts

figure 13.1
The post-production process

Film Editing Glossary

Cut

A visual transition created in editing in which one shot is instanta-neously replaced on screen by another.

Continuity editing

Editing that creates action that flows smoothly across shots and scenes without jarring visual inconsistencies. Establishes a sense of story for the viewer.

Cross cutting

Cutting back and forth quickly between two or more lines of action, indicating they are happening simultaneously.

Crossing the line

Where the camera is moved across the imaginary line drawn between the noses of two characters, disrupting continuity and making an eye-line match impossible. See figure 13.2 below.

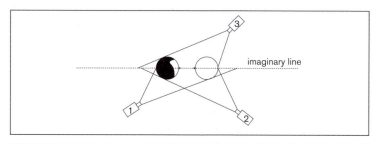

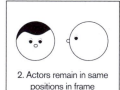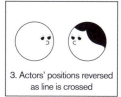

| 1. Actors appear as above in the frame | 2. Actors remain in same positions in frame | 3. Actors' positions reversed as line is crossed |

figure 13.2
Crossing the line

Dissolve

A gradual scene transition. The editor overlaps the end of one shot with the beginning of the next one and as the first slowly disappears, it is replaced with the second.

Editing

Selecting and joining together shots to create a finished film.

Errors of continuity

Disruptions in the flow of a scene, such as a failure to match action, or the inconsistent placement of cast or props.

Establishing shot

A shot, normally taken from a great distance or from a 'bird's eye view', that establishes the location where the action in the following sequence will occur.

Eyeline match

The matching of eyelines between two or more characters. This establishes a spatial relationship of proximity and continuity.

Fade

A visual transition between shots or scenes that appears on screen as a brief interval with no picture. The editor fades one shot to black and then fades in the next. This transition is often used to indicate a change in time or place.

Final cut

The finished edit of a film, approved by the director and the producer. This is what the audience sees.

Iris

Visible on screen as a circle closing down over or opening up on a shot. This technique is seldom used in contemporary film, but common during the silent era of Hollywood films. This transition functions to transpose from one scene to the next.

Jump cut

A cut that creates a lack of continuity by leaving out parts of the action.

Matched cut

A cut joining two shots whose compositional elements match, helping to establish strong continuity of action.

Montage

Scenes whose emotional impact and visual design are achieved through the editing together of many brief shots. The shower scene from *Psycho* is probably the most famous (and one of the most effective) example of montage editing.

Online editing

The term for editing on a computer. The most common computer system is AVID. However, recent developments by Apple and their programme – Final Cut Pro – have revolutionised editing with their robust, quick and cheap hardware and software.

Offline editing

The term for editing on actual video cassettes – usually duplicates of the original material. In order to work efficiently, an editor needs two machines: one to put in the source tape, and one onto which the compilation is made. From this, the EDL is created.

Rough cut
The editor's first pass at assembling the shots into a film, before tightening and polishing occurs.

Sequence shot
A long take that extends for an entire scene or sequence. The scene will therefore be composed of only one shot with no editing.

Shot reverse shot cutting
Usually used for conversation scenes, this technique alternates between over-the-shoulder shots showing each character speaking.

Wipe
Visible on screen as a bar travelling across the frame pushing one shot off and pulling the next shot into place. Rarely used in contemporary film, but common in films from the 1930s and 1940s.

14 Above the Line

ABOVE THE LINE refers to the elements of the budget which summarise the cost of the creative people involved in the project. Even though many people add their creative input to a movie, above the line refers to the producer, writer, actor and director. Regardless of your career ambition, it is essential that each of these above the line jobs or careers are understood.

Producer Credits

Directing is the most glamorous role in the industry, writing is the most creative, but producing is the most important. The irony is that a great producer operates behind the scenes and behind the camera, making sure that everything runs smoothly, and if they do their job well, they are unlikely to be in the spotlight.

When the film comes out, a director will take all the credit if the film is a success. If the film is a failure, the director can usually blame the fickle taste of the general public, and the producer is left to explain the resulting financial disaster to the investors. The director's career can still advance after a failure, especially if the film has a unique 'look' to it. But a commercial failure of a movie can end a producer's career.

The lure of producing is hard to explain. For some, seeing their ideas on the screen fulfils a driving ambition. For others, it is the powerful communication tool of film and television that enables them to reach a great number of people which is the lure. And of course there are the financial rewards; a producer with a single hit film can buy a large house (or two) with the profits. If fame and glory are anywhere in your dreams, then producing will never do it for you. The most you can expect, fame wise, is a grudging respect from other above-the-line people in the industry.

If you have ever sat through an entire movie, it is hard not to notice the title sequences at the beginning and end of the film. The first credits are called the opening title credits. Here the above the line individuals associated with the making of the film are mentioned, either with other names (a shared title credit) or on their own (a single title credit). The credits at the end of the film are called the rear title crawl.

A common complaint of producers and their lawyers is the amount of time it takes to agree the credits in the film. Who comes first, how long one's credits are on the screen, the size of the typeface, and whether or not the credit will appear in newspaper advertising, on cinema trailers, on DVD and video jackets, and on telecasts are all negotiating points.

Naturally, everyone involved in the film wants to be in the opening title sequence because it is more impressive. You will often notice certain people, like the editor, cinematographer and production designer sneaking into the opening title credits – they are people whose career is at the level where they can command and receive an opening title credit in addition to their salary.

A closer examination of the opening title credits will reveal several different categories of producer.

Producer

The producer of the film is the individual who has conceived the idea for the film, found an excellent writer to write a suitable script, hired an appropriate director, supervised the casting process, the shoot and the post-production. The producer will also have a certain say in the marketing of the film. Parallel to all of this worry, the producer is also charged with the responsibility of raising the money for the film and dealing with the investors.

A good producer, like Stephen Woolley, Norma Heyman, Lawrence Bender, Saul Zantz or Nik Powell, has a valuable creative role to play in the filmmaking process.

Each producer spends an amount of time bordering on the obsessive trying to identify new talent. They read galley proofs of unpublished novels, read countless screenplays by up and coming screenwriters, see dozens of theatre productions seeking new actors and writers, and watch countless movies at festivals and at home on preview cassettes.

A producer must also be a master of negotiation and be able to sell the concept of the movie to talent and investors.

Hint A producer's job is to discover and nurture talent. A good producer looks everywhere for it: at theatres, concerts, galleries – anywhere something new is tried that might work in the cinema with a little guidance.

Associate Producer

Suppose you, as a producer, find you have an actor of a certain stature attached to your film, but cannot attract an investor. You may meet an individual who says: 'Based on the fact that your project has these merits, including this actor, I have a client who will invest in your film'. This person makes a formal introduction to a financier who then finances the movie. The person who introduces you to the money is called the associate producer. An associate producer has no other role in the film, and for their services you pay either a flat fee, or a commission based on the amount they raise, and/or a small percentage of the profit you make from the film, if any. The associate producer rarely has any creative input into the film. Associate producers have been compared to real estate agents and accordingly often insist on having a title other than associate producer. In a situation like this, you will usually accede to their demands to be a 'producer' because it will facilitate the financing needed to make the film happen.

Co-producer

Suppose you have an investor who will only fund your project if certain actors are involved. If you do not have a good contact to these particular actors, or are being shut out by their agents or personal managers, you may need someone who can introduce you to these people.

A co-producer is someone who can gain direct personal access to the person or actors you are pursuing on your behalf. A co-producer leads you to talent. Like an associate producer, they have no other involvement in the film and are paid either a flat fee, or commission if the person/actors they introduce you to sign a contract with you. Co-producers have been likened to dating agencies.

Executive Producer

An executive producer is the person who writes the cheques. Sometimes several individuals share this credit. The credit can also be taken by the solicitor who does the paperwork for the company or individual financing the film. An executive producer does not have creative control, technically, for the film. But in reality, the executive producer can dictate whatever they want using the adage of all business: he or she who has the gold makes the rules.

Line Producer

A line producer (production manager in television) is the most anal member of your team. It is this person's job to get you finished on time and on schedule. S/he is the person who goes crazy if you are three minutes late from lunch break. A good line producer will assist in getting you deals, and will have a useful black book full of contact telephone numbers for crew and facilities houses.

How Much You Get Paid

The rule of thumb fee for producers is ten per cent of the total budget of the film. In reality, this is rarely achieved and British television producers have seen their fees cut to less than half that.

As an independent producer, you need to be aware of the demands a project will place on your time. Until *Trainspotting* was in official pre-production, the producer Andrew Macdonald spent a year and a half working with the screenwriter, John Hodge, perfecting the script. During that time he was working in Scotland as a runner. Once you have the script and the money raised, the pre-production phase commences. Until the film is totally complete, the producer will be unable to do any other job. They say in the film business that there is no life after movies. And this is especially true for the producer.

A typical first independent film with a budget of under a million will totally consume the life of a producer for between six months and one year. During this time the producer will not be able to contemplate working for anyone else, or earning revenue from anywhere else.

In order to calculate your fee, simply take your monthly living expenses for six to twelve months. That is the minimum amount of money that you need as your fee. To take any less money means that your work as a producer will suffer while you try and supplement your income from other endeavours. The irony is that producer's fees are usually the most difficult to raise. Investors usually resist the idea of paying a producer's fee to someone who also has a profit share.

Hint Everyone has different lifestyles and different expenses and financial responsibilities. Make certain you have an accurate estimate of what your time will cost you before you submit your producer's fee.

How to Break In

Tim Bevan is the co-founder of Working Title and has an impressive list of producer's credits including *Notting Hill* and *Fargo*. He insists that his smartest move was to befriend the juniors at the main Hollywood agencies (Endeavor, ICM, William Morris and CCA) when he started out in the mid 1980s. Now each of these juniors has risen in rank and they deal with the majority of the big stars in the industry. They all return Tim's calls and make his job of producing that much easier.

There doesn't seem to be any one way that producers break in. Roger Corman was a chemist until the age of forty-seven when he sold a script. With that money he bought a camera and started producing.

Many lawyers end up producing and are remarkably well-suited for the job. They already know how deal structures work and understand the complex money flows involved in the life of a film.

Other producers have broken in by working as an assistant for another producer. Chris Auty, who now masterminds Civilian Content started on the bottom rung at The Recorded Picture Company – Jeremy Thomas's company. As a producer's assistant you will work on someone else's feature as an assistant to the producer, usually for nothing, in order to gain experience.

Or maybe you should produce a short – either for yourself, or someone else to see whether or not you enjoy the experience.

Hint As Robert Rodriguez says in his excellent book *Rebel Without A Crew*, get experience on your own movies, not movie experience (i.e. pulling cables) on someone else's film.

Seven Essential Qualities of a Producer

1 Know your screenplay
A great script is gold dust in the film industry. Finding it can be like finding a needle in a haystack.

Hint Take the time to fully understand screenplays. It will pay dividends in the long run.

---

2 Understand money
Especially how to raise it. This is what a producer must do in order to call themselves producer.

Jeremy Thomas, one of the greatest living British producers tells me every time I meet him, that he is out 'truffling' for money.

Hint The more you learn about money, the better able you will be to understand it and use it.

---

3 Develop excellent interpersonal communication skills
A producer is only as good as their power of persuasion.

Hint Hone your pitching skills. You will have to pitch the film not just to investors, but to cast, crew and finally distributors.

---

4 Have business savvy
No one can teach this, and it isn't something you can buy. It just sort of develops as you gain experience.

Hint Read the trade papers.

---

5 Be organised and able to multi-task
The phone is ringing, the doorbell is chiming, the sirens are wailing, and your lead actor is having a nervous breakdown. All in front of your principal investor. Deal with it.

Hint Prioritise and deal with situations in order of importance. If that fails, remember that the sun always rises tomorrow morning.

---

6 Have boundless energy
Every day during the principal photography of your film you will say to yourself that you have never ever felt so tired in your entire life.

7 Have talent

Talent is a very subjective subject. Number seven should really read: must have producing talent; talent for finding writers; talent for developing stories; talent for working with casting directors; talent in finding financial partners; talent for selling movies.

Hint It's not what you know it's who you know.

The Producer's Contract

On the CD you will find a generic producer's contract. This has been provided by entertainment attorney Philip Alberstat.

The contract between the producer and the production will also need to be agreed by the principal investors. The main points are: time and duration of hire, responsibilities of the producer, clear understanding of how any additional profit (or points) are paid, how the flow of money will pass from the investors to the production company to the producer, and a clear statement of how the contract can be terminated should any party fail in their agreement.

In Conversation with Mark Shivas

How would you describe your role as a producer?

Mark Shivas is a producer at Perpetual Motion Pictures. Both as Head of Drama and later as Head of Films at the BBC, Mark has produced and executive produced scores of telvision plays, series and feature films including: *Truly Madly Deeply, Jude, Hideous Kinky, The Snapper, The Witches, A Private Function* and many more.

I would describe it as a mixture of a cajoler, a wet nurse, someone who raises the money, someone who keeps the movie on track, someone who looks after the crew.

It requires a mixture of skills as well: you're an accountant, you're someone who knows something about scripts, but probably can't write them, you're somebody who knows a little about everything, and not much about anything. No one producer is as good at everything a producer does – some are very good at raising money, some are very good on scripts, some are very good on the set, some are very good at promoting the movies. I don't know anyone who is good at all those things.

My forte is with the script, and on the set, with the cast and getting the right crew, and the right director for the project – keeping everybody reasonably sweet. My forte is not raising money particularly.

What does being a producer involve?

Well I find the project, which often means that somebody comes to me (at least they do now because I've been at it for a very long time), with a book, an idea or a script, and says 'Will you produce this?'. To which the answer is usually no. But sometimes it's yes, and then it's a matter of helping the writer to get the script written, and finding the money for that. Then I find the right director and then make that relationship work between the writer and the director and the script and the director. Then I find the right crew, and so on and so on. That's the bit I know how to do best I think. I'm reasonably good in post-production, not so great on the marketing, not so good at the money raising.

I think a producer ought not to be there the whole time. I think another thing the producer should be, is a kind of 'long stop' for the director. The director is very much focused on what's going on from day to day, and I think the producer ought to be able to be a 'back stop' – stand back, see the wood for the trees, and generally support the director.

On average, how much time does a project tend to take from conception to final product?

I don't think there is such a thing as an average. I was an executive producer on *I Capture the Castle* which I commissioned when I was head of films at the BBC, six years before it actually hit the screen – six years! That's the time it took to buy the rights of the book, to get one writer writing it. Then we had to throw out that script and get another one written, and then the first director who was involved in the project left, so we had to get another director. I didn't actually produce that movie, but I was attached and aware of what was going on all the way through.

I was involved as producer on a television series that came out at the same time, called *Cambridge Spies* – that took four years, from the time the writer came to me with an outline.

Twenty years ago, I made a movie called *Moonlighting* with Jeremy Irons, where I was approached by somebody in January and we had the film made and shot and on the screen in Cannes with subtitles in May!

Those are the extremes. But very few producers only work on one project at a time, most producers have to work on several – so they are in various stages of development.

How many projects normally do you work on at one time?

I have three movies that I'm involved with at the moment, and that's a good number. You could have too many and spread yourself too thinly. These three are at various stages of development – they all have scripts, so I'm now casting for one, looking for a director for the other, looking for money and cast for the third.

How do you go about choosing directors?

You look to see whether they have any kind of rapport with the script and the subject matter. In the case of these three movies, two already have directors attached and the third one's looking for a director right now. And because it's a movie that has a part for a star actor, we probably need a director who is reasonably well known to encourage the actor to take part, so we will need a very sensitive and visual director, with a lot of imagination, who's also had a success or two, who can attract these sorts of people. It's all a matter of whether they are available. The good people who are working, so you have to leap in and hope.

Do you have some favourite directors that you tend to go with?

No, I don't. I've worked with several directors twice or more, but I don't have a director, as it were, with whom I always produce – not like say, Andrew Eaton and Michael Winterbottom or Jeremy Thomas and Bernardo Bertolucci. But I am working on something with Nicholas Roeg at the moment with whom I did a film in 1988, so yes I have worked with directors more than once. Some I would never wish to work with ever again of course, but they are few and far between and they shall remain nameless.

How do you find new projects?

In various ways: I have an agent, who sometimes sends me books and scripts, I read the *Times Literary Supplement* to see what books are coming, then there are friends of mine who come to me with things they suggest – there's no one way. Just occasionally, someone will ring up and say 'Look, I've got this script, will you produce it?' And that's like having a birthday – if it's any good that is. I've had plenty of people ask if they can send me a script, and I almost always say yes, and it often turns out to be something I wouldn't want to do. You have to think that it's going to take years of your time and you have to want to get out of bed in the mornings to work on it, so you have got to be incredibly enthusiastic about the project.

What do you look for in a project?

I don't think there's any one kind of movie that I like to make more than another except maybe black comedies – comedies with an edge, which are incredibly difficult to find, but I've made two or three – *A Private Function* by Alan Bennett with Michael Palin, Maggie Smith and a pig and Roald Dahl's *The Witches* with Angelica Huston. If I could find more of those, I would be very happy – on the other hand, they don't always make money. I suppose you try to find something that is unusual, whatever that may mean, and I couldn't possibly define that. There are certain genres that I don't care for; I don't really like science fiction, I may watch it sometimes, but films where the characters are called X and Y are not my cup of tea. And I haven't made 'big' movies, most of the movies I have made have been of a modest budget. I can't imagine making a movie that cost $100 million.

What is the single most important element in a project?

The script. First the script and then the director. You cannot make a good film without a good script, in my opinion, but you can sometimes make a decent film without a very good director. You can start thinking 'It's not a terrifically good script, but we have got a fantastic cameraman, we've got fantastic actors', and thinking that will raise it up, but what usually happens when the film is all put together, is it comes back and you'll think: 'If only the script had been better' – it usually shows.

Scripts usually take a long time to get right, which is why developing films can take years. A script does seem to take longer to develop now than it did in the past. I think a lot of films used to go into production that were not properly cooked, and I think there are more fingers in the pie now. So many development executives having opinions, so many financiers having opinions. It's as true of television as it is of movies.

Many people look at directors and producers in the film industry and call these 'lifestyle occupations'. How do you react to that?
I can only think of about ten film producers in this country, or fewer, who are making a decent living. I wouldn't describe it as a lifestyle occupation, because there isn't much of a lifestyle – most producers are not making enough money to have a decent lifestyle.

There is much more money in television, I've found. There are an awful lot of people around who call themselves film producers who have made one film every five years. So if you call that a lifestyle, then I suppose that's true.

Am I painting a black picture? There are a lot of young filmmakers and people who want to get into films, who don't seem to know anything about television, or television writers, which seems very strange to me. They might have just about heard of Paul Abbot or one or two others, but they don't seem to watch television to look for directors and writers, and that's a strange blankness, especially as some of the money for making films now comes from television and has done for a long time.

How do you deal with agents?
Well if they are British agents, most of them are quite helpful – not all, but most of them. And if they have some respect for you, then they will usually help you, and indeed find things for you, and point you in the right direction. American agents, I have had less to do with. It seems to be very hard to get past them to their clients and they seem obstructive to people they don't want to deal with. I think some British agents are becoming more like American agents and managers, which is not particularly good. But of course, a lot of people have an agent here and in America – the bigger clients.

How do you see their role?
I have an agent and his role is to find me things and give me advice and to do some of the deals. I would have thought there is a difference between an agent and a manager – and in days gone by, there was more of a managerial role for some of the agents who guided their clients' careers, but these two functions have been split between the agent and the manager – that's more American, but it's coming here too. Producers don't always have agents – they usually have lawyers instead!

Has digital filmmaking changed filmmaking for the better or worse, or not at all?
I don't think it has changed it for the worse, no. I don't think it has changed things greatly. There have been some very interesting movies shot on DV, which, like Michael Winterbottom's film *In This World*, couldn't have been shot any other way. It can be a good thing, but again, it depends on the project and the script.

What are the largest problems you face today?

The scarcity of sources of money to tap into in this country in terms of production companies. There's the Film Council, BBC Films, Working Title and one or two other places, but other than that there aren't that many places to go. Of course there are the lease back organisations, tax breaks and so on. There aren't very many places to go for development finance for scripts either, which is a problem.

In the art film market – by which I don't mean 'art' films, I mean smaller films – it is so difficult to get people to notice them. So much money is spent on big movies and marketing them, that it's hard to get in there and to make people take notice – that's changed I think.

I think the change has happened because the corporations have taken over from the film companies, because of this business that if a film doesn't do well on its first weekend, it gets pulled – I think that's very bad, things can't just take root. It's too expensive to advertise – the amount of money it takes to advertise has become colossal – almost as much as the production of the movie. So we are up against these huge machines really, and I find that hard.

Is finance is the only problem?

Well the more fingers there are in the pie, the more opinions come, and it's possible that the vision of a few people can get diluted by having to dance to the tunes of a larger number of people, and that's the danger in international co-productions; the more producers and the more financial sources you have, the worse it is for the producer, director and writer.

Why do you do what you do? What satisfies you about it?

I like most of the people I work with, it's never the same from one day to the next and it's always interesting and dangerous and funny.

Why did you choose to become a producer in the first place?

I think because I like to be in on a project right from the beginning, and I didn't feel that I particularly wanted to direct actors. The business of working with the script and the writer from the early stages seemed to be something I was quite good at. I liked the movies, I liked television. Once upon a time I thought my life's ambition was to be a film critic for *The Observer* newspaper – but that never happened.

Do you have to make many sacrifices?

Well you are away from home quite a lot. If you're shooting, you're away for eight to ten weeks. That's tough. But every job requires some sacrifices, I don't think producing requires an inordinate amount of sacrifice.

Is there one deal, one project that got away?

Yes but I'm not going to tell you what it was. It's a television series.

Could you have prevented it from happening?

No. I made the wrong decision – I turned it down, which in retrospect, was a mistake. We all make mistakes don't we?

Writers and Buying Screenplays

There are two types of screenwriters: those with a previous screen credit, and those without. As a producer, you could exploit an un-produced writer desperate for an opening title credit quite easily. However, morals and common sense dictate that this would be a strategically unsound approach. In essence, whichever type of writer you deal with, as a producer, you are hiring a creative ally, and, depending on the financial arrangements, are initiating a financial partnership.

Successful producers I know in London, such as Andrew MacDonald, Jeremy Thomas, Richard Holmes and Tim Bevan, have a pack of writers – usually around eight to twelve – who supply them with scripts. Writers all have different work rates, and it is not uncommon for a producer to have several scripts delivered in the same fortnight – and then to have to choose between them. Had the scripts been delivered on time, this situation would never arise.

Development Team

The classic development team consists of a producer, a development executive and an admin support person. The development executive reads and assesses the scripts submitted to the producer for consideration. A good development executive will also take meetings with the writer, and make creative suggestions for the rewrite.

The admin assistant maintains the database, and prepares packages for delivery. They may also help read scripts.

In London, a three-person team like this one, including office rent, telephone and payroll deductions, will cost a minimum of £75,000 per annum and will be able to assess ten scripts a week and see about three stage shows and five preview screenings each.

Three types of script deal

Scripts are bought and sold three different ways.

1 Outright purchase

Suggested purchase price for a screenplay in the UK for a film with a total budget under £750,000 is £14,000 (PACT). In the US, for a movie with a budget under $2 million it is a minimum of $55,000 (Writers Guild of America).

If, as a producer, you find a script, and make an offer of purchase, and if it is accepted and you pay your money, then the script becomes yours. You can do anything you want with the script during production, and the writer has no recourse to dispute your decision. Some producers will buy a script, polish it and then attempt to sell it on for a profit.

2 Option

Suppose you find a script, and agree a purchase price, but want to protect your own cash flow while you are attempting to raise the rest of the finance. The answer to this dilemma is to get the writer to agree to an option period where you pay a deposit against the purchase price. The balance of the purchase price is payable on the first day of principal photography – the day when actors are speaking on set for the first time. The amount you paid as a deposit may or may not be credited against the total amount if you do choose to buy the script.

Should the project not meet its target financially within the agreed option period, then the producer returns the copyright to the writer, and the writer keeps the down payment. Or, the parties may have agreed beforehand to allow for an extension of the option period or a limited and defined period of time for a further deposit.

Hint The Option Deal: Often a producer will wish to minimise his/her outgoings and offer a writer a part payment to be treated as a holding deposit on the script for a period of time while they secure the balance of the finance. The balance of the purchase price is due on the first day of principal photography or on the anniversary of the option, whichever is first. Should the option period expire, it is customary for the producer to arrange for a further payment to the writer for an additional option, with this extra money credited to the original purchase price, or not, depending on the agreement. Most option agreements call for a ten per cent payment for a one or two year option.

---

3 Step deal

When a producer finds a good writer, they may ask the writer to develop an idea into a treatment, and then, after discussion, develop it further into a first draft, second draft, polish, and so on.

A step deal operates on the premise that the writer will be engaged for each step of the process, and also allows for a divorce mechanism should the producer and writer have creative differences. Should they separate (i.e. the writer is fired), the writer keeps the step payments made to date and the producer owns the copyright to the work created thus far.

Hint A good writer's agreement forms the cornerstone of the legal paperwork of your production. Make 100% certain that the script you are buying or developing has the proper paper trail to satisfy the 'chain of title'.

Shopping

This is the fourth way that scripts can be sold, and unfortunately it can ruin a writer's script.

Shopping refers to a practice deplored by screenwriters. It occurs when a producer promises something unrealistic, like a personal contact to Harrison Ford, and manages to get the writer to sign a short option of a few days or weeks while they try to get the star's interest.

They then call every single production company they can think of and pitch the script. Later, when the option has expired, the writer will then find their script on the 'rejected' list of every suitable production company. Sometimes, naïve or poor pitching in a single afternoon can fatally damage a script.

The Writer's Contract

Entertainment attorney Philip Alberstat has provided a full long form writer's agreement on the CD. In order to mitigate your costs, it is advisable to look at this contract and make notes in the margins of any additional comments or clauses you cannot agree to before you go to your legal counsel. Philip has also provided an outline contract for an option deal.

A producer or production conpany needs a contract with a writer that conveys the full copyright of the script to the production company in exchange for a sum of money. Before negotiating with a writer, the producer needs to establish whether or not the contract will be offered under the writers guilds: either the Writers Guild of Great Britain, or the Writers Guild of America. The guilds have an enormous amount of influence with the studios and the large production companies, and have very strict and established guidelines that cover the whole range of writer/producer relationships including the provision for residuals, travel and accomodation expenses and payments for rewrites.

As the writer's contract forms the cornerstone of the eventual copyright of the film, it is essential that you consult and hire an entertainment attorney familiar with writer's rights, and the bargaining chips that you, as producer, have to offer.

In Conversation with Steve Kenis

Steve Kenis is an independent agent and has his own company, Steve Kenis & Co. His clients include Peter O'Toole, Jeanne Moreau, Bruce Beresford and Frederic Raphael. Steve is also a member of both the American and British Motion Picture Academies and PMA (Personal Managers Association) Council.

What is it that you do?

How long have you got? I'm an agent. I represent actors, writers, directors, sometimes producers, in furthering their careers. I would say we are in 'the ham and egg' business – except we have to get both the ham and the eggs! We try to find situations or employment or whatever you want to call it, for our clients. That's kind of basic. In the context of a filmmaker with their own project, my job is to try to help get that financed, move it along, get the picture made. If you are talking about a director who, in addition to having his own projects, is also a gun for hire, it would be to find him a place to shoot his gun.

What do you look for when choosing clients to represent?

Talent. Just talent. At this stage in my own career, I'm looking for more established people. I do have a couple of young, starting out writers, directors – but very few. I'm beyond the stage of taking talented young but unheard of actors and breaking them. I don't do that any more. I will do it rarely with a director and even more rarely with a writer. I would have to be completely knocked out by what s/he's done – and I mean knocked out. I have to be convinced that I can move them. I have to see some of their work and make a judgement. There's not a checklist of specifics that I'm looking for – it's an overall evaluation.

Do you gravitate towards certain kinds of directors?

No. If somebody is good and talented, that's it. Some people are more comfortable working in one genre, be it comedy, melodrama, prefer action. Some people work across two genres, rarely more than two. I don't gravitate towards any particular one. The only area that doesn't interest me that much is horror movies because it's probably the only genre of film that doesn't appeal to me.

Do directors come to you or do you headhunt them?

I used to headhunt them, or they came to me. Now I rely more on re-commendation, referral. Someone will tell me 'Hey I've heard about X, you ought to check them out' – in which case I'll go after the person, find out about them.

Who are your main collaborators?

There are several people I work with regularly; a manager in New York and a management company in LA. In terms of producers, once a pro-ducer gets involved in a filmmaker's project, then I will work with that producer to get it financed – there can be that kind of collaboration, where the two of us are going towards the same goal together.

At what point in a project do you get involved? Can you explain the process of your involvement?

Usually I'm involved at a project's infancy, but each one is individual, it depends on what's involved, who's involved. For example, I saw a TV serial here in Britain and it occurred to me that there was an American movie in that story, so I contacted the producer. It turned out she had the rights for a theatrical feature picture in the material. I got her together with an American producer who appreciated the same thing that I had in it, and we made a deal for her, with him and he moved forward with it then – because he could do things with it that she couldn't do, because she lives here in London, he lives in LA – he brought in a lead actress and set it up at Warner Bros.

I have had other situations where I have worked with a producer here, and if we get something set up over here, we are both moving it forward. We'll be talking to each other all the time, strategising, figuring out who's going to do what. In terms of getting a movie set up, each project is its own role of the dice.

Are you involved in the legal side of things also?

Well, I try not to be. I encourage whoever I'm involved with to have their own lawyer. The TV producer I mentioned earlier has a lawyer here in London, and that lawyer is one of the few people who is also an American lawyer and has worked at one of the major American studios, so he's one of the few people in this town that can look at an American studio agreement and understand it and know all the details and nuances of it. There are few like him; I think people are best off hiring someone in LA, and I encourage them to do that.

I have helped out though. I helped out a young writer-director who had a piece of material and we had an arrangement with some people that fell apart. He couldn't afford a lawyer, but I was able to make sure that the other people who were involved with the project couldn't reach in and grab it. But I don't like to be involved with the legality of things.

Is it very different representing writers than it is directors?

It is different. With writers, if you are talking about an original screenplay and what you are normally doing is trying to find a viable producer who will pay some money for it and has the ability to get it set up. For example, I represented the writers of *Sexy Beast* and I sold that property to Jeremy Thomas. Jeremy got it made.

On the other hand, you might take a piece of material and try to get a director attached and then get that set up, either with a producer or a financier, or distributor.

If you are talking about just a director, presumably who has a piece of material – because a director without a piece of material, is just a director for hire – then if the director is hot and he has got a piece of material then you can go in and get that set up. You are bringing a producer a gift.

What would you say makes a good agent?

Tenacity, taste, knowledge of making a deal, but the most important thing is relationships. Relationships are indispensable in this business – if you can't do relationships, it doesn't matter whether you've got taste and tenacity. If you don't know anybody or people don't respect you, there's nothing you can do. Relationships make an agent. And patience.

What's the difference between a huge company like ICM and a smaller one like your own?

I don't have to answer to a whole level of management – I'm only responsible to my clients, that's the primary advantage. The disadvantage is that you've got to get all the information yourself, which is a pain in the neck and very time consuming. I've done both, and there are advantages and disadvantages to each. Right now, I like doing it this way.

What are the differences between agents here and in the US?

Agents here tend to get more involved with their clients. In America, the expression is an agent 'handles' or 'represents' somebody. Here an agent looks after a client. It's more than semantics: agents here deliver a more personal level of involvement.

In the US they also have personal managers. They are not licensed and they do a lot of the same thing as agents (if they're any good), but they aren't supposed to make deals. Some actors (and some directors and writers as well) have both personal managers and agents. The area of personal management does not exist here except in the music industry. The British don't like paying two commissions, whereas Americans would rather pay the extra money in the hope that they are getting a better shot at success. Also there is a closer level of personal involvement with an agent here in Britain than there is in America – it's not the same, it's not as in depth, but it is an important difference.

Do you think it is easier for a director to approach an agent in the US than it is here?

No. You have got to direct a film that's going to get interest.

The best thing is if you can direct a movie or a short (a feature is obviously best, but that's the toughest) and somebody from one of the distribution companies – whether it's an art house distribution company, one of the classics divisions, or one of the studios or whatever – sees it and gets excited. They will pass the word to a couple of agents – and agents will always get excited if they are hearing that a buyer likes somebody. This is called 'demand pull' (as opposed to having to push yourself). That's the best way of getting an agent. It's the good housekeeping seal of approval!

What are the difficulties you face today in the current economic climate?

I don't relate it to the overall economic climate, I relate it to the state of the motion picture and television business, and if they're making movies, it doesn't matter if they are tearing down all the buildings outside, if they are making movies we'll do OK. The economy can be thriving, but if the number of movies and television shows being made is cut back, we won't do very well. It depends on the market that we have to sell into – if that is strong and vibrant, that's what determines how well we do. Whether that is related to the overall economic climate is something else – that's something you should ask the financiers and distributors.

Is the current climate good then?

It's pretty good – it's been better, but boy oh boy has it been worse – in the late '70s, early '80s and early '90s. *The Crying Game* was a watershed movie – everyone thinks that the watershed was *Four Weddings and a Funeral*, but in my opinion, it wasn't. *Four Weddings* did much better worldwide box office than *Crying Game*, but the watershed was *Crying Game* and then *Four Weddings* consolidated what had already been started. There have been situations like that before; *Chariots of Fire* also started a wave of interest in British pictures.

Following *Four Weddings*, the international motion picture and TV community started looking to Britain again for its movies and more importantly started looking at the talent here. Other subsequent movies built on that success, but then there was, as often happens, a swing the other way, and in the five or seven years following, a lot of movies got made that maybe shouldn't have been made. I think that about two years ago or so, people started waking up and realising that there were British movies that had been made that were sitting on the shelf, without theatrical distribution deals, in the States or even here in the UK, and so things started falling away again.

The various government initiatives – sale and lease back, tax incentives – that's helped to keep the fall from being as precipitous as it has been in the past, when we had over-supply, over-production etc., but still there has been a recession of sorts since that peak. That's probably where we are right now. So it ain't so bad, but it's been better.

The production numbers for this year have been pretty good, so whether it's going to go south or not, I don't know – that's going to depend on the movies that are being made now and how well they do. When a movie comes out and people go see it, that's great, but that's not going to happen to every movie, we all know that – but if it happens to enough movies to keep the pot bubbling, then we'll be fine.

Every once in a while having a 'big British picture' sure helps. I'm all in favour of a *Chariots of Fire*, *Notting Hill*, *Bridget Jones Diary* or a *Billy Elliot*. That's terrific. I mean, thank god Working Title's around. The people over at Working Title have a lot of ability and having a working relationship with Richard Curtis sure helps too. But the other non-Working Title films that have come out and done business in the States, in the UK and other countries of the world are also very important. The more *Sexy Beasts*, *Full Montys* and *Billy Elliots* there are, the better off we all are. Those are the kind of films that keep the British film industry in business.

Why have you chosen to be an agent?
I like it, I like doing what I do, I enjoy it! Why do I enjoy it – I don't know! I just found something that I like doing, so I do it. Being an agent as opposed to selling shoes you mean?

Well surely it must be something to do with a love for film?
Well I've always loved movies, I've loved movies since I was a kid and the process of doing what I do is enjoyable to me. Why? I don't know that's just the way I've popped out of my mother's womb I guess!

Do you like helping a person to achieve their creative potential?
I find show business and the people who populate that business to be a very satisfying arena for me. The people in the business are generally bright, they are generally talented – maybe with some it's artistic talent, maybe with others it's commercial talent. I like it, and I've gotten a great deal of enjoyment out of it, and I see other people who do other things and I wonder if they are happy and satisfied doing it – some are, most aren't, but the people who are in this business all seem to enjoy it.

What's the hardest thing you have to deal with?
Clients who try to rewrite history! People who say that something happened in a different way than it happened. The hardest thing is always dealing with other people's disappointments – nobody likes that, whether it's a director or whatever.

What advice would you give to a filmmaker who is starting out?
Make sure that's what you want to do. Then do every thing you can to be able to direct something, because that's what you are going to be judged on. Whether you do it by going to film school, or conjuring up a short film, whatever, people don't hire people to direct movies that have never done anything before. You have got to be as industrious as possible and persevere and be as tenacious as possible.

The Director

Directing is the most glamorous job in the industry. The most prized is that of writer/director. Writer/directors are considered the most creative people in the film industry, and deservedly so. When contemplating a career as a writer/director, remember that the industry considers writing an excellent screenplay to be extremely difficult and rare. The industry also considers the job of directing a film well to be very difficult. As a writer/director, you are effectively saying to the industry that you are taking on not one of the most difficult jobs in the film industry, but two. There is nothing wrong, or overly ambitious about striving to break in as a 'hyphenate'. If you feel that you have the energy and talent for both, then go for it. The work habits and career paths of writer/directors are very different, however. A writer/director will be able to complete a single project every thirty to forty months. A director can easily direct a film per year, and a writer can complete a script in three or four months.

Everyone wants to direct. It is easily the most interesting job in the film industry, and the most sought after. Create a unique look in your short or feature and the industry will sit up and take notice.

The film industry is noted for glamour. Directing is the most glamorous job in the industry, and easily the job for which there is the most competition. Most people cannot name the writer or producer of a commercially successful film. But most can name the director of *The Blair Witch Project*, *El Mariachi* or *Reservoir Dogs*.

When a director is hired, s/he is charged with the overall responsibility of the picture. The director has to take full responsibility and make the final decision on the visual and audible details of the film. The director also has to coordinate all of the elements of the script, the sets, the lighting, the make-up, the wardrobe and the actors and meld them into a whole. Taking charge of a hundred-strong army of technicians and creatives with their accompanying technologies is a daunting challenge. To succeed at a job that is full of so many variables is amazing.

Hint The director's job is to keep everyone working together and on target, hurtling towards the final destination determined by their vision.

It is no surprise that some directors embrace the French 'auteur' theory that claims the film is the creative brainchild of the director, regardless of the creative input of the actors or the rest of the creative team (including the writer!).

Other directors such as Stephen Frears (*My Beautiful Laundrette*, *Dirty Pretty Things*) refuse to label themselves as artists or auteurs because of the contribution of the writer. These directors consider themselves mere craftsmen.

Hiring a Director

While some movies are produced and directed by the same person, it is most common for a producer to hire a director. A good producer is one who understands the creative vision of the director.

For a producer, choosing the right director is probably the single most important creative and business decision that they will make during the production of their film. The right director will be the creative partner for the producer, and also be able to understand the main elements of the financial Everest that the producer will have to climb. The relationship between the director and producer is also an important ingredient that can determine the outcome of the project. The wrong producer/director relationship will create a feeling of distrust which will permeate the entire set.

The Director's Contract

Entertainment attorney Philip Alberstat has provided a full long form director's agreement on the CD. In order to mitigate your costs, it is advisable to look at this contract and make notes in the margins of any additional comments or clauses you cannot agree to before you go to your legal counsel.

A director's contract needs to clearly define the following points: that the copyright of the film remains with the production company, the terms of hire (dates of employment, and reimbursement) and a means for terminating the contract should either of the parties fail to deliver their services as stated. It is essential that this contract is written and signed by all parties before commencement of the production.

Four Responsibilities of the Director

1 Directing the screenplay

A director's first task is to read and reread the screenplay and look for the visual details that will help to tell the story. Then, a director must decide what visual details need to be added in order to enhance the story. The director often rewrites the script to incorporate these ideas into a new draft, which the producer can use for funding. Producer Jeremy Thomas will say to potential investors that David Cronenberg has looked at the original script and has now added his comments. This is another way that producers add pedigree to the script. If you are a director but are not at that level yet, be prepared to fight hard for any changes you want to make to the script.

2 Directing the actors

Directing for the screen is different from directing for the stage. In stage directing, you work with actors to get them to peak on the first day of the run. In screen acting, you want a performer to stay the same as they were during the audition process. One of the screen director's many tasks is to find out what the cast can and cannot do; and what they will or will not do. This is done during the audition process.

Running an audition

Many British acting performances, either on stage or on screen have been ruined by pale imitations of American accents. Why the fad of American accents? Are there no American actors living in Europe? I am certain no British cinemagoer would accept an American actor poorly imitating Hugh Grant's or Kate Winslet's accent.

Actors will be nervous at an audition, and the director must make them feel comfortable. Perhaps an assistant will welcome the actors in an ante room and take their head shots and costume measurements.

Most auditions consist of a cold reading of two or three pages. The director might read one part, the actor the other. Sometimes you will hire an actor to read a part with the one you are auditioning – especially if you have already chosen an actor for a role and want to see how they compare to another face.

To see what an actor can or cannot do is fairly straightforward: either she can drag the two hundred pound gorilla through the burning embers or she can't. Similarly accents, if required for the part, are either believable or not. If the actor cannot do what is required for the part, then they are not right. If they are right for the part, then a good director will find out what they will or won't do, and find out before any contracts are offered. This is all done during the audition process.

However well or poorly an actor reads the part, compliment them on their reading, remembering that they are nervous, and ask them to do it again, but give them a direction. Have them read standing up, shouting, whispering, walking around – whatever, as long as it is different.

Actors go to acting classes and acting school. They read deep books on the art and craft of acting, and through their training form opinions on how a certain emotion should be acted. If you are not in agreement with this, then you cannot work with that particular individual. And if they argue or challenge your direction in the audition process, you will not be able to direct them during the rigours of the shoot.

It is useful to videotape the auditions as a point of reference. Most actors are happy for you to do this, but it is polite to ask them first.

The evening of the audition is the polite time to call and tell actors whether they have been successful or not. Actors are all too accustomed to rejection, and understand, rationally at least, that they do not fit the part. They will usually tell you that they enjoyed the audition and look forward to working with you on a future project. A personal call from the director demonstrates your compassion for them. If you are unwilling to call, then get an assistant to call.

Not calling an actor about a failed audition is rude; however, most film companies don't extend this simple courtesy to the actors who have given up their time for them.

On the shoot
Actors get over-used and worn out. There is a knack to knowing which actor is good on the first take, which on the third. Use the slower actor for camera tests and preliminary technical rehearsals.

3 Directing the camera

Don't move on until the master shot is perfect. In a worst-case scenario, you may have to rely on the master shot if all else fails. After the shot, the director will ask the camera and sound persons whether or not they are happy. The sound person will always say that they picked up the noise of a helicopter or something, and you will have to decide whether or not to do another take.

Deciding where the camera is placed before each shot is the prerogative of the director. Sometimes a director will consult with the director of photography, sometimes not. Once the position has been chosen and agreed, the director places the actors and blocks the scene while the camera and lights are being rigged.

The DoP watches this process and decides which lens to use. By showing the director a lens, the DoP can then demonstrate the viability of the shot. Often the DoP will suggest an alternative camera position, which gives the director extra time to rehearse the actors while the camera is being moved. Actors will attend the shoot knowing their lines.

Basic Shots
The film industry has terms for the different ways that a person is framed. This makes it easy for film professionals to communicate the type of shot that is expected.

i Master shot
This shot takes in all of the dialogue and any new visual conceived by the director. If the camera is moving at the same time, this is called a fluid master shot.

ii Medium shot (MS)

A shot that is framed from the waist up.

iii Close-up (CU)

A shot of just the face or head.

iv Extreme close-up (ECU)

A shot of just the mouth, or the eyes.

v Cat in the window

The cat in the window shot was named after the shots of the family pet turning their heads during 1950s American sitcoms. This shot gave the editor something to cut to when their was insufficient coverage to cut a scene. Hence, cut to the cat in the window.

vi Reaction shots

Shots of other actors reacting to the dialogue or action off camera.

Hint Allow Max Headroom. Don't cut through the top of the head or through major joints like elbows or knees. Leave space at the top of the head except where you are in an ECU.

---

4 Directing the budget

To demonstrate the challenge of directing a low budget feature film, let us assume that you have a ninety-page script and a 6:1 shooting ratio, and a one week or nine day shoot. That means that we need to shoot ten pages per day. It also means that we can ship no more than 1/9th of the film stock to the lab each day, or 5400 feet of film stock per day.

At the end of the each day, you want to hear the script supervisor say that you shot ten pages and the camera assistant say you have shipped 5400 feet to the lab. That means you are on time and on budget.

If the script supervisor says you have shot nine pages and the camera assistant says you have shipped 5400 feet, you are still on budget, but behind schedule.

If the script supervisor says you have shot ten pages and you find out you have shipped 6000 feet to the lab, then you are on schedule and over budget.

It you shoot just nine pages, and ship 6000 feet, it would seem that you are close to schedule and budget, as you are only over by ten per cent. However, this is a fiasco, and if at the end of each day this happens, it will most likely mean that you will run out of film stock near the end of day seven.

When I worked as a scenic artist, we dreaded day three of the shoot, as it was usually the day that the director was fired. Actually, directors are never fired, they leave due to creative differences. And that usually means that they did not understand how to direct the budget.

On the third day of the shoot, a suit would come to the set. People in

Notice that a 6:1 ratio does not mean that the actors get to say their lines six times each; it means that you have just six minutes in order to get the shots you need to get the editor enough material to work with in post-production.

Remember that we are using the assumption that one page = one minute = 90 feet of 35mm film.

the industry dress according to their jobs. Everyone on set dresses creative-sporting-casual as if to suggest when they woke up in the morning they dressed not knowing if they were going to play polo or go to the set. Anyone in the film industry who deals with money dresses in a suit.

And when the suits came to the set, we feared negative suit burn; referring to the damage the suits would do to the negative.

As soon as the suit would find out how many pages they were behind, they would rip out the next two, three or four pages from the shooting schedule, and presto! We would be back on schedule.

If you find out you are behind budget on a short, low budget shoot, you must make some decisions immediately. It doesn't really matter which decision you make, just make one of them.

The options open to you are:

It is no good talking to the director and cameraperson about shooting ratios and schedules, because whatever you say they will just agree with you, and continue on their way. In the low budget world, your budget is your film stock.

1. Abandon the shoot, return all the equipment and film stock, suffer the loss of a few thousand, and regroup and come back in a few months' time when you are better prepared.

2. Offer the director and cameraperson a 2:1 shooting ratio until they have caught up.

3. Find some more money and buy some more film stock.

4 Fire the director and direct the picture yourself. At least you will understand the importance of shooting ratio.

Shooting a Page

Let us suppose that we are shooting a page of a script.

On this page of script, a wannabe filmmaker sneaks into a bookshop and finds a how-to book on the shelf. A clerk catches him and says that he is allowed a single minute to look at the book. The filmmaker is desperately flipping through it because he is about to meet a film investor, and they have been warned that the first question this particular investor always asks is: 'What is your shooting ratio?'. And this filmmaker has never bothered to find out. A bookstore clerk rounds the corner and sees out hero frantically flipping through the book, and warns the filmmaker that he must pay for the book if he wants to look at it. Our hero replies that he has no money, and pleads with the clerk to let him continue. The clerk agrees, but the fire alarm goes off.

At a 6:1 shooting ratio on 35mm we would have 540 feet of film to shoot this page.

Directing the script

Which visual element, not in the script, if added, will enhance the script? What if we add a ticking clock? After all, the script says: 'You have one minute to look at the book'. Perhaps as a director, you would like to cut to the reader, cut to the clerk, cut to the reader's eyes, cut to the ticking clock, cut to the clerk's eyes, and so on in order to add drama and tension to the scene. For that you need a big ticking clock with a large second hand. At this point you summon the art director and hope there are still a few pennies in the production budget that will allow for a large clock with the right 'look'.

Directing the camera
Again you have to select the shots: master, medium and close-up. You might want to storyboard the scene, or simply list a series of shots and angles, called a shot list.

Directing the budget
We have 540 feet to shoot this scene. All the professionals say: capture the master shot, and then move in for coverage. The master shot is when you place the camera in a position that is visually interesting and which captures all the dialogue, and the extra visual element – in this case – the ticking clock. Call action, and after one minute the scene is filmed. We have now used 90 feet of film stock leaving 450 feet.

Hint If you have to redo the master shot, do it from another angle, which means you might be able to use some of the usable segments from the first take, intercut with the second take.

Then we need to do the medium shot. We need some of the clerk saying his lines, some of the filmmaker saying his lines, and some of each actor reacting to the other's lines. I could easily argue that two minutes would be enough to get these shots, using a total of 180 feet. This leaves a balance of 270 feet, or three minutes.

Close-ups
Before we start doing close-ups, what about the clock? Shouldn't we take some shots of that, because we will need it to cross-cut with the actors during the edit. And how much should we take? The first and the last ten seconds? What about cueing and starting and stopping the camera. It might just be easier to film the entire clock for sixty seconds and reduce the risk.

Which leaves 180 feet. So let's get back to the close-ups. You will probably be moving the camera really tight on the actors' heads. It is considered OK to gently touch the actors' shoulders and head to show them where the frame is. Remember that the depth of field is now getting very shallow, and if their heads move towards the camera, or away, they will fall out of focus. You will also find that when the face is close, and with focus so critical, it is very easy to ruin take after take due to the technical issues of focus and framing.

Before you know it, the director is asking for some more film stock, is pleading with you to let them have another couple of takes – pushing you to 7:1 or 8:1.

How do you answer a director in this situation? Remember that in the film business they never actually use the word 'no'.

You answer by saying: 'Thank you for sharing that with me. We will come back to this shot at the end of the day if we have the time'. And maybe you will. Most likely you won't.

Qualities of Successful Directors

1 Great visualisation
Successful directors absorb the script with such intensity that they are able to visualise the entire film in great detail – down to the texture of the fabric on the supporting actors' costume and the nuances of an actor's speech.

2 Great eye for detail
A great director is notoriously difficult to please. They will not approve any prop, set, costume or camera movement unless it is absolutely perfect – or as perfect as it can be in the time permitted for the shot.

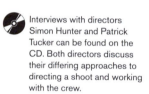
Interviews with directors Simon Hunter and Patrick Tucker can be found on the CD. Both directors discuss their differing approaches to directing a shoot and working with the crew.

3 Great organisational skills
Orson Welles said: 'A poet needs a pen, a painter needs a brush, but a filmmaker needs an army'. The director is the general, and has to keep everyone in the army focused all the time.

4 Great communicator
Great directors are able to communicate their vision to each of the cast and crew on the set, and to the entire post-production and marketing team. A director may not win each creative battle, but is wise enough to know which battles are worth pursuing.

5 Very pragmatic
There are two schools of thought as to how a director should act. One is that of total dictator, where no argument or contradiction is possible or allowed. Any dissent means an instant pink slip from the first assistant director. The other is that each decision should be reached with the consensus of the other creative people on the team: DoP, production designer, editor, and actors.

Either extreme has its merits and pitfalls. The truth is, that a great director, be s/he leaning towards ruthlessness or towards compromise, knows what has to be done in order to get the film completed.

6 Talent
In the low budget realm, as a director you are essentially turning a stage play into cinema. Remember that you what you are most definitely not doing is filming a stage play. Films of stage plays are boring. A director transforms a stage play into cinema.

Consider one of the most dramatic debut features, *Reservoir Dogs*. Would that not make an excellent stage play?

If a director has talent, if a director has the eye and ability to turn a stage play into cinema, Hollywood spots this and calls it talent. They then offer sinful amounts of money, and I think directors deserve this monstrous payout.

Nine Routes to Becoming a Director

There are nine routes to consider when launching your career as a director. Before you decide which route to take, research the careers of directors you admire and see if you can see which route they followed.

Remember, that there is no such thing as the route – only a route that is good for you, one that allows you to maximise you abilities and talent.

1 Studio or guild route

After securing the necessary minimum days of on-the-job training, join the Director's Guild with a signatory production company and work your way up the ladder. Some companies allow you to shadow a director, which gives you valuable training.

2 The independent route

Learn how to identify or create a low budget, ninety-page script which you feel has something controversial to say. Scrape together some money and execute a 4:1 or 6:1 ratio shoot with high production values. Hire a sales agent and sell the film at AFM, Cannes, MIFED or Raindance, and make a profit for your investors. Repeat this process until you are discovered, or are considered a worthy risk for investors.

See Woody Allen, Steven Soderbergh or Quentin Tarantino.

3 Screenplay option route

Write or purchase a script/story and sell it, releasing the screen rights only when you are hired as director. This technique is called holding your script hostage.

This happened with *Return from Alcatraz*.

4 Student or festival route

Make a short film or ultra low budget feature and enter festivals, demonstrating your talent, gaining exposure to future clients and agents on the lookout for emerging talent.

Hire a publicist to promote yourself, even if it is at the expense of your film. You are aiming to achieve notoriety or celebrity status.

See *Buffalo 66*, *Trees Lounge*, *The Blair Witch Project*.

5 Agency packaging route

After associating with celebrity actors or writers from a common agency, convince the agency to represent you as part of a package that they sell directly to production companies with you attached as director. The agency will usually attach name stars to your project as well.

See *Cop Land*.

6 Establish yourself in commercials

By offering to direct test commercials or pop promos for unknown bands, demonstrate your talent and original ideas, and convince a producer to hire you to direct. This is what Ridley Scott and Tony Kaye did.

7 Become a master of the short form

Write and/or direct short films which demonstrate your talent. Enter festivals and competitions. When you have gained confidence, select several of your short films and approach either a production company (number one above) or talent (number five above) and convince them to let you direct a feature. This was the tactic used by Shane Meadows.

8 Start as an assistant editor

This has been the classic route to directing used by many directors from the '40s through to the '70s. Offer your services for free as an assistant editor: log shots and sync sound until you are promoted to editor. When you have cut several films and impressed with your knowledge of shots, get hired to direct a feature. David Lean, Francis Ford Coppola, Martin Scorsese all went by this route.

9 Become a successful stage director

Most stage directors do not realise how well equipped they are to direct film. Blocking, timing, storytelling and working with actors are all essential directing skills that many film directors lack. Why not start a theatre group with a few close friends (like Steppenwolf in Chicago, or Second City in Toronto) and build a reputation for exciting stage shows. Invite reviewers and agents, and wait to be discovered by a producer, or turn a stage show into a movie yourself. This is what Sam Mendes, Stephen Daldry and Andrew Shea all did.

In Conversation with Michael Radford

What do you look for in an actor that you're trying to cast?

Filmmaker Michael Radford is best known for directing the internationally praised and Oscar-nominated *Il Postino* (1994). After a four year break he bounced back with *B. Monkey* (1998), a romantic crime drama starring Asia Argento, Jared Harris and Rupert Everett, which he followed up in 2000 with *Dancing at the Blue Iguana*, starring Daryl Hannah.

First they have to be able to act. It's very difficult to tell from an audition because some actors do good auditions and some do not. So you either have to take it on trust that they can act or you have to agree that if they can't you're going to have to teach them and therefore you'll have to have the time to do it. Some actors you take on knowing that they can't act and then you have to accept that those people have something that you need but don't have a great range. Look, for instance, the girl that played in *Il Postino*, Maria Grazia Cucinotta, she was really not an actress, as such. She called herself an actress but she hadn't done any notable acting. You check her out and her smile lights up the screen and you use that very sparingly through the film at the right moment. When you're directing films you have so many other tools at your disposal that you don't actually have to get the perfect performance out of them – you can fiddle with it later on.

It really depends what kind of role it is as well. Every actor is different. There are actors who have incredible technique like Josh Ackland or Tom Wilkinson. You recognise them when you see them. You know that they have such skill at their disposal that there is very little you have to teach them or ask them to do. They understand the process of acting.

Then there are people who are movie actors who have a wonderful look about them and have loads of experience and they're the kind of people you get to play to their strengths, which is often the fact that they can, by some kind of wonderful mystery, give insight into an alternative life and that, in essence, is the most important part of cinema. When you look into an actor's eyes and you actually see something more going on even when they're not acting. That's what you look for.

I try to cast actors who 'look the part', because you have to start somewhere but if I find someone I like I tend to readjust the role to fit them.

Do you prefer working with actors that have experience or not?
I like working with all actors. I was asked to do a course on acting for thirteen directors. I decided to teach the directors how to act in five days so that they understood what it's like to be an actor and it's amazing what we achieved. It depends how much time you have. If you have no time for rehearsal then you need professional actors because newcomers don't know how to approach the whole process. If you've got the time, you can work through the process of acting with newcomers.

Take *City of God* as an example, which is done with kids, adults, and people from the favelas and shantytowns of Rio de Janeiro. The director went there for six months, set up an acting school and taught everybody how to act. Once he had taught them the process, it's a fantastic opportunity. People who are real civilians and not actors bring a kind of freshness to it that is very difficult to achieve when you have professional actors and they don't have the range you need.

On my last picture, *Dancing at the Blue Iguana*, I had about five months of rehearsal, and when you have professional actors and so much time for improvisational rehearsal you get to a far more profound level than you will ever get when you just go in and do the text. It depends on what kind of film is being made.

I'm about to make a film of *The Merchant of Venice*. I was thinking of going to a small Iranian village and doing it there. That would entail a considerable amount of very rewarding work. That's one kind of movie. Actually I'm doing it with Al Pacino as Shylock, which is another kind of movie. I'll get the chance to work with a great actor and to explore something in a very classical but profound way. Some people don't like to work with big movie stars – it can be a pain in the ass if there is a lot of ego flying around. As the director you want to feel as if you're in charge and if you feel there is some actor in charge then it's tough.

So does it bother you if an actor comes up to you and tells you how they think a scene should be done?
It bothers me if they tell me how they think a scene should be shot. I think actors should know their craft and if they feel a scene should be

done in a particular way they should articulate that. However, one reason that you have a director is because an actor is not always the best judge of the whole. He's following his path and his particular character and, just like we all in our lives try to make ourselves the most important person in the universe, similarly the actor takes his character and makes him the most important person in his universe – in the movie. But that may not be what the movie requires and you have to be able to say no.

I remember when I was making a film called *White Mischief*, I made the mistake of saying to the actors 'Look the dialogue is not necessarily Shakespeare so if any of you feel that it needs altering then go ahead'. The next day, every single one of them had written a new scene for themselves. One of the girls brought me her work and I asked 'Why have you written this extra scene?' I knew she wanted an extra scene but what she said to me was 'Well my character feels this and feels that. This is a scene in which she expresses it, and I don't think that there's one in the screenplay.' I said 'How do you know she feels those things?' She said 'Well, from reading the screenplay.' I said 'Exactly'.

What do you do if an actor is having a difficult time getting through a scene?

You have to look very carefully at what you've done. They first thing that crosses through your mind is whether you've hired the right person. Then you'd have to start all over again. That's happened to me on numerous occasions. When it's a small role I tend to take the quickest route and bring in a new actor. With the bigger roles obviously that's difficult but it has happened to me when I seriously consider, after a week of shooting, restarting the film with a new actor.

If it's a particular scene you have to look at why. You have to ask 'Is it because the circumstances are not right?' 'Is it because we are approaching this scene wrongly?' 'Is it because the actor doesn't understand the scene?' If all those things were true then it's down to me. If an actor is having trouble with the scene not because he can't act but because he's incapable of doing what you asked him to do, then you're in deep shit. But if the actor is sincerely trying to get somewhere then you have to figure out what you have to do to make it work.

I once had a conversation with Denzel Washington about this and we called it the tingle. You get a tingle when you feel the scene come alive. What I try to do is look at all the things in the scene that can make the scene come alive for the actors. Just the choreography of the scene if necessary. But you have to remember not to obsess about things; usually scenes go a bit awry at the beginning of the shoot, before the actors get totally into their characters. You also have to make sure you're not obsessing too much. You don't want to become too much of a perfectionist. Remember that you can cut around the problems in the scene. A director has to be aware of losing perspective himself – you could be looking at this thing and thinking the actor isn't getting it but actually they got it ten takes before and you just didn't recognise it. That's what usually happens. Things are never quite as bad as you thought and if they are you can always loop it in the studio.

I was told that one of things about being a good director is to being able to act yourself. Do you think that's true?

I think you have to know what to feels like to be an actor. One of the ways to do that is to attend a workshop where you actually have to be one. When you play a character and have it judged, you instantly understand what it feels like. You understand how exposed an actor is. I think the secret to all directing is to strip away all the layers of self-consciousness. Everybody walks onto a film set aware that there are 150 people standing about ready to judge you right at that moment – never mind the public. No one is impervious to that. So, what you have to do is just get them feeling really confident about who and what they are. I think you can only do that if you recognise that actors are not like cameras and all the other technical stuff you have in the movies – they're actually living and breathing beings. Often the battles that take place between actors and directors are about the actor fighting to be allowed to act in the face of a director who is not interested in what a performance can bring to their vision. The director needs to prevent the actor from imagining that everything relies on him and helping them to trust all the things that don't rely on him.

I read about a director who said that actors are the most important part of the movie because an audience can forgive any technical mistakes but if the actor isn't on point with his performance then...

I would go further than that and say the audience will forgive even bad acting if they're in love with the story. I mean, look at the Harry Potter movies – nobody gives a shit what the acting is like – it is terrible, universally terrible – but nobody gives a damn because everybody knows the story and everybody wants to go and see it.

I think great acting is one of those things that you don't miss if it's good enough, if it's serviceable, but when it's great, you really do notice it. One thing I don't like is when you get the sense that the actor has one eye on an Oscar™ nomination and they're giving an Oscar™-style performance. Which is why I think a lot of people like to watch non-Hollywood movies – they can be very self-regarding. You don't get that kind of acting where the performers have one eye on themselves all the time anywhere other than Hollywood.

What are some of the techniques you use to put actors at ease?

My methods have changed over the years. You have to be confident with yourself. You have to look like you know what you're doing first of all – that's the most important thing. The way you talk to actors is important – you need a confident tone of voice. You must look like you know what you're doing even though you don't sometimes. If actors can trust you, can trust that you actually understand what they are trying to get at and where they're coming from and all the rest of it, then that's immensely useful. You have to be endlessly patient. There is no point in exploding and making the set into a miserable place.

There really is no point in yelling at actors. I think there are some people who think that gets the best results. I know there are some people who think that the more miserable a film set is the more likely you are to get good results, but I don't believe that. I believe that if people are happy and content they work well. We all get well paid in this business. You want people to put in the maximum. I won't tolerate anybody who doesn't hit that level. The other way you put people at their ease is by giving the actor a feeling of real importance on the set. Often the technicians will take over. They will barge in and do the lighting as though the actors can just come on and get on with it. What I make sure is that the actors are not interfered with. During rehearsal I send everybody out. I don't have everybody standing around watching because it doesn't allow you to work and actually direct the actors. I demand that they have all their stuff ready and they don't come in with all their stuff breaking the actors' concentration. Often the technicians won't be aware of that, but on my sets, they bloody well will be, because I think it's really important that the actors are given the space in which to work. It's not all about the lighting and camera work. The other thing is that if you do have a bit of rehearsal time it makes everybody feel little bit better about things.

What was the most important thing you think you had to learn to become a director?
Choreography. You have to learn to choreograph scenes. The more films you do the better you get at it.

In Conversation with Bernard Rose

What do you look for in an actor?

English director Bernard Rose started out as a music video director, completing his first feature film *Paperhouse* in 1988. He directed the cult classic *Ivan's XTC* in 2000.

I think the first mistake people make – and perhaps this happens in England more than any where else – is the idea that the actor has received some special information or some kind of training that is somehow going to make a difference when you're actually doing a movie and although obviously actors need to be trained to do theatre, they are just people. There isn't some kind of great and mystical difference between someone who is an actor and someone who is just an interesting person. So really what I'm looking for is someone who is an interesting person and who can hold your attention and if they don't hold your attention in real life then they're never going to do it on the screen. And that can be for a whole number of reasons and depends on what you want to use them for. The whole thing isn't mystical or mysterious really it's just you want to get X so you need Y.

So does it matter to you if the actor is experienced or not?
It depends on what you're doing with them. If you need somebody to do like a Shakespeare or some great monologue, you're better off not just picking someone off the street, but if you want someone to look like someone off the street then they are probably better at it than an actor who has been around. So it just depends on what you want to do. I

think each situation is different. There are times when an experienced actor will give you ten times more than a non-actor, but conversely there are times when an experienced actor will not be the right choice.

So, how important is rehearsal?

I think, again, it depends on what you're doing. If it's something that needs rehearsal – like a bomb sequence – then you'd better rehearse it. If it's a stunt or something dangerous or something that requires physical precision then I think that rehearsal is absolutely essential but for everything else it's better not to rehearse at all. I don't even like to block action. I just like to say, 'I'll follow you, you do what you want'.

Does it bother you if an actor comes to you and tells you how they think a scene should be done?

Immensely it bothers me. I would say to them 'I'm not interested in what you've got to say. Just show me and I'll shoot it. If it's any good we'll use it, if not we'll do it again. But let's see it in action and let's see if it works'. From that point of view I always encourage actors to come to work in full make-up and costume because one of the things that I think is really bizarre about filmmaking is that unlike theatre, ballet, opera, clowning or all the traditional forms of dramatic art where putting on the face and putting on the make-up is an essential part of an actor's preparation, film actors don't do their own make-up. If they can't control how they look what are they really doing? I think that they have to make themselves up like they would in the theatre. The process of making themselves up and choosing their clothes and deciding how they're going to look – that becomes their real rehearsal, that's their real pre-paration. They're really making all the key decisions about how they're going to play the part and without it being a rather boring and meaning-less and dry discussion. That's physical and real.

What do you do when you have an actor who is having a difficult time getting through a scene?

Either you stop and try something different or a different approach to the scene or a different version of the scene or you fire the actor. One of a few things has gone wrong if an actor is not giving a very good per-formance; reshoot the scene with somebody else if the actor is bad, redo the scene if the scene is bad, or sometimes it could be the loca-tion that's bad or sometimes it can be something really stupid like the chairs are in the wrong place. I don't block people, but the way you arrange the furniture in the room is essentially telling the actors where to sit. But if someone is having a difficult time the worst thing you can do is ask them to repeat it in the same set-up because all you'll do is make them more aware of their own failure. You have to change some-thing so that it's different; it could be something very simple but if you don't change something physical about either the set, the lines or the lighting or do it on a different day or change the actor then doing it over and over will grind everyone down and they will get very unhappy and not work to their maximum ability.

A lot of times in movies you get scenes of the director jumping up and down, screaming at the actors. That's not true is it?

No, not unless they want to get fired. People do get frayed when they're working on a film but if that was your MO for doing a whole picture, then unless you were paying for it, people wouldn't put up with it. It doesn't mean that you don't sometimes have to be very definite and keep things moving on to get what you want.

One of the things that I like about shooting with DV is the speed that you can work at. I think one of the greatest enemies or problems of any set is when the cameraman takes too long to turn the camera around and to change the lighting and everybody's energy goes.

What was the most important thing you had to learn?

How to use a camera. I don't want to insult the whole profession of directors of photography, but the DoP is basically a filmmaker who decided to stand up and commit to content; but they're just going to be hired for their filmmaking ability. Essentially a director who doesn't know anything about a camera is somebody who is placing their entire film in the hands of the DoP so your film's success depends entirely on the guy you just hired. That is an incredibly dangerous situation to put yourself in because you're not in control of your set. He might say he needs another half an hour to shoot the scene and you don't know if he's lying or if he just wants to get overtime for his buddies. You're really up shit creek without a paddle. The most important thing, now that the market has changed, is to be able to use the camera and do it yourself so that you're not relying on anyone else. I don't think in the future that the jobs will be separated in that way any more. I think that the person directing the picture will be the person who shoots it and that will be how it works. There won't be that kind of separation of specialisms any more. I think that is really a thing of the old technology.

Do you think that a lot of young directors seek the glamour?

I think there are a lot of people who get into the movie business because they want money or glamour but it is a terrible business to earn money in. That's not a good idea and it's not really all that glamorous. That's why I'd say, that if you want to be a director, you should grab a MiniDV and shoot as much as you can and realise that that is the same as making a film. That is making a film. The idea that someone is a better director because they sit in a chair watching a monitor while everybody else runs around and does the work for them – that's not directing. That's being strapped in a front of a train which might be okay but you don't know who is driving the train or whether they're going to slam you into a brick wall. There are some people whose talent as director is just being the head of the crew and doing a job and that's legitimate. There's lots of filmmaking that is essentially just that but if you want to actually make films that are different or that have something to say, that have more substance, then you're going to have to do it yourself and that might very often mean doing things that are completely not glamorous and poorly paid too.

Actors

In the realm of low budget film production, actors are the most exploited group. This is almost certainly because there is an oversupply of actors trying to break into the industry. Often, in micro and no-budget film productions, the actors are referred to as the moveable props. This is partly because they have little or no rehearsal time. They are moved around the set like pieces of furniture.

How Actors Break In

Stage

Many British screen actors started out in theatre.

Some actors train for theatre and perform a succession of roles in increasingly high profile productions until critics, audiences and film producers notice them. If a producer or casting agent spots them in a stage production, and think they might suit a part, they will contact the actor through their agent and arrange for a screen test. Often an actor trained for the stage will not know the different techniques required for a camera. Sometimes an actor will look good on stage, but will not be photogenic and therefore be unsuitable for the screen. Other actors work equally well on stage and screen.

Once the actor is discovered in theatre, they then become a movie actor. Rachel Weisz is an example of a stage actor who has become a screen actor.

Television

Actors dreaming to become movie stars will typically move to LA and get a job as a waiter, and then try to hunt down work in television. Television work may not be as glamorous as movie work, but it is much more abundant and, by restaurant standards, extremely well paid.

Fortunate actors will get the odd commercial to supplement their income until they get the golden call from their agent that they have an audition for a test pilot TV show. If they succeed in getting the part, they will get Screen Actors Guild minimum payments for the show. The test-pilot producer has probably received funding from a TV network to produce the show, and everyone concerned with the test-pilot wants the show to be re-commissioned thereby guaranteeing more work. The assumption is, that if a test works, the networks will want to use the actors in the test.

A very small percentage of tests actually get aired, and an even smaller percentage of the ones that are aired get commissioned. The producer will probably get a commission for a half season (thirteen shows). If that tops the ratings chart, then they might get a commission for a full season (twenty-six shows). Up until this point the actors are probably still receiving SAG minimums. But at the twenty to thirty episode level, actors' salaries start to balloon. At this point they might go to ten or twenty thousand dollars per episode. As the total episode count nears a hundred, the show is considered a huge American success, and the producer can now start to sell the show to other countries. As their original commission and budget was for the USA only, any foreign sale goes directly to the producer's bottom line. Actors then have the leverage to increase their payments to huge amounts, such as the reported $600,000 per episode the *Seinfeld* stars were getting.

But the actor is still a TV star, and although they are now well established on television they are still unable to get work as a movie actor. And regardless of the amounts of money they are making in television, many TV actors have career ambitions of working in movies because of the glamour.

TV stars vs movie stars

No matter how well known and successful a television star is, they cannot get starring roles in movies because audiences are used to seeing them at home on television where they can watch them for free. A movie star is an actor you can only see in the cinema, and whom you are willing to leave your home, go to the movie theatre and pay money to see.

Certain actors cross from television to film. Although it took George Clooney several years, he did eventually make the switch to being a big movie star. Helen Hunt, Will Smith, Bruce Willis, Demi Moore and Johnny Depp are other examples.

Certain actors attempt to cross from television to movies and fail. David Duchovny is one example of a television star who has had tens of millions of dollars spent on advertising him as a movie star, and who failed to win audience recognition. Michael J Fox is an example of an actor who went successfully from television to movies and then returned to television.

How to Treat Actors

Actors and producers are all aware that every low-budget feature has the potential to explode and propel the participants into glory. It is precisely this expectation that producers exploit.

Producers must be aware that creative people involved in the production, including directors, writers, composers, camerapeople and actors automatically own the copyright to their performances or creations. But the producer must own the copyright 100% if the film is to be sold. Accordingly, actors must enter into a legally binding agreement with the producer that gives the producers 100% of the copyright to their performance, even if they are not being paid.

The Actor's Contract

Contracts exist to protect both parties – the actors and the producers – in an agreement. A good contract lays out the ground rules so each party knows what is expected of them and is protected in case the other party fails to deliver.

Hint Always use a written contract with actors, no matter how informal the shoot is. This will save misunderstandings and disagreements later.

Basic conditions

Overleaf is an example of a basic actor's contract. Terms included are:

1. Pay for the travel and food expenses of an actor.

2. Provide public liability insurance to cover cast and crew for any accidents during the shoot.

3. Provide the actor with a copy of the finished film after post-production is complete.

Rights and payment

You must obtain the rights to distribute and exhibit the film, even if you want to put it on your website for free. As a producer, you try and get actors to agree to assign all rights in a short or no-budget feature film to you for nothing, or next to nothing when you sign the contract. Actors usually are aware that there can be little or no revenue from films like this, and are generally willing to sign agreements like this if they feel that their performance will get exposure.

Whenever you are forced to be specific about distribution rights, you may want to include the specific rights you want the actor to assign to you as 'cinema, television, home video, DVD, Internet and film festivals'.

Hint It is a reasonable request that the producer is making here. Without this film, and unless you are allowed to get it as much exposure as possible, an actor may not get the chance to progress their career.

Deferred payment contracts

Sometimes you will need the services of an actor who will only agree to assign their rights in the film if you agree to a deferred payment. In this scenario, you negotiate additional payments which become payable if and when the film achieves a certain level of sales.

Equity

Equity is the British actors' union, which lobbies for actors' rights and have made agreements on minimum actors' payments with other organisations. Thatcher's reign in the UK reduced the power of the trade unions, including that of Equity. Presently, not every actor is a member of Equity, nor do actors need Equity cards to work on film and television. Equity does not blacklist members or companies who pay below Equity rates. Equity have negotiated agreements with the organisations behind the film and TV industry to ensure a minimum wage for their

BASIC ACTOR'S CONTRACT

Actor's Name   Producer / Production Company
Actor's or Agent's Address   Production Company Address

Date [dd/mm/yyyy]

Dear [Actor],

This letter confirms our agreement that you will take the part of [character name] in the film [title of the film] (henceforth referred to as the 'Film'). I am letting you know in advance that the title of the film may change, but if it does, I will let you know by sending a letter to this address, making clear that the name change will not affect our agreement.

I am writing to everyone taking part in this production to make clear to everyone, including you, the basis upon which the Film is being made. If anything is unclear, or if you would like further discussion, please contact me.

Once you have read the entire letter, and agree to it, please sign both copies, retain a copy for your records and return a copy to me.

1. I, [name of actor] will make myself available for the shoot dates of [start date] to [wrap date].

2. I, [name of actor] will attend the following locations for the shoot: [list them].

3. I, [name of actor] agree to give over any rights I may have in the finished Film to [name of production company or producer].

4. I, [name of actor] will be paid a fee of [amount] per day for my performance in this Film. The fee is payable within [number] days after the performance was given.

5. [The production company or producer] will ensure that [name of actor]'s working days are not longer than ten hours.

6. [The production company or producer] will use our best efforts to ensure [name of actor]'s health, safety and welfare during the shoot.

7. [The production company or producer] will have public liability insurance to cover [name of actor] during the shoot.

8. [The production company or producer] will provide [name of actor] with food and refreshments throughout the shoot.

9. [The production company or producer] will either provide transport or pay travel expenses to and from the location of the shoot. These expenses will be agreed between us in advance.

10. [The production company or producer] will be provide [name of actor] with a VHS of the finished Film within three months of the completion of all post-production. Upon receipt [name of actor] agrees in advance to sign a piracy waiver.

11. Should [name of actor] require access to the rushes for the purposes of [name of actor]'s showreel, we will make them available at cost price.

Signed by [name of actor]   Signed on behalf of [The production
                                                company or producer]

_____   _____

Clause 3 will allow you to distribute the film in any and every way you can.

figure 14.1
Basic actor's agreement

For the latest details on
Equity day rates contact
them on 0870 9010900 or
see their website:
www.equity.org.uk

members. These rates are obligatory in some circumstances and dis-
cretionary in others. There is a certain unwritten standard that you
should pay Equity minimum rates, and if you intend to pay less, you may
have to vigorously defend your position. If you are partly funded by public money, you will have to pay Equity minimum rates.

PACT

To register your production
with PACT, you need to be a
limited company (see Chapter
11) and to agree to pay the
PACT levy. For more
information see the PACT
website: www.pact.co.uk.

PACT is the producers' association that represents most TV and film
producers in the UK. Most TV stations in the UK have signed the PACT
agreement that includes minimum payments to actors. If your production is registered with PACT, then you must use their simpler minimum
payment system. If not, then Equity's standard should be adhered to.
PACT minimum payments are £100 per day or £400 per week.

Film rates

Equity had a bitter dispute with PACT which was resolved in 2002 after
nearly two years of wrangling. The basic minimum rate was set as
above, and the agreement reached allows for two methods of payment
of actors for use, net profit share and royalty payments. You, as producer, must decide which of the options to use at the time of engaging
the actors and must apply the same option to all performers in the film,
and you can't change your mind afterwards. Producers can no longer
buy out all rights in all media in perpetuity; artists will now share the
success of a film either through royaltys or net participation.

Option B relates more to the large studio pictures that come to be
filmed in the UK. This is mandatory for production with a budget of over
£20 million. This option relates to royalty payments.

'Use fees' are the rights to sell
or exhibit the finished film in a
certain media/territory. To
exploit the film in any market
and by any media the
producer must make the
appropriate use fee payments.
The payment is calculated as
an extra percentage of the
total basic salary: if it's 50%
extra on a salary of £100, the
actor will be paid £150.

Option A is the most relevant for independent producers. In addition
to day rates that start as low as £37.50 for school productions, performers are entitled to 2% of the net profit of the film. There is also a
sliding scale for pre-purchase of other territories. There are also rules
about the minimum 'use fees' that you must pay. You must pre-purchase
a theatric use at 37.5% of the total fee. If your budget is under £1 million, then you must pre-purchase other uses up to a minimum total of
50%. If your budget is over £1 million, then you must pre-purchase
uses to a minimum of 75%. Other uses are in the chart below.

Market / Medium and Territory	Use Fee %
Theatric North America and non-theatric worldwide	37.5%
Theatric world excluding North America and non-theatric worldwide	37.5%
Videogram	90%
UK premium pay, pay per view and on demand TV	25%
UK network terrestrial TV	20%
UK secondary TV	5%
USA major network TV	25%
USA non-major network TV	10%
USA pay TV	20%
World Television excluding UK and USA	10%

figure 14.2
Option A: Net profit share

Finding Actors

PCR (Professional Casting Report)
This weekly publication charges a subscription to actors and lists forth-coming auditions. It is printed on dark red paper (to prevent copying) and is mailed every Monday morning. Producers can list auditions free of charge. It is a highly effective service – be prepared for a deluge. I once advertised a half-day's work for which I was offering a fee of £50 ($75) and received 850 letters the next day. Include as much information as you can to ensure the responses are appropriate to the role.

Fax your audition to 020 7566 8284 or telephone 020 7566 8282 or look at www.pcrnewsletter.com.

SBS
Where PCR is sent to actors, SBS is a weekly publication sent to agents. Most actors believe the information in SBS is more current than in PCR, but SBS tends to scorn student and low budget productions, because there is very little money in them for the agents. Call 020 8459 2781 to submit information.

Equity
If you believe that an Equity card makes a better actor, and just want to reach Equity members, then call 020 7670 0242. The ad is free to place, and only Equity members will see it advertised, either at their website, www.equity.org.uk or on the Equity hotline 0870 9010900.

Shooting People
Shootingpeople.org publishes a daily list of casting sessions and auditions. If you wish to post to the list, you must join (£20 per year).

Fringe and local theatre performances
Tuned in producers and directors comb the fringe theatre productions looking for new talent. The actors in these productions are very approachable and open to deals. Many have yet to find an agent, removing another layer in the negotiation process.

Drama schools
The National Council for Drama Training has a good website which lists all the drama schools in the UK: www.ncdt.co.uk. A canny producer will watch drama school productions, with an eye to spotting the next big performing talent.

Spotlight Casting
Spotlight Casting Live offers a premium service which costs £30 + VAT for a three month subscription to their database. Once you have access to the database, you will be able to browse over twenty five thousand actors. The entries are divided into handy groups like age, hair colour etc. to help keep auditions as efficient as possible for you and the actors. Go to www.spotlightcd.com/spotweb/records.asp

Hint When you approach an actor or their agent, you need to have a sheet of paper with the following:

– The name and full contact details of the production company
– Summary information about the film – length, shooting format, shooting dates, funded or unfunded
– Appropriate information about the roles available giving age range and meaningful physical and character detail
– The location of the shoot
– Details of the payment on offer

Working with children

If you are filming for three days or less, no licence is needed.

In the UK, it is a criminal offence for a parent or guardian to allow a child to take part in a publicly shown film or TV programme without a licence, or for any person (i.e. you) to encourage or employ a child to do so. All children under the age of sixteen need a licence to perform if you ever intend to show your film to a paying audience, on television, or sell videos/DVDs. This also pertains to family members, preventing you from using your own baby in a film unless you obtain a licence.

A licence is obtained from the local authority where the child lives. The application is made by the producer and countersigned by the parents and/or guardian.

It states the length of the engagement, and includes two photos of the child and a copy of their performance contract. If the child is under fourteen a licence will only be granted if the role can only be performed by a young person of that age.

The authority will only grant a licence if they believe the child to be healthy and fit, that the filming is not dangerous, that their education will not suffer, and that they will be treated with care.

In addition to the licence, there are strict regulations relating to working hours and rest periods. A young person over thirteen cannot work more than seventy-nine days per year; under fourteen they cannot work more than thiry-nine.

It is also an offence to allow or cause a child to go abroad for the purpose of 'singing, playing, performing, or being exhibited, for profit' without a police magistrate's licence.

Hiring a Casting Director

Landing the right actor for your film is usually the key to securing finance. In order to get the right actors for your financiers, hiring the right casting director becomes another of the essential ingredients to the film package.

Once the right actor has agreed to be in the film, there begins a delicate balancing act between the actor's demands, the needs of the producer to satisfy the financiers, and the director's creative demands.

Consultation with an experienced entertainment attorney is an essential element of this process.

A good casting director juggles these variables and delivers the actor to the set on time, drug-free and ready for work. This will cost you a weekly fee of £1000 to £3000 per week. Most film projects will require their services for at least six weeks.

Summary

1. Choose the best above the line people you can.

2. Offering an opening title credit is a huge inducement for new talent.

3. Deferrals can be helpful, but can also cause problems.

Enough talk. Let's get into action and sell the movie.

In Conversation with Ewan McGregor

What makes you choose to take on lots of independent films when you could be making commercially big films?

Well, I've only ever really seen them as, certainly the ones I've chosen to do, I've only ever seen them as stories, and I'm in the business of telling stories, so whether it's a huge budget Hollywood picture or whether it's a low budget British picture makes no difference to me. What's important is, is it a good story and do I want to be part of telling that story. Really that's it. I've always seen it that way. I would never want to narrow my horizons because the great thing about being an actor is you can get an opportunity to play all kinds of people in all different kinds of movies. And to kind of narrow that down would be foolish as far as I'm concerned. Initially, I suppose I was almost the other way around. I didn't want to be involved in Hollywood pictures. But I've learned that that's stupid too, because, you know they make a lot of pictures in Hollywood, why would you not want to be involved in them; if they do have stories to tell? Yeah, the more the merrier, really. It shouldn't be, or I don't think it should be a reason for doing a picture anyway, what size the budget is. It's irrelevant to me.

Since he burst onto the film scene in *Lipstick on Your Collar* and *Trainspotting*, Ewan has recently starred in Baz Luhrmann's Oscar and BAFTA winning *Moulin Rouge!*, *Young Adam* and *Down With Love* to name but a few of the broad range of roles Ewan takes on. This year, he has shot Tim Burton's *Big Fish* and Marc Forster's supernatural thriller, *Stay*. Ewan is recognised as one of the finest British actors in the world and has been described both by *Vanity Fair* and *Time Out* as 'the saviour of the British film industry'.

Does what you're looking for in a script differ now from when you were starting out?

No, no, no. It really doesn't. And in fact I'm in the best place that you can be as an actor. I've got choice, and that's all you can ever hope for as an actor, is to have choice in your work. So I'm really fortunate. So now more than ever I'm in a position where I can do whatever I want really, independent or studio or whatever.

And I still don't get offered all the studio stuff, you know, I'm not saying that I do, but some of it I do.

What's the process that a script would go through to get to you? Does somebody else read it first? Does it hit a lot of hands before it gets to you?

In my case, yeah, I have an agent in Los Angeles and I have an agent here in London and they get sent all the scripts. Some people hand them to me at festivals and things like that and I'm terrible at reading them. I mean, I'm just lazy. Also with me I get kind of – all next year is booked up. I'm making three films almost back to back next year, so the scripts that are on for next year, I can't do them anyway. So there's really no point for me reading stuff for the moment, and I'm not. I suppose the normal process would be, my agent would be sent the script with a breakdown of who's steering it and who's involved in it and whatever. My agent here in London knows me inside out. She's known me since I was nineteen, and she's been my agent since then and she knows exactly what I'm about. You work closely with your agent, so she knows what I would be interested in and what I would not, and sends me the cream of the scripts that she gets given, 'cause there are a lot of them, because there are a lot of people trying to make films, which is great. But I just can't read all the scripts I'm sent because I just haven't got enough time. She also doesn't make any decisions based on budget, because she knows I'm not interested in that.

The film I just made in Scotland, *Young Adam*, was very low budget, and also we lost a lot of the budget so it didn't have the money, and I was already attached to it. And I went out to look for the money myself, in America and here and went talking to people to try to regain the budget that we lost. *Young Adam* came in a bunch of scripts, and she sent it because it was a Scottish piece and also it was a terribly well written script. It was the first I read of that bunch and that was it. Just because it was a great story.

Once the script gets to you, what do you look for?

First and foremost is the story. I don't have any system of choosing scripts. I don't have a check list – does it have this, this, and this? And I'm not particularly knowledgeable about them. I'm very easily pleased. I'm very easily pleased when I watch movies and also when I read them. And I can read a script and other people go, well you know it needs a lot of work, and I would be quite happy to go shoot it right there and then. I'm glad those people are around. They've obviously got a higher standard of script reading ability, or whatever, than myself. But it's really just like if you're reading a novel and you don't want it to end. I just look for that. If I feel that way reading scripts and I'm really enjoying it; if I'm looking forward to seeing what's happening to the character next – I'll know within about ten or fifteen pages. Sometimes a character doesn't appear then, but you're kind of engaged after that short amount of time in the script. If it's well written you can tell right from the beginning.

I think what turns me off from a script these days is that, and especially American scripts, there's a tendency at the moment for very clever writing; for the writer to make a lot of comment to the reader. I hate that because I'm sensible enough to be able to read it on my own. I don't like stage directions that are directed towards the reader. And I don't like reading stage directions for actors, because you're going to hire actors to be in your film and it's really up to them to decide whether to close their eyes at a moment or not. It's not really up to the writer. 'He closes his eyes, turns to the left and says...' – you think, 'How do you know?' And so I find that rather frustrating and it will put me off a script, if there's too much in writing. I was sent the script for *Xxx*, and it was just fucking abysmal. I mean, I don't think I read 15 pages of that before I gave up. But there was stuff like 'No James Bond, this movie,' and I was thinking, 'Yes it is – it's just James Bond on fucking roller skates'. And there were lots of in-business jokes which just are a waste of time. Tell the story, and tell us what happens to the characters in your film and don't be too clever about it. You find that with the best writers – a Tom Stoppard script won't have any directions in it for anybody. It'll say 'Park – Night.' And there's the dialogue, and that's kind of what it should be. It should be just that because the writer isn't the director, the writer isn't the designer, the writer certainly isn't the actor, usually, and so they should leave that to the people who know best. It's kind of juvenile. It's like control freakish, to be writing everything for everybody. You don't need that. There should be room for imagination.

When a script comes to your agent, does she take into consideration who's sending the script?

Yeah, it's like, say Mark Herman had written and was directing another film and he sends it to me, then she'd send it to me because we've done two films already. And yeah, that'll happen; if there's any history there or if one of my friends was in it. There's a constant dialogue between an actor and an agent, and she'll very often be sent a script, and say 'I don't think it's very good, do you want to read it?' and I'll ask about it and then say no, just because of time. I can't be only making films and reading them because I've got other stuff to do, you know what I mean? But I don't think there's a risk of things slipping through the net. Very often people come up to me and say, 'We were going to send you this, but we thought your agent would never give it to you,' and that's just not the case. My agent will give it to me if it's very good, you know, if it's a very good piece of work. If it's being made for £5.50, but it's a great story. I'll get sent short films if they're good. I had a meeting with a director who was making his first film. I got sent this short script. It was ten pages long, but it was good so I met him, and then it didn't end up working out for one reason or another. I think there's a common misconception that you can't get scripts to people. Well, that may be the case with other agents, but certainly not with mine.

So as long as it's a good story, it doesn't matter to you if it's being directed by an established filmmaker or a newcomer?

Yeah, yeah if it's good. Oh yeah, absolutely, I like that. The exciting thing about being an actor is you get a chance to meet a whole bunch of other great people. A lot of my films have been with first time directors, I mean a lot of them. And continuously. With David Mackenzie [director of *Young Adam*], it was his first – he's made, he's made a digital and a bunch of shorts, but this was his first feature film on film. And that's exciting. It's really exciting to be working with someone who's directing for the first time – watching them suffer – [laughs] as the director.

As an actor, what is the most important thing you feel the director has to do?

The most important thing for us is that they know what an actor does. That they understand – well, you can't really understand the acting process because every actor has a different process, I believe that, I don't think there's anybody that goes about it the same way – but some of the directors I've worked with whom I'd say are poor directors, it's usually down to the fact that they have no idea what you do as an actor, and they've no understanding of acting.

It's a very interesting relationship between an actor and a director. It seems to me that the best directors are the ones who have the best character. It's funny, it's just so much to do with their character. It doesn't matter if you know all the names of all the filters and all the lenses – it's irrelevant to me. And really if you've got a great DoP, he's going to be in charge of all of that anyway. I really think the biggest mistake a director can make, a new director can make, is to feel he's got to be in charge, that everything's got to be his idea. It's a huge mistake, and I've seen lots of directors do that, because it's terrifying, there's no question about it. It's terrifying to be standing on a movie set and it being your movie. It's scary. You've got time against you – everything's against you. You've got thousands of questions being fired at you, right, left, and centre. But the biggest mistake is not to use the talent of the people around you. And the easiest thing, and the thing that makes the best director, is somebody who stands in the middle of this creative process, and uses the talent of the people he's employed. You know, he won't know as much about how a camera works or what stock to use as the DoP, because it's the DoP's job. So he should rely on the DoP to help him out. He should rely on the sound man to help him out and all of the actors to help him out. And to stand in the middle and kind of orchestrate it, you know, like a great conductor won't necessarily be a great clarinet player, but he'll be able to guide the clarinets. It should be like that. I have directed myself, and I think it's a terrible thing that there's a sense of failure if you ask someone else's advice, and it's not the case.

It is a collaborative process, and it should be, it should be one. They should at least have an understanding of what acting's about. I get more and more frustrated. And it's funny, it's getting worse and worse on all levels, in big films and small films, the crew's frustration with actors. If you want to discuss something with the director you can see people in the crew rolling their eyes. You think, this is what it's about, this is what people come to see. They're not coming to look at your set. I mean, I hope not, anyway. They're coming to see people, and they're coming to relate to the people on the screen. And that sometimes can take as much time to get right as the DoP took to light the set. It's very often the case that the DoP will light for 45 minutes and we'll come on and be expected to shoot a five page scene in five minutes. I really believe it's all about mutual respect on a film set between actors and the crew, and the crew to the actors. I would never dream of going up to the DoP while he's lighting to have a chat. I would never do that. But in the same respect, I wouldn't want someone in the crew to come up and start rapping with me when I'm trying to get my head around a death scene or something, you know what I mean? I deserve my space around me at that moment, the same as the crew does when they're setting lamps, or whatever they're doing.

Do you ever see yourself directing yourself in a film?
I think it would be very interesting. I actually think it's quite a good place to do it from. I'd have to speak to somebody who's done it. I think Johnny Depp did it. Kevin Costner does it a lot [laughs]. I think it'd be fascinating. Certainly it comes in the editing, because you've been in the scene. I learned this when I co-produced a film called *Nora*. I was involved in the post-production of it. And I would be sent, you know because I was in Australia at this point, I was sent tapes weekly of the latest cut. And I'd know where the errors were in the timing in the edit because I'd been in the scene and I remembered the beats. I remembered exactly how long pauses should be, you know. And I was able to say, 'Hey look, there's a really nice pause there and you're nipping the end off, and that's why the scene's not working'. And they'd put it back in there and suddenly it would work. That's only because I was in the scene and I would remember how it should feel. I don't know about the logistics of being on set and shooting and directing and being in the scene yourself. I don't think it would be a problem. It might be difficult to direct the other actors because you're in the scene with them, and the take would finish and then you'd go up as an actor giving other actors notes. I don't know how that would work. I have to find out.

What is the most important thing, in your opinion, that a producer has to do?
Keep out of my fuckin' way [laughs]. Yeah. Fuck off, mainly. I don't know, I don't know very much about producing. I've worked with some great producers. I think it depends on the project really. Because sometimes the producer is there and shelters the actors from any of the concerns going around about the production. Sometimes that's a very good thing. And other times it's nice to feel that you're really involved in it, and that you're an active participant in making this movie. It just depends. And I've worked with producers who are on set all the time. I've worked with those producers who you never see. There's no right or wrong, really, I don't think. I've worked with Jeremy Thomas, he produced *Young Adam* and he's got to be the best producer in the world, I think. He's got a CV of some incredible movies that he's produced. And he's still an independent film producer and Britain's finest, I'd say. He would pop in and out of set because he was working on other things at the same time as *Young Adam*. Again it's something to do with the character of the man or the woman, you know. He's a great bloke, and it's always lovely to see

him. Then there's other producers that you only ever see ten minutes before you're due to wrap. They come on to put pressure on the director and the crew to get it done quicker. But at the same time they're putting pressure on the actor in front of the camera and it's best not to do that, really. It's terrible when you suddenly catch the producer out of the corner of your eye, and you know it's because he wants you to get on with it. I don't know, it's a difficult job. Thank god they do it because otherwise we wouldn't be making movies at all. I have very little to do with the producers of films, really. You know, they take you to dinner, but that's it.

When you were starting out, what were some of the things you had to learn about the craft of acting, and then the business side as well?

Well see, I'm still learning every time I do a film, I think. The very first time I sat in front of a camera was in *Lipstick on Your Collar*, which was the first job I did, a Dennis Potter series on the television, which was shot on single camera as a movie. I think I felt absolutely that I was ready for it, and I didn't doubt I was going to be – I was very arrogant I suppose, but I never doubted I would be good in it. Or at least I was driven to be good in it. At the same time I had absolutely no technical knowledge at all, and I'd spent four years training in theatre. And even through three years of drama school in London we did nothing – we didn't touch movie work at all, which is insane and stupid, really. British actors have the luxury of being able to do television, theatre, and film all at the same time, so we should be trained as such. I had no technical background. And just even down to things like the names of who people are; what's a best boy, who's the gaffer, you know. Hitting marks, shooting tables up and down, cheating eyelines. The technicalities of filmmaking I was completely clueless about. Had it not been for my uncle, who's an actor, who kind of took me to his flat a couple nights before I started that project – I remember he put a pair of socks down on the floor and he said, 'OK, deliver this bit of dialogue and walk towards me while you're doing it but stop when you hit the socks' – he taught me how to hit marks and it gave me a head start. One of the things I love about my job, is that it's absolutely fifty-fifty split. It's absolutely a two-sided thing in that, on the one hand it's emotional, you are emotionally exploring a character moment to moment. And at the same time, you're technically making sure that that emotional performance is ending up on film. You rely on those two things to different degrees. I mean you can't hope to emotionally hit the mark every take of every day of every shoot. It's not going to happen. So sometimes you rely more on your technique than your emotions and sometimes it's the other way around. But I enjoy that. I really do enjoy working with focus pullers and operators and making sure that everything works the best it can and making sure I give them an option that's easy to get focus marks, and working with them. I really enjoy that side of it. And tricky tracking shots – making sure you're always seen by the lens, while you're playing a part. Maybe you're upset or something in the scene; while you're upset there's always part of your brain that's making sure you're still on camera. What's the point otherwise? There's no point in being really upset and crying beautifully if the camera can't see you, you know. I like that, but at the same time I've seen actors who think it's completely the technician's side to make sure you're on film and it's got nothing to do with them. And I just don't agree. I think we're all working together to make a movie. Things like standing up, slowly, or something, you know. If you in a scene in a tight shot, sitting at a table, and you suddenly stand up really quickly, the operator hasn't got a chance of keeping you in frame. And I've often heard operators saying, 'Look, can you just stand up a bit slower?' And I've heard actors saying, 'No, I can't. I'm feeling this at this moment so I can't.' And I think, 'Well good. You stand up as quickly as you like and you won't be on film at that moment.' Because, you know, they won't be able to get you. I think it's always better to find a way to stand up slowly, you know. Find a way to work together to make it all happen.

Are there any mistakes you've made that you wish you hadn't, or you would recommend to somebody not to do?

Not really. No, because I think everything's part of you. I can't think of anything that I wished I had – I would have gotten more sleep at times. I really mean that. There's films that I did where I think I should have spent more time asleep in my bed before going to work. But I've learned that lesson. It's important – there's a magic that happens in front of the lens and it's a shame if you waste it. It's a shame if you're not present for it or if you're exhausted. You're tired making a film any-way, but you have to look after what happens in front of the camera. But there's nothing I regret, there's no mistakes. There's not a moment in any of the films where I go 'Aargh', because it's all kind of fine. I'm not too critical about myself when I watch things, not really. The best thing about it for me is that I still can't believe I'm up there. When I sit down in a preview cinema or in a cinema and the lights go down and the film starts and I'm up there, I still can't believe it's me. I get such a kick out of it. And I've never not enjoyed watching something that I've been involved in for the first time. Not really.

Are there any other favourite directors you've worked with?

Yes, and they've all been very different. I've never worked with a direc-tor and thought 'Oh he directs like so and so.' That never happens. Everyone's always completely unique. I love working with Danny Boyle, because there's a connection there that was built over three movies, and I don't know what it is about him other than I would do absolutely anything. I'd want to be my best for him. And he works you – he pushes you; every single take of every set-up, he would be working you. So as an actor you're very satisfied. You'd never hear him say, 'OK, that was great. Let's just do another one.' He'd always have something for you to try. It's another note for directors, I think, base your direction on what the actors have just done. There's nothing more frustrating for an actor than doing a take and then getting a note that's got fucking nothing to do with what you've just done. That means you're left wondering if the director's watching, you know. Which is terrible if you think, 'God, is he watching what I'm doing?' If you get a note out of left field it's very frustrating. It's much better to build a performance through the takes based on what the actor's giving you. I think that's an important note for directors. Danny certainly did that. I loved working with Peter Greenaway, and he's a completely different animal all together. He'd give you very little direction, if at all. And at the same time I had such trust in him because I knew his work, and he's such an amazing, intelligent man. That film, *The Pillow Book* is one of my favourite pieces that I've done. Mark Herman I've worked with. I've enjoyed working with all of them in different ways. I think Danny and I had a real special thing going on and I was very happy that he was there. I will always remember the feeling of, if I turned around and saw him on the set, I'd feel happy that he was around. And that's a really nice thing.

In Conversation with John Hubbard

John Hubbard and his wife Ros run Britain's premier casting agency, Hubbard and Associates.

How important is casting in a film?

The thing is about getting the talent to get the money. Nobody gives you money now without knowing who the cast is, even if you have a really good director. They say in Hollywood these days that the only reason you hire an A-list director is to get A-list talent. They would rather not hire an A-list director, they would rather work with a first timer, somebody that is a little more cost effective, because it is all about money. Hollywood is, without a doubt, all about the dollar.

At what stage do you like to get involved in a project?

We like to get involved in the very early stages of a project's development. Sometimes people come up to us and tell us they are thinking of buying the option to a book, and ask us if it is castable. Sometimes we are second in. The producer will have a script or an option to a book, we will have a synopsis or just an idea of the story and they will come in to talk about it. They will say 'Do you think an A-list cast would like to do this?', 'Do you think people that would get the film funded would want to do this sort of subject?'.

Sometimes a director or a producer will get very fixated on one person, and that is very terribly dangerous because you are most likely not to get that person. Then they start saying 'If I don't get so and so then I can't make my film' and it just doesn't work that way. It can be the same with every project no matter the size. We are just about to start *Tomb Raider 2*, it's a big budget very attractive film, its Jan de Bont directing, who is a very big A-list action director. It's a big studio, lots of money and exposure. But I know that we're going to have to work down a list of actors because our first choices are going to be unavailable or too expensive or they'll pass on the script or won't want to do an action film.

The earlier we are in the better, because then we can control the casting and make a big contribution right from the start of the process.

Is there any one of the many films you've worked on that you have found particularly rewarding?

The favourite has got to be *The Commitments*, because Ros [Hubbard, John's partner] and I had so much fun working on it. Our day started at around seven or eight o'clock in the morning we would start workshopping at nine with the actors and the musicians that we met two or three nights previously. We would do that until five o'clock. Then we would have a break before we went out. Every night we went to all the clubs in Dublin, Cork, Limerick, and Belfast listening to the great music, the awful music; we would have a video camera and film each member of the band in close-up as they were performing to play them back later and decide whom we wanted to bring into workshop. Because Ros and I just love music, it didn't feel like work, it wasn't like a holiday because the hours were very, very long, but we got a total buzz out of going to see bands and working with music.

Lord of the Rings was an incredibly satisfying film to do because it is a very spiritual film. In fact Ros did an interview in a couple of weeks with a magazine that I have never heard about called *Bible Today* and they wanted to talk to her about her beliefs and her life and *Lord of the Rings*, because Tolkein was a Catholic. I think the strength of the movie comes down to its spiritual aspects not being obvious, but it is about human beings and is about their place in the world, it is about fellowship, and about humans coming together to beat off a mass evil. And I think one of the reasons why the film has been so successful is that it's a true story about people's beliefs and feelings and relationships towards each other. Also it was great working with a genius director like Peter Jackson who is one of the very few truly visionary directors. I read the script and was not be able to see a cinematic possibility, I could not see the massive success that it could have but Peter sees something. He saw the power it would have on the screen, how he would multiply the power of the words in the script to make it visually and emotionally moving. *Evita* was fantastic because we were all over the place like America, Argentina, Budapest, and Spain.

The less satisfying ones generally had a script that was not that good, but unfortunately you have to do a few of those when you have a business to run and are training people, and when you have to keep an eye on the turnover.

Out of the 100–150 films that we have done, somewhere between fifty to sixty of those have been the most amazing experiences. I am about fifty-eight now and I am still learning all the time. Everything that happens, every job I do, I learn a little bit more. That is very satisfying – when you still get excited by something.

Can a person with no experience in casting be able to just have the eye for the business, or do you need the experience and training to be successful?

It is primarily about instinct, either you have an instinct or you don't. I think you can have no experience but still have a good instinct about good actors. We work with film students all the time who have never made a film and a lot of them have never worked with actors, but some of them come in and you see that they have a natural instinct. I was talking to a young film student the other day, and he just seemed to go to movies twenty-four hours a day which is a very good learning tool. If you have an instinct that is how you develop and strengthen it. I think if you were going up a mountain and you had the choice of somebody who has been up fifty times or someone who has just started I think you would go with the older and wiser person. However, the media loves youth. Dan, my son, is twenty-seven. Clients call and say that they are going to use Dan to cast a film because it is for young people. And I say 'But Ros and I just cast The Commitments – I don't understand. Just because you are over thirty doesn't mean that you can't cast a nine-year-old.' First of all it's instinct then it is experience; meeting thousands of actors, seeing thousands of movies. I believe that my instincts are more highly trained than most people who have only done a couple of films – that's not to say that they don't have the instinct or the talent.

If a producer came to you with a limited budget would you get involved? Would you accept deferred fees?

It would entirely have to rely on the script and director and the producer and the team. If my instincts say that the script is really interesting and I am dealing with realistic and intelligent people, then yes we will get committed and we will say OK we will do guaranteed deferments, or share success in the film, or help you out for nothing. I have to do it less and less, because we are so busy with what we call the day job that it is very difficult to set aside that kind of time, and people can be very demanding when you are working for them for nothing. I sometimes do it, but it absolutely depends on the conditions, my judgement about the script and the people that are associated with it.

Do you join projects based on working with directors and other crew from previous films, or are you individually hired?

The answer is yes to both, so for example you will work with Ron Howard and then he will never use you again, I'm not sure why – he just doesn't. Whereas people like Alan Parker, and Bruce Beresford will fight to have casting directors. There are just a lot of directors that want us for the team, without a doubt we will do Alan Parker's next film and Paul Greengrass's next film and that's very satisfying. It also has to do with how much power that the directors have because a director can go into a meeting and say that they want to use the Hubbards and the studio may say they want to use someone else. Alan Parker will fight for us but some directors may not be able to or don't want to make waves.

How long do you stay involved on a project?

Until you finish casting the last person that has to be cast. Some casting directors will only cast leads, some may do the children and day players as well. When I go to the preview, I want to know that I cast everything that moved. Even if it is two people who have a couple lines each, I want to cast them, because I want the best people there.

How to you attract big names to low budgets?

It is really difficult to get big names in low-budget films. A lot of it is about the right approach – not being stubborn with agents, having respect for them and what they can do for you. Always be pleasant and always be realistic. The agents have to read the scripts as well, so they have hundreds of scripts in their office and what I resent is the arrogance of producers who think that theirs is the only script, or the only important script. If you're approach is like that you will just get rejected, because the attitude is all wrong. Being stubborn and unrealistic is also a problem. Saying 'I have a really good script, I have a really good part for Art Malik' is OK and you have to aim for those big names, but you have to be prepared to cast someone else. Your script should be just as good without the big name. Use people like us, also respect our presence and position and also the power we have to help you have the right attitude and approach us in the right way.

Have you ever worked on a low budget film, if so have you ever cast any big names?

One or two, not very many. Gossip about established stars 'looking for a different kind of part' is generally nonsense. Take Daniel Day Lewis – that kind of rumour circulated about him, but he is retired and is not working unless the director is Martin Scorcese or Jim Sheridan. It took Michael Mann about a year to persuade him to do *The Last of the Mohicans*, ending in a four-hour lunch. And this is Michael Mann, this is a man who makes fantastic movies, and he found it difficult to get this guy. So coming in with that sort of line is complete rubbish. It is hearsay, somebody making it up, somebody being dramatic, being misinformed. Usually projects need a hook; like a director or writer that actors respect. That is what moves a project up; because agents are engaged by the clout a respected (not necessarily big) name can have.

At the level of low-budget scripts it is extremely difficult to get big names. It's a matter of having a fantastic story and characters. For the big name factor, you just have to bash away at agents and use every means you can to try to get it to the actors. There are a lot of actors that don't open the script and send it to their agents. I would never do that myself – eventually you are going to end up talking to the agent, so why make them angry. If you talk to Richard E. Grant at a party and he says he loves the sound of your script, he will give you his agent's number. But then you'll call the agent and he'll say they're not interested. Actors do want to help out; they are very generous and they don't want to say no to your face! But it's hard and getting harder at the film markets to sell anything. In the old days if you had just one name that, would be just fine, but now the market want two names or five names because they need to get more attention and publicity than other films. The more names you have, the more publicity you get and the more people take notice. It has become frustrating and painfully hard to make any movie.

Moving the Budget Up

I am always asked how much a low budget film costs. The question should be: how much do you have?

AS THE CASH BUDGET for your film creeps upwards, certain elements of your budget may remain the same even though the budget increases in value. You might be faced with the prospect of having a hot project where you suddenly raise more money than you anticipated. Or you may decide to ramp your budget higher in order to attract different types of crew or talent. The exercise below is an interesting and useful way to see what happens as your movie budget inflates.

Hint Making low budgets work depends on two elements. The cash you have (budget), and the amount of time you have allocated for the shoot (schedule). You must negotiate with your cast and crew and convince them that you can complete the entire film with the amount of time and money you have in your budget.

Basic Considerations – Film Prints and Blow-ups

No matter how low or high your budget, when you are finished you will have to make a 35mm internegative. The following budgets do not include this final step in the filmmaking process, which costs roughly the same whichever budget you use to shoot your film.

Similarly, if you shoot on a tape format, the cost of transferring to film is not included. Again, this is more or less a standard fee regardless of the type of DV camera you use.

It is a common myth that a distributor will pay for your transfers and blow-ups if they like your film. In truth, they simply lend you the exact amount of money you need to blow up your film, and then add on interest and charges that somehow seem to leave no money for the filmmaker.

Hint If a distributor pays for your blow-up, you may not make any money, but you will get your film into cinemas.

Moving a £100,000 ($150,000) Budget Up

Key Elements

Producer
As a producer, you will have a nominal fee. The more money you demand as a producer the less likely you are to maintain a profit share of the film once made.

Script
The script requires self-contained, minimal locations and a handful of actors. You will also limit in the amount of special effects and stunts required to tell the story.

Writer
At this budget level, most writers will also want to direct. If you are buying a script from a writer, it is unlikely that you are going to be able to pay more than £1000 ($1500).

Remember that you also have to allow for the costs of registering your script at the US Copyright Office (about £25) and of photocopying the script. You will need about a hundred copies to give to potential investors, sales agents, cast and crew.

Actors
Most likely you will be using semi-professional actors.

Originating format
There are three choices at any level. It is important to choose the format that suits your story and budget. While you may be attracted to shooting a high quality film on a 35mm format, it could be that you will have to sacrifice mobility and speed to the detriment of your story.

i 35mm
- one-week (nine-day) shoot at a challenging 3:1 shooting ratio, and finish the entire film
- two-week shoot, 6:1 shooting ratio and enough money to complete the edit up to the point of the final mixing and neg cut
- three-week shoot at 6:1 and enough money to cut a trailer with which you attempt to raise the money to finish the film

ii 16mm
- two-week shoot, 6:1 shooting ratio, start to finish
- three-week shoot at 8:1, raising more money later for post-production

iii Digital

– Two- or three-week shoot start to finish, without having to pay for a tape to film transfer

---

Hint The longer you have to shoot, the better looking the film will be.

Crew

In Chapter 12, 'The Shoot', there is an illustration of how a crew can grow in size as the budget increases.

You will be working with a small crew of four or five people: producer, director, first assistant director, DoP, sound recordist, and one or two production assistants who will double as boom operators or camera assistants when necessary.

Hint The truth is (at the time of writing) that when you shoot on film, be it 16mm or 35mm, you will attract better people – both cast and crew – than if you are shooting on tape.

Post-production

You will try to get the film edited with pictures and sound to a 95% completed state. You can then present your film to sales agents and potential buyers on a high quality tape format, avoiding the expensive final 35mm process.

Moving a £250,000 ($375,000) Budget Up

Key Elements

Producer

One could reasonably expect a fee of £10,000 at this budget, partially to acknowledge the increased responsibility and the larger cast and crew.

Story

The script you choose can handle locations within a major city, with the possibility of two or three days in another town or village.

Writer

This budget could carry a fee of up to £15,000 for the script.

Actors

Genre definitely dictates the type of actors you will use. No names will work in sci-fi and horror, where the type of story will make the film sell. Other genres will sell much more easily if you spend a large portion of your budget on named actors. You may choose several known (but not really well known) actors and go for an ensemble piece. Often you will see a film with several actors that you remember vaguely from other movies, but the title and logline of the film are what sells it. Audiences might choose to see the film based solely on the fact that the actors, although not widely known, are likely to turn in solid performances.

Perhaps you are in contact with an actor with a bigger name, and choose to surround them with experienced but unknown actors. In this case, the film might be billed as 'Starring X'. Or you might be able to get an actor with a very large name to do a cameo role.

Whatever level of actors you use, it would be wise to spend at least £50,000 on actors at this budget level.

Originating Format

i 35mm
- Two-week shoot, 6:1 shooting ratio and enough money to complete the edit up to the point of final mixing and neg cut
- Three- or four-week shoot with a 9:1 ratio and enough money to cut a trailer, with which you attempt to raise the money to finish the film

ii 16mm
- Although cheaper than 35mm, shooting on this format at this budget is not really an option unless demanded by the story

---

Hint It is easier to get good actors if you shoot on 35mm.

---

iii Digital
- A two camera HD shoot is often used at this level

Crew
The crew will rise to nine or ten.

Post-production
It is possible to completely finish the film with this budget, although finishing the film to a fine cut, showing it on tape and hoping to raise additional completion funding is also an option.

Moving a £500,000 ($750,000) Budget Up

Key Elements

Producer
One could reasonably expect a fee of £20,000 at this budget. Again, this is partially to acknowledge the increased responsibility and the larger cast and crew.

Story

The additional script payment of up to £25,000 allows you to consider more experienced (and expensive) writers, or acquire the screenplay rights to a novel or short stories. The story possibilities are still limited, however, in terms of locations.

Writer

This budget could carry a fee of up to £25,000 for the script.

Actors

Depending on the genre and script, it would be possible to spend up to £250,000 on actors (see above) or with a horror or sci-fi script, spend as little as £25,000 with the balance of the budget below the line, in either art department or special effects.

Originating Format

i 35mm

- Three- or four-week shoot at 12:1, through to completion of the film

ii 16mm

- Three- or four-week shoot at a ratio of 12:1 through to completion of the film, with enough money for a blow-up

iii Digital

- Shooting on HD, for three or four weeks at a ratio of 12:1 through to completion of the film

Crew

Up to thirty people including a driver, art department assistants, runners and other support personnel.

Post-production

Edit the film to completion, including clearing all music rights.

Summary

1. If budget permits, spend on talent. It makes the film easier to sell.

2. Try to add money to the art department and special effects budget. A better looking film is easier to sell.

3. You will never, at any level, have as much money as you need to do 1 and 2 above.

When you're finished you need to decide how you will sell the film.

Account	Description	Page	Total
	Raindance Film Producer: Elliot Grove	The Living in the Home of the Dead HD 30 day shoot 12:1 shoot ratio Director: Simon Rumley	
500	script	1	25,000
600	producer/director	1	40,000
700	talent	1-2	65,000
800	fringes	2	6,500
Total above the line			**136,500**
900	production staff	2	11,500
1000	camera dept	3	7,000
1100	camera	3	6,000
1200	art department	3-4	14,000
1300	art/props	4	12,000
1400	electrical department	4	5,400
1500	grip department	4	2,000
1600	grip electrical package	4	8,500
1700	production sound	5	5,750
1800	stunts/SFX	5	14,500
1900	police/fire/safety	5	1,000
2000	craft service/catering	6	17,650
2100	wardrobe/make-up	6	8,675
2200	location manager/scouts	6	2,700
2300	locations	7	21,000
2400	transportation	7	12,500
2500	picture vehicles	7	200
2600	accommodation	7-8	8,500
2700	general office	8	12,750
2800	transfer to 35mm	8	75,000
2900	insurance	9	15,000
3000	legal	9	10,000
Total production			**271,625**
3100	editing	9	25,000
3200	music	9	5,000
3300	post production sound	9-10	45,000
3400	answer print	10	10,000
3500	titles and opticals	10	10,000

Misc		0
Total above the line		136,500
Total below the line		366,625
Above and below the line		503,125
Total VAT within budget		56,400
Contingency		20,000
Total (UK sterling)		**523,125**

figure 15.1
Budget top sheet for The Living in the
Home of the Dead

In Conversation with Nick O'Hagan

Nick O'Hagan produced *Pandaemonium* (2001) and was an associate producer on *Solitaire For Two*. He was the co-producer of *Young Adam* starring Ewan McGregor (2003).

How would you say different budget levels affect the story?

You tend to look for stories that are contained, have fewer characters, don't have big set pieces, that will only take place in a couple of locations – low budgets tend to be more character-driven or have something very unique about them. What I would encourage though, is even when you're just using a couple of locations, to be a bit creative – you should push the boundaries a bit. People tend to think they are only going to be able to shoot in one room, but you could be on the moon in the story, and then in some field out in the middle of nowhere; or you could go back in time. Don't limit yourself when you are thinking about budget. Sure you are limited about the set pieces, but there are ways of not allowing yourself to be limited by a smaller budget of £200,000.

How would a budget increase from £100,000 to £500,000 affect the film you made?

It would probably not make a huge difference to the script, but to the elements, yes. I would always say cast as best you can, and as high and as sexy as you can in terms of profile. Always go for the best actors. Crew I'm less concerned with.

So you would pay extra to get 'named' actors?

Well, good actors – not necessarily 'names'. Because low budget films are limited with cast as they are with crew, they tend to just go for people who are willing to do it. And the actors who are willing to do it – OK, some of them might be the greatest actors, but they haven't had the experience and they don't have the power yet, or they don't have the presence yet. It's just fact. I find that with a lot of British low budgets the acting is just not accomplished enough.

So you could have a great little script, but you do tend to get let down by some actors. Because they are the ones who are telling your story, they are the ones who have got to be up there. On a low budget, you haven't got much time – you are having to shoot a lot, and quickly. If you put in someone who is experienced, they will quickly get to the level of acting that you require and you'll get a better powerful performance on film. If you don't have someone who is a bit more experienced, you may not be able to give them enough time to get into their part.

I make sure that I can pay actors a reasonable amount, so that I'm not getting someone who just wants a part in a film because they are not getting any other work, and so are prepared to do it for nothing. That said, some great actors are still prepared to do things for almost nothing. Other than cast, things don't change much at this level of budget.

Do things change when the budget goes from £500,000 up to £1 million?

I think it only really starts changing when having the extra money allows you to shoot for longer. But sometimes, allowing you to shoot longer isn't necessarily going to make it a better film.

So given the option, would you prefer to shoot for longer, or spend the extra money on getting a good actor?

I would prefer to spend it on a good actor. But shooting longer can obviously help. It allows the director and everyone to get it right, and not be so rushed and compromised. So yes, going up to £1 million is going to improve the production values.

I wouldn't be changing the script dramatically. I would focus on more time, and maybe instead of shooting digitally, I would decide to shoot on 35mm – which means that you need more time.

And of course, people can get paid better. This means that you can probably get more out of your crew because you are at least paying them a little bit. And when the going gets tough – which it invariably does, people don't feel so bad about doing the hours. But, that said, once they are in on a film, they are in – they believe in it, and are doing it for various other reasons, so that extra £100 a week isn't going to make a big difference.

How does an increased budget affect your choice of originating format?

I really have no preference. Format does not change according to budg-et – it changes according to what the film requires. I will say that if you are shooting on Super16 and you are blagging a Super16 camera and film stock, you might as well blag a 35mm camera and stock, once you are in for blagging stuff for the film, I think that if you want to shoot 35mm, then shoot 35mm. It is not the budget that is going to tell me what format to shoot on.

What I will say is that sometimes budgets are just unreasonably high. I think what a lot of people do is say 'I'm going to make this film for this price', and just jot a figure down, but they don't know why they are doing it for that price. I do think that if you are a first time filmmaker, you have to try and make it for as little as possible, and don't kid yourself that you are going to make a £300,000 film. Too many people think 'We are going to need £3 million to make this film'. I hear it all the time: 'Look, I've done a really nice budget'. But that's a waste of time! It's got nothing to do with anything – we don't make budgets, we make films! No one is going to give you £3 million. So I suggest that people do it for as little as possible. And then there is a point where they might say 'I can't make the film then' – then you can't make that film now. Put that one aside I'm afraid – write another script, do something else first.

You have got to think how you are going to get the investment to cover that budget, and it's just not possible if it is too high. The only way it is possible, is if you have an A-list cast – and even then it is some-times not possible, because you have a first time director.

If you are a first-time filmmaker, you should be making something for £100,000 because then you might just get the investors' money back. You have to think about what the bottom line is. You could create the most brilliant piece of filmmaking but ultimately not make the money back for the investors. If you don't make the money back, you are not a good bet and are not going to get another chance either from the same investors or from others. First time filmmakers really need to look at making films for as little as they can.

First timers should not write things that are mainstream. One reason is the cost, but the other thing is that anything that is mainstream is never going to get you noticed, unless you are exceptional – but even then you can't compete with the mainstream in terms of an A-list cast.

Take the filmmakers of *Lighthouse*. They had very little money when they started out, but they eventually got a bit of money to help finish it – and that is often what happens. But they've done really well because they did it for almost nothing. With that film, if they had gone out and tried to raise money the traditional route, it could have cost twenty times more than it did – because that's how much you would have thought it would have cost. Then they wouldn't have been able to make it. But what's happened now is that they got to make it, and climb up another rung, and then they get asked to make a bigger film.

A first time filmmaker shouldn't do something that is financially risky – that's the bottom line: the script shouldn't be financially risky, it should-n't be too big a budget. You want something that is quirky, and edgy that will get you noticed. Keep the budget down, and someone might be prepared to take a risk on it, as it just might pay off.

What are the differences between films you have produced for only a few £100,000 and those made for £1 million or more?

More money does and doesn't change things, because I think you never have enough money. No matter what your budget is, you never have enough money to do everything you want to do anyway, so in a sense, you are always limited. In fact, having less money can make you do something more original, because you are pushed and you can't go the easy route. You need ambition. And never having enough money does challenge you. With less money, never is your ambition more apparent. You are immediately feeling the constraints and fighting against them – so you are having to work harder and be more ambitious in order to achieve your goal. You should never lose that ambition. That's what good filmmaking is: pushing the boundaries.

In Conversation with Simon Rumley

How important are 'named' actors in your films?

Simon Rumley is the director, producer and screenwriter of *Strong Language*, *Club le Monde* and *The Truth Game*. He is currently working on his fourth film.

I suppose it's good when you get names, everyone feels a little more confident and excited about having them on board. But frankly, whether 90% of the British acting 'names' other than Hugh Grant or Ewan McGregor will make any difference to your box office is debatable.

I have always worked with lesser known actors. Mainly because what I've done is a youth trilogy of films, set in London during the 1990s, where most of the actors ranged from the ages of about 18 to 30, and in this country, there are very few actors within this age group who are well known. There are maybe a few from TV whom I have used, but in terms of British public awareness, you have really got maybe only a handful of actors who are known. And even if you take actors like Andrew Lincoln or John Simm – good actors who have done quite a lot of stuff, if you were to stop the average person on the street, and ask them whether they had heard of them, they would probably say no, and even if you showed them a photograph, it's likely that half of them would still not recognise them.

Arguably the named actors are actually better actors, so the quality of acting will be better – but that is not necessarily true, perhaps it is for some of them, but certainly not all of them.

How would a budget increase from £100,000 to £500,000 affect the film you made?

It very much depends on who you are talking to and depends on how much you are going to push the low budget nature of the film. But in my opinion, there is not much difference in making a film for £100,000 than for £500,000 as far as the script goes, other than having more money to spend on a good crew. The real difference starts to occur when the budget rises from £500,000 to £1 million and upwards.

In the last year or so I have written two scripts: one was for a £3 million type film, and one was for a £500,000 type film. The point is to ask yourself 'Would I prefer to get another film made in the next year, or would I prefer to try and get a higher budget, and get paid more money, but maybe not make another film for the next two or three years?'

Ultimately it really depends on what the requirements of the script are. In the end you have got to work to what your story is, and then hope for the best. I have tended to write scripts that I know can be done for not much money, which is why I have managed to do three films when a lot of people have only managed to make one in the same amount of time.

In terms of getting to the next stage, there is no real reason why for instance, you should need to spend a lot on locations. If you look at a film like *The Shining* – that is only one location. Or this horror film that we are doing at the moment, again that will be one location. *Reservoir Dogs*, was essentially one location really, with just a couple of exteriors. So there is no real reason why if you are limited to just a few locations it should be a bad film. If you are a good filmmaker, you should be able to rise to the challenge of making something interesting, wherever it may be – whether it's set in a bar, an aeroplane or a town. Again, it depends on what, as a writer/filmmaker, you are looking at first: whether you are writing because you know you already have a lot of money, or you are writing because you just want to make a film.

For example, for the first film that I made, I knew I could only raise a small amount of money and wrote accordingly. For my second film, I was told that if I could make a film for about £100,000, someone would finance it and they would underwrite it – so I then wrote a script based on that. My third film *Club le Monde* I had written the script for ages ago. It could have been made for £1 million but we did it for just over £400,000. It comes down to me feeling that it is a lot easier doing something on a lower budget than a higher budget.

Why? What complicates things when the budget is higher?

You have more people on set so you are going to have more problems with communication. If you have a lower budget, then theoretically you have a smaller crew, so there are fewer people to actually communicate with and deal with. And then there's the logistics of it all: if you have a bigger budget film, then it's going to be a longer shoot, so you have got to have more coordination and more people. If you have more money then you have more complications and more that can go wrong.

This country is quite interesting in its attitude to work, because I think a lot of people now will only work on a film if they are paid. One always gets the impression that in the US people are more enthusiastic to work for nothing on a low budget film. I remember watching a documentary about the making of the film *Pi* and seeing over fifty people working behind the scenes, and thinking 'Hang on, no one got paid for any of this'. Yet everyone was still very excited about doing it. In this country you generally don't get this kind of attitude, which is a shame.

On my last film, I had a few problems behind the camera for various reasons, and at times I was thinking: 'For god's sake, you are working on a fairly reasonable script, it is low budget, but so what? You are working on a film, and let's get together and make this a positive experience.' But the attitude in this country does not seem to be very gung-ho, it's very much 'How much am I going to get paid?' and 'God, that's not very much money'. At times it is worth cutting the crew down to a minimum and just doing it with a bunch of mates over a few weekends – my first film was a bit like that. There was me, the cameraman, camera assistant, a first AD, a sound man, and about sixteen actors.

Do you think if you had been offered a few hundred thousand more it would have become a different film?

No, not really, because I wrote it very specifically to be made with virtually no money whatsoever, and if I had got more money, then everyone would have just got paid more, but it still would have been the same script. We may have shot it on 35mm as opposed to Super16, but beyond that, no other changes.

What is your preferred originating format? How does that change as the budget increases?

Format has big implications on the budget. What has become interesting over the last four or five years – maybe with the advent of Dogme more than anything, and the technology – is that it is becoming more and more acceptable to shoot your film on DV. Mike Figgis has been a keen exponent of this as well. That now means essentially that anyone can make their own film: you can shoot it on a camera that you can buy for as little as £1000, you can edit it on your equipment at home, and you don't need all the crew. But you will still have to blow it up to 35mm – so there remains a barrier of money at the end of the process.

In low budget films, the theory is that you shoot them, edit them to tape or digital, and then you take them around and hope that someone is going to think it is really good, and give you the rest of the money to enable you to blow it up to 35mm, so that you can then release it. But you could probably count on one hand the number of times that has happened in this country. It happens more often in the US because there is more of an infrastructure to encourage that kind of thing, and there are more festivals.

But if you don't have a budget for 35mm, you shoot on the cheapest medium that suits your film – which until recently, has been Super16, and then you hope for the best. All my early films were shot on Super16. My first was Super16 and Hi-8 video, and my last two were Super16. This came down to money – not having enough.

If you have 35mm, you need more cameras, and more crew etc., so you could just be complicating issues. And to be honest, with most low budget films, it doesn't really matter if the images are not pristine. It's not like they are going to be shot in the desert *Lawrence of Arabia* style. And the public who are going to see them are probably more interested in character development and the story, and dialogue. So actually, the fact that it may be a little grainy, or some scenes are a little darker than others shouldn't matter. The 'look' is important, but it is less important to me than other things. If a film looks great, but has a really poor story and is not well acted, frankly who cares! With low budget films like *El Mariachi*, more than anything it is the energy and the passion that gets the film onto the screen in the first place that is important.

Shooting format is important, and often different formats obviously suit different stories, but it comes lower down in the scheme of things than a lot of people think.

My next film is going to be shot on HD. I would definitely consider making a film on DV though – it creates more energy behind the camera, and you can do it quicker. For the kind of films I want to make, DV is a reasonable medium. But of course, it doesn't suit everyone.

I think it's quite exciting to make a film on DV. The quality is such that you look at some DV films, like *The King is Alive*, *The Intended*, *Dancer in the Dark*, *28 Days Later* and see a negligible difference once they have been blown up to 35mm. It doesn't affect your viewing experience – the audience gets involved with a film because of the characters, not because it looks pretty. DV may well be an option for my next film, especially as I personally prefer to make one film a year on low budget, than one film every three years on a higher budget and have that energy to move the camera around.

Which genres do you think are especially suited to low budget production?

Some genres lend themselves more easily to low budget than others. Horror films like *The Blair Witch Project* testify to this, since you don't need much money to create an atmosphere. You can do a romantic comedy with no money. But you can't really do science fiction or action on a really low budget. Although *El Mariachi* is an action film which was made for very little money, in general, you cannot make an action film on a low budget, since as an audience, we have come to expect the big bangs and big car chases, You're thinking *Bullet*, you're thinking *French*

Connection and it's these kind of things that you can't do for free, and you can't get away just with writing a good script, because an explosion is an explosion on screen, no matter how well you write it.

What impact does a budget increase from £500,000 to £1 million have on the kind of film you would make?

I would allocate the extra money for a good music mix ,which in low budget films seems to get skimped on, because it is the last thing.

I would increase the shooting schedule from four to six weeks, or would increase pre-production time, or probably do both. So instead of paying for a pre-production team of twenty people for two weeks, you would suddenly be paying a pre-production team of twenty for four weeks instead. And if you are adding another two weeks to the shooting schedule that would increase the budget by about a third.

More time means that everyone isn't under so much pressure and the actors have more time to prepare. It should mean that things work better. It also means the director can try out more set-ups or be a bit more experimental with the camera. It just means that everyone has a little more luxury to do better stuff. Then again, the script shouldn't be so ambitious that you require more time anyway.

So by the time you have paid the actors more and the crew more, that will have already brought your budget up to £1 million, and it is still exactly the same script.

How often is it that an original budget is increased?

Never happened to me. But when you go to the UK Film Council they might say let's raise the budget a bit more and therefore get higher profile people on board, so it can happen that your budget is increased, but very rarely. It's very much like a game of chance that you play. For example, with this horror script, we could have gone for a £1 million budget. We could have paid ourselves more, we could have got more well known actors, but then it would have meant that the money we were getting from one source, which would have covered 50% would now be only 30% and actually, the other thing with a £1 million budget is that you need to bond it, and will also have to bring in various Skillset levies, which are not that much, but a percentage here and a couple of thousand there adds up pretty quickly. So if you are making a film for £1 million, you could probably make it for £500,000. It is nicer to have more money, but again, it depends on what you are looking for out of a film – are you looking for a quick return for your investors, so that you can then go on and make more films, or are you just happy doing things more slowly, with more money, and making it that bit more polished? I'm all for making as many films as I can.

Obviously, I would always take the higher budget if it was offered, as any filmmaker would, but it does add complications and can bear no relation to how good the film is. But everyone gets paid a little bit more, which is nice. For a £500,000 film, you don't get paid that much in proportion to the time and effort you put into it, but you are always hoping that this film will be the one that takes you to the next level.

Seven Essential Steps for Becoming Rich and Famous by Making a Low Budget Film

Step 5 Savvy

Savvy comes from the Spanish word sabe meaning 'to know'. It has two meanings. When used as an adjective it means well informed and perceptive. As in 'S/he is a savvy film producer'. When used as a noun, it means practical understanding or shrewdness. As in 'A producer known for their financial savvy'. Savvy cannot be taught; it can however be learned by following three simple steps:

1 Knowledge is power
Become informed. Learn as much as you can about every aspect of the industry.

2 Read the trades

All trades are structured in a similar way. The first section deals with news stories of films in production, festival news, business updates and scandal. The next section has articles and analysis of current issues. This is followed by a production focus section, which lists films currently in production and post-production. The final section is a listing of all the box office reports from around the world. Filmmakers with savvy read the trades and look for news stories which track new trends. The production notes will show which movies are getting funding, and the box office charts will show how different films are released, the number of screens they are playing on, and the decay rate of their box office take.

The three main trade papers are: *Screen International* (for British and European news) *Hollywood Reporter* and *Variety* (for a combination of American and European news). For web-based news, go to the magazines' websites:
– *Screen International* www.screendaily.com
– *Hollywood Reporter* www.hollywoodreporter.com
– *Variety* www.variety.com
    These sites all have daily updates, some are free and some are subscription based. For news of independent film production, awards and festivals, subscribe to the excellent free service www.indiewire.com for a daily email update or www.filmthreat.com for a weekly news service.

3 Internet
This invaluable resource can get you information on any topic or person in a matter of seconds. Before you go to any meeting, you should do a quick Internet search on the person you are meeting. Search for both the company and individual: check with a normal search engine (like Google™) and also use www.imdb.com, the movie database. You will find their credits (or lack of) as well as the details of any current productions they may be working on. This way, you may also find their own website, which can be a very useful tool in sussing a company out.

16   Preparing the Marketing Plan

IF ONE LIVES AND WORKS as a filmmaker in Europe, the entire film-making process, from start to finish, is described as falling into three stages, although many new filmmakers neglect the third:

Pre-production	Production	Marketing
The script is developed and financing is raised	The film is shot and edited	The marketing materials and press kits are prepared, the film is taken to festivals and markets and sold

figure 16.1
Pre-production, production and marketing

This is 100% accurate. It describes the filmmaking and marketing process in chronological order: in pre-production one develops the script and finds the cast, in production the film is shot and edited, and at the marketing stage the film is promoted and sold. Independent filmmakers describe the progress of their projects in this way as well.

In Hollywood, the process is divided into two parts:

figure 16.2
Make and sell

The film bosses argue that it is senseless to make a movie unless you know it will sell. And to do this, they spend vast resources on trying to predetermine what the public wants to see/buy next. One can imagine a harried junior executive racing to the office screaming 'We have an entire warehouse full of dinosaur t-shirts. What are we going to do?', and the answer coming 'We better make a *Jurassic Park IV*'. The actual shooting of the film is usually the last element of this process, and ultimately the least significant, as far as the marketing and selling of the film goes. So the process looks more like this:

figure 16.3
Sell and make

The Competition

If you were contemplating manufacturing a chair, wouldn't the first thing you do be to go to the local furniture stores and see what sorts of chair were on sale? You would probably look at the materials and design and try to calculate the cost of manufacture. Even better, wouldn't you try and talk to the manager to see what the customers said about the chairs, and find out what types of chair sold best?

In order to see what our competition is, let us analyse who else is making movies.

The Majors

Dreamworks operates as a major studio but is accommodated by Universal Studios.

UIP represents MGM, Sony and Universal outside the United States.

There are eight major studios, and all of them are based in LA; they are who is meant by the catch-all term 'Hollywood'. They are called major studios because they make movies and own and operate cinemas all around the world. Warner Bros, for example, own and operate cinemas from Britain and Germany to Brazil and India.

The major studios make about forty films per year at an average budget of between $50–80 million per movie. On rare occasions, two of the majors will get together and produce a mega budget picture, like *Titanic*, to minimise the attendant risk. The majors are Buena Vista, Columbia, Dreamworks, Paramount, Twentieth Century Fox, United Artists, Universal and Warner Bros.

The Mini-Majors

Mini-majors make and distribute films like the major studios, but in just their home territory and one other. Pathé makes films and distributes in France and Britain, Alliance Atlantis in Canada and the UK. There are approximately twenty-five mini-majors around the world.

The Independents

An independent (not to be confused with an independent filmmaker) makes movies and distributes them in their home territory. In the UK, Entertainment, run by the Green brothers, make movies and distribute in the UK only. A recent start-up UK company, Fruit Salad, made two movies for distribution in the UK: *Human Traffic*, and *South West Nine*.

Optimum Releasing, a UK niche distributor, is considering production, and the most interesting distributor in the UK, Tartan Films, distributes a wide range of American independents, Asian and European films, as well as producing its own slate of films including the recent titles *Ted Bundy* and *Kissed*.

Film Production Companies

These companies make movies for theatrical release and are funded by a combination of the companies listed above and/or private investment and/or stock market offerings. These films are usually made on the sell then make principle. About 300 movies per year are made at budgets of $3–10 million. Scala Productions, Company of Wolves, Working Title and Recorded Picture Company are some of the larger film production companies in the UK.

Independent Producers

Technically, most producers are independent as they rely on multiple source financing. But in terms of researching the marketplace, we will consider only those working outside of industry financial support. This is most likely to be the category that you will fall into unless you are financed by one of the above companies.

Every year in the English-speaking world it is estimated that 3000 films get made at budgets ranging from less than £10,000 to more than $1 million. These films are financed with the filmmakers' own money (85%), by wealthy benefactors (10%) and with soft money from government agencies or tied sponsorship from music companies and product placement (5%).

Genre

Lloyd Kaufman and Michael Hertz's Troma Studios are an excellent example of a highly successful B-movie studio.

Genre or B-movies are making a strong comeback because of the attractive financial returns. They can be shot cheaply and sold at a profit sooner than larger budget films. There are approximately 500 English language B-movies made every year.

Adult Movies

Porn is sadly the most successful industry in North America, out-stripping defence, education and medicine in terms of profitability.

Bollywood

India creates more films than any other country. Film companies range from small to branches of the major studios such as Sony. The recent successes of crossover films such as *Asoka* and *Devdas* have proven that Bollywood films have an international appeal.

Exhibitors

Exhibitors do not make films themselves, but they own the cinemas that are hired by distributors. They have a vital role in the distribution process because, in the end, it is the exhibitors who will look at your film in a special exhibitors' screening and decide whether it has enough appeal to the local audience to merit a playdate. Without a playdate, your film will not be shown in a cinema.

Who Buys Films?

A good example of a negative pick up is *Sister Act* (1992), which was produced by Touchstone Pictures, and distributed by Buena Vista in the US.

The majors, mini-majors and independents all buy films for distribution in addition to the films they produce. The strategy is to acquire a back-up film that can be released quickly in order to minimise the damage of a blockbuster disaster. The majors will look at all the other companies making films and see if there is something affordable and good that they can use. When the distributor finds a film, they negotiate a price with the producer, called a negative pick-up, where the producer is paid the cost of producing the negative plus a profit, which is contingent on the quality of the film.

In order to find the right film to buy, each company hires an acquisitions executive (film buyer) whose job is to source and negotiate the purchase of quality product for their company. And this is the person that you must get to see your film, and buy it. There are really only about a hundred people in the world that you want to see your film. They are the acquisitions executives hired by the majors, mini-majors and independents to acquire product for their cinemas. Each acquisitions executive is subjected to a barrage of sales materials from other majors, mini-majors and independents seeking to sell their films.

The difficulty an indie producer faces is that s/he is stuck in the same group with so many other films by other equally talented and passionate filmmakers. But to an acquisitions executive looking down, it can look like a blur. Your job as producer is to catch the eye of the acquisitions executive.

What Screenings do You Want Buyers to Attend?

The ideal place for a film buyer to see your movie is in a preview theatre during business hours. Book a preview theatre such as Mr Youngs in London. Create a list of potential sales agents, distributors and acquisition executives from the guides published by *Screen International*, *Hollywood Reporter* and *Variety* for the major film markets. Prepare an invitation about four weeks prior to the screening and send faxes and make telephone calls to get a list of names of those coming. It is worth making a follow-up call closer to the date to remind busy executives. Your goal is to get the most senior person from each company to see your film. On the day of the screening, prepare refreshments. You can start the screening five or ten minutes late to allow for latecomers.

Many sales agents and acquisition executives will leave after the first twenty minutes or half hour. This doesn't necessarily mean that they dislike your film. More likely they have another screening to rush to.

Attracting Acquisition Executives

Remember to ask yourself three questions whenever you see a movie, short or feature on the TV or in a cinema:
1. Does this demonstrate talent?
2. How did they do that?
3. Could I make that?

Executives rely on a weekly newsletter service called filmfinders to list all new and upcoming productions www.filmfinders.com

There are two job titles a producer will look for during the course of producing a movie. A development executive is someone who works with the financier or production company at script stage. An acquisition executive is a film buyer and watches new films at festivals, film markets and at private screenings. A development executive is usually very difficult to meet. You communicate with a development executive by post or telephone. An acquisition executive is much easier to meet. It is their job to find you. It is your job to intrigue them with your pitch, with your marketing materials to get them to your screening.

It is at this juncture that most indie producers make a serious error of judgement. Most filmmakers will tell you that they envisage hundreds of people lined up around the block in order to see their film. They have aimed their entire film career at this (as well as every single penny they can borrow). Certainly, this is the wonderful conclusion of marketing the film — but is the end result of a successful marketing campaign, not the start of one.

Experienced filmmakers make their movie with about a hundred film executives in mind: the film buyers that are employed by the majors, mini-majors and the independents. Every aspect of their film is aimed at the acquisition executives they want to entice to a preview screening of their film with the sole intention of selling it to them.

A successful filmmaker will research the distributors most likely to buy films of the same type as the one they are planning or have made. Some go as far as to meet the film buyers directly and pitch their project in the hope of securing financing. If the acquisitions person thinks that a written or verbal pitch contains merit, they can then refer the filmmaker to the appropriate development executive.

It is easy to forget that the acquisitions executive is hired as the eyes of the distributor and when s/he discovers an interesting film, they will have to refer the film to the marketing and ultimately the financial directors of the company. Obviously, small distributors have as few as two or three employees, where larger ones, like Pathé have dozens in their acquisitions and marketing departments.

But the most important fact is that most acquisitions are simultaneously tracking hundreds of films exactly like yours. You must constantly make them aware of your uniqueness.

Career Route of Acquisitions Executives

An acquisitions executive is one of the most accessible people inside the industry. It is their job to find new talent and sign it before it disappears to the competition. Accordingly, they attend private screenings, go to film festivals and scour the trade papers for news of anything new and interesting. A successful acquisitions executive must have excellent communication skills, be able to negotiate, and have a grasp of basic business and legal affairs. They are hired because of their feel for the marketplace and what will or will not attract an audience.

Acquisition executives come from a variety of backgrounds.
- Festival director: after proving an ability to programme a film festival that becomes successful and demonstrates a feel for the marketplace
- Cinema programmer: after proving that they can deliver audiences to films, they are then head-hunted by distributors eager to capitalise on their ability to pick audience-pleasing films
- Talent agent: after learning the business and signing undiscovered talent, and proving they know what is hot

- Preview screeners: after watching many films they demonstrate that they can sort the wheat from the chaff
- Journalists in style or trend press: after publishing perceptive reviews they demonstrate that their taste is relevant to a larger audience
- Assistant to sales agents: learn the business from the inside out

Choosing Your Niche

Niche filmmakers like Hal Hartley and Woody Allen make the films they want to make knowing that enough film buyers will buy their films, justifying their production and marketing budgets.

One of the priorities for selling a film is to know the marketplace. If you can identify a sector of the market and predetermine what they will buy, then the choice of film and filmmaking techniques becomes much easier. British filmmaker Jake West was born a horror fanatic. Obsessed by the genre he lived, breathed and dressed as a goth until every aspect of the genre and its audience became second nature. After writing a screenplay he assembled a minimal cast and crew, secured financing from a private investor of about £15,000 ($22,000) and shot his first feature, *Razor Blade Smile*. He edited it over the course of a year and sold it to Palm Pictures who in turn collected over $1.2 million from sales to countries around the world. Although the picture was modest in it's scope and in the filmmaking techniques employed, Jake knew that if he could deliver a finished film it would find an audience.

Another filmmaker, Ottawa-born Lee Demarbe, created a fantasy horror film called *Jesus Christ Vampire Hunter* for a little under £10,000 ($14,000). The film was shot on 16mm and edited at Lee's apartment on an abandoned Steenbeck. To date the film has recouped over £30,000 ($50,000) from limited releases in Canada and is slated to join the Troma Studio label for further distribution. Described by one journalist at the screening at the Raindance Film Festival in 2001 as 'a fun loving romp by a group of talented filmmakers', Lee always realised that he had a film that could find an audience. Even a limited audience could guarantee him a profit.

Key Artwork

Dimensions of theatre posters in the USA are 27 by 40 inches, and in Europe are 30 by 40 inches, and are known as quads.

Before your film reaches an acquisitions executive, key artwork for posters, theatre billboards and VHS/DVD jackets will need to be generated. If you sell your film, the distributor may decide not to use your artwork – in the way posters for American films are rarely the same in Europe. Not to have artwork makes it more difficult to sell your film. Artwork will always give a visual treatment of your ideas for the marketing plan, and can inspire the prospective buyer.

If you are mocking up a video jacket, be sure you include a strong graphic image on the front, and on the spine put your contact details. On the reverse, include a paragraph summarising the film as well as complete credits and an idea of the rating: PG, 12, 15, 18 (in the USA: G, PG, PG-13, R, NC-17).

It is also a good idea to buy some blank video jackets and slide the printouts of the jackets into the sleeve to complete the illusion of a finished product. Remember that certain countries have different video box sizes. The largest is Australia, the smallest America.

Creating a one sheet

A one sheet is sent to prospective buyers, or can be sent by a buyer to exhibitors to inform them of a screening. The one sheet will also be useful in submitting to festivals and markets (discussed in the next two chapters).

Overleaf is an example of a one sheet created for *Tromeo and Juliet*, an adaptation of the Shakespeare play from Lloyd Kaufman's Troma Studios. The film was shot, and a four minute trailer was prepared. This poster was taken to the Cannes Market. This low six-figure budget film was marketed as costing over $1 million, and on the basis of this one sheet and the trailer, Lloyd sold the film for a low seven-figure number.

Trailers

At Raindance we are constantly asked what makes a good trailer. A trailer is a key marketing tool that can be used to sell your film when complete, or to raise additional finance before the film is finished. Given that a trailer is a mini-movie used by filmmakers to demonstrate their ability to the film industry it is shocking how many poor trailers are made by so-called talented filmmakers.

Trailer checkpoints:
— No more than two minutes
— Has great ADR and foley
— Good musical score
— Little or no dialogue
— Mysterious and intriguing
— Clear, short titles i.e.: 'A film by ...'
— State the delivery date

Summary

1. Understand the competition and try to work out what your unique selling point will be.

2. Choose a niche market and deliver a product tailored to it.

3. Make fresh and bold marketing materials.

In order to attract the film buyers to your screenings, you need to make a press kit.

1. Choose a title that is taut and tense and tells the story of your film

2. Graphic images that illustrate the story of the movie

3. The log line or strap line usually contains no more than ten words that give further detail about the main thrust of the movie

4. Credit principal cast and crew

5. List any outstanding artists or bands contributing to the soundtrack

6. Company logo if relevant

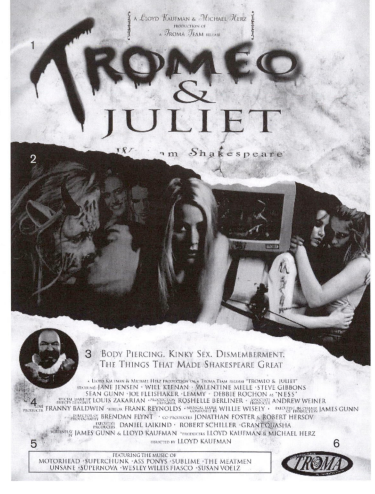

figure 16.4
One sheet deconstructed

In Conversation with Graham Humphries

Graham Humphries is an illustrator who does work for The Creative Partnership and has worked on poster designs for many Tartan Films titles.

What are the usual stages you go through on a project?
Usually things start with a script or even just a treatment. Either the client will have an idea for a basic visual concept or they will ask me to come up with one. I'll design a basic image or logo, maybe a script cover or display, or basic storyboards to indicate how a film might go.

At what stage in the process do you get involved in a project?
It depends. I am working with someone at the moment who came to me with their film when it was in post-production with a rough cut. They were still mixing the sound and had yet to commission some of the soundtrack work. They were looking at producing a poster, which they would take to Cannes, MIFED and other festivals. At that point they

1. Short synopsis of the film

2. Additional graphics

3. Additional paragraph outlining the artistic merit and credits of the filmmaker

4. Contact details of filmmaker

figure 16.4
One sheet decontstructed continued

had some visual material – just photographs, stills – and a loose idea of campaigns they'd seen elsewhere. So it was just a question of coming up with three or four ideas for posters. That happened a year ago. They just got back to me two days ago to say they've finished editing to a final cut. Now we're going to look again at producing a poster as a sales tool, as well as a logo which will go onto the beginning of the film, which will be animated by somebody else. The identity of the film is the logo and the visual feel of the film is translated into the poster.

What makes you turn down a project?

I tend not to turn down work. I usually get excited when anyone approaches me. It's very flattering for them to choose you. So I very rarely turn down anything. It's important to have a mix of everything – a whole spectrum of projects with different ideas. The more you have, the better, because each job helps influence the next.

How do you present roughs?

It can be anything from a sketch, to an almost finished concept, rendered on a computer. I might just place images together and put them with colours. It could be a verbal presentation of an idea and if the idea's strong enough, then we'll take it further. Sometimes money won't be available to go ahead, but you'll talk about a job until some money comes in later that will take things a bit further. If the film goes to a distributor and is a finished product, then you'll present a finished poster.

One romantic comedy I worked on had a series of production shots that they chose and a certain number of pictures from the film. It was just a matter of scanning those in, compositing images onto the computer and adding in other frames to get the texture of the film. I presented four different poster options for that film. But sometimes, filmmakers aren't too sure how to visually present it to the public, so I will show them the options. Usually they have an idea of what sort of films they like in the area in which they think their film is in, and they give me the names of three or four films that have been successful and say this is the sort of thing we want to go for.

What happens when the production company decides to change the title or the lead image on a project?

That happens a lot. Quite often in script stage, the title is just a working title, and it's not until the final stages – when I'm working on the finished poster – that they go to a different title. That's sometimes to do with screenings, and the way the audience reacted to the name of the film; whether it let the film down or took particularly wel. Films can even be released in one country under one name, and then be retitled for release in other territories just because of the audience.

Another thing that will happen from territory to territory is that a campaign might be figured as ineffectual as it moves from place to place. Sometimes we do adaptations of other campaigns and just change the format a bit. Traditionally British posters are in landscape format [horizontal] and American and international posters are in the portrait format [vertical]. So we change those formats often between the countries. Perhaps it's a cultural thing – a poster which, in one place really works is going to miss in another country. It happens all the time with Asian films for example. You just have to look at the material and think that the audience here is going to react differently to this image than that in another country. Cultural triggers change from place to place.

What do you do when a client picks the layout that you like the least?

That happens a lot. You try to think to yourself that even if you didn't like that idea especially, you did put the image on paper. That happens often. All you can do then is the best you can. You can shift the colour use, title treatment and things to make it better. You learn to reject all the other ideas you had about it. And you recycle ideas as well. You think, well, that was my favourite, yet they didn't like it. So put it away and someone else might like it for theirs.

17   Publicity

The American movie *The Cable Guy* starred one of the most famous men in the world at the time – Jim Carey – the film was wrongly publicised as a comedy. In fact it is a brilliant horror film. As a result, the film scored a mediocre box office run in America and Europe.

THIS IS THE MOST important element of the filmmaking process, and ironically, the one most often overlooked by new filmmakers. If you hire the best cinematographer, screenwriter and actors in the world to work for you, they will make you a film: eight thousand feet of celluloid with absolutely no marketable value. You cannot sell a film. You can only sell a movie. You turn a film into a movie by using publicity to create a buzz, or hype for your film. Additionally, publicity will attract acquisition executives to your movie.

Like other elements in the filmmaking process, you must develop a publicity strategy. Your film can suffer irreparable damage with the wrong publicity plan.

Creating a Press Kit for £1500 ($2000)

The single most effective tool in creating publicity is a press kit. A press kit is used to send details of the film to journalists and acquisitions executives. Creating a press kit is made simpler by following these basic steps:

Step 1 Create a Folder

Folders:
100 x 50p = £50 ($65)

Embossing:
£50 ($65)

Total cost:
£100 ($130)

A stationer will sell stock folders with flaps in which newspaper clippings and press releases can be organised. Ultra low budget press kits use stock folders from stationers with self-adhesive labels on which the name of the production company is printed. Self-adhesive labels went out with Margaret Thatcher. A better alternative is to get a printer to emboss the folder with the title of your film. Acquisitions executives are notoriously snobbish. The flip side is that they are easily impressed, and you would be amazed what the effect of a little bit of gold embossing can do for your press kit.

For the low budget press kit you will need to buy one hundred folders. A normal film might send out a thousand or more press kits – beyond the reach of lo-to-no budgets. Through skilful manipulation, you aim to create the impression that you have mailed a thousand press kits to international executives and journalists, and so create the impression that your film is hot.

Step 2 Write a Synopsis

A synopsis is a summary of the story of your film told in an engaging way that captures the reader's interest and makes them want to see the film. A synopsis should never sound like 'and this happened, followed by this, and then this happened'. This type of synopsis is certain to bore. A well-written synopsis should be a teaser. There are three kinds of synopses that you should include in your press kit.

Hint You are writing a synopsis that should sound like the paragraph on the back of the DVD or video jacket. The point of the synopsis is to make the reader want to see the movie.

---

i The long synopsis
A single page, double spaced, in which the story is summed up in three quarters of the page, and the last three or four lines of the page contains an anecdote from the making of the movie which demonstrates your incredible talent.

ii The medium synopsis
Three quarters of a page long, in which the story is summed up yet again, only more concisely, with the last two or three lines devoted to another production anecdote which again demonstrates the talent you know you have.

iii The short synopsis
A half page, in which the first three quarters is a tight and punchy story summary, followed by another production anecdote, this time a mere line long.

The reason you supply three synopses to journalists is because you want to make it easy for them to write a review of your film, and you offer three different lengths of synopsis because you don't yet know how much space they have in their publication.

These are now ready to be photocopied.

Step 3 Write Cast and Crew Bios

You should include brief biographies of the key people you worked with on your movie. Actors' bios should include previous film roles (if any), stage work, and awards they may have won. Key crew bios like director of photography, production designer, editor and composer should detail other directors and productions they have worked on, or work-related experience. For example my DoP shot a commercial for Burger King and my production designer designed a table for Ikea.

Be certain that you have a brief, concise and interesting biography for yourself. If this is your first film project, and you have absolutely no other film experience, then you could include your work in your previous life. For example: Elliot Grove, an ex-carpenter, produces his first feature film using project management and organisational skills he learned on building sites. If your previous work experience, like mine, sounds too lame to be of interest, you might simply list your education credits. Your total cast and crew bios should run to no more than three or four pages and when photocopied should be stapled together to keep them separate from the synopses.

Step 4 Create Ten FAQs

Creating hype and publicity for your film means that you have to give precise direction and guidance to the people who hear about your film: film festival programmers, film journalists and, of course, acquisition executives. I was in London during the launch of Quentin Tarantino's *Reservoir Dogs*, and was fortunate enough to see his press kit. Scanning it reassured me that Tarantino was not relying on the judgement of film critics or even the film going public to determine that he was an amazingly talented filmmaker. He was printing it himself in his press kit, under the guise of the Ten Most Frequently Asked Questions of Quentin Tarantino During the Making of *Reservoir Dogs*. Immediately following the questions was printed his answers.

Hint Film hype is not earned. It is manufactured by you. It is you who has the power to turn yourself into a cult filmmaker, and your film into a cult movie.

Doing this for yourself will be an easy thing to complete, because the ten questions will be the same ten questions that everyone has been asking you during the making of the film. On my film, the questions were: what was it like working with non-professional actors? If you had to do it over again, what would you do differently? What did you learn about directing films? How did you get the notorious Mad Frankie Fraser to star in your film? Who are your influences? Where do you see the future of British filmmaking?

List your ten questions on a page, and after each question type an answer about five lines long. You are hoping that a journalist will be intrigued by your film, but for whatever reason be unable to reach you in time for their press deadline. If this happens, then the journalist could write: 'Contacted today from New York, Elliot Grove said…'

By listing these questions and answers you are also giving the journalist a taste of how you will react to similar questions, and accordingly how you will appeal to the readership of the particular publication.

Step 5 Get Publicity Stills

The picture editors of the trade papers frequently bemoan the poor quality of publicity stills available to them. Screen International looks for a production still to appear on page three of its weekly and finds this the hardest still to find.

Although your press kit has a slick, glossy cover, three synopses, cast and crew bios and FAQs, you still need to have photographs. Getting a good publicity still is a true art form. The right still can be used on the poster, in newspaper ads, on video and DVD covers, on T-shirts – in fact, everywhere your movie is mentioned. Truly memorable images, like the eyes from *The Blair Witch Project*, cross into popular culture and are mimicked and satirised by others.

Publicity stills that work are photographs that include action. The stills photographer you hire should have a portfolio of stills that demonstrate movement and action within the frame. Ask the stills photographer to attend the shoot on the days that the most action is happening. Perhaps it is the day with the duelling swordsman, the pistol shot or the day you managed to get a large crane onto the set. The photographer needs to take four kinds of stills:

To hire a stills photographer for three days and get contact sheets or jpegs on a CD-Rom cannot cost more than £500 ($750) on this budget.

1. Stills of the cast re-enacting key moments of the movie. The photographer cannot click away during the shoot because the microphones will pick up the shutter noise. After a suitable take, ask the actors to hold their marks. You can then rearrange the actors to suit the frame, and get the photographer to capture the moment for posterity.

2. Stills of the cast and crew showing off the production values of the movie: show as much film equipment as you can, show the fake head being glued onto the actor, the finger nails being ripped off, whatever – but make sure it contains loads of action. Journalists and the public all concur that a picture tells a thousand words.

3. Get pictures of yourself producing. If nothing else, you will want a record of your efforts to prove that you actually produced a movie. But photos of a person producing a film are pretty lame: generally they are shots of them reading a script or signing a cheque. In order to make the photos of yourself more dramatic, turn to the theatre and use a stage trick used by accomplished stage actors when they are on the stage with another actor and wish to upstage them. They pull out their finger and point. Try it. Look at some photographs of filmmakers and they are invariably pointing. Take your stills photographer to the set, tell them that every time you point, you want to hear the shutter go. You can point at anything. You can point at a speck of fluff on someone's jacket, you can point at the sun, you can point at your foot, you can even point at your nose. It doesn't matter. Point and make sure you hear the click of the camera. In actual fact there are really only two times that you point when you are on the set as a pro-

ducer. The first is when you say 'You, with the attitude – you're fired. Off the set. Now.' And the second is: 'Thank you for sharing that with me'. At this point you will usually wander off to watch a movie for an hour or two until things cool down.

4. Photos of yourself with celebrities. Even if you do not have a celebrity working on the film, try and convince a local celebrity to attend your set, again on a day with a lot of action. When they show up, give them a polite tour of your set, introduce them to the key people on the crew and allow them time to ask questions. For many, this will be the first time they have been on a film set, and your lo-to-no budget shoot may not fall into their pre-conceived ideas of what a film set should be like. At the appropriate moment, ask them politely if you could have a picture or two with them. If necessary, offer to send them a copy. When you are ready, make sure that you are standing stage right (camera left). And point!

Hint Always stand on stage right to have your picture taken. Why? Captions run left to right, and this position guarantees that your name will appear first.

If you start studying the publicity stills used by successful film people you will see that they follow these rules.

Step 6: Include Reviews and Third Party Endorsements

Third party endorsements always work wonders in the world of promotion. All commercial enterprise uses third party endorsements. You may use toothpaste recommended by the British Dental Association, eat a certain breakfast cereal on the recommendation of a leading nutritionist, and see a movie because a certain journalist – probably well known for their taste and judgement – has put a film onto their own 'must-see' list.

By getting a journalist to see and review your film you are starting to create buzz for your film. Make a copy of the review and include it in your press kit. Even if the journalist disliked your film, the review they print will most likely include a superlative somewhere in the opening one or two sentences. Film journalists have careers too. They want to be quoted and have their name splashed on the poster. If they didn't like the film and include a superlative, they know that you will quote them out of context. So 'an amazingly inept first film' becomes 'an amazing first film'. When you print their name and publication after the quote, you are helping them with name awareness of their magazine and themselves. Journalists are always trying to increase their stature among the readership, or get a better job. With your poster in their portfolio, their reputation is enhanced and they have an even better chance of moving their career upwards. Essentially, you are helping each other.

Journalists and film festivals

Journalists have love-hate relationships with film festivals. On one hand they enjoy and thrive in the glamorous atmosphere of a film festival. If the right filmmakers come to their festival, they will be able to do many interviews in a short space of time that they can warehouse until needed. What they dislike about film festivals is the fact that they have to watch movies – and lots of them. Usually they screen these films alone at home from cassette. Few festivals have the resources to screen the films ahead of time at private screenings for journalists. Supposing you have entered a small regional festival in Europe or America in a town or small city that has a weekly community paper. This paper will have an entertainment section devoted to printing the press kits and photographs of films released by the distributors in the area. The entertainment editor probably has another area to cover as well: perhaps it is sports or holidays. When the local film festival arrives, this film journalist will be asked to cover the festival and preview all the films. When they reach your film, they discover that your press kit has three synopses: long, medium and short. The journalist knows that their work will be made easier by this simple addition to your press kit. Next, they discover the cast and crew bios which are short and succinct.

Finally they see the ten FAQs. Now they can watch the film, make notes and know they have ample information on which to base their review. And even if they hated your film they will be able to write an intelligent article based on the information you have provided. Journalists tend to include a superlative in the review of a film they dislike, because they know you will quote them out of context. For example: 'Elliot Grove's first film was an extraordinary example of incompetence'. The quote out of context would become: 'Elliot Grove's first film was … extraordinary…'

Journalists want to be quoted, they want a big line printed on your poster, and they want their name printed underneath the quote. They are hoping to get a job on that city's daily paper, or maybe move to a national paper or magazine.

Step 7 Create an Electronic Press Kit

A Unit Publicist films key moments of the shoot and key interviews on a MiniDV camera. These materials can then be edited together for the electronic press kit.

An electronic press kit (EPK) is a set of videos and CD-Roms with photos, interviews with the principal cast and crew, duplicated and distributed to appropriate people. It is difficult to accomplish on a lo-to-no budget.

During the shoot, hire a documentary filmmaker to take a high quality video footage of the shoot. Include interviews with the key actors, director, producer and other principal crew where appropriate. For example, if your film features prosthetic heads being lopped of, interview the prop-maker and the special effects artists. You are looking for angles that might help you sell in the story of the film later.

When doing interviews, have someone ask key people on the cast and crew questions from your ten FAQs. Then film the answers. If possible, set up some of the interviews in front of a simple cloth or curtain with a poster behind the interviewee. In this way you can deliver the interview to a television station and they can cut in their own reviewer making it look like they were in the same room, when in actual fact they have never met.

You should make VHS copies as well as Digibeta copies (for television). The tape can also include a short trailer for the movie.

Broadcasters welcome EPKs because it represents free content. You will have to guarantee to any television station that the music rights are cleared for broadcast.

There is a list of which countries are NTSC and PAL on the CD.

Hint Make certain that you also have a NTSC copy of the EPK for use in USA, Canada and Japan.

Title (Genre)

Production company/ies, Lead production company address, telephone and fax

Shooting locations

(Shooting start date)

Cast: [Up to twelve principal cast members' names]

ExPrd., [Executive Producer's Name]; Prd., [Producer's Name]; Dir., [Director's Name]; Scr., [Writer's Name]; DP, [DoP's Name]; Ed., [Editor's Name]; LinePrd.,[Line Producer's Name]; AD, [Assistant Director's Name]; PrdDsgn., [Production Designer's Name]; Art, [Art Director's Name]; Set, [Set Designer's Name]; Cstm, [Costume Designer's Name]; PrdCoord., [Production Co-ordinator's Name]; Snd., [Sound Recordist's Name]; Cstg., [Casting Director's Name]; Publ., [Publicist's Name]

figure 17.1
Example of a production listing

Publicity Strategy

Step 1 Get Listed in the Trades

Once you are listed in the trades you will start to get calls from acquisition executives. They will always ask to see rushes or a rough cut. Politely put them on hold and contact them when you have finished your film.

About three weeks before the start of your shoot, contact the production listings editor of the trade papers and submit to them the details requested. Here it is important that you have a unique fax number. Companies with a telephone/fax number will not be taken seriously. A company with its own fax number looks professional. The trade papers have very little space, and they want to make sure that they only list professional productions. See figure 17.1 for an outline of the information that you will need to provide for a listing.

Hint Who reads production listings? Crew (by the time it is published it is usually too late to get work), and the acquisition executives.

Step 2 Create a Website

Check out the *Memento* website (www.otnemem.com) and the *Blair Witch Project* website (www.blairwitch.com) for excellent examples of web marketing.

Creating a website for your film has numerous advantages. You may want to publish a diary of your project on the site, create quizzes and games relevant to your movie and start a discussion group about your film. Some filmmakers put up clips from the movie, or out-takes and filmmaker's mistakes if they relate to the tone of the project. Make sure anything you include fits in with the tone and 'brand identity' of your film.

It is a good idea to use an area of your site to hold your press kit. Here you can include a photo gallery (make sure each picture is captioned clearly with names). Your website can also hold high quality, print ready stills for publications and film festivals. These same stills can later be used to satisfy the demands of a potential distributor.

Hint The perfect website contains the following elements:

- An easy to remember name
- Simple and fast loading
- No black backgrounds with white text. It takes too much ink to print out
- A press release section
- Other professionals will research you and your movie via your website, so include specific details of the film
- A newsgroup so you can keep everyone updated on the developments with your film

You should:
- Assess the competition
- Experiment with the best video compression technologies for your clips
- Plan for the future development of your site

Step 3 Press Release

There are three times that you will be able to issue a press release.

The first time is on the first day of principal photography, the next time will be on the last day of principal photography, and finally, on the last day of post-production, when the film is effectively complete. The press releases you write should also be archived on your website, and ready for inclusion in your press kit.

The trades will also be able to print a still each time you print a press release, if the film is interesting enough, so make sure that your unit publicist has taken enough high quality stills to offer the press a different still each time they receive a release.

A good press release will give background information on the project and the filmmakers, and provide specific details on the who, what, where, why, and when of the film. Keep them as brief and as clearly written as possible. See figure 17.2 opposite for an example.

figure 17.2
Sample press release

Step 4 Distribute Completed Press Kit

The first press kits are distributed to the trade papers. You will probably also want to distribute to independent film magazines, such as *Filmmaker* and *Raindance Film Magazine*. As your scope widens, you might want to include some of the influential websites, such as indiewire.com and filmthreat.com. Other magazines such as *Hot Dog*, *Total Film* and *Empire* might also be convinced to run a story on the making of the film.

Consumer magazines might be interested if you have a story specific to their readership, or an actor who is newsworthy. If you do have any big name actors, then make sure you state whether they are available for interview; this is not only more interesting to journalists, but makes for more effective publicity for the film.

Make sure that you are distributing it effectively. Rather than spending a huge chunk of your publicity budget sending press kits to every publication you can think of, target your mail out to appropriate titles, whether you are aiming highbrow, lowbrow or anywhere in between.

Approaches To Publicity

The most valuable asset of any PR company is their database of contacts. To do your own PR, go to a bookstore and buy every single magazine that has a film section, and copy down the names of the journalists along with their contact details. Then telephone each publication and verify their details.

Making Contacts

A blind fax landing on someone's desk is not the best way to get noticed. The two most effective ways of promoting your film are:

Phone/fax/phone

Make verbal contact, pitch the story, whiz the fax through, and then call back to close the deal. Doing this, it's possible to contact a hundred people a day, however, if you miss someone, and leave a message, they may call you back while you are on another call, thus starting a frustrating game of telephone tag.

Lunch/fax/phone

Go to the time, trouble and expense of setting up a lunch meeting, then fax and phone for follow up. This is intimate and personal and you're likely to close (once you have paid the restaurant bill), however you can only do one meeting a day.

Summary

1. The right press kit will enable you to sell your film.

2. Excellent photographs and images are an essential part of a good press kit.

3. Always search for elements of your project that could attract either notoriety or celebrity status to your film.

If you want to complete your press kit, you will need to be reviewed and interviewed. To do that, you will need to go to a film festival, and you might even win an award!

In Conversation With Phil Symes

Phil Symes is the director of The PR Contact. He has been a key player in film public relations since the early '80s when he formed his own agency. Phil specialises in working with independent producers on a world-wide basis. Recent international launch campaigns include films such as *The Son's Room* (Palme d'Or, Cannes) *City of God*, *Spirited Away* (Golden Bear, Berlin), *Irreversible*, *The Magdalene Sisters* (Golden Lion, Venice), *The Brown Bunny*, and *At Five In The Afternoon* (Jury Prize, Cannes).

How early on in a project do you get involved?

It comes in various stages; sometimes a producer comes to us with a script idea, and is looking for support in putting the project together, so we help them to find financiers, production partners, distributors. On a number of occasions we have introduced producers to financial partners, production partners, and sales agents. Largely, that work is done at major festivals like Cannes or Venice. For example, we put together a major project with Phil Collins for one producer, Norma Heyman. It was a script called *Buster*; Norma wanted to make the film and had Phil Collins on board, but she didn't have any money for the project. We worked with her at Cannes and introduced her to a number of partners. The film was made and became one of the biggest grossing films in British history. That's one requirement of clients who come to us.

Another situation is a film that is about to shoot and they want a publicist on board to help put together the publicity during production. The main aim there is to interest potential buyers around the world and get them involved at an early stage to pre-sell the film. Everybody wants to have a film ready for release with distributors on board for major territories. A lot of those sales are effected during the period of production. The aim is to get very positive pieces in the key international trades, *Variety*, *Hollywood Reporter* or *Film France*, as well as trying to create some major consumer publicity. We would always go to magazines like *Vanity Fair* or *Harpers & Queens* to position the film as a much sought after product. During that period we will also work with the producers in putting together the press materials that they'll need to deliver to the buyer who is taking the film for a territory. That material is normally the EPK, the electronic press kit, which will feature B-roll footage shot during the production and interviews with the director, producer, set designer, hair and costume, production designer, and key cast. Then you'll have the written press kit, which we put together, and that will again be the same thing – a written report on the production, background information on all the people involved, all actors, production people, director, plus stories which can be planted along the way, stories that happened during production, and cast biographies. We will also supervise the photographic material, colour transparencies and black and white images. Our role is to work with the photographer to make sure he covers all the days that should be covered, those that are photographically interesting. We make sure that he has enough photos of the key players and that he has images of the director working on set. The normal delivery requirement is 100 colour transparencies and 100 black and white images. At the end of shoot we will make those selections, get all the principal actors to approve the images, and then we will supply the captions, identifying what's happening in each image.

Sometimes during a production we will be involved taking journalists onto set. That's another phase of publicity, and what that all leads to is publicising films at key markets such as festivals. Once a film is finished, and if it hasn't been sold for the world then the sales agents will want to take it to festivals and markets for further sales or they will want to take it to festivals for the potential glory of winning a prize or creating international awareness of the film. And the biggest and most important festivals that we cover are Berlin, Cannes and Venice.

If you get a call from a prospective new client, a new filmmaker, to go to a private screening is there anything that makes you more or less likely to accept the invitation?
We always go and see a new film and base our judgement about whether we will work on it and what we would charge according to our enthusiasm for it. If we are excited about it then we will work on it.

What is the most important element of a press kit?
I think the most important elements are the production story which is the front piece of the press kit, which explains the genesis of the project, gives quotes from the director, producer and some of the cast and is the tip sheet for most journalists. It explains the project to them and provides them with material for editorial they may be writing themselves, and then it should also include up-to-date biographies on the key actors, actresses, and the director.

How do you go about putting one together?
Well first you call all the agents of those involved and get their current CV and photos so you know what they look like so when you go on set you can identify them, and also so that you have some background information on them. We will then interview each of them on set during production and those interviews become the basis of the press kit.

Do you gear your press kits differently for different clients?
I think if you're good at PR (I hope we do this) you get a good sense of how the producers or director wants it written. They all have a signature style and we try to adapt each kit to the way we feel each director or producer would want it written. And you determine that from a conversation on set, from knowing what kind of newspapers, magazines and books they read, and you can identify the style that would suit them best. Some like very flowery descriptions while others like their press kits very sparsely written, with just the basic information. You try to judge what the director, producer and sales company are looking for.

How much input do clients have on their own press kits? Do they finalise it? Do you they approve it before it is sent out?
We do it in different stages. During production we will write a preliminary production kit which is a very basic, thin information pack that we put together to get a sense of whether we are working in the right direction. Once they have given their comments on that, we then make that into a much more detailed document. We will then, before delivering it to the producer or sales agent, get the cast to approve their biogs. And then it will go back to the producer for their final draft comments. There

is always tweaking to be done. We haven't yet had a situation where we've had any document thrown back at us. If you get a sense of how they want it written, you will normally get it right as long as you are willing to work with them.

You've mentioned a lot of skills that a film publicist needs like being able to talk to people, being able to write, having a good eye for a publicity still etc. What are the most important skills for someone who wants to work in your business?
I think it's always helpful if you have experience of journalism. It's journalistic skills that apply: getting to know people, being able to talk to them, being able to get information from them, and then being able to translate or convey that information to others. And also knowing how to be persuasive without being a nuisance, aggressive, or applying too much pressure on someone is important. There's also some instinct to it; knowing who is the right journalist to approach on a particular subject. But that comes from having read their columns on a regular basis and also being very conscious of what's happening in the bigger picture of the world. There are events outside of the film industry which relate to the subject matter that you're dealing with that you can use to get your message across.

How important is the right exposure? Is 'any publicity good publicity'?
No. Well-considered publicity works but badly-considered publicity doesn't. If you are getting a message to the wrong market sector then you are not going to be successful. We work on a diverse range of films; from the German director Werner Herzog to something as popular as *Dancing at the Blue Iguana*, which starred Daryl Hannah and was directed by Michael Radford, who was very successful with *Il Postino*. This is a more mainstream film. This is going to appeal much more to an older woman, a wide range of men, and it will be publicised in the mainstream whereas the Werner Herzog film campaign would be directed to the Herzog specialists, enthusiasts, a smaller market, but a very specific one. So I think you have to get your market right. It would be pointless calling *The Daily Star* or *The Sun* about Werner Herzog – there would be no interest. But they would certainly be interested in Daryl Hannah in the kind of costume she wears in *Dancing at the Blue Iguana*.

Instead of sending out three hundred press releases, we try to determine from among those three hundred, who the key fifty players are – whether it be magazines, newspapers, radio or TV – and just concentrate on those fifty and forget the others. There's no point.

Do you consider your company different from other publicists?
I think one thing we're very fortunate about is that almost all of the people that work in the office are very, very keen on film. They love working with filmmakers, actors and actresses. They really are enthusiasts for what they do. So to them it's not really just a nine to five job. It's something they love doing and I think that comes across. And they're not the

kind of publicists who just want to work on big Hollywood studio pictures. We will get involved with something that seems odd or strange because we think it's exciting. For example at the Berlin Film Festival we were offered a Japanese animated film and a lot of other agencies said 'Oh, is that all you have to work on?' and we said 'It's interesting, it's exciting', and it won the Golden Bear.

Is there a direction that you see filmmakers heading in or that you would like to see?
Originality is very important. We have a lot of first-time producers or filmmakers coming in with scripts and almost every script you read is derivative of something else that has come before. It seems very hard to find a very good, new, original script. So many times we read scripts in our office and say, 'Well that is *Matrix* meets so and so meets so and so'. In terms of the industry, there don't seem to be many independent filmmakers around. Most of them are attached to a consortium company or they are with Film Four, or they're working with Working Title. There is no Palace Pictures out there, there aren't so many talented young independent companies as there were in the '80s.

What's the best thing about your job?
Seeing it work. What I love is if I've worked very hard on a project that was totally unknown such as the Indian film *Asoka*, then seeing it become something much talked about, much admired and successful at the box office. From a starting point where people were saying that Indian films don't work in this country, we took the film to Venice and it was a huge success and then did very well.

Does it become difficult to find original ways to present a new movie?
I find that if you do work on a certain style of film you get lots of offers of repeat business of that particular genre. And we wouldn't be excited if we did twenty films that were all of the same type and I don't think we could get the journalists interested. For example we are working at the moment on a very controversial French film called *Baise-Moi*, it's interesting because it is the first time we've worked on a film of that type and we hope it will be successful. But thereafter we will want to go on to do something else that we're interested in.

Do you take on a lot of challenging or controversial films?
I think challenging films are more interesting because you don't do a formula job repeating everything that's been done in America. If the film is untested, then that to me is much more interesting. For example at Cannes this year, our slate of films was a French film, an Italian film which won the Palme D'Or, an Iranian film that won a major prize, a Japanese film, a film from Kurdistan, an American film and a film from China. At Venice we had an American film by Larry Clark, a very challenging filmmaker, an Indian film, a German film and a British film from the man who made the *Full Monty* so, quite a mix.

In Conversation with Tom Charity

Tom Charity is Film Editor at *Time Out* London magazine and the author of *John Cassavetes Life Works* (Omnibus Press) and *The Right Stuff* (BFI Modern Classics).

What do you think the role of the film critic is?

I think film critics are important. In a way I have misgivings about being lumped in with publicity because what I think is important about film critics is they offer an alternative to publicity, to the hype. It depends on the critic and the publication. But I think you have this big Hollywood machine which has enormous financial resources trying to lure 'punters' into the cinemas, regardless of what the product is. And the most useful, direct role of the critic, is to offer an objective analysis of that product; a guide to consumers as to the quality and the nature of what the film might actually be, and also as a kind of cultural commentator, to stand back and look at a wider picture of what might be going on in the movies. Because *Time Out* is one of the few independent publications – we're not owned by a big corporation – we can write exactly what we think without any pressure whatsoever on us from our employers. I think that's a really valuable freedom to have. We can lead our review section with any film that we choose, and that's the film editor's prerogative, which is not necessarily the case in national newspapers where there's a lot of pressure to go for the biggest Hollywood film as the lead review.

How did you start out in the business?

I did a course that was split fifty-fifty between film and English and the film component was also split fifty-fifty between film history and theory and film practice and production. So I had experience from both sides. I kind of realised that I didn't have the patience or the wherewithal to go into filmmaking and kind of fell into film writing. But I can't say I feel very frustrated about that, I think it's worked out pretty well. When I came out of college I applied for a job at *Time Out* that I wasn't really qualified for and didn't get interviewed for. But the film editor liked the samples that I'd sent in and agreed to meet me to talk about whether I would be interested in doing freelance work for him and yes, I was. I always felt an affinity with *Time Out* and I was kind of lucky in that that's where I got a break, almost right at the beginning of my career in journalism. It was actually the first place I was professionally published, so I had an emotional attachment to *Time Out* anyway.

If a new filmmaker invites you to a screening, what makes you more likely to accept?

Well, it happens a lot, specifically with short films. With short films, I invariably say no. And the reason is that I am just too busy. As it is, I have to see three or four films every week for the job. So I don't have the time to go and see extra films just because someone's made them. There's not much I can practically do to help a short film. What I will say to people in that position, short and feature filmmakers, is that it is much easier for me if they send a tape. I am very happy to give personal feedback but there's no way I can get anything in the magazine unless there is a public screening.

So how does it work with the big releases?

What happens with mainstream releases is that they organise press previews which might be anything from six months before release to a week before release. That's how I see most of my films, but we run copy in the magazine with release.

How important is a press kit for a filmmaker and what should they include in their press kit?

A press kit is useful but I don't know how important it is. The most valuable use that it has is a list of cast and crew with everybody's name spelled right. And maybe a brief synopsis of the plot with the character names. Sometimes it's useful to see a brief CV for the talent. But that's it really. It's less useful now for mainstream films because that information is generally available on the Internet.

You and Geoff Andrew have been called the most important film critics by distributors; they are seeking your approval to increase box office.

Er, I don't think it's true [chuckle]. I think *Time Out* is important to a certain sector of the film distribution-exhibition industry. Art house films rely on independent voices like *Time Out* because they can't afford to buy the publicity that Hollywood can. Because Geoff and I are pretty open to art house cinema I think that has attracted a readership that is interested in that kind of film, and that's good for independent distributors.

Our readership, the circulation of the magazine, doesn't compare with national critics or with Alexander Walker in the *Evening Standard*. Anything with TV coverage is going to reach many, many more people than *Time Out* will. But our readers go to the cinema a lot, which is nice. We are a London magazine and London is a huge percentage of the box office particularly for independent films. For that sector, our importance is out of proportion to the readership because Londoners tend to be much more cosmopolitan than people outside London and because these films don't get distributed properly outside of London.

How do you feel about being quoted out of context?

It's tricky, really. Quite often, PRs will phone us up to ask for quotes for their films and obviously they do it when they know that we liked the film. I feel a bit torn because you want to support those kinds of films but in the end it's my name on it and I have lost count of the number of times people have given me a hard time over a film I have recommended because it's been quoted on the poster. Often they end up telling me their reservations about a film which I've shared in my review but they haven't read the review they've only read the poster. So I do have mixed feelings about it.

My rule of thumb now is I won't give a quote unless I have written the review and they're not allowed to quote anything that isn't verbatim from the review. Some people are more generous than that – some people will give them a quote and work it into the review. But I think that's the tail wagging the dog.

Is there a certain type of film that you are more likely to give a good review to?

I don't know. I like to think I have very eclectic taste but some people might disagree. Somebody said that there are only two kinds of films: good and bad. And I don't agree with that. There isn't a genre that I feel unqualified to review a film in. But one of the things about working here and being a film editor is that we have a team of freelancers to call on so if I don't think I am going to enjoy a film, then why should I put myself through that? I would rather give the film a better chance so I'll assign a freelancer who I think would enjoy it. If it's a film about the rave scene – I'm too old! So I'll find somebody younger and hipper!

When you review a film do you assess it against your personal tastes or do you try to make a judgement about how the film will be received generally? Do you believe that the readership trust your opinion?

I think it's impossible to try to second guess or generalise public opinion because everybody has their own opinion and no two people are going to see eye-to-eye over a film. So the only way to do it is to be honest about your own reactions to a film and hopefully you can write the review in such a way that you can put the film in context so that people can see where you're coming from and form their own opinion not only on the film, but on the review.

Are you concerned with how other people review the movies that you review? For example, you weren't too enamoured by *A Beautiful Mind* but it won a Best Film Oscar™.

I wish I could say I didn't care at all about what other people thought but of course I do. You're in a pretty exposed position as a critic. I do read other people's reviews before and after writing mine, and I always did, because I am fascinated by films. I like to be aware of what other people are thinking, what my colleagues are thinking. The crucial thing is not to be swayed by that because, if you end up second-guessing, you are not being true to yourself and if you're not true to yourself, how can you expect your readers to trust you? A film like *A Beautiful Mind* is going to get very mixed reception. There is a very polarised reception to films – what's a perfect film for the Academy is not necessarily going to be a very hip film in London. I would have trouble, probably, being a critic in LA because it's a business town. I don't think that my perspective is close enough to what the citizens of LA actually want from a movie. Here there is a great cynicism about what Hollywood does, which I think is a healthy thing, and I do my best to promote it.

What advice do you have for independent filmmakers?

I am surprised how little sense of film culture a lot of young British filmmakers have. I don't think they see enough movies, particularly older films. I don't think they have enough curiosity about cinema as an art form. They seem to me to be very fashion led. You get a seemingly endless run of Tarantino rip-offs and gangster films. There's nothing wrong with doing a gangster film, but do they all have to be the same? You just get the feeling that they've seen *Lock, Stock, and Two Smoking Barrels* and they're going to do their version of that. I'm sure they've seen *The Godfather* but have they seen Cagney movies? Have they seen Fritz Lang movies? Do they even know who Fritz Lang is? They should; this is how you learn. You look at a Scorsese — I mean he didn't just pick up a camera and do it. He studied film, and I don't mean in college; I mean in a cinema. And they're lucky these days because everything is available on tape, on DVD. You can do a film school at home.

How are photographs picked for *Time Out*?

I pick them. We're generally sent a pack of photos or they're on the Internet. More often they're just on ImageNet, which is a website that all the main distributors use. And it might vary from a choice of two or three stills, through to fifty. Personally I think it's a mistake to only send a couple of stills because you'll just see the same pictures everywhere. And if I have to drop a picture because of space limitations, then I am going to drop a picture that I've seen everywhere else and am bored by. Pictures are important and equally, in a way, it's a mistake to send out too many because you want to have some control over the visuals, over the message that the pictures send out because they are as strong as the words. It's important to let the stills reflect what the film is. I think that's good advice to a young filmmaker: to get a decent stills photographer because you do need about six to a dozen really strong shots.

What about any advice to a young writer?

You know, it's one of the truisms of film criticism that you will constantly find yourself saying that the script wasn't ready and I know how frustrating that is for a writer to hear! I think the most important lesson the film writer can learn is that there can't be too many rewrites; everything can get better. You can listen to other people's opinions but you don't necessarily have to follow their advice. I think a lot of screenplays coming out of Britain could use a little polishing. There are a lot of stereotypes and people are very lazy. One of the things that Americans have done better in the independent sector is that they are more open to putting a fresh spin on stuff whereas a lot of British scripts just tend to recycle but that's not what you want from the independent sector. Originality is key, and I don't know why that doesn't come through more. Everyone seems to be on the fast track to selling out. Independents should use the freedom they have to be outside the mainstream; experiment, and that's what will actually make you stand out. Some kind of flare and originality really does stand out.

What about someone trying to get into film criticism? Do you have any advice for them?

Don't do it. [Chuckle.]

18 Film Festivals

FILM FESTIVALS ARE the result of corporate, civic or national ego. Film festivals are founded by corporations, municipalities or nations to demonstrate their cultural ethic and prove to a larger community that culture exists in the company, city or state.

A city like Leeds for example has a museum, an art gallery, a symphony orchestra, an opera and a film festival. The city fathers who assist in funding the Leeds Film Festival, can certainly claim that the city of Leeds is a cultured place, and therefore more attractive to tourists. The revenue generated by the extra tourist traffic thus justifies any public money given to the festival. However, a film festival is usually last on the list of cultural events funded by public money.

Bermuda has a film festival that is part funded by the country's tourist ministry. Tour packages are sold to film fans include film tickets and accommodation during the end of the low season. In this way the film festival – a cultural event – is used to promote the island's tourist business and fill its excellent hotels and restaurants with customers.

Other film festivals satisfy corporate needs. In London the Sci-Fi Festival used to be sponsored by the Sci-Fi Channel to create awareness for the Channel, and its specific programme of sci-fi films.

In industry terms, film festivals are usually used as launch pads for films. Attended by acquisition executives and talent scouts, festivals are full of new product and fresh talent. Acquisition executives rely on the choices made by festival selectors (called programmers) to filter through the vast array of material in circulation. Individual festivals have built reputations based on their programming. In Europe, Rotterdam, Berlin, Raindance and Cannes all have unique programming choices that distinguish each festival from the other. In America, Toronto, Telluride and Sundance are well known for their programming, while smaller festivals like Montreal's excellent Fantasia Film Festival present unique and original material themed around horror and science fiction.

A film festival's role is to provide an audience of receptive and appreciative filmgoers to view your work. Distributors can also use the festival to build publicity for their film before its commercial release. A festival is also a place where acquisition executives can discover new talent as they have a platform to screen their first shorts and features.

Start Your Own Film Festival

If you have a burning passion for cinema, and you would love the organisational challenge, there is nothing to stop you from starting your own film festival. All you need to do is contact the owner of a cinema in your area, and see what they charge for a week-long hire. This is four-walling: you buy all of the tickets for the cinema for that period at a discount. This is exactly how Raindance Film Festival started.

In 1993 there were no other film festivals devoted to first time film-makers or to British films. In that year there were only six independent films made in the UK – probably the low point in British filmmaking history. The major British film festivals in 1993, Edinburgh and London, specialised in European and world (i.e. American) cinema. British film-makers were considered freaks with the exception of Ken Loach, Mike Leigh and Derek Jarman. The uniqueness of Raindance Film Festival was to feature British films and films by first time filmmakers.

Hint In order to make your film festival successful, create a business plan.

Creating a Film Festival Business Plan

Step 1 Determine the unique selling point of your festival
With so many new festivals opening every week (and closing a few months later) it is more important than ever to find out how your festival will be different from any other festival currently playing in your area. Perhaps your area needs a specialist festival to broaden the range of films for certain key audience groups, for example Asian audiences? Or perhaps you live in an area where there simply aren't many films being shown and audiences could be found for a variety of film genres.

Step 2 Is my festival original?
You do not want to do something that someone else is doing in your area or has done in the recent past. Festival listings are published by *Variety*, *Screen International* and the British Council. You should study them and try to get a feel for the different types of festivals already established.

If you attempt to start a festival that is not original, you are likely to fail.

i Limited amount of both private and public funding
In a climate of so many competing festivals, funders are unlikely to back a festival if they perceive it to be similar to another event. This is mainly due to limited resources and a need to balance provision.

ii Competition for audiences from other established festivals
Most people will not travel long distances to go to see films except in the case of the very large or specialist film festivals.

iii Competition for film prints and distribution difficulties

Well-established festivals always get first choice on titles as distributors or sales agents will be confident that the film is going to be seen by a large number of people.

Step 3 Form alliances

Determine what other arts organisations or cultural embassies might exist in your catchment area in order to allow you to share the workload, and perhaps raise sponsorship. If you live in a capital city, then you might consider approaching the cultural attaches of various government bodies. Countries like Germany, France, Italy and Sweden have strong filmmaking traditions, and have aggressive cultural policies where each nation is trying to export its own film culture. Of course the drawback is that you will be limited in some respect by the types of film you can screen. If your festival was funded by the Israeli government to screen a series of Israeli films, you may not be able to screen a series of Palestinian films.

Step 4 Choose a time

This is probably the most important step of all. If you chose a time near another festival, or during a time in the calendar year that has frequent high profile sporting events, you are less likely to succeed. Similarly, scheduling a film festival during a religious holiday like Easter or Christmas would be foolhardy.

Step 5 Draw up a budget

At Raindance, we have calculated that each 120-minute slot costs £4000 ($6000) to run.

Running a film festival isn't cheap. It takes a lot of time to trawl through submissions and select film you want to screen, it costs money to contact the producers, sales agents and distributors and convince them that a screening at your film festival will help their film, and it casts a small fortune to pay for the print to be shipped to and from your festival. Add to that the cost of the cinema, the cost of running ads, printing leaflets and catalogues, not to mention bringing over a filmmaker for a special event, and it is easy to spend £100,000 ($150,000) on a week-long event. Whatever you decide to do, you have to assess the financial impact and cost. Put it on a budget, and then see if you can raise the money to pay for it. See figure 18.1 overleaf for a festival budget.

Step 6 Draw up a marketing plan

Marketing and sponsorship go hand in hand. A sponsor may have a marketing budget of their own that they can use to enhance your event.

When you are considering your marketing budget, try and see which local groups can assist you in marketing events within your festival. If you have a German film – try the German cultural organisation, if you have a film about animal cruelty – contact the local humane society, if you have a film or series of films that portray the evils of racism – contact the local commission for racial equality.

You should also consider alternative forms of marketing such as street marketing.

Film Festival Budget	Budgeted	Actual
Income		
Box office		
Merchandise sales		
Submission fees		
Grants		
Sponsorship		
In-kind sponsorship		
Total income		
Expenditure		
Venue hire		
Film print transport		
Equipment		
Guest speakers		
Hospitality		
Marketing/PR		
Printing:		
Flyers		
Tickets		
Posters		
Catalogue		
Office expenses:		
Telephone		
Rent and bills		
Postage		
Salaries:		
Director		
Programmer(s)		
Assistant(s)		
Total expenditure		
Total profit / loss		

figure 18.1
Festival budget

Considered mainstream now, street marketing is a surefire way to get punters into the cinema. Whether it is a few people standing on a street corner near the cinema handing out flyers, a unicyclist juggling fire near the box office or a signwriter chalking on the sidewalk, anything will get people into the cinema. A simple photocopied flyer with the title of the film, the time and place it is screening and a few good one liners about the film can really get people into your screening. Another alternative would be to print an image on a postcard. The cards can be left for collection, or used in a mailout.

Consider putting together a catalogue containing all the films you are screening. This is another useful way to get people into your screening, and it also provides a base from which you can sell advertising.

Step 7 Get listed in the directories and websites

Dull and boring as it may seem, it is important to get your festival listed in all of the trades and on the different websites that contain film databases. If you give awards and have a celebrity jury, listings come easier.

figure 18.2
Secretary postcard:
British distributor Tartan Films used this
simple card for Secretary in 2003. The
postcard is cut around the shape of her
legs and bottom and folds just above the
log line, so that it pops up, like the
secretary in the movie. The film became
the number two film in London

Step 8 Raise the money
However you do it – public funding, private investment, sponsorship, cultural grants – you must raise the money. Submission fees and box office will cover half your costs if you are lucky.

Step 9 Programming a film festival
Let us suppose that you have hired your cinema for one theatrical week: from a Friday morning to the following Thursday night. The cinema is now yours to do with what you want.

A film festival has several key elements. Film festivals show movies, they hold talks and seminars, they pay tributes to filmmakers, they throw parties and they create atmosphere. It is important to plan your festival time out to the minute, and make certain that you have each of the ele-

	Fri	Sat	Sun	Mon	Tue	Wed	Thu
10.00							
12.00							
14.00							
16.00							
18.00							
20.00							
22.00							
00.00							

figure 18.3
Festival schedule

ments at the correct time. It would be difficult to run a film festival successfully with the elements in the wrong order. A party at 9am would do little to enhance the atmosphere, and a series of Jewish films on Passover would also be disastrous for the potential Jewish audience at the box office. Remember that festivals need to be innovative and original. Do not copy the efforts of other established festivals. Be original and fresh.

i Devise a schedule

Draw up a screening schedule of available time slots. When the cinema is not a festival cinema, its first showing probably is at noon or two o'clock. Since you have the cinema for the entire week, you can start the screenings earlier if you want. See figure 18.3.

ii Decide on strands

An efficient way to make your festival stand out from the competition is to choose a strand. Strands can feature the works of a single filmmaker, the films of a country, films made by an ethnic minority, or a genre. At Raindance we have had strands of films from countries like Japan, Canada and the Balkans, and filmmakers strand with movies by Roger Corman and Shane Meadows. We also have had B-Movie strands which show late nights on Friday and Saturday. Strands make your marketing tasks easier, because you are marketing a collection of films, not a series of individual titles.

Premieres, World Premieres and Festival Politics

Film festival directors, like myself, will always choose a world premiere over a national premiere. It is simply more glamorous. As a filmmaker, you have certain trump cards to play with when you submit to film festivals. When you are accepted for the first time to a film festival, it technically is your world premiere. But if that festival is a small festival, you may choose to give that festival a national premiere and save the world premiere for a festival in another country.

Festival politics also kicks in. If a film screens at Edinburgh, it is ineligible for the London Film Festival – which only screens UK or world premieres. If it screens in Edinburgh, it can screen at Raindance. A film premiering at Raindance is not eligible for Berlin because Berlin specialises in European premieres. A film can screen at Raindance and then Rotterdam however. A film cannot screen at Berlin and Cannes. Sundance winners are usually excluded from the Cannes Film Festival – not because they are ineligible – but because the directors of the Cannes Film Festival would rather screen world premieres.

On the other hand, in order to illustrate how ego boosting the so-called premiere drama is, allow me to relate some stories about my first-hand experience with premieres and other festivals.

We screen many shorts at Raindance. One particular programme a few years ago contained several truly outstanding shorts that were also selected for another British film festival. Screening in our festival would normally have disqualified these shorts, but the producers were eager for them to screen at Raindance because they supported a series of feature films in development and it was important that certain financiers and talent agents saw the work in front of a paying audience. In order to show the shorts, I simply told the festival programmers of the competing festival that we had not received the prints. This bare faced lie was enough to convince the other festival that these films were not shown at Raindance thus preserving their world premiere status.

Although I am not proud of this episode, I did it in order to protect the integrity of the filmmakers and of our festival. I also have been the victim of several world premiere pranksters myself, advertising world premiere screenings at Raindance when in fact the films had played in dozens of other festivals.

Playing premiere roulette is becoming more difficult as festivals become more web-literate. At Raindance we routinely do a web search on new film titles, and will know in a matter of seconds which film festivals you have already screened at. We also do not put as much emphasis on premieres at Raindance – preferring to screen work we determine is worthy of an audience.

Staff Needed To Run A Festival

Festival Director

The festival director needs to be able to run the festival like any other well-run business. S/he needs to understand commerce as well as being able to communicate persuasively and effectively with potential sponsors, and filmmakers. Sponsors need to know what benefits they will derive from giving money to the festival that are unique and different from sponsoring another type of event, like a sporting event. The festival director also needs to be able to persuade distributors to screen high profile films at the festival, in order to give the festival a cachet that can be used by the marketing people.

Above all, the festival director has to have a vision that will lead the festival to a new plane, and give the festival a position different from any other festival.

11th RAINDANCE FILM FESTIVAL SUBMISSION REVIEWS

Reference number: _____
Title: _____
Country of origin: _____
Running time: _____
Originating format: _____
Screening format: _____

Category: Narrative / Documentary / Pop Promo

Genre: Thriller / Drama / Comedy / Animation / Romance / Experimental /
                  Horror / Sc-Fi / Family / Musical / Mockumentary

Theme: _____
_____

Brief Review: _____
_____
_____
_____
_____

Rating: Excellent / Festival must
                 Consider as possibility
                 Weak

Shortlist for Jury Prize: Official Selection Feature
                              Official Selection Short
                              UK Feature
                              UK Short
                              Digital Feature
                              Digital Short
                              Debut Feature
                              Documentary

Reviewer: _____

figure 18.4
Raindance film evaluation form

Programmer

The programmer(s) are the people who view all the preview cassettes
and shortlist films appropriate to the festival.

Before you hire a programmer, give them a cassette of a film that you
have already seen and formed an opinion on. Ask them to evaluate the

film according to their tastes, and then compare their review with your own. If you don't, then you could miss out on some gems.

I experienced this embarrassing situation in 1993 when a programmer for Raindance in New York turned down a black and white film shot with a wobbly camera. The film turned out to be Kevin Smith's *Clerks*, which premiered at Sundance in January 1994 – a mere three months after Raindance. Make sure you trust the taste of the programmer(s) you hire. Typically, the programmer of each strand in your festival will make their individual shortlists and then confer with the festival director and make a final decision on the films.

Publicist/Head of Marketing

This is probably the most important job on the festival team. The publicist has the daunting task of releasing, not one, but dozens of films (not movies!) with no stars to the unsuspecting general public. The publicist will also need to decide how to approach the trade papers as well. It is one thing to get good reviews for your festival's films in the local weekly newspaper – it's quite another to get a positive notice in one of the trades, like *Variety*, *Hollywood Reporter* or *Screen International*. Good coverage in the trades will elevate your festival to the point that acquisition executives will start to attend – which in turn enhances your reputation amongst filmmakers eager to do a deal for their film.

Print Traffic Coordinator

This is the second most important job in a film festival and the most underrated. The print traffic coordinator is the person responsible for insuring that film prints arrive at the festival in time for the screening, and leave the festival to the next destination in time for that screening. The PT coordinator has to make sure that the prints arrive in the correct screening format along with the right sound format. S/he also has to make sure the prints clear customs (a process that can take hours or days) and allow time for the film print to arrive at the cinema in time for the projectionists to 'make up' the film into a single projection piece. After the screening, the PT coordinator makes sure that the film print or tape is packaged and sent to the right destination for its next screening. Dealing with other film festivals, film producers and boring customs officials are all part of the PT coordinator's job.

If you enjoy endless telephone bashing and email correspondence with people whose first language is other than yours, then you may be right for this job. If film traffic is sorted, then a film festival runs smoothly. If it isn't, then the festival collapses into a chaos of delayed and cancelled screenings, and if you let down other festivals that follow yours by not getting prints to them on time, then you will be tarred with the unreliable brush, and it tends to stick.

Sponsorship Coordinator

Ah! A luxury – to have a full time person who raises sponsorship and makes sure that there is enough cash to meet the budget of the film festival. In reality, this essential role is often overlooked in the rush to launch the festival, leaving the organisation exposed to financial ruin. Most festivals never run past their third year, due principally to the financial problems that lack of funds create. Sort this out if you want your festival to succeed.

Runners

The lowly runner can make or break your festival. A runner will pass out leaflets as part of your street marketing campaign, deliver heavy 35mm film prints to the cinema, answer hundreds of telephone calls and do anything else you can imagine. What does a runner get out of it? A job reference from your newly prestigious festival on their CV is one benefit that most interns or runners desire. Of course that helps anyone trying to break into the industry. The real value of a runner/intern is the fact that they get to watch you cave in under the enormous pressure, and learn from your mistakes. If they can give a good neck massage, then their letters of reference will be the most glowing imaginable.

Types of Film Festivals

Film festivals are divided into categories based on the number of acquisition executives that attend.

Majors

The major film festivals, in rank, are: Cannes, Toronto, Sundance, Berlin, Rotterdam and Venice. Cannes is undoubtedly the premiere event. Toronto and Sundance vie for the number two spot, but since Sundance has become a launching pad for Hollywood films, I personally give the number two spot to Toronto – if for no other reason than the important slots it gives to foreign language films. Rotterdam is an amazing festival hosted by an amazing city. Berlin has an excellent festival with Europe's most energetic and charismatic director. Venice is an important festival as well, but is becoming dangerously corporate.

Mini-Majors

Mini-major festivals are also excellent festivals to launch your films, and vie with the majors for industry and celebrity turnout. Festivals such as

Locarno, San Sebastian, Tribeca and Karlovy Vary have hundreds of celebrities and paparazzi attending and can be a useful springboard to getting your film noticed.

City Festivals

There are many city festivals that attract the attention of filmmakers and filmgoers alike. They do not have a sizeable industry presence, very few acquisitions executives and are designed to appeal to the cineastes within their borders. Edinburgh, Leeds, Cambridge and London are some of the important UK festivals designed for local residents. Palm Springs, Telluride, San Francisco and Montreal are a few of the many in North America.

Mom and Pop

At the risk of sounding patronising, mom and pop festivals are small festivals that were created simply for the enjoyment of cinema. They are usually run by one or two people, and can be themed, such as the Frightfest and the Sci-Fi Festival, in London. Sometimes they offer wider themes, such as the Human Rights Festival or the London Lesbian and Gay Festival (run by the British Film Institute). These festivals attract local press, but very few if any industry people and virtually no acquisitions executives attend.

Independent

There are only three truly independent film festivals in the world: The Los Angeles Independent Film Festival, held each April in LA, the Slamdance Film Festival held each January simultaneously with the Sundance Film Festival, and Raindance in October in London. Each of these film festivals treat submitting filmmakers with a great deal of integrity and each prides itself in viewing every single submission many times until a quorum of programmers decides whether or not the film should be screened. These three festivals are also classed as mini-majors according to the number of acquisition executives who attend.

Presenting Yourself to a Film Festival

Most film festivals only accept films that come by personal recommendation. In order to be seriously considered for a festival you must form a personal contact with one of the festival programmers and convince them that your film will reach an audience. While this may seem a daunting and unfair process, it is, unfortunately, a part of the film festival game. If you are targeting a specific festival, then it is prudent to find out which individual is programming the specific strand that you want to screen in, and make sure that you speak to, and form a personal relationship with that person. When that person screens your film, you want to make sure that you are able to communicate with them after the screening and find out precisely what they felt about your film. At this point too, one needs to be persuasive, but not desperate. Nothing will turn off a festival programmer quicker than the whiff of desperation surrounding a film project.

In order to develop a festival tour, you must do some careful research. Observe what sorts of films a particular festival screen before you submit. Find out who the programmers are, either by calling the festival directly or by looking at their websites. Once you have decided that the festival you are pursuing is appropriate to your marketing plan, request the correct application forms and submit your film.

What it Costs

Film festivals usually charge submission fees. At Raindance the cost is £15 for a short under 15 minutes, with an additional charge of £1 per minute. The larger festivals like Toronto, Sundance and Cannes do not charge a submission fee, but will may not look at your film on cassette. You need to hire a screening room when the festival director is in town and wait for them to see the film on a cinema screen. This does sound terribly old-fashioned (it is). So the free festival submission really boils down to the cost of duplicating the submission form, and hiring the preview cinema for the screening of your film £150 plus per hour.

Attending a Film Festival

When you get a call or email from a festival offering a screening slot, you will have to make sure that you have a film print, or high quality tape in the required format. Some festivals screen VHS, but others do not consider it a professional exhibition format (which it is not). Your film print will need to be shipped to the festival to arrive some days before its first scheduled screening. If the film print is travelling from outside the EU, then customs forms will need to be completed, and a customs broker hired to clear your film through customs. The festival you are screening at will usually provide you with the necessary paperwork and broker details. Technically, when your film arrives in the UK from outside the EU, it is assessed for value and VAT is charged to the film festival as a temporary importer. Once the film has been screened and returned to the filmmaker, the festival can reclaim the VAT. Once your print shipment details have been finalised, it is time to think about your own personal plans, and whether or not you wish to travel there as well. If you do, the festival may have low-cost accommodation organised, and have preferential rates on airlines. It is generally a good decision to attend festivals, provided you can cope with the financial cost.

Four Reasons to Attend Film Festivals

1 Do a deal

Love and Human Remains and *She's Gotta Have It* were both sold immediately after their festival debut screenings. *Love and Human Remains*, was in such demand at Raindance an extra screening which was laid on also sold out. A deal memo for world rights was agreed on a coffee table outside the cinema.

The primary reason for submitting your film to a film festival is to have it screened in front of acquisition executives who will 'discover' your film and make you an offer on the spot. If you are attending one of the smaller festivals, it is unlikely that this will happen. Film buyers travel through the major and mini-major festivals and would only consider a side trip to your screening at a smaller festival if you carefully planned the publicity surrounding your screening. They might reasonably ask why you had not been accepted into a larger, more convenient festival.

2 Win awards

If you read bios of filmmakers, you will often see the phrase: an award winning filmmaker, but the names of the awards won are never mentioned. That is because there are only three awards worth mentioning on a CV.

The most prestigious award is the Oscar™. Even a nomination is mentioned on a filmmaker's CV. The Academy has carefully presented itself to the industry as a credible event, although in recent years it has become known as a marketing contest with the cleverest and most expensive marketing campaigns winning the awards. Following that, the Palme d'Or at Cannes is highly esteemed. Its cachet has become established because it is judged by very high profile industry jurors at the most important film festival of the year. The third most sought-after award is the Golden Bear presented at the Berlin Film Festival.

Many festivals offer awards to any filmmaker attending their festival as a means of attracting entries. A friend of mine, Dov Simens had a 20-minute live action short starring William Forsythe. He submitted to the Montreal Film Festival knowing that they had a 35mm live action science fiction short film category and gave out gold, silver and bronze medals. There was one other entrant and he won the bronze. A few weeks later he did the same thing at the Cincinnati Film Festival and now calls himself a multiple award winning filmmaker.

3 Sit on a panel

If award winning is not your thing, then get yourself invited to sit on a panel. Not only will it help you hone your public speaking skills, but you can then claim that you were directly involved with the festival.

4 Getting reviewed

Film journalists really do not enjoy film festivals. Suppose your first film festival is a small regional film festival, a mom and pop film festival. The local weekly newspaper will have a film journalist who creates the weekly centre spread on movies from the press kits supplied by the major distributors. But with the film festival approaching, s/he will have to watch all the films entered into the local film festival and write reviews of all of those as well. As a producer, you want a good review, and hope and pray that the pictures you sent to the festival with your press kit are attractive enough to get printed in the newspaper.

The film journalist for this small weekly newspaper also has career aspirations. S/he would like to work on one of the daily papers, or get a job reviewing films on a radio or television station. Because the newspaper is so small they also have to cover the horse racing, but a festival really gives them some hope of a ticket out of Smallsville. Journalists have learned that they should always print a superlative in their review, even if they hate it, because they know you will quote their review out of context. For example: 'Elliot's first film is a fine example of how not to make a movie' becomes 'Elliot's first movie is a fine example'.

When you quote the journalist out of context they then can include your quote in their portfolio. If their quote makes it onto your poster, be certain you include their name and publication and send them a copy!

Cannes Film Festival

The Cannes Film Festival is arguably the largest and most exciting film event in the world. I heartily recommend that every writer, director, producer and actor go there at least twice: the first time just to be awed and to discover how the festival works, and the second time for business or pleasure depending on what your ambitions are.

Cannes is composed of four things: screenings, parties, tradeshows and networking. It takes place in mid-May and is actually an amalgamation of several festivals: The Directors' Fortnight, Un Certain Regard, the main festival competition, shorts and classic films. Admission is free, but to get a ticket to the screenings you need an invite.

Routes to a Screening Ticket at Cannes

Go to a sales agent
Get your hands on a copy of the official catalogue, and find out who the sales agents are that are handling the film. All or most of the sales agents with films in the festival also attend, and find out where their temporary offices are, and go and use your powers of persuasion to see if they can get you a ticket.

Go to the festival office
The film festival hands out tickets for the evening screenings each morning. They only give tickets to people with passes. The passes are free. To get a pass you must register about two months in advance. You can register with any one of the French guilds or unions as a special guest: producer, writer, director, cinematographer, journalist, cultural representative etc. Each French guild or union has an alloca-

tion of tickets which they dispense on the morning of each screening. To add to the confusion, each organisation has a different office in the festival building (called the Marché) which you must locate. Then you stand in line and hope they aren't 'sold out' before your name is called.

Stand outside the cinema
Stand outside the cinema in a tuxedo or evening dress and hope that one of the invitees who shows up doesn't make the dress code and is barred entry. When this happens, politely ask them for their ticket.

Routes to a Party Invite at Cannes

Cannes is a party festival with upwards of two dozen parties every night. The trick is to get invited to the party to enjoy the views over the harbour, the free drinks and food and to be impressed by the guest lists. Getting a ticket to the party of the moment is a fine art. Some travellers to the Cannes Film Festival spend their entire day trying to get a party invite.

Go to a sales agent
There will be parties after the screenings of many of the top films in the festival. Go to the sales agent, see if they will give you an invite. In the worst case, if you can't get an invite, see if they will give you the location of the party. Then it is up to you to see how successful you are with the bouncers at the door.

Go to the event organisers
Few companies have the wherewithal to actually organise the party themselves. Indeed, many of the American companies would be lucky to have a single francophone employed by them. They hire the services of one of the professional event organisers. Many of these party and event organisers are based in London. Call them up, and either offer your services in exchange for a ticket, or see if you can convince them that your presence will enhance the atmosphere of the party.

Go the national film organisations
The Irish, the Canadians, the British and the South Africans are just a few of the many nations with formal film presences in Cannes and they all threw parties in 2003. Walk into their pavilions and ask for an invite. They are usually easier to get than film parties.

Hang out at the *Variety* or American pavilion
The *Variety* and American pavilions are the hangouts of the serious Cannes partygoers. Attend either of these pavilions early enough in the morning, and not only will you get a free coffee and croissant, but will hear about any upcoming parties. It is not unknown for serious party-ticket-trading to go on. You'll overhear bartering along the lines of 'I'll give you two of my Sony boat party invites for one of your BBC Films lunch tickets.'

Trade Show

Cannes is really all about the trade show. While the festival is about the glamour, the red carpet and the celebrities, the trade show is a terrific place to make useful contacts.

Stroll through the Riviera or along the Croissette into the lobbies of one of the luxury hotels and you will see display after display by broadcasters, distributors, producers, sales agents and manufacturers. In 2003 over 1700 companies exhibited in Cannes. If you do want to go to the trade show, you will either need your pass (which you must arrange two months before the festival) or have a letter from one of the exhibitors inviting you to a meeting within the trade show area.

Networking

Another great reason to go to Cannes is to meet fellow writers, directors, producers and actors – all of whom are trying to do what you are. Meet at the cheap bars like the Petit Carlton away from the action, or just stroll along the beach with a bottle of wine, and see if you can find someone to collaborate with.

Business Cards

Whatever you do, do not go to Cannes without a couple of hundred business cards. You will need them to introduce yourself to everyone. Business cards also make you look professional.

Getting Your Film into Cannes

Every January, Thierry Frémaux, the artistic Director of the Cannes Film Festival visits London to view the year's British submissions to Cannes. The screenings take place at Mr Young's, a private screening room in the centre of Soho, London.

In theory, if you are a British film, in order to be considered for entry to Cannes you need only get your film to Mr Young's and M. Frémaux will see it, love it and screen it at his festival. It's even free to submit.

Here are the hiccups. The films can only be previewed on celluloid, so your film has to be at print stage. Mr Young's charges £150 for a two-hour screening slot. M. Frémaux has to watch dozens of features on a single weekend. Imagine how many times he says the word 'next' before he stretches his legs and waits for the projectionist to thread the next film. And would you like to hazard a guess at how many of the features he watches all the way through?

Maybe a better strategy is to submit your film to a smaller festival; the programmers are more likely to watch your film all the way through, and if it is selected, it won't be lost amongst the thousands of others.

Hint The ten top film festivals by acquisition executives

- Cannes
- Toronto
- Sundance
- Berlin
- Rotterdam
- Venice
- San Sebastian
- Tribeca
- Los Angeles Independent Film Festival
- Karlovy Vary

Summary

1. Understand how festivals work so you can make them work for you.

2. Do your homework, and help the festival promote your screening.

3. Go to Cannes.

But what if you still haven't sold your film after attending film festivals for a year. Should you panic? Of course not. Go to a film market.

Seven Essential Steps for Becoming Rich and Famous by Making a Low Budget Film

Step 6 Bottom

By bottom I mean energy, and plenty of it.

Bottom is a term I learned growing up on the farm. Whenever we needed a new horse, my father and grandfather would go to an auction, and look at the horses on offer. After the health of an animal was checked, the owner was always asked if the horse had bottom. Because bottom is a subjective quality, it was usually better to see the horse before the auction in a working environment, but this wasn't always possible.

A horse with bottom knows when the chips are down. There are still a good six hour's work left to do in the field, the storm clouds are gathering, and there are at best only four hours of good light left to get the job done. A horse without bottom will just sit down in its harness and refuse to go any further. But a horse with bottom will knuckle down and strain, trying to get the job done in impossible circumstances.

There will be many times during the course of getting your movie made when you will have to work well past your level of endurance. When I am working on a production, I wake up each morning saying: 'I have never been this tired in my life!'

When Roger Corman visited Raindance he was in his late seventies, and still producing over thirty movies a year. I asked him what his secret was. He said: 'Getting and having energy means following a few basic and simple rules.'

He never drinks before his evening meal and then he drinks as much as he wants, and he has a power nap every afternoon. I found him behind the screen at a cinema where he was about to give a talk, lying shoes off, face down on a sofa. I coughed. he opened one eye and leapt into action.

19   Film Markets

SUPPOSING YOU ATTEND several film festivals and execute a finely planned sales and marketing programme and still do not sell your film. Should you despair and give up? The answer is: not at all. Film markets are there to serve you.

There are three major film markets:

AFM is playing a high-risk game of politics, hoping that the proposed 2004 market will obliterate MIFED

AFM

The American Film Market runs in January and November.

AFMA, 10850 Wilshire Boulevard, 9th Floor, Los Angeles, CA 90024-4321, T: 001 310 446 1000, F: 001 310 446 1600, E: info@afma.com, W: www.afma.com

AFMA Europe, 49 Littleton Road, Harrow, Middlesex HA1 3SY, T: 020 8423 0763, F: 020 8423 7963, E: afmaeurope@attglobal.net

Every year at Raindance we publish the names, contacts details, and reasons why we meet people in Cannes. This year's edition is on the CD, or for future editions go to www.raindance.co.uk

Marché du film

Held during the glamorous Cannes Film Festival in mid-May, the Marché du Film is perhaps the most important of the three film markets.

Cannes Market, 3 rue Amélie, 75007 Paris, T: 00 33 1 53 59 61 30, F: 00 33 1 53 59 61 50, E marketinfo@festival-cannes.fr, W: www.cannesmarket.com

M.I.F.E.D.

Milan host the M.I.F.E.D. market every year at the end of October.

FMI – Fiera Milano International, Palazzina FMI, Largo Domodossola 1, 20145 Milano, Italia, T: 0039 02 4855001, F: 0039 02 48550420, E: miffed@fmi.it, W: www.mifed.com

How Film Markets Work

Film markets are no different than any other type of market. There are goods, vendors and buyers. At a market, an organiser books a convention space and screening rooms. The organiser then lets out these spaces and screening slots to interested film sellers, and advertises the companies and films attending in the hope of attracting film buyers.

At the AFM, the market organiser books the Loews Hotel in Santa Monica. The bedroom furniture is replaced for the duration of the event with office furniture. Film vendors book bedrooms, and install TVs and VCRs. The entrance to the hotel has a large board that lists the companies attending, along with their suite number. Interested buyers can then locate the temporary offices of the companies selling the films they are interested in.

As each buyer enters a suite, they present their business card and take a seat. The film sellers will have prepared a one sheet and a trailer for the film. The buyer will then watch the trailer. If the asking price for the film is above $50,000, the buyer will then usually demand to see the film in a cinema. The vendor then contacts the market organiser to schedule a screening (if one hasn't already been set up) and the buyer will attend the screening, along with other prospective film buyers. Following the screening, a deal is made.

Who Attends Film Markets?

Have you ever gone into a photocopy shop, opened up the flap to get a copy of a letter, and found someone else's paper in the copy tray?

This is what happened to my friend, Dov Simens when he attended the AFM. On the right is what he found.

This represents the high and low estimate for what a low budget feature expected to gross at that year's AFM. Buyers from each of these territories were attending. A buyer from Korea could be the owner of a small cinema chain, or of a major cinema chain that also owns a television station and a home video distribution label. In all, every year at the major markets, between 4000 and 6000 film buyers attend.

How to Attend a Film Market

If attending a market is so simple, why aren't all independent filmmakers attending film markets with their finished films? Like most things in filmmaking, it's down to money. It costs to attend a film market.

First you need to join the market. It costs between $15,000 and $20,000 to join the market. Then you need to rent the display space. On top of that there is the cost of shipping film prints to the market, and of paying for screenings at the official market screening rooms.

Having spent all that, you need to create a presence for your film by buying advertisements in the trade papers clearly identifying the screening times and location of the screening. On top of that you may want to have a party or event to promote the film.

It is said in the industry that in order to make a minimal presence at Cannes, AFM or MIFED will cost a minimum of $50,000. Given the increasing importance of Cannes as a launch point for films with distribu-

	Low			High
Argentina	4,000		Ar...	5,000
Australia	25,000		Australia	35,000
Belgium	3,000		Belgium	5,000
Brazil	5,000		Brazil	10,000
Chile	3,000		Chile	5,000
Colombia	5,000		Colombia	10,000
East Africa	7,000		East Africa	10,000
Ecuador	4,000		Ecuador	5,000
England	25,000		England	40,000
France	15,000		France	30,000
Germany/Austria	30,000		Germany/Austria	50,000
Greece	4,000		Greece	7,000
Holland	6,000		Holland	10,000
Hong Kong	5,000		Hong Kong	12,000
India	10,000		India	20,000
Indonesia	5,000		Indonesia	15,000
Israel	4,000		Israel	10,000
Italy	10,000		Italy	20,000
Japan	20,000		Japan	40,000
Mexico	5,000		Mexico	10,000
Middle East	4,000		Middle East	5,000
Pakistan	7,000		Pakistan	10,000
Panama / Cen. America	2,000		Panama / Cen. America	3,000
Peru / Bol'/ Ecuador	6,000		Peru / Bol / Ecuador	8,000
Philippines	8,000		Philippines	12,000
Portugal	2,000		Portugal	5,000
Scandinavia	35,000		Scandinavia	50,000
Singapore / Malaysia	6,000		Singapore / Malaysia	10,000
S. Africa	3,000		S. Africa	5,000
S. Korea	35,000		S. Korea	50,000
Spain	15,000		Spain	25,000
Sri Lanka	4,000		Sri Lanka	5,000
Taiwan	8,000		Taiwan	15,000
Thailand	4,000		Thailand	6,000
Turkey	2,000		Turkey	4,000
U.S.S.R.	15,000		U.S.S.R.	20,000
Venezuela	4,000		Venezuela	6,000
West Africa	6,000		West Africa	10,000
West Indies	2,000		West Indies	3,000
Yugoslavia	7,000		Yugoslavia	10,000
TOTAL:	370,000			611,000

figure 19.1
The high and low sales estimates for a low-budget feature at AFM, as found by Dov Simens in a photocopy tray

tion, films aiming to make a sale are having to spend more on getting noticed. Most independent filmmakers cannot afford this. This fact has given rise to a new film professional: the sales agent.

Sales Agents

Sales agents represent several different films at a film market in order to balance the cost of attending the markets against the potential income from several films. In fact, sales agents are usually foreign sales agents. The USA and Canada territory is always referred to as the domestic sale. The USA dominates the film industry, and prices are always quoted in US dollars. Even if you live in Chile, and sell the film to a local Chilean distributor, that is still considered a foreign sale, even though it would be your domestic sale. A domestic sales agent, by definition, would only sell to American companies, while a foreign sales agent would sell to any non-USA country.

Sales agents charge commission on the sales of your film, and also charge their expenses: a portion of the cost of going to a market, telephone calls, advertising expenses, travel and accommodation.

Living in the Home of the Dead		
Asking Estimates		
All US$		
Budget approx £500,000		
Territory	**% Witholding Tax**	**Projected Sales**
Europe:		
Belgium & Luxembourg		20,000
France		80,000
Germany/Austria/German-speaking Switzerland	25.00	85,000
Greece & Cyprus		15,000
Israel	5.45	15,000
Italy	8.00	85,000
Netherlands		15,000
Portugal	5.00	10,000
Scandinavia & Baltic States		70,000
Spain	10.00	90,000
Switzerland		20,000
Turkey		15,000
UK		Financing Territory
America		
North America		300,000
Argentina/Chile/Uruguay/Paraguay	15.00	15,000
Brazil		30,000
Columbia	25.00	15,000
Mexico	15.00	20,000
Others		30,000
Asia		
Japan	10.00	125,000
Hong Kong		25,000
India		
South Korea		80,000
Others		50,000
Australasia		
Australia & New Zealand		50,000
Miscellaneous		
East & West Africa		
Middle East		15,000
South Africa	20.00	20,000
Eastern European Territories	15.00	60,000
Others (including all non-theatrical rights)		50,000
Total Projected Asking Sales (with W/H)		**$1,405,000**
(Not splitting Scandinavia)		

figure 19.2
Asking estimates for a £500,000 film

Living in the Home of the Dead		
Settling Estimates		
All US$		
Budget approx £500,000		
Territory	**% Witholding Tax**	**Projected Sales**
Europe:		
Belgium & Luxembourg		10,000
France		65,000
Germany/Austria/German-speaking Switzerland	25.00	70,000
Greece & Cyprus		10,000
Israel	5.45	10,000
Italy	8.00	75,000
Netherlands		10,000
Portugal	5.00	5,000
Scandinavia & Baltic States		45,000
Spain	10.00	60,000
Switzerland		15,000
Turkey		10,000
UK		Financing Territory
America		
North America		150,000
Argentina/Chile/Uruguay/Paraguay	15.00	10,000
Brazil		15,000
Columbia	25.00	7,500
Mexico	15.00	12,000
Others		10,000
Asia		
Japan	10.00	80,000
Hong Kong		20,000
India		
South Korea		65,000
Others		30,000
Australasia		
Australia & New Zealand		25,000
Miscellaneous		
East & West Africa		
Middle East		
South Africa	20.00	10,000
Eastern European Territories	15.00	45,000
Others (including all non-theatrical rights)		40,000
Total Projected Sales (with W/H)		**$904,500**
(Not splitting Scandinavia)		

figure 19.3
Settling estimates for a £500,000 film

A sales agent can also invest money in your film by advancing a portion of the money estimated for the sale of your film. This money might be for part of the production budget, for completion funds (to be used for the editing and post-production budget) or for the relatively simple and inexpensive process of completing your press kit.

In order for a sales agent to advance funds they will want to read the script, meet the filmmakers, and be satisfied that their investment plus interest, plus profits can be recouped. In addition of course, the sales agent will charge commission on monies from the sale of the film.

Tips and Strategies for Cannes

The Cannes Film Festival is the largest and most prestigious film festival in the world. Each May, hordes of filmmakers, international sales agents, distributors, film financiers, film entrepreneurs, producers, writers, stars and cineastes descend on the seaside port of Cannes for a ten-day marathon of screenings, parties and workshops. There are several competitions running in the festival, and in addition, the Marché du Film operates at the same time.

If one is serious about a career in film, a trip to Cannes in late May is simply imperative. To make the most out of your trip to Cannes, consider following one or more of the following strategies for financing or selling your film.

Have a Plan

Although Cannes looks glamorous and casual, astute insiders plan their trip beforehand. Get a copy of the trades about a month before the event and email and call to set up meetings. Actual meetings in Cannes are very fluid, and it can become difficult to adhere to a schedule, but at least you have a strategy in place from the moment you arrive.

Have Something on Paper

My movie, *Table 5*, was edited for free on the condition I gave the editor the Romanian television rights – since he owned a late night Romanian cable station at the time.

Cannes is not the place to bring your seventeenth draft screenplay; people are too busy rushing around to even consider reading scripts.

Instead you should prepare a one-sheet which includes a summary of the project, the pitch, key personnel and a brief description of what you are looking for, be it investment (include a brief budget), or a sale.

If you are aiming to sell your film at Cannes, include phrases like 'All rights available except Romania', (if that were the case).

If you aren't able to get a sales agent, then you'll need to prepare your own sales estimates. See figures 19.2 and 19.3 on the previous pages for an example of asking and settling sales estimates for a £500,000 movie.

Play Ping-Pong

There are always an incredible number of people at Cannes, and you can have more one-on-one meetings in a day than you could in a year back home.

The ping-pong theory is that if you hang out in the right places you will bump into people with whom you could, given a little charm and a producer's savvy, develop useful relationships.

You might have blagged a ticket to the legendary MTV party, you might be on the red carpet at the Palais, you might be nursing a drink on the terraces of the Majestic, or getting plastered at the Petit Carlton. In any of these places, it is likely you will bump into film executives. Get their business cards, and chat them up.

Make sure that you maximise the benefits to your film from your time in Cannes. Make the most of your little black book of new contacts. If you talk about a treatment that you have, and the contact says they'd like to read it, make sure you follow that up quickly and politely. Even if you just send a brief email once you're back home to say how good it was to meet them, this will help to distinguish you from the vast numbers of new people that all film executives meet every year at Cannes.

Hint Cannes is a marathon that tests your ability to go without sleep and the recuperative powers of your liver. Whatever you do, pace yourself, or you will burn out.

The Nick O'Hagan Method

Nick is a Raindance favourite and is one of the most happening producers in the UK at the moment. He has researched the people who book offices in Cannes and discovered that most of them book rooms at the Grand. His strategy is to get a table in the shade at the Grand Hotel, and order a coffee. Sooner or later, anyone he wishes to see will walk by, and he jumps up and offers them a drink. If he needs to meet someone, he always says: 'Meet me at the Grand'.

An advanced method would be to take a table at the Carlton or Majestic bars, sit there with your lawyer or head of business affairs, hire a bevy of buxom beauties and then wait for everyone and anyone to drop by and see what the action is all about.

The American Pavilion Strategy

To pitch, you need to know where to pitch and who to pitch to. The American Pavilion, along with the other national pavilions like the British, German, Canadian, South African and European Media pavilions are excellent places to meet other filmmakers at your level.

A few strategically placed drinks should enable you to garner hot tips on who is looking for what. The pavilions also become a trading market for party tickets. Desperate pleas along the lines of 'I'll give you three Kodak tickets for one Soho House invite' will become familiar.

Pavilions all run business centres and for a relatively small fee (I paid €300) they offer a service providing free coffees and croissants (useful for meetings), Internet access and conference rooms. They will also receive your messages and mail.

Sellers Sell

Film sellers attend Cannes to sell completed pictures. They are not there to look at new projects unless they have brought along an acquisitions or development executive. Remember that making a bad contact can be worse than making no contact at all; don't pester someone to listen to your pitch when they are not buying.

Check the guides; these people will be listed, with their job title (buyers are highighted), in the guides supplied by the main trades before and during the market.

Dress Code

Cannes is casual, and whatever you do bring a very comfortable pair of shoes along. If you plan to go to evening screenings at the Palais, or some of the parties, you will need formal dress.

Formal dress for men means a tuxedo, and a slinky dress for women. Trainers and sandals are forbidden at many of the late night venues.

Publicists Can Help You

Publicists rule Cannes. It is they who control the guest lists of all the top parties, they manage the major stars and know where they are staying, and, they can sometimes get you a ticket to an incredibly glamorous event if you treat them properly.

Bring Your Lawyer

If you are really serious about doing a deal at Cannes, it is essential to bring your lawyer along. Not only will they have many useful contacts, but should the need arise, they can rough out a deal memo on the back of a menu or napkin, polish it up on a laptop at the hotel, or on one of the computers at a pavilion.

While it might appear that the added expense of bringing a lawyer is too rich for your budget, you never know when you might strike gold and need a lawyer on the spot to finish off negotiations.

The Hotel du Cap

About four kilometres east of Cannes is a swanky seaside resort called Cap d'Antibes, or Cap for short. The Hotel du Cap is where the A-list talent and players hang out. No trip to Cannes is complete without at least one visit to the glitzy bar of this power pen full of the likes of Weinstein, Elwes, Bruckheimer and co.

Parties

Most of the serious networking takes place at any one of the hundred-odd parties that take place during the Cannes Film Festival. Your first job on arriving at Cannes is to discover what parties are to be held, assess which ones are the likeliest to offer you a real chance of meeting people, and then trying to get an invite or ticket.

Getting into the right party involves a fair amount of social nous and a degree of luck. One tactic is to walk up to the maitre d' or security guard at a party venue, present your business card and barge through. This technique will work at lower echelon parties and afternoon drinks soirées on the terraces overlooking the sea.

To get a truly hot ticket in Cannes, like an invite to the MTV party, requires some successful pre-planning. Unless you know one of the party organisers, or someone in the upper levels of MTV, your best bet would be to make friends with a publicist or other insider who might be able to give you a tip.

Once you have your MTV ticket, you have to decide whether to go and network, or to trade your ticket for other parties which might also be difficult to get into.

My friend Rinaldo Quacquarini of the Screenwriter's Store in London attends Cannes with filmmakers software company Final Draft. During Cannes I would see him several times in the course of the day as our paths crossed on the Croisette as each of us raced from meeting to meeting. When he found out that I had not one but two MTV party tickets, he started pleading with me to give him one.

About six hours before the party started I got a text message offering me £500 worth of software for the tickets. I then passed him in the Market, and said: 'Sorry, Rinaldo' and he laughed and said, 'I'm only kidding'. Then, around an hour before the party was due to start I got another text message, this time offering me £1000 worth of software for the pair of tickets.

The next day he sheepishly grinned and said 'The sick thing is, I would have given you a grand's worth of software. And I don't care if the party was crap! I just wanted to be able to say I went!'

The MTV parties that I have been to actually are quite disappointing. Held in various venues around Cannes, including Pierre Cardin's futuristic house in Miramar, the MTV party tickets are hot simply because there are only a thousand of them, and there are over forty thousand delegates at Cannes.

Summary

1. Decide which markets you want to attend, and make a plan.

2. Having a sales agent is beneficial.

3. Film markets can be useful for attracting interest in your film before it is shot.

Selling your film means getting distribution.

20   Distribution

IT IS THE AIM OF every filmmaker to sell their film to a distributor. The distributor, theoretically, pays the filmmaker a sum of money (the advance) plus a percentage of box office receipts as the film passes through the various stages of release (the windows).

Cinemas, hotel premium screenings, airline, pay or premium cable, home video, terrestrial television and ancilliary markets such as schools, prisons, oil rigs, and cruise ships all contribute money to the distributor. From this money the distributor deducts their expenses and the amount of the advance, and then pays to the filmmaker the money as agreed in the distribution agreement.

A filmmaker needs to understand how distributor's work, and what they need in order to do their jobs properly. Despite the mistrust filmmakers have of distributors (and distributors of filmmakers) this understanding will make money for both sides.

Delivery Schedule Basics

Delivery marks the start of the distribution life of your film. The distributor who has purchased your film will have a list of items that they require from you. This list is known as the delivery schedule, and you will not be paid for your film until you have provided the distributor with everything that they ask for.

Hint A basic delivery schedule will include

- a master of the film, be it on film or on tape
- copies of the contracts with the actors
- proof of the clearances of any music
- publicity stills
- out-takes and other material relevant to a DVD release
- a script with the dialogue as shot
- other related promotional and publicity materials

How Distribution Companies Work

Distribution companies make money on the difference between what they pay for a film, and the money they receive from the box office returns and the returns from television, home video and DVD sales. A distributor buys films for their country or territory. Some distributors distribute in more than one territory.

How distribution companies see films

Before a distributor buys your film, they must see your film. Each distributor has an individual in charge of recommending films. This person is called an acquisition executive, and it is their responsibility to track up and coming films through the pre-production and production process. If the film is hot, the film can be bought in the pre-production or production phase. Sometimes, the producer will create a teaser or trailer to entice film buyers.

i Festivals

Filmfinders lists all the festival screenings of every film. Make sure they know about it by sending details to www.filmfinders.com.

More often than not, the first time a film is screened is at a festival. Buyers attend film festivals to discover new films. Festivals are also a good chance to see how a film plays in front of an audience, and gives a distributor a chance to see how the filmmaker's marketing materials are working.

Hint Acceptance into a festival is further proof of the provenance of your film. Make the most of festival screenings. If a film buyer cannot attend, send a festival report. If the screening is sold out, or critically acclaimed, or if you win an award, send this information as soon as possible to the appropriate buyers.

---

ii Markets

Film market screenings rely on the advertising of the film in the trade press. The three major film markets, Cannes, AFM and MIFED are crowded with product, with as many as 1500 films vying for buyers' attention. Buyers at a market will only see the most distinctive films. It is at market screenings that the pedigree of a film becomes important: be it because of the stars in the film, or the director.

iii Private screenings

It is possible for a filmmaker to go to a major city like LA, New York, Paris or London and set up a private screening at a preview cinema and invite acquisition executives to attend. Since it is not as competitive as a film market, one theoretically has a better chance of attracting acquisition executives. If the person cannot attend, they will often send a junior to watch the film, and recommend it or otherwise.

A ploy often used by filmmakers is to call such screenings a world premiere trade screening in order to attract the attention of film buyers.

iv Submitted tapes

Even if your film screens at a selection of markets, festivals and industry screenings, it may be impossible for certain distributors to see your film. In such instances, call and find out if the company accepts DVD or VHS screeners, and submit it along with your latest press kit.

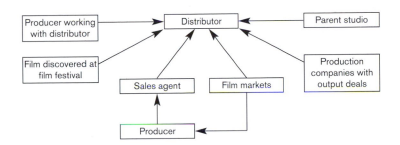

figure 20.1
How distributors acquire films

Preparing the Distribution Marketing Plan

For every film, the distributor's sales department negotiates an individual and strictly confidential deal with each exhibitor's booking department. Under English law, the maximum is two weeks. After two weeks the distributor and exhibitor can continue playing the film if it has reached a sufficient audience.

Once a distribution company has acquired a film, they need to prepare for the marketing and launch of the film.

The creative process of planning and executing a marketing campaign can have a huge effect on the performance of a film at the box office. A good marketing plan will create visibility, awareness and interest in the new film, peaking with the opening weekend. After the opening weekend, the distributor hopes that the film will get good reviews and word-of-mouth. In fact, distributors place far greater value in word-of-mouth than ads and trailers on television to create good box office numbers. Hence the need for the right hook for a film.

When a new film is acquired, the distributor will hold a private screening for their marketing personnel to decide how to position and market the film for maximum audience appeal. The marketing team will then develop a strategy on how to reach this audience.

A total budget is then agreed for the cost of advertising the film and the duplication of 35mm prints for the cinema. This is the P&A budget – the prints and advertising budget.

P and A Budget

Marketing and media costs have risen dramatically in recent years. Cost of paper has doubled, cost of radio and TV advertising has sky-rocketed.

When your film goes to a cinema for release, the following costs need to be budgeted for:

Cost of prints
About £1000 per print.

Booking fee
A distributor will pay £2–5000 to a booking agent to schedule your film within the appropriate cinemas. A good booking agent will know which cinemas are likely to attract better audiences for your film.

Distribution fee
Usually one-third of the box office gross is charged by the distributor.

Posters and quads
Quads for the cinema foyers are a very effective way of promoting your screening. Hung a week or two before the opening, they will have a 'coming soon' paper shoved under the glass, removed and replaced with 'now showing'. Four colour quads cost £10–15 each depending on the quantity you order.

Trailers
Certain cinemas and chains will show trailers of your film in the weeks before it opens. Copies of the trailer cost about £10–30 each.

BBFC
For the film to play in the UK cinema, it must have a censorship rating. The censorship criteria has relaxed over the past few years in the UK. BBFC charges £28 per minute plus VAT.

Publicity
A good publicist will promote your film for between £2–3000.

Advertising
The sky is the limit, but £10,000 should be spent here for basic ads.

Marketing Terminology

Marketability vs playability
Marketability is how easy the film is to sell to an audience, whereas playability is how well the film stands up to an audience and so how well it performs in the marketplace.

Hint Marketability and playability are not necessarily the same thing.

Does the film work, does the film grip audience's attention, does it deliver what it promises in the title and the marketing campaign. For example, *The Cable Guy* was marketed as a comedy starring Jim Carey. It was in fact a horror film starring Jim Carey in a diversion from his usual role as a comedian. The film disappointed at the box office.

Blockbusters with top stars need heavy marketing budgets to publicise their releases. As competition between films and distributors increases, marketing decisions become more crucial. Inspired marketing cannot save a bad film. A fine film can be lost in the melée if it does not have a clear, distinct promotion.

Word of Mouth

The most effective form of publicity is word of mouth. If your best friend goes to a movie then calls you up and says 'Hey you have got to see this' you are much more likely to go and see the movie. In America, independent filmmakers have tried a version of this with the Take One programme, where everyone who saw the movie was encouraged to send one more person, effectively doubling the box office.

Buzz

Distributors hire research companies to track the awareness of an approaching release in the months and weeks coming up to a new release. A film is competing not only with other films, but with other leisure pursuits. It is effectively a new product launch.

Often a distributor will use several film festival screenings as an attempt to create good word of mouth. UK distributor Pathé's head of marketing did this with the English premiere of *The Blair Witch Project* at Raindance, and Tartan Film's Hamish McAlpine and Laura de Casto did the same when they screened *Secretary* at Raindance East. Both screenings were a way of drumming up interest. Fortunately for Raindance, both films had exceptionally successful releases.

Promotions

Major promotional partnerships can involve a year's forward planning. Sometimes a film will partner with a product or an event. In America, the Oscars™ offer an obvious marketing hook, and certain films are carefully (and expensively) positioned according to their nominations. Distributors can often use extra press advertising and quotes from reviews following awards won or nominations. These ads are usually turned around the very night they are won in order to meet newspaper ad deadlines. Some distributors use award wins to help push new release windows. See figure 20.2 for an example.

Opening weekend

The total box office take from each cinema screen showing a film on a Friday, Saturday and Sunday is added together to calculate the opening weekend gross. Sometimes this amount is inflated by including the box office take from preview screenings in an attempt to catapult a film into the coveted number one slot.

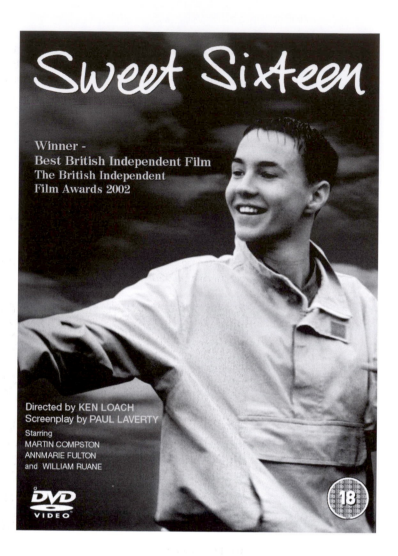

figure 20.2
Sweet Sixteen DVD cover citing British
Independent Film Awards win

Distributors are sent the weekend figures late Sunday night, and live in dread of the 3am fax call. By the time business opens on a Monday morning, exhibitors and distributors know whether or not the film is a hit.

Holdover meetings

On the Monday following a film's release, with the opening weekend box office figures at hand, the distributor's marketing team meets to discuss the film's performance and to decide what (if any) changes need to be made to the marketing campaign, and more importantly whether or not to continue the film's run in cinemas.

If the film is deemed to have legs, then the distributor's sales people will call each of the exhibitors and try to convince them to hold the film for another week's run. If not, the film may be pulled from the cinemas before its scheduled run is over.

Exhibitor

An exhibitor is the individual or corporation that owns the cinema. While they make money from a percentage of the box office take, they also make a considerable amount of money from the concession booth. Hence, an exhibitor is more likely to consider a lower percentage from the box office if they can see a large advertising and promotion campaign guaranteed to get people into the cinema.

Distribution and Marketing Tools

Poster

The poster is arguably the single most important marketing tool. The right image can create an enormous amount of interest, both in the media, and in the general public. *The Blair Witch Project* used a single still in its campaign. If you contacted Pathé for images, you were sent just this single one.

figure 20.3
The unforgettable Blair Witch Project
publicity image

Media advertising

Depending on the budget of the film, the distributor will book advertisements in magazines, newspapers, television and radio. As the cost of these ads spirals, distributors usually limit themselves to a few well-placed ads. In London, the ads are placed in *Time Out*, *The Guardian Guide* magazine on a Saturday, and *The Evening Standard* (afternoon newspaper) for a single insert on the day prior to the film's opening. Television spots are reserved for the big budget Hollywood movies, or high concept films.

Trailers

A well-cut, succinct trailer can play in cinemas in the weeks running up to a film's release to create interest. Even though the trailers are in the exhibitor's best interest as well as the distributor's, cinemas often charge a screening fee for the privilege of showing it.

figure 20.4
Front and back of the eyecatching
Tartan Films postcard for Ivan's XTC

Hint Try to avoid making a trailer that is so explicit that the audience feels like it has seen the movie in its entirety.

Publicity

A well planned release will include a PR campaign to promote the director and lead performers in the months before the release of the film. A good publicist will seek to find any unique hooks that can be played to the local press.

Different publications have different lead-in times. The style monthlies, like *Dazed and Confused* and *Tatler* will have a three-month lead-in time. The film magazines like *Hot Dog* and *Empire* will have a six week lead-in, while *Time Out* and the daily newspapers need a week's notice. A distributor will often need to fly in the lead actors twice: once for the long lead-in publications, and then right before the opening of the film for the dailies, and possibly the premiere.

Promotions and merchandising

Distributors often try to tie in the release of a film with a product release or re-launch and offer a price incentive. For example, Pret à Manger, the British sandwich chain, offered a discount for anyone who bought a sandwich who also wanted to see the Robert Altman film *Pret à Porter*.

Postcards

Postcards are a cheap and effective way to market a film. A good post-card has a visually pleasing image, a great title and logline. The reverse of the card can also offer a brief summary of the film, and still leave room for a mailing label. They can also be left in cafes, bookstores and cinemas to help promote the film.

Hamish McAlpine of Tartan Films used a clever postcard for a UK marketing campaign which the American filmmakers had used to market the screenings of the film *Ivan's XTC*. By doing a series of targeted mailings before the film opened, the distributor managed to create memorable word-of-mouth buzz based solely on the image (see figure 20.4 opposite).

Preview screenings

Several weeks before the opening of the film, and timed to coordinate with the lead times of various publications, the distributor will arrange for preview screenings for journalists to come and see the film. Even if a particular publication's deadline is not for several weeks, preview screenings allow a journalist to see the film, write the review, and save it for publication just before the film's official opening.

The trick is to get journalists to attend the screening, and distributors will usually offer light refreshments, including ample amounts of alcohol.

Premieres

In London, the latest James Bond premiere was held at the Royal Albert Hall and tickets sold for £1000 each. The event was sold out, and after the huge expenses of bringing in a 35mm projector, turning the Albert Hall into an ice palace, flying in the stars and feeding the 5000 strong audience, the charity Cinema and Television Benevolent Fund raised over £500,000. The distributor was delighted with the front page coverage as well.

Official premieres are another chance to create attention, especially if the stars can attend. Big Hollywood movies usually use this occasion as another chance to get coverage and build hype for their movie. Premieres usually hit the news bulletins on the evening they happen. Often a distributor will choose to partner with a charity. Tickets for the event will be sold at a premium, with the proceeds used to defray the cost of hiring the cinema, flying in the talent, and with the all profits going to the charity.

Festivals

Prestige festivals like Cannes, Sundance, Toronto and Berlin offer another celebrity opportunity for distributors to create hype for their films. These festivals stage heavily publicised gala screenings where the stars attending are interviewed by scores of journalists and, with newspapers ever-hungry for a 'starlet on a red-carpet in a jaw-dropping dress' shot, the screenings become front page news around the world.

Internet

Distributors often mistrust the Internet as a medium for promoting their films. Part of their fear is based on the threat of piracy, and also the fact that a distributor in one territory cannot protect their territory from encroachment from web-based viewers abroad.

Done correctly, and with sensitivity, the Internet offers unlimited low-budget opportunities for promotion.

The classic example is *The Blair Witch Project*, which used the Internet to create a whispering campaign about the fate of the three filmmakers. The makers of *Six String Samurai* discovered that the word 'samurai' is one of the most popular words entered in search engines and managed to create a huge interest in their film (which sadly failed to deliver at the box office).

Secretary, a film full of sexual oddities, was promoted on the net in the UK using a series of quizzes about which letters on the keyboard got the secretary spanked or pinched.

Summary of the Distribution Process

A studio is a vertically integrated film company that makes films and distributes films in every territory. There are seven majors – Buena Vista (Disney), 20th Century Fox, MGM/United Artists, Paramount, Sony (Columbia TriStar), Universal Studios and Warner Bros – which finance, produce and distribute in the States. Dreamworks which also finances, produces and distributes in the States, but does so from accommodation provided by Universal Studios in LA.

- Producer/studio acquires rights to film a story from true life story, treatment, adaptation or screenplay
- Screenplay is developed/rewritten
- Casting and production finance are confirmed
- Principal photography takes place, in studios and/or on agreed locations, followed by post-production and editing
- Master print delivered to distributor
- Delivery determines release strategy, release date
- Distributor presents the film to exhibitors and negotiates agreements to have film shown in cinemas
- Marketing campaign to create buzz
- Film festival debut
- Test screenings used to judge audience reactions or to evaluate alternative marketing
- Prints delivered to cinema
- Run may extend subject to demand
- Film prints couriered to other cinemas
- A film print goes to rep cinemas
- Excess film prints destroyed
- Remaining film prints retained in archives of distributor
- Film distributed on home/video/DVD and/or pay cable
- Film distributed on terrestial television
- Film released in ancilliary markets (prisons, schools, nursing homes)
- Copyright returns to the filmmaker

Studio distribution

Of the majors all distribute themselves in the US, yet only Fox, Sony, Warner Bros and Buena Vista International distribute internationally. The rest (Universal, Paramount, MGM/UA and Dreamworks) distribute internationally collectively through UIP (United International Pictures).

Distribution Terms

Opening weekend

The cumulative total of the tickets sold to a film in all cinemas in a territory on a Friday, Saturday and Sunday.

Wide release

A film released immediately on 300 plus screens in the UK and 1000 plus in the US. At £1000–2000 per print, wide releases can cost a lot of money, and so are reserved for those films most likely to enjoy big box office openings. If the film is likely to benefit from word-of-mouth, distributors may open it on the Wednesday or Thursday ahead of the first weekend to encourage this.

Saturation release

A film opening in many theatres in one area (for example London's West End) supported by extensive regional advertising and publicity.

Platform release

Intends to domino the audience, perhaps beginning with a two or three cinema release, building over subsequent weeks to nationwide coverage. In the UK distributors often open a film in the West End, even on just one screen, for a week before nationwide release.

Miramax used this strategy brilliantly with the release of *The Crying Game*, which opened on two screens in New York. The distributor didn't book additional screens until the film was sold out for every screening, and then opened the film city by city.

My Big Fat Greek Wedding is a recent example of a film that opened slowly to a large number of screens and then built its release as the film received high audience figures.

Wide-multiple release

If a distributor has a film with a major star which they fear will get bad reviews, they will often open the film in as many screens as possible, knowing they have a limited number of week(s) to earn box office revenue before bad word of mouth damages the film's revenue.

Exclusive engagement

Sometimes a film opens exclusively at one cinema, or a number of screens at a single cinema, perhaps ahead of extending the run or broadening the release.

Distribution Deals

When a distributor agrees to distribute a film, they sign an agreement with the producer that sets out the different aspects of the deal. The deal you make will be based on one of the following six principles.

i Studio
The company you are producing for is owned by a studio which will handle all aspects of the distribution.

ii Output deals
A distributor agrees to handle the entire output of the production company making not only your film, but other films as well. For example Buena Vista International has an output deal to distribute all Miramax films in Europe.

iii Pre-sales
Distribution rights are sold during pre-production, usually for a cash advance. For example Buena Vista bought the rights to *Pulp Fiction* before the film was made, thereby ensuring that there was enough cash to make the film.

iv Negative pick-ups
The distributor agrees to hand over an agreed cash price on delivery of the completed film (the negative).

Often the major studios and major distributors will have several films available on short notice to open quickly to plug a blockbuster disaster. *Sister Act* is an example of a film that was quickly released with minimal publicity, only to succeed beyond the distributor's wildest expectations.

v Outright acquisition
Rights for a territory or series of territories are purchased after production is completed.

These are agreements signed with distributors whereby they agree to hand over money when a completed film (i.e. a negative) is delivered. These agreements are signed prior to completion of the film.

Both parties need to come to a common understand of what quality the completed film should be – including script, cast, technical and production standards. A completion bond will need to be in place to ensure that if the film runs out of money, or unforeseen events occur to prevent the film meeting its required standard, reshoots and re-edits can occur until the delivery requirements are met.

After a third party (e.g. a lab) agrees that the film is satisfactory, the distributor pays the producer. This payment is usually the costs of production plus any interest on loans accrued. In some cases an advance on the film's potential profits may be paid, although the higher the advance the lower the profit share of distribution royalties.

vi The standard deal
In a standard distribution deal, a distributor will agree a non-refundable advance payment to the producer of the film in exchange for the rights to distribute the film in a certain territory. The distributor then attempts to recoup the money and a profit through the money taken during the release of the film.

Once the distributor has recouped the advance and the expenses of releasing the film, an agreement is made where additional profit share is paid to the producer.

As part of the agreement, the distributor will also commit to an amount of money spent on prints and advertising for the film. The producer will also have to agree to a delivery schedule of when prints, soundtrack, publicity materials and other items will be handed over to the distributor. The distributor will also agree to the distribution fee – approximately 30%.

Anatomy of the Box Office

Let us assume a £1 million box office gross based on a 100 print release in one week. The table below demonstrates how a film that grosses a very respectable box office income could end up making a loss of £1000.

Box office gross		1,000,000
Less VAT	149,000	851,000
Less exhibitor cut	425,000	426,000
Less print cost (100 @ £2k each)	200,000	226,000
Less (minimal) marketing expenditure	100,000	126,000
Less 30% distribution fee	127,000	
Total profit (loss!)		(1,000)

Why Films are Released in Cinemas

The reason so many films are released in cinemas despite the fact they lose money is to turn the film into a movie. When members of the public see the advertisements and reviews, they think of the film as a movie because it has, or it will, play in a cinema. Even if they fail to see it in a cinema, the cinema release will enhance the other release windows. Distributors also know that a television or home video sale will be more valuable should the film be released in a cinema.

Other Release Windows

Pay hotel or airline

Martin Myers, a colleague of mine, negotiated the airline rights for *Withnail and I* with a major British airline to coincide with the tenth anniversary of the release. He achieved a low six figure number on intercontinental flights departing from the UK for a six month period.

This small and short window is positioned directly after the theatrical window. When screened on airlines, a film is sometimes still being screened in cinemas in the destination country.

Luxury hotels also show near first run movies. Suites and bedrooms have several free-to-view channels and then several pay-per-view movie channels, including two or more porn channels. The movies shown are recently screened theatrical releases. The distributor, hotel and producer split the revenue from this window.

Home video and pay cable

The operators of these two windows dislike each other. If you go into a video store, you will see titles with disclaimers like: 'not to be seen on TV for six months'. Conversely, on premium channel TV channels you will often see the phrase: 'exclusive to Sky TV'. A savvy producer will take the highest offer, and then use the other operator for the next window. So he will sell to home video for a nine-month window, followed by pay cable for another nine-month window, or vice versa.

Terrestrial television

It is difficult for many independent filmmakers to place their film on terrestrial TV because of the populist demands on all of the mainstream stations. No matter how worthy and intelligent your film, it is probable that the programmers for these channels will give your movie a miss in favour of a film with real movie stars and expensive production values.

If your film does find a home on terrestrial TV, it is likely that the distributor who has purchased your film will already be looking for the TV rights fee to offset potential losses from the cinematic release.

Ancillary

Ian Kerry's innovative Flicks in the Sticks programme exploits this window by using a mobile digital projector which tours small communities in the west of England. Last year he organised 500 screenings with the box office divided between the distributors and local organisers.

Many producers overlook the revenue that can be gained from screenings in prisons, hospitals, cruise ships and schools. Should a film become very successful in other windows, it is almost certain that receipts from this window will escalate dramatically.

Some UK producers are creating movies based on adaptations of public domain novels which appear on high school English literature courses knowing that they will have a certain number of DVD sales. This helps to explain the great number of Thomas Hardy novels filmed, and also makes Merchant Ivory productions of E. M. Forster novels look like ancillary marketing genius.

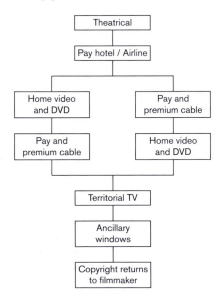

figure 20.5
Release windows

In Consultation with Claes Loberg: Branded Entertainment

Claes Loberg is an international expert in branded entertainment, who divides his time between London and New York.

The market for films (and film concepts) is becoming increasingly complicated; it's no longer just studios that are interested in great ideas.

The media world has fragmented in recent years: we have seen the emergence of the Internet, mobile/cell phones have become commonplace, and the number of television channels has proliferated. These developments have had a tremendous impact on the media and entertainment industries, with the ramifications still not fully understood.

For the film industry these new media represent new channels with which to reach the public, an opportunity that the industry has been quick to recognise: *The Blair Witch Project* famously exposed the marketing potential of the Internet, Hollywood has turned multi-channel television into an important distribution outlet, whilst mobile phone technology is now reaching the stage where mobile video is a mass market reality.

However, although new media have so far benefitted the film industry they are now ushering in changes that will undermine many of today's conventions. Professional piracy and amateur file swapping have decimated the music industry; the film industry will be next – there are serious doubts as to whether there will be audiences willing to pay $10 to watch a film in ten years' time.

Depending on where you sit today that may be a good or a bad thing: if you're sitting in a grand office built on the profits of film distribution then this change is one to be feared, if you're a young filmmaker struggling to get an audience for your films then this change will bring opportunities. For now, the route to the largest audience (and the greatest income) is still to produce a film so good that people will pay money to watch it in a cinema but other ways to become a profitable filmmaker are emerging.

Alternative Buyers of Your Film

As a filmmaker, your 'customers' have traditionally been the studios and distributors – if you couldn't sell your concept or film to them then your masterpiece remains forever yours. Television has long provided an alternative avenue to mass audiences (though not an easily accessible one); the Internet has also provided an alternative method of finding an audience but carries the significant disadvantage of also lacking any kind of remuneration or funding.

Studios and distributors will remain as potential customers but their buying power will fall as they lose control of the audience. Professional piracy is growing and file swapping of feature films is growing as consumers get the bandwidth to be able to download them. Hollywood will fight the trend, using technology and the law, but there are currently no indications that this is a fight that they can win.

This does not mean that the film industry will die but it does mean that it change: budgets are likely to decrease, films will increasingly be marketed as 'events' and simultaneous global release dates will become more common. Film styles may also change: the studios may increasingly look for films that 'need' the big screen experience, or for films that appeal to audiences that are most likely to be tempted out of their homes and into the cinemas.

Although Hollywood will evolve to find its niche – the demand for the films we enjoy will not change. Instead other buyers will emerge to fund the projects that Hollywood can't.

Branded Entertainment

In 2003 Raindance embarked on a series of branded entertainment spots for Nokia. Their tagline is 'sharing the moment', and we ran a competition for filmmakers to create fifteen-second short films for the company. The best ten were screened at the Raindance Film Festival. In 2004 we plan to do a series of these competitions around the UK in order to promote this exciting new short film format. Fifteen seconds is the amount of video information that will fit on their new generation mobile telephones.

It was rumoured that the Bond film *Tomorrow Never Dies* was the first film to reach profit before release solely due to product placement income. Brands or companies that own them have been funding films and content for many years: the product placement industry has grown rapidly since *E.T.* drove the sales of Reese's Pieces candy, and many television and cinema adverts have legitimate claims of artistic merit.

In 2001 BMW commissioned a series of five short films using David Fincher as Executive Producer. These films, directed by a number of first class directors including Guy Ritchie, John Frankenheimer and Ang Lee, starred Clive Owen as a driver for hire. Each film was approximately eight minutes long, and was exciting and stylish. In the films the Clive Owen character drove a BMW but the films lacked any logo close-ups or lingering shots of the car. The aim of the films was to communicate what BMW 'means' not what the car 'does' – it showed that BMWs are stylish, are exciting and some of the films also illustrated other facets of what BMW means including safety and reliability.

The BMW films are great examples of branded entertainment – quality films that attract an audience whilst representing a 'brand world'.

Every brand is defined by a number of attributes that are created by the company's activities, products, services and marketing. These attributes are typically adjectives such as 'quality', 'fun', 'cool', 'trustworthy' or descriptive captions such as 'value for money'. Marketing professionals group these attributes together to define the 'brand character'. For example, the brand character of Nike could be 'skilled', 'sporty', 'fashionable', 'athletic' and 'winning' – from these words alone you can almost picture the character that Nike customers aspire to – the toned athlete breaking first through the finishing tape.

The 'brand world' is an extension of the brand character to include the setting: the Nike brand world might be 'skilled', 'sporty', 'fashionable', 'athletic', 'winning' and also 'everywhere' and 'anywhere'. The Coca Cola brand world could be 'fun', 'friends', 'satisfying' but also 'endless vacations' and 'beautiful places'. The brand world provides important extra information when you're creating entertainment.

Creating entertainment that reflects a brand world is very different from product placement. Entertainment can reflect a brand world through a setting, through one or several characters, through a plot line or device, etc. For example, BMW films conveyed the BMW brand world by using a character that BMW drivers could identify with and by showing the performance of the car. The short film/trailer 'Lucky Star' communicated the Mercedes brand world by depicting the world of the man who knows everything, and showing that he drives a Mercedes. More famously Tony Scott's *Top Gun* illustrated the brand world of the US Navy by showing its men to be brave, honourable and daring (the characters in *Top Gun* may fall out with each other but they all do the right thing when America is threatened...).

Is Your Script Branded Entertainment?

Some film ideas lend themselves to branded entertainment (*Top Gun* being the most obvious, though there are others such as *The Italian Job*). Other films have been able to accommodate branded entertainment (the recent Bond films, Robert Zemeckis' *Castaway*, and Steven Spielberg's *Minority Report*) but increasingly scriptwriters are writing films with potential clients in mind.

To understand whether your film concept could work for branded entertainment you first need to understand the brand world that you believe your film could reflect.

Branded entertainment is different from product placement. This means that it can be more difficult to assess which films will be appropriate for which brands. With product placement, this can be easy: if the scene requires a car, a beer or suit then it is likely that Ford, Budweiser or Hugo Boss would be potential brands for placement. For branded entertainment, you must take a step back from your film and evaluate the messages that it communicates: is it an anti-capitalist lesson? A warning of the perils of love? A celebration of friendship? It is the messages that your film communicates that will dictate whether it could become great branded entertainment.

A celebration of friendship? Then it might be right for Coke or Vodafone. A favourable view of the surfer's lifestyle? Then Quiksilver or Billabong might be interested. A tale showing that a man has to do what a man has to do? Potentially perfect for Marlboro.

A note of caution: companies are used to advertising – they define the audience they need to target, they find an angle that will appeal to that audience and create content that will exploit that appeal. They are not used to buying or investing in films that are in the can or halfway through shooting. Major advertisers are targeted with hundreds of ideas and concepts every year – the ideas they commission are the best – getting an advertiser to spot and invest in the branded entertainment potential of your idea is not easy.

Advertisers are increasingly using advertising agencies and specialist branded entertainment agencies to assess the merits of entertainment ideas. If you believe that your idea could reach the mass market as branded entertainment then the best preparation you can do is prepare a treatment (as per usual) but also identify as fully as possible the branded entertainment angle you see within your film and the brands that you see it being relevant to. If you can get a branded entertainment agency (such as Cocojambo) to read and represent your idea to the major advertisers then you're on the road to creating branded entertainment.

Self-Distribution

Many filmmakers are considering distributing their movies directly to the public, thereby cutting out the expense of dealing with a distributor directly. While on the surface this might seem an attractive possibility, most filmmakers take this route for one of two reasons: either their film failed to attract the commercial interest of a distributor, or their film is too specialised or covers too narrow a field of interest to attract a distributor. Although many filmmakers might consider self-distribution an option of last resort, through new distribution opportunities offered by digital distribution and the web, this can be a viable option.

Digital Distribution

There are many ways to use digital distribution to get your film out there. You could use digital technology to pipe a movie straight into a cinema. You could distribute your movie straight into consumers' homes using a cable, or on DVD disc (a home video right) or over the Internet using broadband. Broadband already hosts a multitude of websites where you can download movies, or can access them using one of the streaming software technologies.

In the past few years, various private proprietary internets have launched or are being planned such as eKIDS Internet, Verizon and the new venture by Blockbuster. Additionally the major studios have announced joint digital ventures which will take until the end of the decade to materialise.

Distribution on the Internet
There are three ways to get your film on the world wide web.

1 Get your film accepted by an established film site
You simply supply them with a master tape and they do the rest. The most famous is Atom.com and having your film accepted by them acts as a reference for your CV, like having a film accepted by a major film festival. There are hundreds of others, including Brit Shorts, shortbuzz.com, ifilm.com, mediatrip.com and thebitscreen.com.

Many of the less well known film sites are hungry for new content and may take your film even if it has been turned down by other bigger sites. They won't pay but they will put your film up there. They may require you to compress it and deliver the file rather than the master tape.

Raindance organises the British Independent Film Awards and in 2002 we created an award for Most Effective Distribution Campaign to recognise the ingenuity of British filmmakers in the face of the adverse market. In this first year, the award went to the filmmakers of *Christie Malry's Own Double Entry* – a film which was self-distributed by the filmmakers and its star Nick Moran. They toured the film around cinemas and promoted screenings in the pattern of a series of music gigs.

The UK Film Council has announced in late 2003 that 150 UK cinemas will be fitted with technology capable of accepting picture download files, and equipped with high quality digital projectors.

2 Win a commission to make a web oriented film

Examples are projects such as Dazed and Confused's Stop For a Minute a site made up of thirty one-minute films. Directors Ang Lee, Guy Ritchie, Wong Kar Wai and others were commissioned by BMW to make films for their widescreen player at www.bmwfilms.com.

3 Make your own micro site

There are many companies who you can pay to build and host your micro site. Design will cost you £100 upwards, depending on how many pages and your friendliness with the designer. You could also use Macromedia Dreamweaver or Adobe GoLive to produce a web page yourself.

Once you have your movie on the web, it is your job to publicise the site, and to try to drive traffic to your cinema.

You can then attempt to sell videos, DVDs and merchandise associated with your film from the site.

Censorship

The British Board of Film Classification, 3 Soho Square, London W1D 3HD,
T: 020 7440 1570,
F: 020 7287 0141,
webmaster@bbfc.co.uk,
www.bbfc.co.uk

In the UK film censorship classification costs the same whether it is a no-budget feature intended for release on one screen, or the latest Hollywood blockbuster. The costs are per minute and run as follows:

Type of film	Fees (in £ per minute)			
	First hour	Second hour	Thereafter	Minimum fee
Shorts, features and trailers for theatrical release	10.20	7.50	5.60	102.00
Shorts and features for video release	11.68	7.75	6.48	116.80
Shorts and features for video release, previously classified for film	7.80	5.20	3.47	78.00

Summary

1. Make it your business to find out what distributors need.

2. Consider the publicity required by a distributor/

3. Don't underestimate the importance of an original hook.

Now let's put together a plan of attack to create a viable business plan.

In Conversation with Simon Franks

Simon Franks is the chief executive of Helkon SK. He is one of the UK's leading film distributors and producers. He was the executive producer of *Spider* (2003) and *Bend It Like Beckham* (2003).

What does your production company do?

Basically our production business is linked to our distribution business and the idea of it is to bring product into the distribution entity. We look at the production business effectively as a supplier for the distribution arm and we try to focus our production efforts on movies that we have an interest in from our distribution point of view. So we are really a very marketing-driven production company because when you are distribution focused you are starting off with a customer and working on what they want to see and then working backwards. Rather than coming at the industry from, let's say a more artistic point of view, saying, 'What movie would we love to make?', the first question for us is, 'What does the audience want to see?'. In terms of what we actually do, we make about three to four movies a year. Either fully financing or co-financing, co-producing and we hope over time that could rise to maybe five, six, but I don't really ever see it going beyond that. Four really is the number we're happy to stay with.

What does your job here at Helkon entail?

Well, I started this company. Originally we were called Redbus and we did a deal with a German business, so we changed our name to Helkon because they were partners with us. My job really now is, I'm chief executive. I run the operations of the business, both on a day-to-day level, and also on a strategic level. That encompasses overseeing the people who run the marketing group, the people who run the production group, the people who run the finance group, they all sort of report into me. My job really is to coordinate all their efforts.

Can you give us a run down of a typical day at Helkon?

A typical day for me. I can't really give you a typical day because, you know we have a lot of staff. We have offices around the world so I do lots of different things a lot of which are very boring and one of the things about my job is that it's probably one of the least sexy media jobs. Because a lot of it is about running a business and we're a business more than we are anything else and as a business there's a lot of administration, there is a lot of quite tedious effort that has to go into making sure the business ticks. But if I was to give you for example a cross section of a week, you would get a more interesting flavour. I probably, two or three times a week, go to a screening or a movie that has been made but that doesn't have distribution. I probably read three to four scripts a week, which is nothing, like our head of production and head of development probably read twenty a week. But I read three or four which will be scripts they passed onto me which will have gone through all the readers and they've read them and are seriously considering. I will also sit in the marketing meeting, which is where the distribution group talk about movies we are releasing and schedules and P&A (prints and advertising) spans and things like that. I will probably have maybe a meeting with a head of an exhibition, for example the head of Warners or Odeon or one of the cinema chains. I might have a meeting with someone at the UK Film Council, which is the government body that supports the film industry. I will most probably be involved in one or two meetings with our investment bankers. We are quite an acquisitive company and we look to maybe take stakes in other production companies or even buy out other distribution businesses, so we might be doing that. So those are kind of the things we do, so obviously that changes around the market time. During the markets, I'm obviously in Cannes, I'm in Venice, I'm in Toronto, I'm in Sundance. So for the festivals and the markets I'm obviously away and my day during those times changes dramatically cause I'm out there meeting filmmakers. I'm out there meeting producers. I'm out there trying to spot up films that haven't been noticed and I'm trying to spot talent that hasn't been noticed.

What would someone do to get your job?
Well, really I wanted this job. So I started a company to get it. You can't really get this kind of job because I own the controlling share of this business. So, on that basis I control the company. So to have a job where you control the company, you have to start it I guess.

Well, how did you go about starting the company?
Well that's a fairly long story. I mean it doesn't happen overnight. It involves a lot of luck and a lot of hard work. I was in investment banking and I was quite fortunate. I left university, got a good job and I'm sure you know you can make quite quick, big money in the city. I got to a situation where I was twenty-five, twenty-six and I had made quite a lot of money, not enough to retire but enough to start a business, which is what I always wanted to do. My only real passion was films. I love watching movies. I love the enjoyment and the buzz of creating movies and unfortunately I didn't have any other way to express myself creatively other than coming from the business side. But, that is enough for me to be involved in the films and that way has been great. I decided I would leave banking and start a business. I was very lucky and because I worked in banking I knew lots of people, my age, who had also spare money that I could get them to invest and I set up a tax scheme and we raised about $3 million and started the business. We just got lucky from day one. We picked up a few projects here and there. We started off picking up a project for $50,000 and probably made $300,000, which is not big money, but if you do that a few times a year and it starts adding up. Then a few banks started having confidence in us and starting lending us money. Now today we have revenue in the tens of millions. I think probably this year, $14–15 million. There is a linear progression in the business and we have grown at a steady pace. I'm happy to say the rate of increase is growing as we get more and more talented people on board.

Whenever I get asked to look back how I started it, the key is to find people and we were very lucky, because Universal Studios bought Polygram, which was the big European studio effectively and they were certainly the leading independent in Europe and in the UK as well. What happened was, we did a deal with the head of the UK business and took over the entire Polygram group, which was the head of theatrical, the head of distribution, the head of marketing, the head of PR. Overnight that brought us the profile and the prestige and most importantly it brought us a skill base that meant we had experience beyond our years, because most of these people had been distributing movies for seven, eight years. So we grew, had a few hits, and you make a lot of money in this business with hits. The rest is history.

What projects are you currently working on? What would you say is the biggest thing?

I don't think I can answer that question. You have to understand, our production business is attached to our distribution business, and they are very strategically linked. So the main focus is not one or two key projects of the year. It just isn't that way. The distribution team will tell you they focus on every movie exactly the same. They're doing twelve movies, or thirteen, fourteen movies this year and they give the same amount of commitment to each of them. Each one is important for them. I think obviously on our own productions, we probably work that little bit harder and obviously *Bend It Like Beckham* is an example of that. We were involved from the earliest stages in the development of the movie throughout production and then distributed the movie. I think it has been a huge success. I think part of that is down to how early we got involved in the marketing stage and how hard we worked on it. So I can't give you projects. I mean because, right now we have a kids' movie that we hope we're going to production with by the end of the year called, *Tooth*, which we are very excited about. But we also have a movie that we did with Lakeshore called, *The Hunted*, which is a $70 million budget, action movie. They're both very exciting to me, but then again we have a couple of smaller films, I have *Spider*, I was one of the producers on the David Cronenberg movie, *Spider*, which I love. We're going to make a lot less money from that, but I love it as a piece of filmmaking. So there's no real pinnacle. There are lots of different things in the year and some I like, some I hate, some are going to make us money, some aren't.

We just try and enjoy them all, if we can.

21 **Best Laid Plans**

THE ROUTE TO FINANCING your film can be a meandering, confusing and tiresome one at the best of times. Approach this journey without a map, and you will wander and become so disoriented and discouraged you will almost certainly give up. In order to successfully achieve your goal of financing your film, you must develop a strategic plan to assist you. Accept the fact that you will need a business plan, and you are already well on the route to successfully financing your film.

Creating a business plan is a special skill that requires a combination of ruthlessly detailed financial calculations, creative thinking and blind luck. Over the past ten years I have presided over the development of countless business plans for shorts, documentaries and features. Here is a distillation of what I have learned.

Power Tools for Creating a Business Plan

Tools are created in the mind in order to assist you with your work. Here are specific tools designed to assist you in the task of creating a business plan for financing your movie.

Any business plan is developed using certain techniques, or tools. These tools are effective in business plans for any business. The only difference in a film business plan is some of the technical detail.

1 Pedigree

This is the most important aspect of preparing your project for financing: building pedigree. The trick is to get the right people to comment favourably on your product as it stands, be it in the script stages or the finished film.

A good, well-made film, properly marketed can return an enormous amount of money to the production company that made it, and the investors that backed it. But before an investor backs any project, he/she will want to be satisfied about the project's pedigree.

Film financing is most commonly arranged by experienced producers and entertainment attorneys through existing industry funds and established film investors. Each of these people or organisations represents a filter that is trusted by an investor and once they have approved the project, they enhance the pedigree of it. In your own life, you probably act in the same way. If a friend you trust calls you and says 'I have just heard a fantastic song by this new artist. You must get their CD.' Chances are, the next time you are in a music store, you will search out the CD and even buy it.

However, it is very difficult for a new producer to attract the interest of an established film investor or production company. So the catch 22 is how to market your project to a production company on your own.

Building the pedigree for your project

When you start out on a project for the first time you have no pedigree because you have never done it before. Your first task is to convince the people that you are pursuing for money that your project is worth considering and financing despite your inexperience. To accomplish this, you need endorsements from people that potential investors respect.

However, getting the right people to comment on your project can be difficult unless they are approached in the correct manner, up the steps of the ladder, so to speak. Below is an expanded version of the pedigree advice I gave for screenwriters trying to sell their scripts in *Raindance Writers Lab: Write and Sell The Hot Screenplay*.

i The receptionist theory

A useful ploy for developing contacts with receptionists was used by Raindance producer Oscar Sharp who regularly lunched with receptionists around London until he furthered his career.

The bottom rung in the film industry world is the receptionist. This is the person who controls access to the company they work for, and most critically, they control direct personal access to the person you are pursuing. The receptionist also possesses a great deal of very personal information pertinent to the company they work for. Details like executive travel plans, anniversary parties, special event the company is planning and inter-office personal relationships will all filter down to the receptionist after a period of time. Your goal with the receptionist is to make them your friend, and then court them with your project. You are really hoping that this lowly employee will brag about having heard about a really fantastic film project, and being overheard by one of the moguls next to the coffee machine.

Hint The receptionist theory is that this person can refer your project higher up the food chain. Make sure you say thank you properly to any receptionist that helps you.

---

ii Film organisations

Align yourself with a respected film organisation like the Independent Feature Project or Association of Independent Film and Video in America or Raindance or the Script Factory in the UK. Perhaps you will employ the receptionist theory, or simply join and attend various events and meetings.

Get someone from a film organisation to champion your project to industry funding sources. Organisations like the IFP and Raindance in are respected by the industry. Try to get a letter of reference from one of their employees about your project. If you can persuade them to call up the head of development at a film company and recommend your project – fantastic. If you succeed in this, the production company will consider your project – usually by paying one of their freelance script readers to read your script and offer their opinion about the quality of the script. Some film production companies have close ties with film organisations. In the UK, Working Title, Red Mullet, FilmFour, BBC Films, Civilian Content, Tartan Films and Pathé are a few of the production companies with close links to Raindance. In America, Fine Line, NextWave and Sony Pictures Classics have ties with the IFP.

Hint A film organisation will only recommend your project if they really like it and they feel that a recommendation will enhance their reputation.

---

iii Stars

Get a star to read and recommend your script – even if they are unable or unwilling to play one of the parts. Another approach would be to persuade a star physically unsuitable for the part to read and recommend your script with a line like 'if only I had stumbled across this screenplay in 1955 when I was younger – it would have been perfect'. Based on this recommendation, you search out a production company with access to an actor similar to the aged one in their youth.

iv Business, cultural or community leaders

Which community or business leaders do you know? Perhaps your local car dealer, local councillor, pastor, sheik, bank manager, could consider and evaluate your project.

Do you think you could get Sir Richard Branson, Bono from U2 or Donald Rumsfeld to read your project and like it? Names like these would almost certainly guarantee a positive reaction from any number of film production companies. If you get them to write a letter of reference – even better.

Remember that half-hearted endorsements are as damaging as a negative one, and should be excluded from any promotional literature you may prepare.

Hint Never exaggerate anyone's enthusiasm for your project. Investors have a secret weapon that they use to suss out referees: a telephone!

---

v Producer

Producers of successful films are often open to becoming mentors on other projects, especially if there is a benefit to them.

The theory is that since they have already succeeded in producing a film – even if not a good one – they will know how to select material and prepare a financeable package. Successful producers may also allow novice producers to work under their wing and use their name to present projects for financing. This will instantly add industry-recognisable pedigree to your project.

Hint If a producer likes your script then everyone in the industry will associate your project with that individual and your project will rise to the same level of pedigree as that person.

---

vi Financiers

Any financier, but especially a film financier, has the potential to endow your project with impeccable pedigree if they love it enough. So start bombarding your local credit controller with your package.

If you know anyone who works for one of the film financing banks, or the insurance bond guarantee companies, so much the better. If they read and love your project, and will agree to be quoted, your project starts to take on the pedigree of old leather topped desks, waistcoats, Earl Grey tea, and – most importantly – of money. This helps make your film bankable.

vii Reader's report

By acquiring a positive professional reader's report on your screenplay you will be able to prove that an independent film professional has favourably judged your screenplay. Financiers will often request a copy of the reader's report from which they will make their initial judgement about the quality of the script, and by association, the project.

Hint Never forget that the raw material of any movie is a well-crafted and original screenplay.

---

viii Film festivals

Raindance is continually being called by producers and financiers who ask about the pedigree of various filmmakers. If the producer or director has previously had a short film or feature in the festival, we will be asked our opinion of the film, and the audience reaction during the screening. We are often asked if we have an archive copy of this original material on cassette. If the filmmaker agrees, we can then provide this material to the potential investor or production company.

Hint Acceptance to a film festival along with a positive screening report will enhance your pedigree for subsequent projects. You may even win an award – include this in the package you present to financiers to convince them that respected programmers like your film.

---

2 Creating Comparisons

Most business training programmes tell you to execute a thorough business plan when you are contemplating a start-up business.

A good business plan assesses the risks and opportunities associated within the venture, creates a realistic profit and loss account as well as an example of rate of return on investment.

Comparisons are always used in traditional business plans to verify the profitability of a project. Specific profit assumptions are supported by comparing the start-up project to other similar or established businesses in other areas. For example, Bob's Easy Clean earned £100,000 after expenses, is similar to my proposed business and is based in central Glasgow. Therefore, it is reasonable to assume that my business, Elliot's Dirt-Off could expect to do similar business based in central Brighton. These assumptions and supporting evidence are then available for investors to consider. The investor then decides whether or not to make the investment based on whether or not the investment proposal described in the business plan meets with their investment criteria, and is not too risky for their personal taste.

Creating a business plan for a film, however, is rather different from preparing one for another goods or service-based industry. The reason is that each film that is created is essentially a prototype, and cannot be compared directly to any other. And unlike the clone of a cleaning shop (above) your project has no direct business example to draw from, meaning that you have to create a brand every time you start another film project.

3 Creating a Brand

Advertising executives guesstimate that for an average release, each dollar spent on advertising nets $2–$5 in the cinema.

Each film project is essentially a new brand. The reason Hollywood is so successful in marketing their movies is simply that they have a knack of creating a brand out of each of their new films. The weapon they use is money – and lots of it. It now costs over $20 million to market an average Hollywood film. Essentially these film companies are creating a brand with money – money which buys up billboards, newspaper and magazine ads, TV and radio spots.

Part of your challenge when you are creating a business plan is to start creating the brand within your package. Being genre-specific not only focuses your investor immediately (i.e.: I hate horror/I love horror), but allows the investor to visualise the type of film, and the look of the film from the simple question of genre.

Creating a genre-less film is an almost certain kiss of death. A film that we often see at Raindance that falls into this category, is what the American screenwriter William C. Martell calls 'the dying grandmother' movie – where a twenty-something male, struggling to discover the true meaning of life is denied enlightenment until his grandmother becomes ill and dies a slow lingering death. A film such as this has little or no interest to anyone except the filmmaker.

Other low-budget filmmakers like Lloyd Kaufman have created whole careers – even dynasties – by understanding and creating genre-intense brands.

Of the Hollywood companies, only three market their films as 'Made by ...'. They are Disney, Dreamworks and Troma. These companies have established brands that say to the cinemagoer that a Disney, a Troma, a Dreamworks picture represents a certain type of experience.

Hint One of the most powerful tools for creating a brand for your film is genre. Is your film horror? Action? Crime? Adventure? Thriller? Science fiction? Fantasy? Or is it a combination of genres like romantic comedy, action-adventure, or thriller (crime plus horror)?

---

4 Running a Business

The minute you take on an investor, you add a new dimension to your business and to your life. You are no longer a one person show. You can no longer make decisions on your own. You must now conduct every aspect of your business in a slick and commercially sound manner. Record keeping, tax accounting etc. When you have financial partners, they can exercise creative control as well, whether or not you have allowed for this element when you signed the deal.

If you have accepted industry money then it is far more likely that a particular investor will want to exercise precise creative control. This often means that they, or a representative, are on the set during the shoot, accompany you to rushes screenings, and monitor the entire post-production process as well. In extreme cases, if the production falls behind schedule, they will have the right to fire you and finish the film with their own personnel, in order to safeguard their investment.

Beware the private investor with a creative agenda: 'I'll invest in your movie, but only if my son/daughter gets to direct and they are sixteen. You get to advise them.' All money comes with strings.

This is an argument for going outside the industry to seek finance, and in the process keeping creative control. By going outside the industry you are playing on the fact that film-illiterate investors will not know what shooting ratio means, and preying on the mystique that surrounds the film industry. Although you will still have to operate your business professionally, private investors will usually allow you total creative freedom.

Contents of a Professional Business Plan for Presenting to Private Investors

The document you create will be slick and glossy. The irony is that although investors probably won't read it, it needs to look like something that they might want to read. It needs to look so professional that they are convinced of your pedigree without needing to read it.

i Executive summary

This top sheet contains the key elements of your movie in a few tightly worded paragraphs that summarises what you have, what you are offering and what you are looking for.

ii Talent summary

A one sheet. Briefly sum up the key talent and production team with credits. Only include recognised shows, radio plays or TV unless the individual has won an award in something pertinent to your production.

iii Budget one sheet

A summary of your budget, condensed into thirty to forty line items. A sample budget top-sheet can be found in Chapter 3.

iv Start date/delivery date

Put down the best and worst case scenarios. An investor will like to know when you have physically completed your film in order to know when they can expect to see the start of a return on their investment. If you include these dates in your business plan, it will also motivate you to get the production off the ground.

v Brief synopsis of your project

One paragraph long.

vi Investment merits

List the positive elements like talent attached, deals done, distribution guarantees, or simply your firm statement that you believe that this is a commercially viable project.

vii Press release

On another company's letterhead, preferably that of a PR company, stating the start date, and listing the key elements, including synopsis. See Chapter 17 for more advice on press releases.

viii Media publicity plan

Outline when press releases will be issued i.e.: first day of principal photography, the wrap, first day of post-production etc.

ix Risk factors

Outline the ways this project can fail, despite the good intentions of all involved, and offer contingency plans for these eventualities.

x Organisation and operations

Brief biographies of key people involved.

xi Appendix

Include a quick primer on how revenue is generated and collected in the film industry or supplementary materials such as press clippings relevant to the project.

Presenting to the Private Investor

It is very easy to try to impress a film-illiterate private investor with a dazzling array of special effects. This rarely works. People with cash to invest in the film industry have their cash because they have shrewdly and creatively run their own businesses and are rarely dazzled by fluff. Best to keep it simple: present no more than ten pages, including press kits, synopses and budget outlines and key summaries.

It is better to distil this from a large quantity of material, with the spare information neatly organised in a presentable way that can be delivered to the investor in a day or two. The cute approach – a CD of songs you would like to use, or a trailer of the movie only works with first time investors.

Become familiar with the Securities Exchange Commission (SEC) regulations, and understand how and when you are allowed to approach private investors before you need to become a Public Limited Company (plc). For this you will need the advice of a lawyer.

Business Plan Mistakes

Here are some common business plan mistakes that might enable you to swindle the life savings out of an elderly widower, but are more likely to result in a firm door slam from a seasoned equity investor.

1 Unrealistic revenue projections
Creating graphically pleasing four-colour bar charts illustrating income potential relevant to long-past commercial successes might impress a member of the opposite sex at a night club, but in an investor meeting will make you look like a dud.

A better strategy is to list worst case scenario income projections, coupled with a strategy for managing this: i.e. web sales, DVD and self-distribution strategy.

2 Misleading foreign sales charts
Every year the trade papers publish sales revenue projections territory by territory around the world. Including these in your low-budget financial calculations means that you are comparing yourself with large budgeted and slick productions from established producers. Relying on these trade projections will make you look amateur.

3 Hyping the audience

Comparing the fact that football (soccer) is the world's largest sport with 100 million players and that your film is about football players does not mean that you have a ready made audience for your movie. This would only have relevance if you were producing a how-to movie about football, not a dramatic feature. No audience will watch your film unless there is a story in the movie worth watching. Marketing money draws an audience to your film, and word of mouth and reviews keep the box office coming. This can only be achieved with a great script.

4 The actor's influence

Relying on the market appeal of a name actor can actually harm your project by creating expectations for its financial success. Just because Eddie Izzard or Mathew Modine are in your film still doesn't mean that anyone is going to want to buy it. It is a well known fact that all actors make a large percentage of terrible films. If you are able to cast a named actor in a part that makes them look good, as well as manage to tell a story, then you have a better chance of selling your movie. If an actor threatens to hold your project hostage because of their name value, then drop them. The movie will still work if you have a great story.

5 Mentioning *The Blair Witch Project*

Mentioning this unusual success at all in a business plan is a bad idea. *The Blair Witch Project* did not cost $35,000. The filmmakers who created it planned each and every frame of the film. They had a great script for a unique market, and they were able to market the movie successfully using the then relatively untried Internet marketing strategy. Successes where all the elements are lined up at the same time, like *The Blair Witch Project*, happen about once every ten years. Keep your expectations, and those of your investors firmly in the real world.

6 The promise

Skilled salesmen never promise anything directly, because a failed promise will always come back to haunt you. You are simply looking through life with blinkered eyes if you think that promising the earth to an investor will leave you better off. It is far better to share the burden of possible failure with your investor. They may be able to utilise their business and marketing skills to help you.

Hint The only things you can predict are death and taxes.

Presenting to the Industry – the Package

Cute doesn't work with industry people – they have seen and heard it all before and only want to see what you have on paper. Serious investors will respect you more if you tone down the hype and present the dirty truth about your project.

The 'package' is the following bundle of pre-production documents designed to answer questions any investor, but particularly a film investor, might have.

There is a script format guide on the CD.

i The script
The script must be properly formatted. As the industry becomes more institutionalised, screenplays must conform to the standard. Failure to do so means that your entire package, no matter how excellent, will look amateurish. Don't use cone bindings; use an Acco clip.

ii Chain of title documents
Proof that you own the screenplay.

iii The budget
Properly typed, and covered with a one sheet or top sheet budget, which summarises the entire budget. Include details of above the line (costs of the talent) and be prepared to justify your fees as producer. In the below the line section, specify any unusual costs such as stunts or special effects which might affect the look of the film.

iv Discussions with potential cast members
Include a diary of availability, and copies of all correspondence.

v One page cover letter and a short synopsis of the script
Do not reveal the ending. You want them to read the script. End your synopsis or cover letter with a teaser like 'Our movie ends with an explosive song and dance number that reunites the romantic leads in a scene similar to the ending of…'.

vi Head shots
Include them if you feel they are pertinent.

vii Résumés of creatives on production team
Keep them brief, but highlight key work and awards for each crew member. The fact that Jane DoP is embarking on her first feature might seem a bit more acceptable to an investor if you also correctly state that she was the second assistant camera on *Mad Max 3*.

viii Revenue projections
Keep them realistic. It is better to say you have no idea how to get a distribution deal, but feel that you are in a strong position to recoup investment plus profit because the film will only cost £200,000 to make.

Hint Only send out the business plan where the investor asks for it, and then keep it to a short distillation of around ten to fifteen pages.

Issues You Must Address

Put yourself into the shoes of the person you are pursuing and you will be able to understand their reservations and be better prepared to answer their questions and minimalise their concerns.

i Industry scepticism about low budgets

At a meeting with several low budget filmmakers and industry producers, I was admonished by the comment from a producer of several well-known British films that 'your £50,000 budget wouldn't even cover the cost of catering'. I was also told by a civil servant, employed by a now-bankrupt government-funded film organisation that my £300, 35mm feature film budget would not even cover the cost of insurance.

Producers and investors within the industry will be sceptical about your ability to make a movie at a tenth to a twentieth of their production budgets. You are challenging the very foundations of their careers and their businesses. Tactfully outline exactly how you will save money. List production freebies in detail. They will admire your production skills at blagging a £12,000 camera package for nothing. It is something they can relate to. Demonstrate that you understand the logistics of a big-budget shoot, and illustrate how you will be able to achieve similar results using your cottage-industry style production techniques.

ii Marketing plan

Industry financing sources are more willing to accept marketing and publicity plans that break the traditional mould than innovative production techniques. Marketing plans that use the Internet and other low cost or free techniques like guerrilla marketing to create buzz are proven winners in the entertainment industry. Demonstrating your understanding of new media techniques will add value to the package.

iii Successes can be box office failures

Equity financed projects need to sell for more than their production budgets to offer a return to the investor. So if the distributor pays an advance greater than the production budget, then the film is in profit. If the film fares poorly at the box office, the distributor loses money, but the film is still in profit. All films have a certain revenue and the producer's trick is to bring the film's production budget in under that revenue level. The skill is knowing where that level is, of course.

iv What happens if you don't get a theatrical distributor?

Tertiary distribution refers to schools, prisons, hospitals etc.

Traditional industry financiers are paralysed when their projects fail to get a distributor with an accompanying advance. Fail to secure this elusive prize, and you will need to override a fundamental concern of all industry investors. Be quick to fill in the financial gaps with alternative means of creating revenue: self-distribution, foreign VHS and DVD rights, Internet distribution, and tertiary revenue streams.

v Be well versed in the mechanics of the film industry

The more you can learn to love the business side of the film industry, and understand the workings of it, the better you will be able to use that knowledge to maintain your creative control.

At any meeting with industry people you must understand how the industry works and how money flows during the pre-production, production and distribution processes. You also need to make sure that you have a clear grasp of the roles of the people you are negotiating with, not only so you can properly pitch your project and answer their questions, but to make sure that you are talking to the right person.

vi Don't quote *The Blair Witch Project*

Pulp Fiction was made for $8 million and took over $200 million world-wide box office.

Comparing your project to *The Blair Witch Project* or to *Pulp Fiction* implies that your investor will be part of a similar box office success. Industry professionals are all too aware of what this doesn't mention. The following are the fees that will eat away at that box office total:

- Exhibitors fee: this can be up to 75% of the box office take in the UK
- Distributors fee: this can be a further 10–35% of the remaining money
- Deferral payments to cast and crew
- Interest: the bank charges and cost of your overdraft
- Bonus fees to investors
- Your producer's fee (see Chapter 14)

Legal advice

Before you hit the investor trail, be it private funding or industry money, review your project with a media lawyer who will know which details will need to be included in your business plan to make it squeaky clean from a legal and accounting point of view. A lawyer will be able to advise about Securities Exchange Commission rulings. Breaching these rulings is a serious criminal offence.

Blue sky rules

Most countries have regulations limiting the promises you can make to an investor. Although you can argue that common sense should prevail, simple omissions like declaring that your second bedroom is a paid production office, or hiring your nephew as assistant director can expose you to legal action from a disgruntled investor.

Hint Don't become filmmaker as poseur! Just because you have a business plan doesn't entitle you to hang out at media cafés with a smug look on your face. A business plan is just one small part of the process. Many filmmakers grasp their business plan so tightly that they never make the film! Scripts are the currency of the film business. Better than spending months writing a business plan would be to polish the script and get it out to established producers who are expert at getting money for you. After all, the script is the ultimate business plan.

Summary

1. Learn as much as you can about how money flows in the industry.

2. Prepare a lean business plan and relevant supporting material.

3. Never overestimate your return, or underestimate your investor.

Turn the page for the ten tricks and traps of producing.

22

Ten Tricks and Traps of Producing

PRODUCING FEATURE FILMS is an occupation fraught with danger, and prone to mishaps and misfortune. As Shakespeare said: many a slip twixt cup and lip. Here are the ten basic areas where new producers trip up.

1 Measure Success by More Than a Theatrical Release

The times are a-changin'. The costs and associated risk factor of releasing a film theatrically are so onerous that it is becoming virtually impossible to secure a theatrical release for independent films. Your film might not be right for a theatrical release. Astute producers in the 21st century explore other avenues of distribution including self-distribution, ancillary markets, television and home video. Another drawback with traditional theatrical distribution is the fact that financial and creative control of your movie can easily pass to the distributor, who can often treat a filmmaker as a necessary evil in their business.

The innovative British writer/director Mike Figgis has been campaigning for an alternative distribution strategy since 1999. The advent of digital technology has opened up new exhibition formats by allowing for high quality projection from tape. Figgis proposes using alternative venues to cinemas. By wresting control of exhibition from traditional cinemas and exhibitors, Figgis hopes to bring cinema to a new audience, and to keep control of the film with the filmmaker. His approach, championing alternative exhibition venues and creating a new cinematic tradition following the model of fringe theatre, is an exciting new opportunity for producers.

2 Learn How to Use Agents

New producers treat agents poorly. The common tactic new producers use is to expect assistance from an agent who represents the talent whom they are pursuing for their poorly paid project. Often a producer will make an approach to the agent without proper preparation.

Before you approach any agent, find out who they represent and what sort of material they need from you to secure their clients. Then find out how to approach them in a way that they will say yes.

Remember that when you approach an agent with a minimal budget, they are working for you for free and need to see what other benefits you can bring. For example, you may have a part for their client that shows off a new skill: a comedy actor playing the tragic or evil character. By taking this role, even for a token payment, the actor may expand their repertoire and/or develop their acting skills. The unusual casting may also help to get your film noticed later on.

If you approach an agent professionally, with a clearly thought out plan (as dealt with in Chapter 21) you are far more likely to be taken seriously and treated with the same respect that is reserved for established producers. Remember that if an agent is unhelpful or treats you with disrespect it may have nothing to do with them and everything to do with your approach.

3 Pre-Sales

Pre-sales are a thing of the past and are virtually impossible to secure for a new producer without a proven delivery record. Learn to do without on your first project. Make your film, sell it, and then use that film's record for your next financial model and to enhance your pedigree.

See Chapter 21 for tips on demonstrating and improving your project's pedigree.

4 New Money vs Old Money

Established industry investors are a conservative lot and will try to exercise creative as well as financial control on your project.

It is true that they have systems in place: application forms you can use, a clearly defined evaluation procedure and enough production savvy to know what can happen during the rigours of production. But they are deluged with material from established producers whom they have already worked with and whom they trust.

Keep your eyes open for the new players in town, and pursue them with the attitude that you are willing to take a risk with them if they are willing to take a risk with you. Remember that you cannot skimp on legal representation at this point. Engage the services of an experienced entertainment attorney who will have the expertise to close the deals while protecting your interests.

Private investors new to the industry are less likely to involve themselves creatively, and may have other agendas prompting them to invest in your film. Try to find out what ancillary services you can offer to your investors (while maintaining your integrity).

5 Festivals Besides Toronto, Cannes and Sundance

Most filmmakers argue that unless they are accepted into one of these festivals they will be unable to secure distribution. This is possibly true. But films like *Girls Don't Cry*, *Broken Vessels* and *Amores Perros* didn't preview at these festivals.

There is no doubt that many films entered into the big three do get distribution, but the odds are stacked against getting into these festivals. Very often films programmed at these festivals are included because the festival programmers are pressurised by sponsors. The programmers' decisions often bear no relation to the quality of the film.

It is also worth bearing in mind the promotional machinery behind many of the films at these festivals. Increasingly, films screened at Sundance already have distribution and the festival is merely used as a launch for the ensuing publicity drive. You may get more coverage at a smaller festival where your film has more chance to stand out.

It is also a fact that many of the supposed hot films at these festivals die an anguished box office death. Although a place at Toronto, Cannes or Sundance is a wonderful thing, investigate other launch possibilities and develop a strategy to accompany them.

6 Sales Agents do Not Advance Money

Assume that you will not get a financial advance from a sales agent who is taking your film to a market. Instead of focusing on the advance, ask yourself if the company you have chosen produces good marketing materials. A good sales agent is capable of supporting a European and American festival tour.

It is more important that they understand your film and are in tune with your creative objectives than that they advance you cash. If a sales agent advances you cash, you can run the risk of incurring vast and onerous interest and penalty payments as they recoup. All this before you see another cent.

7 Big Sale vs Big Career

Sales agents sometimes pay a big advance for a hot film in order to keep costs down. Then they bundle your film with several others and dump them on distributors. Although you have the kudos of landing a big deal, you lose the one-on-one relationship with foreign distributors.

Hal Hartley is an example of a filmmaker who has managed his career successfully by developing individual personal relationships with small European distributors who understand him and his films thus giving him the attention his films require in order to succeed.

8 Success is Relative

Holding out for the big deal at the expense of time can be a fatal error. Better a small deal now, than one in two or three years' time when all of the efforts behind your festival and film market strategy has evaporated. Always look at the year ahead and determine where you want to be.

9 Get a Sales Agent Early on

The sooner you find a sales agent the better. Sales agents do more than sales negotiators. They offer excellent advice on how to position films at festivals and markets. They also give invaluable assistance to build profile for the film and for you and then maximise exposure. In many ways, both the sales agent's and your own career benefit equally from the success of the film. If you wait until the big festival premiere, you are reducing the time available for a sales agent to do their job. You also are gambling on whether or not you are accepted into a festival, and whether or not your film is properly promoted at it.

10 If it ain't on the Page it ain't on the Stage

The screenplay is everything. Successful producers read, read, read. They read galley proofs of novels and short stories, spec screenplays, and stage plays. They go to the theatre looking for material and new acting talent and they watch movies, movies and more movies. A good producer always has several scripts in development, and is always on the lookout for a hot new writer and a great new script.

Make absolutely certain that the script you want to produce has that one impossibly bold, fresh, original, dynamic idea that nobody else has but which everyone wants. If you have this you will finance your movie.

23

The Development Process

MOST FILMMAKERS ARE constantly in the development process. The second you have a good idea for a movie, and think about it again, you are really in the development process. In the film industry, development refers to the process of getting a screenplay to the point where it can be presented to financiers and investors, directors and actors. You try and create a package that, when shown to any prospective investor or talent, you will hear the magic 'yes'. This is known as the green light in the film industry.

The Development Path

The simplest way to proceed with the development process is to write your own script without any co-writer or partner or investor paying your rent while you write. When you do this, the legal rights to the script are clear and easy to understand and to explain to distributors once the film is finished.

It starts to get complicated when you write with someone else, when you base your story on a newspaper article or person's life, or adapt a novel into a screenplay, or base it on a television show or video game.

The ultimate barrier in the development process comes after the film is made when a film buyer will ask you to prove that you own the rights to the story 100%. If the answer is no, then you need to acquire the underlying rights to your story, and secure them in a written form acceptable to your investors and potential film buyers.

Securing Story Rights

1 Public domain

Suppose you have found an old book and want to turn it into a movie. You cannot assume that merely the fact that it is old gives you the right to turn the book into a movie.

Public domain laws vary from country to country. In the USA, for example, the 1909 Copyright Act gave the copyright to the author from the date of publication for a total of twenty-eight years, and then, upon proper renewal, for a further twenty-eight years. This act was in force in the USA until 1st January, 1978. Since then, US copyright law has gone through a series of changes. Works created in America now are deemed to have a copyright duration from the date of creation until seventy years after the death of the author.

Other countries vary, and certain countries have one law for their own territory, and another for other territories. The point is that you will need a lawyer to search the rights for your story if you are basing it on an old book or magazine article.

For general purposes, you will be safe to assume a work is in the public domain if the author has been dead for one hundred years.

Hint A useful resource is the United States Copyright Service: website: http://www.loc.gov/copyright.

---

2 Copyright reports

If you have doubts as to the copyright of your project, you must get a copyright report. These reports don't guarantee the safety of your copyright assumptions, but list all copyright facts from public records.

This is a fictional example of an initial script clearance report provided by Gregg Millard, who offers an excellent and thorough script clearance service. His contact details are as they appear on the top of this document, and on the CD you will find a summary of his services.

Gregg Millard

T: +44 (0) 77 10 56 27 74
F: +44 (0) 20 73 54 02 51

E-mail: gregg@boltblue.com

FICTIONAL EXAMPLE OF INITIAL SCRIPT REPORT
(Based on commonly found script clearance items.)

CHARACTER NAMES / ADDRESSES
Listed in the order they first appear and apply to all script references of same.

SCENE	PAGE		STATUS
1	1	GREGG MILLARD (London Lawyer) Numerous listings for exact name match in London for both full name and G. Millard. Exact Name match with professional listings.	
			not clear for use

Suggestions with no exact name match by address or professional listing:

SAM DANIELS
TONY JACOBS
ANDREW GONSHAW

cleared for use

2	1	ELISA No specified address. First name use only	
			no clearance required

<u>SCRIPT REFERENCES TO INDIVIDUALS/BUSINESSES/ORGANISATIONS</u>
Listed in the order they first appear and apply to all script references of same.

SCENE	PAGE		
3	2	GEORGIO ARMANI	
		Dialogue reference only to international	
		clothing designer and associated products/brands.	
		No derogatory or defamatory use.	
			no clearance required
		DAVID BECKHAM	
		Dialogue reference only.	
		Possible defamatory remark.	
			pending producer's legal advice

<u>BUSINESS/ORGANISATION/PRODUCT NAMES AND LOGOS</u>
Listed in the order they first appear and apply to all script references of same.

SCENE	PAGE		
4	3	AMERICAN EXPRESS	
		Featured use of existing, registered and	
		protected business name and logo.	
			clearance required
5	3	SOFT DRINKS	
		Possible featured use of existing registered	
		and often highly protected soft drink product,	
		brand name and logos.	
			clearance required
6	3	UNICEF CHARITY	
		Possible featured use of existing registered	
		and internationally protected organisation name	
		and logo.	
			clearance required

Suggest copyright free name created, cleared and agreed for use.

7	3	PAPERWORK and BILLS	
		Possible featured use of existing, registered and	
		protected names and logos as well as names,	
		addresses, telephone numbers, websites.	
		Possible use of data-protected names	
		and addresses.	
			clearance required
8	3	USE OF HOME PC	
		Possible featured use of existing registered	
		and protected business, product and logo.	
		Possible associated use of copyright protected software,	
		images, website addresses/names.	
			clearance required
9	3	MANCHESTER UNITED FOOTBALL CLUB	
		Features use of highly protected registered business	
		and football club name and logo.	
			clearance required

Recommend name created, cleared and agreed for Art Dept use to avoid high
licensing-in costs.

<u>LOCATIONS</u>
Listed in the order they first appear and apply to all script references of same.

SCENE	PAGE	
10	4	LONDON AIRPORT

LONDON AIRPORT
Possible use of existing registered and
protected business names and
logos including on uniforms.

clearance required

Recommend clearances incorporated into location agreement.

SCENE	PAGE	
11	4	HOTEL and RESTAURANT

HOTEL and RESTAURANT
Possible featured use of existing registered
and protected business name, logo
and address.

Recommend copyright free name created, cleared and agreed for use.

MUSIC
Listed in the order they first appear and apply to all script references of same.

SCENE	PAGE	
12	5	CANDLE IN THE WIND

CANDLE IN THE WIND

exploitation agreements required

| 13 | 5 | TWINKLE TWINKLE LITTLE STAR |

TWINKLE TWINKLE LITTLE STAR
Music composer deceased and music composition
and lyrics out of copyright unless using an existing
arrangement that remains protected.

Producer to advise

| 14 | 5 | MUSIC AND SINGING |

MUSIC AND SINGING
Possible use of music and lyrics that
are copyright protected.

Producer to advise

Re: MUSICAL RING TONES ON MOBILE PHONES AND OTHER DEVICES

Musical ring tones are subject to all usual musical copyrights.

FILM FOOTAGE & PLAYBACK
Listed in the order they first appear and apply to all script references of same.

SCENE	PAGE	
15	6	TV NEWS and SPORTS BEING WATCHED ON HAND HELD DIGITAL DEVICE

TV NEWS and SPORTS BEING WATCHED ON HAND
HELD DIGITAL DEVICE
TV Playback use of protected materials

exploitation agreements required

FLASHBACK TO DIRTY DANCING FILM
Exploitation of protected filmed work.

exploitation agreements required

BENNY HILL SHOW CLIP
Exploitation highly protected filmed works.

exploitation agreements required

NEWSPAPERS, MAGAZINES, WEBSITES, BOOKS
Listed in the order they first appear and apply to all script references of same.

SCENE	PAGE	
16	7	THE DAILY MIRROR

THE DAILY MIRROR
Possible featured use of registered

newspaper title and all associated
copyrights such as text and images

clearance required

VOGUE
Possible featured use of registered
and protected magazine title from 1920.
Possible use of images and text that
remain copyright protected.

clearance required

17   7   **AMAZON.CO.UK WEBSITE**
Possible featured use of existing, registered
and protected business domain name and logos.
Possible featured use of book titles, images, authors
that are copyright protected.

clearance required

THE CLIENT by John Grisham
Possible featured use of title, image and content
that is copyright protected.

clearance required

TELEPHONE NUMBERS

All featured land-line and mobile numbers for filmed use are controlled by OFTEL in the
UK and other similar authorities in overseas territories.

VEHICLE REGISTRATION

Vehicle registration plates are usually included in hire agreements, exceptions may
include plates created say for historical or period authenticity which do require clearance
with the relevant administrations.

POLICE / OTHER ORGANISATIONS

All police, doctor, professor and other similar names should be checked against records
where they are available.

If using Metropolitan Police, London:

All / any police use(s) including names, logos, locations, identity cards, documentation
require licensed-in paid for agreements.

Using police / other public services from other countries may require local agreements.

Pending decision and advice from Producer

QUOTES/OTHER EXTRACTS FROM PROTECTED WORKS
Listed in the order they first appear and apply to all script references of same.

SCENE   **PAGE**

47   35   ROMEO AND JULIET (William Shakespeare)
Writer deceased and out of copyright.

no clearance required

ARTWORKS & OTHER IMAGES
Listed in the order they first appear and apply to all script references of same.

SCENE   **PAGE**

22	21	BRYCE MILLARD

Copyright and reproduction protected work.

exploitation agreement required

44A	29	PHOTO OF FRANK SINATRA

Possible use of copyright protected image.

clearance required

Note: Works that would normally appear to be out of usual copyrights can be subject to reproduction rights clearances from galleries and museums for example.

LIKENESSES

Likenesses of real and fictional characters can be subject to copyright protection in some American states. Likenesses of well known people and characters can require clearing and/or exploitation agreements if the film, TV, Commercial or other production is to be exploited in the North American territories.

Suggestion avoid the use of likenesses of well-known real-life or fictional characters where possible.

SOURCES: Gregg Millard Experience and Imagination!

NOTE FOR PRODUCERS:

All checks and clearances undertaken using best endeavours to undertake all appropriate traditional and electronic searches using existing databases/directories/listings that do not incur paid-for access, unless expressly agreed in advance with the producer.

The service is undertaken for and on behalf of producers. It is not an insurance or a guarantee against liability and neither does the service or work of Gregg Millard take the place of recognised legal opinion or advice.

3 Chain of title

Oral permission to use material is totally worthless. You must get everything in writing.

As you proceed to verify your claim to the copyright in a story, a novel, a short story, or an original screenplay, you must provide written proof from the copyright holder at each step of the way. These written proofs, along with the consent from all the other creative parties in the film (cinematographer, composer, director, performers) form what is called chain of title.

Hint   Without a satisfactory chain of title, no one will finance or distribute your film.

4 Fact-based stories

a) Based on deceased characters

Until recently it was a legal maxim that nobody can own history. However, in America there have been several instances where states have passed laws protecting famous residents. For example, the state of Tennessee has special laws prohibiting the use of Elvis Presley's likeness without permission, and the same goes for the state of Georgia and Martin Luther King. California also has a law prohibiting unauthor-ised use of the likenesses of Charlie Chaplin and others.

b) Based on living characters

If the person is still living you need their written permission to tell their life story. You cannot hide by changing the person's name, or transporting them to another locale.

c) Son of Sam laws

New York State passed a law preventing any profit from publication of the notorious serial killer David Berkowitz passing to him. Instead, the money is to go to his victims and their heirs. Most other states and countries now have equivalent laws, meaning that the movie based on the life story of a criminal, still living, becomes extremely complicated. And to complicate matters further, these criminals could still sue you for defamation if they are represented unfairly.

Writer's contract

A producer must be certain that the format of the writer's contract follows the industry standard. If your contract with a writer is written on the back of a napkin, or contains unusual clauses, the lawyers for any potential financier will peruse them for days and weeks, trying to understand them, and trying to find any reason to get them redone.

The writer's contract is discussed in full in Chapter 14: Above The Line.

E&O

Your financiers and potential distributors will ask you for errors and omissions insurance (E&O). E&O insurance applications ask whether or not you have depicted any real people, or thinly disguised real people. The insurance company will hire a lawyer to read an annotated copy of your script. In it, you will have marked the script with each case of a scene or character based on fact, and if you are attempting to disguise it, the documentation or proof that you do not need a release.

Additionally, the E&O company will want to see the signed releases from all the characters on which the film was based.

It is relatively easy to get the signatures of the people portrayed in a positive light in your film. The difficult consents are the ones who are portrayed in a negative light, such as the drunk train driver, the corrupt politician, the careless dentist. These signatures should all be collected as soon as possible at the outset of the writing process.

Your lawyer will be able to guide you through the creative boundaries of your story should you be unable to collect certain signatures. In this case you would need to rely on other sources, such as newspaper articles and television and radio news reports.

Copyright registration

The law in most countries states that you own the copyright the minute you create a work. There is no legal requirement to file your work for copyright registration. All copyright registration does is provide you with a birth certificate.

One of the most useful services is the US Copyright Office, which is a central clearing house that records copyright dates, and subsequent liens or other legal charges and agreements against a title. It performs much the same function as a registry for land titles.

Most producers file the so-called short form agreement with the US Copyright Office because it merely records the fact that the sale or option has proceeded and does not disclose any personal details such as price or term.

Hint US Copyright Office www.loc.gov/copyright

Titles

Titles are not eligible for copyright. This helps to explain why so many songs use the same or similar titles. The only way to protect a title is to trademark it.

The major film studios and production companies have a system whereby they agree not to use other companies' titles, and have created their own system to resolve and mediate disputes.

Independent filmmakers usually obtain a title report (that is different from a copyright report), which is based on searches for similar titles in the entertainment world. Financiers and distributors will want to see a clear title report on the title chosen for the film.

Development Financing

You have scoured underground theatre and have a list of actors so sizzling hot you can hardly wait to launch their careers in the movies. At film festivals you have seen scores of shorts and debut features from which you have short-listed several directors you would like to work with. All of this has been at your own expense. Finally, after meeting dozens of writers and reading hundreds of screenplays, you finally have a script that you really believe in. You visit a printer and get some flashy business cards made up with your name as producer on them. But this is still no guarantee that you will get your movie made.

You need money.

What is Development Money?

Development money is the sum total you need to invest in your idea until it is in a form (a package) suitable for presenting to investors where it can attract production financing.

Development money is used to pay the writer while the screenplay is being rewritten, the producer's travel expenses to film markets to arrange pre-sales financing, location scouting and camera tests. It also covers the cost of administration and overheads until the film is officially in pre-production.

Typical Development Budget

While there is no such thing as a typical budget, most development budgets will include the following items:

- Script payment fees agreed under the terms of a step deal or option deal
- Producer's fee
- Travel and accommodation expenses for the writer and producer to attend development meetings with investors
- Location scouting and camera tests
- Creating a budget/schedule
- Script readings with cast
- Script editor
- Cost of duplicating scripts and postage
- Cost of developing concept for website
- Production of key art work
- Office overhead usually no more than 15% of the budget
- Producer's legal cost
- Research expenses

How Development Finance Deals are Structured

Development money is the most expensive and financiers who put up development money typically expect a 50% bonus plus five per cent of the producer fees. The bonus payment is usually scheduled to be paid on the first day of principal photography along with the five per cent of the producer's profits as the film starts to recoup.

While development is the most essential money for a movie, it is also the most difficult to raise. Financiers, be they private or industry, consider this money to be the highest risk, and therefore the least attractive from an investment point of view. From a practical level, the more time (and therefore money) that can be put into a film before financing is sought, the better the chance of finance, be it development or production. And the further you can carry the project along without resorting to outside finance, the greater your profit share will be when the film finally comes into a revenue stream.

Case History – *The Living in the Home of the Dead*

Carl Schönfeld, a friend and producing partner came back from the Berlin Film Festival in February 2003 with the exciting prospect of working with writer/director Simon Rumley, whom he had spent time with in Berlin. Simon had just completed a screenplay based loosely on his experience nursing his ailing mother, and also influenced by his interest in horror films.

Simon had already made three low budget features, two of which, *Club Le Monde* and *Strong Language*, had played at the Raindance Film Festival. *Strong Language* had been nominated for a British Independent Film Award in 1998 – although Simon and I hadn't known each other personally then.

Carl and I met with Simon in late February. Simon, very unusually, had producer Nick O'Hagan attached to the project and cut a deal based on the producer's profit share of the film. Carl and Nick would produce, while I would handle marketing and promotion. I then approached a private investor, Brian Hamilton who was willing to invest £10,000 into the project on the basis that he would share equally in any profit share that Carl and I had in the film.

The £10,000 was paid into the account in early April.

The money was dispersed as follows:

Option on screenplay	£2000
Copying and mailing screenplays	£500
Casting agent fee	£1500
Office expenses specific to the project	£300
DVDs of Simon's previous films	£350
Key artwork	£1000
100 A4 four colour one sheets for Cannes	£200
Location scouting	£1000
Office assistant (6 weeks)	£1200

The deal was organised as follows:

The investor was present at the early negotiation meetings between Simon, Nick, Carl and myself. He was also party to the negotiation of the deal and the profit split structure. Several times one of the parties needed to concede, but the final deal was signed in the first week of April.

From there, I approached a UK distributor, and managed to get the UK rights sold for an advance of 10% of the budget. Simon at this point had been shooting some promo reels for the UK Film Council, which had gone extremely well. Based on Simon's success, and on the basis of his previous three features (all of which made their money back) we decided to approach the UK Film Council for funding.

At the same time, we negotiated with Dean Goldberg of Park Caledonia to raise the balance of the budget under the UK tax laws. He was able to commit funds rather early because of the involvement of the UK Film Council and because the film had a UK film distributor.

As part of the exercise, we approached Douglas Cummings of Axiom Films and asked him to provide sales estimates. These arrived with a low estimate of $900,000 and a high of $1,400,000. We then went back to the UK Film Council armed with 50% of the budget in place as well as sales estimates well in excess of the proposed £400,000 ($600,000). To our surprise, the UK Film Council had pages of notes on script changes they insisted on before our application could proceed. Meanwhile, we had been incurring expenses with a casting agent and location scout, trying to get the film shooting by the end of September.

Simon decided that the changes demanded by the UK Film Council were far wide of the mark, and would destroy his creative vision for the project. We decided to abandon the government funding, opting for a series of private investors, where the project currently languishes.

Sources of Development Finance

1 European film industry money

See the CD for information on European funding.

Many film production companies in Europe have their own in-house development departments, which work on script evaluation, and rewrites. The money used to fund these ventures can come from a variety of sources, including private investment, share offerings, European government money and profit from previous projects.

Hint Get a production company interested in your project. This will usually be triggered by a certain actor attached to your project, or because you have already secured a distribution deal in one or more countries allowing the production company to see a potential recoup.

---

2 Housekeeping deal

Sometimes a major distributor or production company will really believe in your ability to find the next hot project. They will offer you money to pay for your time, office expenses and writer's fees. In return, they get a first-look or right of first refusal on anything you develop. If they pass on the deal, they will then expect to get the cost of developing that project, plus 50% profit from whom ever you eventually sell the project to.

3 Distribution companies

Distributors may read your script and agree to pay for a number of rewrites in order to turn it into a more marketable commodity. When the film is finished, they will take back this money with an agreed profit.

4 Government finance

The UK Film Council is known for believing in writers and creative producers. They finance a wide range of scripts and production slates. Details of their application requirements, and their compensation expectations are at their website: www.filmcouncil.org.

The UK Film Council

Film council development funding is available for all stages of development up to pre-production. Funding is available for the following costs:

- Writer's fees
- Research fees
- Reasonable overhead costs of the producer
- Payments to acquire and option rights to adapt works for the screen
- Producer fees
- Producer's reasonable legal costs
- Script readings with cast
- Script editors
- Executive producer/mentor
- Other specific requirements, e.g. special effects/storyboarding
- A 'package' to present to potential partners
- Budget
- Schedule
- Casting duly available
- Training courses to aid project development
- Other legitimate development costs at the discretion of the fund

In exchange for its investment the Film Council expects its money back on the first day of principal photography, with a 50% premium.
Film Council Application documentation checklist

- Details of the key creatives involved (writer/director/producer/actors) with biographies/filmographies
- One page synopsis
- Treatment
- Draft screenplay (in the Film Council preferred format)
- Underlying work (novel/stageplay etc., with relevant option)
- Draft development budget (see sample development budget)
- Example of director's work
- Details of any cultural, social or economic diversity elements (e.g. people working on the project, characters/settings in the script etc.)

5 Private investment

Occasionally you will find investors who love high risk, high potential investments, who are willing to finance you and/or your writer until the script is up and in production.

These investors would be called angels in theatre, and if they finance a successful film, stand to earn many times their investment.

Typically, they can command a producer or executive producer credit as well as the usual high interest repayments and a percentage of the producer's net profits in the film.

6 Talent

Successful actors often fund development of projects with their eye on a potential starring role. Entertainers in other industries, such as music or sport, are also turning to development as a way to guarantee them the appropriate vehicle in which to launch a movie career.

Tools for Raising Development Finance

The package

Some talented DoPs have no desire to diversify as they have based their career on a certain technique that they are satisfied and comfortable with.

Add as many elements as possible. At the very least you should have a director. If you are having difficulty attracting a named cast, surround yourself with a veteran and seasoned crew. Get the best-known director of photography (DoP) you can. Convince him or her that you have the finance in place to pay them at least part of their salary. And emphasise that this will be a chance for them to experiment and diversify.

1 Key cast and crew bios

Create a list of the people involved, and list a two- or three-line bio on each, including their most impressive credits, and listing any awards or newsworthy achievements.

2 Promo tape

A good promo reel is short and to the point. It has clear titles and contact details and contains key scenes that demonstrate either the director's ability with actors, or the 'look' of the film if it is for a DoP.

Hint A showreel is different from a promo reel. A showreel contains a series of short scenes, usually with a single track of music from beginning to end. A promo reel is a series of scenes assembled to show a certain skill.

---

3 Development budget
This budget can be done in several ways:

- It can be the projected total budget of the film from start to finish
- It can list the amount of money needed to finance the project up until the first day of principal photography
- It can list the specific costs of getting the package ready for investors including option payments, travel expenses and so on
- Or it can include all of the above

Making Your Project Attractive

How you state your case and present your position will predetermine the success you have in raising finance. Here are a few tips on how to present your project.

1 Start date and completion date
List and aggressively repeat the specific start date of your film. While working on *Living in the Home of the Dead* at Raindance's production company, we kept repeating the start date of 4th August. Even when it ended up moving back two weeks, we waited several weeks before we told anyone, because we wanted to keep the pressure on the lawyers. We were always asked in meetings with financiers and sales agents for the completion date. It became automatic to respond that 'according to our schedule, the completion date, which allows for a standard ten weeks of post production, would be October 31st, in time for final selection screenings at Sundance Film Festival'.

These two hard dates give any one looking at the project the confidence that we knew what we were doing, plus it allows them to visualise the end of the project, and to start to get an idea of when their revenue stream might start.

2 Creative casting
Perhaps your investor has some ideas for casting. You should listen carefully, and keep them informed of the casting process. If a financier starts to feel that they are involved in the creative process, you know that they are hooked on the project, and the rest of the process with them will be much smoother.

3 Start at the top and ski downhill

This is the advice given to me by Dean Goldberg, co-director of Park Caledonia, one of the most exciting financing companies in the UK.

It is far better to ask for more than you need, and then negotiate downhill. Your financier will enjoy taking out the red pen and stroking off certain items saying: 'You don't need this, and you don't need that'. Of course, since you have already started high, you are more able to deal with this financial downsizing.

Pitfalls to Raising Development Finance

Investors seeking to park funds in high risk ventures such as development finance often resist because of the unproven track records of the talent and producers.

This was one of the guiding principles we had when we created Raindance Film – a production company combining investment with the unlimited pool of undiscovered talent, passing through our auspices. However you do it, you will need to demonstrate to potential investors how you are able to overcome this obstacle.

Untried talent

No one was worse at pitching than Guy Ritchie. In fact, he was so poor at this essential skill that Duncan Heath of ICM took pity on him and helped him in every way he could. That doesn't mean to say that he didn't have passion or commitment and energy for his project. Those qualities he had in abundance. It was just the verbal communication skills that he lacked.

Your investor may not believe that your director or actors are sufficiently experienced to handle the rigours of the shoot and post-production schedule. Your investor may want to suggest a more experienced director or actors.

Remedy

The classic way to demonstrate talent is to have a portfolio of previous work, be it short films, reviews of stage work, or other demonstrations of experience that will help persuade an investor that you deserve to work with a reasonable budget to demonstrate your talent further.

If you are fortunate, your writer or director will have already written other scripts, now made. In this case, include copies of these films on DVD. If your director has already directed a series of short films which you can supply on DVD. A film already made in a retail DVD package created by a distributor is a useful asset to your package.

Naturally, you will be unable to advance unless you are able to pitch – to impart your passionate enthusiasm for your project.

Unproven producer

Film financiers are always sceptical of new producers, especially when it comes to entrusting them with a large sum of money. With the risks involved in the creative, financial and creative elements that are combined in the filmmaking process, financiers usually are leery.

Remedy

The easiest way to convince a shy investor that you are a good producer is to do your homework, and to be able to quickly and succinctly demonstrate that you are able to adapt and handle every business and creative variable likely to be thrown your way.

Try to create trust so your investors believe that you can and will meet requirements and delivery schedules demanded throughout the production process. Remember to always take your financier's requirements into consideration.

Another tack would be to surround yourself with veteran accountants and line producers with whom the financier has already worked, or who are experienced in making the type of film you plan.

Summary

1. Create, market and successfully adapt your package.

2. Shoot a promo tape.

3. Create a professional development budget, and raise the finance and make your project more attractive to investors.

Lets raise some more money and spend it on shooting the film.

In Conversation with Tracey Scoffield

How would you describe your job and what do you do ?

Tracey Scoffield joined the BBC as a Script Editor, and is now Head of Development for BBC Films. In the latter capacity, she has executive-produced Richard Loncraine's award-winning *The Gathering Storm* (broadcast in the U.S. on HBO), Stephen Frears's *Dirty Pretty Things*, Thaddeus O'Sullivan's *The Heart of Me*, and Roger Michell's *The Mother* (which stars *Sylvia* leading man Daniel Craig).

Well my official job title is head of development and executive producer for BBC Films. So in the head of development role, my first responsibility is to manage the development team within the BBC, because we have a project slate with about sixty-five theatrical projects on it, all of which require some level of editorial assistance. And that's something that we do pride ourselves on here, is our ability to develop new talent – producing, directing and writing, and that's what the development team do, they are there to give that kind of support and advice. I manage the team and the development slate. I keep an eye on the development slate, and make sure that they are all moving along at a decent rate, and along with others here, I'm involved in the selection of projects – either from the independent sector, or generated in house.

I commission projects from writers, producers and directors – anything from a draft screenplay, right back to basic pitched idea. Like a lot of film financiers who are involved in development, we prefer to come in early on a project, simply because then we have an opportunity to shape it in a way that we think is appropriate for our market.

As executive producer I'm attached to some of the projects which I have been personally responsible for commissioning and developing. That means that I get an opportunity to see them through the whole process. Usually people who work in development are heavily involved in the script process, and then they should look at rushes, and should also be involved in looking at assemblies and giving notes on the different cuts of the film. But they won't necessarily be involved in the choice of director, the casting, or budgeting discussions. Those are the things that an EP is involved in – from development to delivery.

Dirty Pretty Things was a script sent to me out of the blue – it was an unsolicited script. This year, I have worked on *Sylvia* right from scratch with Alison Owen who is the producer. So I get a very nice handful of my own projects to follow right through the whole process.

On average, how much time does a project take to develop?

They can be really fast; if there's a fair wind behind a project and some really hot talent attached to it, and other co-producers in the market place want to invest in it, they want to be attached – then a project can happen quite quickly. But most theatrical projects take much longer.

If you are developing a feature length screenplay with a well-known writer, most good writers are really busy most of the time, so quite often you have to wait for them, and then that process is slow. The standard contract provides for two drafts and two sets of revisions, but I've very rarely seen a script go into production without at least six drafts.

The development of a project can be held up by the slowness of the writing, by raising the funding, and attaching directors to the projects. A lot of directors are either busy or are holding out for other projects that they want to do, and are not available to come on board when you want them to. We don't fully fund any films, we have to find co-production partners, so we always have to have a director who they want to back as well. And quite often, if it's somebody who is new, and it involves taking a risk, we can give them the courage of our convictions if they are right for the project, but for a lot of projects which are of a medium budget, by which I mean about £5 million, people would prefer not to take a big risk on them.

In the case of *Dirty Pretty Things* there were various hold ups which were not the fault of the writer, Steve Knight, but it took three and a half years before it went into production, because there were numerous hold ups, a lot of it was unfortunate, but it was all unavoidable.

How do you find new projects ?

We find new projects in a number of ways. Firstly, we have a very efficient submission system, so that anybody can submit to us from the film community – be it a treatment, or a script, or a proposal for an idea – we will consider it. We do pick up some projects this way.

We generate our own ideas from inside the department. We will think of an idea for a script and attach a writer to it and then a producer later on. On other occasions, writers or directors or producers will come to us with a verbal pitch and we might take it from there.

We have to be very selective because we have a development slate with sixty-five projects on it – that's a rolling slate, and in theory we invest in between six to eight films a year, but you can see how selective we have to be about ideas.

What is it you that look for in a project?

Good quality, obviously – in terms of the idea and the execution. I'm always looking for things that are different. I look for stories that open up new worlds to audiences, because I think that's what people really want these days. I look for an antidote to Hollywood films – because we can't compete with Hollywood in terms of their stars, or the scales of their budgets, so we have to do something different.

I also bear in mind the things that we've got on the slate already – so sometimes we have to regretfully pass on something that's good, because we have something similar.

It's always very interesting for me to notice trends in proposals and screenwriting – you'll notice one year that there are lots of projects around about serial murderers. This year there seem to be so many projects going round about troubled teenagers. We have made quite a few ourselves actually, both for TV and cinema – *Sweet Sixteen*, and the Dominic Savage film *Out of Control* – it's a very popular theme at the moment, which started with *Billy Elliot* I suppose.

Are there certain stories or genres that you won't touch?

Ultimately, BBC Films is delivering these films for broadcast, so we have to be sensitive to what is broadcastable. Obviously that's getting more and more relaxed as time goes on, but we do have to be careful about stories that are either sexually very, very explicit, or very graphically violent – but actually, I would not be attracted towards a very graphically violent story anyway, because I don't think people want to watch them, I really don't. It's impossible for us to take on Hollywood genres and play them at their own game, so we can't do action-adventure or large scale science fiction films, or any of those big, expensive genres. But interestingly, Michael Winterbottom's *Code 46*, which has just screened in Venice and Toronto, is a love story, set slightly in the future. It's not a science fiction film, but it's in a future world – and you can do that sort of thing in a low budget way, just with a very imaginative story, and creating something that looks a bit different.

What is the single most important element?

Well the single most important element for me in any project is the script. If you don't have a good script, you won't get a good director, and you won't get a good cast, and you won't get the money to make the film. I think a director can mess up a good script, but they can't really make a good film out of a bad script. The script is king!

Do many of the directors you work with come from TV?

They come from a variety of backgrounds. The new directors we work with have either worked in television, or a lot of them have had a documentary background in fact. Paul Pavlikovsky and Dominic Savage both have documentary backgrounds, and interestingly, will often work in an improvised way with their cast, instead of with a formal screenplay, so their work has a completely different feel to it. We think that documentary filmmakers have a very good instinct for story and can often tell it in a very immediate way – which suits our budget levels and the sort of stories we are looking for.

How closely do you work with writers?
It depends on the project. Some writers are very independent and don't take notes and will hardly come in for meetings. Other writers are very collaborative, and in fact, require that kind of support in order to get from draft to draft, and will want more hand-holding. It just depends very much on the personality of the writer and on the project.

How many different writers do you work with at the same time?
Well we've got sixty-five projects on the theatrical slate, and I don't work with all of them, because there are other development producers within the department attached to some of the projects, but I'm constantly looking at new work and meeting new writers – whether or not we commission anything from them, it's my job to be aware of who's out there and try and identify new writers who we want to work with. I'm supposed to know everybody really.

On a single project, do you have several writers working on the same script?
That's very unusual – comedy writers often tend to work in pairs, but no, we don't work with writing teams actually. That's a feature of American TV series, it's not a feature of the sorts of writing we commission because really, the screenplays we commission feel more like 'signature pieces' – they couldn't really be written by committee.

Many people look at directors and producers in the film industry and call it (negatively) a lifestyle occupation. How would you react to that?
Well it's a part of it, isn't it? It's the reward. If you make a film which people love, then you get a lot of attention, and with that comes what people perceive to be glamour – premieres, award ceremonies, parties. But you have to work hard to achieve that, I don't think it happens by accident, you might have a fluke but you can't sustain that by accident. I think most people actually deserve it – if that's what they want, then they deserve it.

How do you deal with agents?
Well it's very important that we keep up to date with every agent. We talk to agents both in London and in LA about their clients, and we are constantly looking at their work and receiving proposals from them, because they need their clients' work in order to survive, but we need to know who the new people are who they are digging out as well. American agents tend to be a bit more rigorous, and a bit more attentive than London agents, who give the impression of being rather more passive about their clients' work, but at the same time, it's a style that is more relaxed and friendly actually – American agents are rather aggressive. My preference is more for English agents – because they are more

like me! American agents are a breed unto themselves, I mean they are mind-boggling. They are very, very insecure and paranoid. You can tell that when they are ringing you up about a project, and they are hassling you about something, it's because of some paranoid, insecure reason that's got nothing to do with the project that you're actually discussing – they always have multiple agendas. Often they will do this classic thing of sending you stuff that's completely rubbish and inappropriate, because they feel that they have to tell everybody about their clients.

You get these hilarious letters from American agents: 'Dear Tracey, I have great pleasure in sending you this script which I'm sure you will think is absolutely marvellous' – and you can see at the bottom that they have cc'd about twenty names, just to show the client that they are sending their script out! English agents can't be bothered with all that. Sometimes English agents are infuriatingly lazy and basically can't be arsed to represent their clients, and I find that, at the other end of the scale, really unforgivable.

What exactly is the role of an agent?

Well I think that many agents have different roles in their clients' lives, and a lot of them partly take up the role of editor really, and will look at their work, and comment on it. Lots of agents don't really go all out to find their clients work – their clients find the work, and the agents just do the deals. So agents are all very different, and you have to find the right agent for you, you have to decide what you want. If you are young, and you've got a couple of pieces of work under your belt, but you need the agent to sell you – there are certain agents who are good at that. But there are certain agents who really wouldn't go out and find you work, they will do the deal once you have found the work. Most people consult quite widely before they approach agents.

Do you think digital filmmaking has changed filmmaking for the good, the worse, or not at all ?

I don't think it has changed things yet in any way – but it will. I think everybody is obviously aware of this and is kind of waiting for the impact, but I don't think the impact has yet been made. I think it's very useful for people who are just starting out and they can obviously make a film incredibly cheaply and it doesn't involve the selling of the family silver in order to make a film.

I can see that as far as people like me are concerned, it's going to become highly problematic – with a sudden welter of movies from young people that we will be expected to look at and file comment on! I don't think the impact has yet been felt, we will just have to see – there is bound to be an explosion of some kind.

It will change things once the movie houses decide to spend the money on the equipment so that the product can be exhibited easily. In terms of the sorts of opportunity it offers to a filmmaker, then obviously it offers fantastic flexibility and enables filmmakers to achieve things they have never been able to achieve before, so it's very exciting, but as yet, the projection equipment doesn't exist in the movie houses.

Is it difficult to raise money in today's economic climate?

It's pretty tough at the moment and has been for the past couple of years. Since FilmFour closed down its big operation and there was all that nervousness about films that were being made that were not getting distribution, there has been a real anxiety about investing in films – there is still money around, but it's very cautious. It's taking a long time to settle on projects, and the money is really trying to find projects that are considered risk free – so it's quite tricky for either more unusual projects or more ambitious projects to find funding at the moment. But it might start to pick up, because FilmFour is back in business, albeit in a much more modest way – but there is money there. There are new deals being signed, like DNA signing a big deal with Fox, so there is a lot of production and acquisition money coming into the industry through them, and British films are performing well in the box office and I think that might encourage investors. There have also been about two or three tax funds that have been set up over the past six months. Maybe 2004 will see more money coming into the marketplace. It has been bad. We were the only game in town, apart from the Film Council, which is not a production outfit, and Working Title. Between us, we have been the only real ports of call for people looking for investment.

What is the largest problem that you face today?

Finding really good projects. There are too many projects that are either bad, or are just not good enough.

Is there one project that got away?

There are loads of things that you pass on, that then get made and you can see the point of them, you can see why perhaps you should have invested in them, but at the same time, there are always reasons why you don't – like you are doing something else. I mean, we've all got stories about things we turned down that then became box office smash successes. Someone you spoke to for this book turned down *Lock, Stock And Two Smoking Barrels* – we have a letter to prove it in the files, but I don't think anyone at the BBC regretted that, because it was such a terrible film, and it's not what we are here for really, though Alan Yentob will probably kill me for saying that. There are others – I turned down *Saving Grace* but I don't really care – there are other reasons for making things apart from commercial reasons.

The fact is, nobody can see the real commercial potential in an early script because films have such a long journey to go on before they become commercial properties. If it was possible to identify what that big commercial key was, then only commercial films would be made. You have to think that you see something in the script that other people will want to go and see and will find interesting and engaging and tell their friends that they have to go and see it as well.

Why do you do what you do?

Because I have always loved watching films and my mind works with words and pictures – it's the perfect fusion for me.

24

Production Financing

THERE ARE MANY WAYS to finance the production costs of a film. I will attempt to discuss the various ways films are financed based on the chart below.

Sources of Funding	Development	Production	Distribution
Private Funding	common	common	rare
Friends and family	common	common	common
Lenders	unusual	common	rare
Pre-sales	unusual	rare	common
Gap finance	rare	common	rare
Euro tax incentives	common	common	common
Other tax incentives	rare	common	rare
Equipment charge deferrals	n/a	common	common
Crew deferrals	n/a	common	unusual
Talent deferrals	common	common	rare
Producer deferrals	common	common	common
Soundtrack album	rare	rare	rare
Music publishing	rare	rare	common
Gaming rights	rare	rare	occasional
Product placement	n/a	rare	rare

figure 24.1
Sources of independent film financing

Private Funding

Loans or equity investment from sources other than bank loans and money from distributors who acquire distribution rights to your movie are referred to as private investment. There are elementary distinctions between loans and equity finance.

Loans

A loan carries an obligation to repay a fixed amount plus interest. The original amount of a loan is call the 'principal'. Simple interest is calculated just on the principal. Compound interest is calculated on the principal and unpaid interest. Loans for movies often contain other costs. These can include a commitment fee and the legal costs for drawing up a loan agreement. A loan is documented by a promissory note which is a brief document that spells out the interest rate, repayment and default terms of the loan, and a lending agreement which is a long-form agreement which spells out the details of the promissory note in great detail. This lending agreement can also contain details about warranties, representations, completion bond requirements, collateral, security, and takeover provisions.

Most film finance promissory notes prevent the investor from reclaiming their money from the film, although it is not unusual for a film producer to offer their home or other possessions in a last ditch effort to salvage a deal – often with disastrous results.

Loans are relatively simple to negotiate, and are virtually unregulated, although each country has usury laws governing the amount of interest that can be legally charged.

Equity Investment

Securities are investments in which the investor has no say in the running of the business. Securities are heavily regulated.

An equity investment gives a return to the investor only if a profit is earned. In order not to offer an equity investment that would expose you to securities laws, producers and their lawyers often structure these investments to give the investor some control over business and creative matters and endow them with producer or executive producer credits.

If you choose to solicit funds from the general public, say by way of newspaper ads or bulk mailshots, you have to satisfy government regulators that you are a bona fide investment, and prepare a prospectus of investment in which you detail all the risks and benefits of investment. This document must also contain official back-up to any claims you make. For example, if you claim that your film will achieve a certain income potential from sales, you must include sales projections from a reputable sales agent. Once you have this complete, you publish a public offering document. This can also be sold through financial brokers.

If you choose to approach wealthy individuals one-on-one, you must also prepare a prospectus and create a private placement document.

Hint The key to structuring film financing is to maintain a clear picture of the order in which your investors get paid. Distributors, banks, talent deferrals, completion guarantors and private investors will all be clamouring for money. Make certain that each investor's place is clearly assigned when you start to dole out the cash.

Equity pitfalls

Every year at Cannes there seem to be wild rumours circulating about a group of financiers, usually ensconced on a huge private yacht, who have secured hundreds of millions of dollars for equity finance. Usually

Get the bad news early. You meet a self-proclaimed financier of independent film at a cocktail party who promises you the earth. Ask these simple questions: Who is your lawyer? Who are your accountants? What movies have you financed? Who can I talk to at your bank to verify available funds? Are you a principal?

they entertain producer after producer and make promises of financing pictures in the $5–10 million range. Only after the dust has settled are the producers called upon for finder's fees of between a half and three percent of the total budget of the film. A few more months pass, and the financiers disappear with the producer's money.

Hint The Golden Rule of Equity Finance: Deal with principals, not agents or brokers.

Family and Friends

Friends and family finance most low budget independent films. Even though you are dealing with people you know very well, there are still legal requirements governing what essentially are securities. But dealing with people very close to you can result in ugly situations should the deal or the movie go south.

The basic rules of engagement for raising money from family and friends are:

- Be professional. Create the appropriate paperwork and get it signed.
- Risk. Make certain that each individual understands that they could lose their entire investment, and make sure that they can afford to do so.
- Disclosure. Keep all of your investors informed of the progress of your film. Do not try to hide bad news.
- Use the investors' expertise. If an individual has the ability to fund a film, they usually have financial savvy that you can tap into if problems arise. Don't be afraid to ask for help.
- Use an entertainment lawyer. Get all the legal paperwork done by a professional and cover your back.

Hint Always act professionally with family and friends.

Pre-sales and Foreign Sales Agents

Sample sales estimates are to be found in Chapter 19.

Another financing route is to convince a distributor in another country or territory to purchase your film before it is made. This is called a pre-sales agreement. The distributor will assess your script, look at your cast and decide what the value of the film will be when it is finished, and offer to pay a Minimum Guarantee (MG) to you upon delivery of the film.

This presales agreement is then taken to the producer's bank who will loan all or a portion of the value of the MG as part of the production loan to the film.

A foreign sales agent's function is to find foreign distributors for your movie and then negotiate and document the terms and conditions of the distribution agreements. When you are arranging finance, a good foreign sales agent will provide a sales estimate for your film, territory by territory. This estimate can then be used to demonstrate the viability of your project to other investors, banks and gap financiers (see below).

Gap Finance

Often there is a gap between the amount of money offered to a producer in equity loans, and the value of the guarantees of the pre-sales contracts, and the actual budget of the film. In order for the producer to make the film a 'gap' loan will need to be raised by the producer from a specialised entertainment lender. Only specialist lenders will consider a gap loan, as there are specialised skills involved in analysing the risks of the loan. The lender will evaluate the credit worthiness of the companies who have already bought rights in the film, as well as decide how much income will be derived from the sale of unsold territories. Factors considered include cast and production values of the film. Once a positive decision has been made, a commitment fee (in points or percentage of the final loan value) is agreed, a loan is arranged, banking fees are added, legal fees, and security agreements are lodged over the company to ensure that the gap lender will be repaid, usually before any other investor in the film is paid.

Hint Gap finance is usually the last route a producer will take due to the high cost of arranging the loan. However gap finance is not an equity loan, and once repaid, the gap financier demands no further part of the proceeds of the film.

Completion Guarantee

If you finance a film using a combination of equity investment and loans, you may be required to provide a completion bond which insures the investors and lenders in the event of the film running over budget and/or over schedule.

The producer generally approaches a completion bond company at the outset of the financing process when they have a script, schedule and budget in place. The completion bond company will assess the material and decide whether or not the film can be completed as set out in the budget and schedule and will offer a bond based on the budget plus a ten per cent contingency.

Sometimes a completion bond company will have a representative on the set to make sure that the film is running smoothly. Should a film go over budget, the completion bond company has three options. The first is to loan additional money to the producer to finish the film, the second is to take over the picture and finish it, and the third is to close down the film and repay all the investors.

Completion bonding rarely exists in the low budget realm for several reasons. First, the bonding companies have strict rules about the amount of filming that can be done in a day. These limits are based on large budget Hollywood films, and there is no allowance (or tolerance) for the amount that a small independent film might be able to achieve in a day. Secondly, the crew that is 'bondable' is a seasoned, veteran (and expensive) union crew that the bonding company recognises from other shoots. Your bonding fee might be £50,000, but you will need an additional million to fund the crew and additional days on the shoot.

Hint If an investor is insisting on a performance bond, try first of all to convince them that you are able to complete your film with the amount of money and time allocated in your budget and schedule. Try to demonstrate that your production will be adequately crewed and that health and safety measures will be adhered to.

Co-productions and European Tax Incentives

In its simplest form, a co-production is created by two producers who wish to pool their resources – creative and financial – in order to make a film that otherwise could not be made.

In the current marketplace, which is dominated by scores of territorial grants, subsidies and tax concessions, a co-production between two or more producers from different countries allows a film to take advantage of the benefits from a number of territories while still being considered, for tax and grant purposes, a national film of the particular country of each producer. This arrangement allows the film significant financial benefits which can be shared between the producers.

There are two main types of treaties that co-productions can exploit: bilateral treaties and European Conventions. Bilateral treaties are agreements between countries that create financial incentives for a film to be made in each of the participating countries. European Convention co-productions which qualify under a point-scoring system are able to benefit from a series of grants and tax benefits.

Bilateral treaties

A typical Canadian/UK co-production would benefit from the UK's Section 42 and Section 48 tax credits as well as obtaining Canadian labour tax credits resulting in soft funding of between 14% and 40% of the budget.

Bilateral treaties exist between countries that recognise the benefits for the local film industry if local producers work with producers from another country. These treaties set out the conditions that must be met in order for the project to qualify. Only recognised co-productions are able to attract national benefits.

It is possible to create a film produced by a variety of partners from a host of nations by combining various bilateral treaties and the European Convention in one co-production agreement.

General treaty restrictions
- Independence of co-producers: there must be no common management or control between the co-producers
- Creative, artistic and technical contribution: this contribution, usually measured by a minimum production spend in a territory of at least 20%
- Labour: cast and crew must be residents of the co-producing nations. Some treaties allow for leading actors, writers and directors to be from a non-co-producing country
- Use of facilities/studios: must be situated in the respective co-production countries
- Financial contribution: the financial contribution of each co-producer must be in reasonable proportion to the creative, artistic and technical contribution for each country

European convention of cinematographic co-production

Text of the European convention is available from http://conventions.coe.int/treaty/EN/cadreprincipal.htm

The Council of Europe established the ECCC in 1992. The European Convention does not apply to bilateral co-productions between countries that have already established a bilateral treaty. It does have many similar points to the bilateral treaties. In addition it operates a European points system. A film needs to score a minimum of fifteen out of a possible nineteen points to qualify under the European Convention. See figure 24.2 opposite for a break down of the points system.

An important distinction between bilateral treaties and the European Convention is that the ECCC allows for financial investment from key non-European territories such as USA and Japan without risking the production's eligibility for tax benefits and subsidies.

Production Sector	Points available for	
Creative Group	Director	3
	Screenwriter	3
	Composer	1
	Total available	7
Performing Group (performers' roles ranked by number of days on set)	First role	3
	Second role	2
	Third role	1
	Total available	6
Technical Craft Group	Cameraman	1
	Sound Recordist	1
	Editor	1
	Art Director	1
	Studio or location	1
	Post-production location	1
	Total available	6
Maximum points available		19

figure 24.2
European points system. Points are scored for European elements of the production.

Finding a suitable co-producer

National industry bodies regularly publish guides to co-production in their country. These often include information on producers with a track record in co-productions. The UK co-production guide is at www.bfc.co.uk

The ideal co-producing partner will live and work in a territory with available funds, and in a territory that can contribute to your film in terms of locations, cast or crew. Finding the right co-production partner for your project, or for a series of projects is a key element in your project's potential success. A good co-producer will meet your requirements in the following areas: expertise, credibility, pedigree, commercial standing, and most importantly, compatibility with you and your project.

Structure of the co-production agreement

A competent authority in the context of a co-production refers to the national body in charge of authenticating a film project under the national guidelines. In the UK the competent authority is the international department of the Film Council.

There are certain minimum requirements for a co-production agreement to meet the requirements of the European Convention and/or any applicable treaties. The arrangement between the co-production partners should cover:

- film title and key creatives including writer, director and producer
- production budget, which should be split by territory to show the national spend for each co-producer
- financial contributions of the co-producers and an agreed method of apportioning overspend
- method of division of receipts
- start and delivery dates
- ownership of rights and terms and conditions of their exploitation
- provisions for dealing with the failure of any of the co-producers to obtain co-production status from their national competent authority

Application procedure

Once a co-production partner has been secured and the terms of the agreement negotiated, each partner must submit their proposal to their national competent authority. The application must include:

- completed application form
- co-production agreement
- finance plan
- budget showing the spend in each co-producing country and in any non co-producing country
- plot synopsis
- chain of title

Competent authorities often consult each other before granting provisional status – a time consuming process. Veteran co-production producers suggest submitting applications at least two months prior to principal photography. Upon completion of the film, a final submission is made along with a detailed cost report. The final cost report needs to be accompanied by an independent accountant's report – one for each of the countries involved.

Bilateral treaty competent authority contact information

- Australia / The Australian Film Commission / www.afc.gov.au
- Canada / Telefilm / www.telefilm.gc.ca
- France / Centre National de la Cinematographie / www.cnc.fr
- Germany / BAFA / www.bafa.de
- New Zealand / New Zealand Film Commission / www.nzfilm.co.nz
- Norway / Norwegian Film Fund / www.filmfondet.no
- United Kingdom / UK Film Council International Branch (formerly the British Film Commission) / www.bfc.org.uk

---

Hint As new countries join in bilateral treaties, and tax laws are negotiated frequently, producers should note that these guidelines are frequently updated.

Sale and leaseback

A tax deferral deal will only work if the investor has a tax liability which they would normally have to pay to the government. This payment can be avoided (mitigated) or delayed (deferred) by using a variety of tax products, some of which can be exploited by the investor by putting money into film.

Sale and leaseback is a financial instrument that began with the shipping industry. A shipping company would commission the building of a new ship, and on delivery sell it to the boatyard, and then immediately lease it back over a period of years. The rental payments would retire the original purchase price as a loan plus the interest.

In 1997, the Labour government instigated legislation governing the sale and leaseback of films. The legislation is due to be renewed or retired in 2005. In the intervening eight years, hundreds of films have benefited from sale and leaseback.

A typical sale and leaseback transaction involves a seller (usually a production company wishing to refinance a project) and a buyer (usually an individual or a company which has taxable profits sufficient to absorb the tax relief offered). The purchaser then immediately leases the film back to the seller for an annual rental (typically ten to fifteen years).

Benefit to purchaser

Provided that the transaction meets certain government regulations, the purchaser can deduct the entire cost of the acquisition from taxable profits in the year the film was acquired, and in certain cases against profits from prior years. The tax saved in the current year is eventually repaid out of the income from the rental meaning that the purchaser has, in effect, an interest free loan from the Inland Revenue.

Benefit to seller

The seller benefits from the receipt of the purchase price. However, this is not an absolute gain, as the seller must secure the rental payments with a Letter of Credit (LC). In order to secure the LC the purchaser must lodge a large portion of the purchase price in an escrow account from which the bank can guarantee that the seller can pay its rental payments. The interest accrued on this account plus the capital will be sufficient to retire the lease payments owed. The balance of the money (14 to 19%) not required as a security deposit represents the net benefit to the seller (producer).

- ### Main conditions for a sale and leaseback
- The film must be completed after 1 July 1997 and no later than the end
- of the financial year in which the film is acquired
- Production expenditure must not exceed £15 million
- The purchase price must be incurred between 2 July 1997 and 1 July 2005
  The purchaser must carry on business which consists of or includes the
- exploitation of films
  The film must qualify as British (see below)

In Consultation with Dean Goldberg

Dean Goldberg is a UK based financial advisor and director of Park Caledonia. He is a film finance specialist and has raised over £50 million for investment in British films.

In 1997 Gordon Brown introduced tax relief on qualifying British film productions. Investors could treat as revenue expenditure the costs of acquiring a film's rights or the costs of actually producing a film under Section 48 of the Inland Revenue Tax Exemption. By leveraging this properly an investor is able to get a hundred per cent write-off against tax owed.

An investor entering into a business that either acquires completed qualifying British films or that produces qualifying British films can set off any expenditure in the year in which they are delivered, effectively meaning that the person investing the money can write off every single penny against tax.

By gearing these investments through bank borrowing, it is possible for an individual to get a tax cash flow advantage.

A sale and leaseback is a very simple arrangement.

Suppose an investor invests 25p in a qualifying British film. They then arrange for a bank to loan an additional 75p, based on the lease. The film is purchased for 100p. The investor buys the film for 100p. The entire 100p can be written off against tax meaning that the investor gets 40p for an investment of 25p.

The film producer receives 100p of the budget, but must lodge 75p with a bank to guarantee the lease payments to the first bank, typically over a fifteen year term. The interest from this deposit will pay the interest on the loan from the investor with a matching loan arrangement.

After legal, brokerage and banking costs are deducted, the producer receives approximately 19p. Of that 19p, 6p of it is recoupable, the rest of it is clearly soft money and is not recoupable.

The lease payments coming from the guaranteeing bank are regarded as being income in the hands of the film investors. Therefore they have to pay tax on it as they receive it. So over the next fifteen years the 75% is gradually paid back and tax is incurred on that money. The film producer ends up with 19%, of which, as I said, 6% is effectively recoupable.

The other 13% is free money as far as the film producer is concerned. He can either use that as his backing money, as recoupment, or he can use it as production collateral up front for actually getting his movie off the ground in the form of a pre-sale. This 6% is recouped out of the income that comes into the film. The investor will stand in a preferred recoupment position and that preferred recoupment position will be first or first behind any GAP bank.

From the client's perspective they have an investment in a film in which their initial investment is covered, and they have the possibility of additional revenue if the film makes money.

The main benefits are for the producer, who can attract investors into the film by offering a 100% tax write off by creating a trading loss which can be offset against all other income and capital gains going back up to three years.

But there is income tax payable on the lease payments amounting to 30p over fifteen years, assuming he takes no other tax planning advice, no other tax avoidance. In other words, he has to invest that £15,000 and make sure that he actually gets the use of that £15,000 and actually turns that £15,000, over the next fifteen years, into £30,000 to make this thing work. The level of return that you need to get from here to there is called the Hurdle Rate.

The Hurdle Rate is the rate of return required to turn your cash flow advantage into enough money to cover the tax repayments over the next fifteen years.

The Hurdle Rate in this example, with the additional recoupments, is 3.6 per annum, assuming the investor has no other tax planning strategies in place.

As interest rates have come down, the Hurdle Rate has become harder to achieve, meaning that film producers are not getting enough money. In order to maintain the amount of money available to the producer, a higher Hurdle Rate has to be established, meaning that what once was a pure tax deal now has an element of risk. Accordingly, many investors are demanding an equity stake in the film as well.

See below for the definition of a British film.

When an investor is offered equity over and above their tax deal sale and leaseback stake, a new tax product – a production partnership – is created where the tax advantages will only partly offset the investment.

Now, production partnerships are exactly as their name implies, they are partnerships formed for the production of qualifying British films. An investor can get a 100% write off as before. This works in a similar sort of way – it's geared to a sale and leaseback. But in this instance, the client will tend to have to come up with more money and normally speaking you're looking at them having to come up with anywhere between 30–40% of his contribution (rather than the 25% in the example above).

If the tax deal is dropped by the government in proposed legislation in 2005, producers would be much better off concentrating on trying to get their products involved in production partnerships than in sale and leaseback. Sale and leaseback is quick, cheap money but it's just a tax deal. Production partnerships, on the other hand, make use of the tax deal but then hopefully will educate and can show investors that this is a good alternative investment as opposed to just stocks and shares or equities. It's an asset class in its own right. And it's a long-lived asset class as well if you get it right. If you have a good movie, it's always going to be a good movie. A good movie is always going to make money and it's going to continue to make money and it's going to have legs. So it's a completely different way of thinking. Producers need to get their head around it as well.

Now, one thing you might think, is why would a producer do that? I'll give you an example of a film that we've been looking at and the finance structure. This film has basically got 65% of its budget already sourced. And it's already sourced out of pre-sales in Italy and some grant money and some money coming out of some east European countries. They have on the table an offer for a 15% sale and leaseback, which actually gives them 80% funding. They also have an offer on the table of 25% GAP finance. Now, they'd be silly to take that GAP finance when they can do the sale and leaseback. So they could just take 15% on the sale and leaseback and 20% bank GAP.

Right, so this film is 100% funded. All right, we've come along and said to them, 'Right, we're prepared to give you 30% of your budget.' So we come along and we give them 30% of their budget and that's net of costs. 30% net. They've already got their sixty-five, and then in that instance, they only require a 5% bank GAP. The sale and leaseback's now gone. We take the sale and leaseback. So, from their perspective, they're actually better off because they've got rid of 15% of the bank, so it's cheaper up front for them. We're covering their costs. And we're covering their costs out of the sale and leaseback money that we're going to get. We want to recover our 28% of investment. 2% of it can stay from the sale and leaseback. So we'll sit behind the bank and the bank will be in there for five, we're in there for twenty-eight. So if that film only recoups, the first 33% it recoups we're out with our twenty-eight. But we've done a 15% sale and leaseback deal which goes to the partners as recoupment.

So if the film only recoups 33%, we end up with thirty-three. However, we get the sale and leaseback. Let's say the costs involved in this whole deal are actually 6% of the budget. Well, we pay them. That leaves us with 9% of the sale and leaseback. But we've left 2% of the sale and leaseback in the film so that leaves us with 7% of the sale and leaseback. 7% of the sale and leaseback as a percentage of our twenty-eight is actually 25%. So if the film recoups 33%, we, i.e. the partnership, are out with a 25% premium. So from our point of view, it's a good deal for us.

It's a good deal for the producer up front because he's having to put less security up. He's having to give less away to the bank up front. He's having to come up with less up front. Plus, he's got his costs covered. So if he's doing it with bank GAP, and the bank are obviously going to want a premium on this money, and also you've still got to find all your bank financing costs and everything else like that. Well we're saying that with the deal we're doing, it becomes cheap money to you up front.

Now, whereas the bank would be out after 20% and then that's it, they're gone, goodbye, we're obviously not. We come back in after the film has recouped and we want our share of profits. And our share of profits is effectively 20%. The reason being, because we've had 7% out on the sale and leaseback net, then we've actually really only put in twenty-one and that's all we think it would be fair for us to get. But we'd still get our share of profits and we'd want 21% of that.

And that's it, in a nutshell.

The Definition of a British Film

Tax relief for sale and leaseback, as well as grants and other public monies for films produced under co-production treaties, is only available to a British producer if the film qualifies under the Films Act 1985 revised 27 August 1999 Schedule 1. The requirements for a British film relate to three aspects of the film:

- the nationality of the maker
- the percentage of the production cost spent in the UK
- the percentage of labour costs paid to residents of the Commonwealth or the European Economic Area (EEA)

The maker of the film
This is the producer of the film, and the person who makes the key executive decisions about the film. The maker must be incorporated in a member state of the EEA and must operate under the rules of the state. The location of the office is considered to be the location and thus nationality of the producer. Accordingly, the nationality of the producer and the location of the production company is important.

The maker of the film may be incorporated and managed in certain non-EEA countries which have association agreements. These are: Bulgaria, Czech Republic, Estonia, Latvia, Lithuania, Poland, Romania and Slovakia.

UK production spend requirements

At least 70% of the production cost of the film must be spent in the UK. Certain costs are disregarded when calculating total production cost:

- any expenditure incurred on the acquisition or licensing of copyright works other than those created for use in the film
- any expenditure, including interest, incurred for the purposes of raising or servicing finance for making the film
- any business overheads not directly attributable to the film
- any amount which is deducted by the filmmaker when calculating the requisite amount of labour costs which must be spent on qualifying labour (see below)

Hint The figure of 70% relates to the amount of money actually spent in the UK and not to the cost of goods or services supplied from the UK. A producer must track the amount of money spent in the UK and non-UK. For example: If the film is shooting in the UK and the USA, the costs of camera hire, props, wardrobe, sound and lighting equipment are apportioned according to the amount of time spent in the USA. Certain costs are not easily split according to the amount of time spent on them. The script may be written by a UK resident, for example. In this case, the amount of money spent on acquiring the copyright for the script would be apportioned by the amount of time spent filming the project in the UK and the USA.

Labour cost requirement

Labour is treated differently under the labour cost requirement and the United Kingdom production spend requirement. Under the production spend requirement, the cost of labour must be split between UK and non-UK activity in the same way as the other costs of production. Under labour cost requirement, there is no apportionment between UK and non-UK production activity. If the person engaged falls within the definition of qualifying labour, all payments made form part of the production cost.

The requisite amount of labour cost that must be spent on qualifying labour is the lesser of:

- 70% of the total labour costs after deduction (if necessary) of payments made in respect of the labour or services of one person who does not fall within the definition of qualifying labour
- 75% of the total labour cost after deduction of the payments made in respect of the labour or services of two persons who do not fall within

the definition of qualifying labour and at least one of whom is an actor (and is engaged in making the film in no other capacity).

Issues for British Producers Entering Sale and Leaseback

There are two issues that a producer of a co-production must consider carefully before entering into a sale and leaseback.

Firstly, the seller of a film for sale and leaseback must own 100% of the copyright of the film so it can transfer ownership of the film to the purchaser. If the film has been financed under a co-production, the copyright of a co-production is owned jointly by the co-producers. Thus each co-production partner has to assess the tax consequences of agreeing to a UK sale and leaseback. One solution is for each co-production partner to grant to the UK producer a special licence so it can enter into the sale and leaseback agreement. Secondly, the purchaser will wish to be assured that any such assignment or licence by the co-producers will not undermine the official co-production status and therefore the British nature of the film. The purchaser will therefore require a statement to that effect from each of the co-production partners in each territory.

Other Tax Incentives

Various local authorities in Europe and America offer tax incentives for filmmakers to shoot in their locations. Often it is a simple rebate on sales tax spent in a local jurisdiction. Some localities, such as the Isle of Man offer generous inducements to filmmakers. As this is an ever-changing issue, contact local authorities in advance of any shoot, and regularly check for the latest changes.

Deferrals

Deferrals rightly have a nasty reputation about them, in the industry. In the UK, the crew who worked on the highly successful *Four Weddings and a Funeral* have just been paid their deferrals – some ten years after the release of the film. And the *Lock, Stock and Two Smoking Barrels* crew have yet to be paid and never will due to the bankruptcy and litigation problems that are now in the hands of the receivers of the production company.

Deferrals are simple in theory but complex and difficult to implement. Pay someone later out of profits, offering them a financial inducement to wait, possibly paying them a small percentage of their fee up front.

Hint Avoid deferrals where possible.

Equipment and Lab Charge Deferrals

Labs and lighting and camera hire facilities may offer to take a deferral on rentals in certain circumstances. Your success at getting these fees deferred depends on your negotiating and sales ability.

Hint Facilities and services have three prices:

1. The cash on delivery price

2. The 30 day invoice price (usually higher than the cash price)

3. The deferred price (which can be much higher than the cash or invoice price)

Crew Deferrals

A friend of mine produced a low budget feature with deferrals. The film opened to critical acclaim. Late one night, the producer received a call from the DoP who couldn't understand why the deferral was unpaid when the newspaper stated that the film had taken half a million at the box office!

Often a producer will negotiate a high weekly salary for a cameraperson and then offer a tenth of the salary in cash, and the balance on a deferral. The upside is the producer can claim a higher budget which might benefit if the film is to be sold under certain tax schemes. But most often, the producer simply has the egoist desire to feel the sound of large numbers rushing through their lips. Far better to negotiate a fixed fee, no matter how low, and then pay it. Deferrals have a habit of haunting the producer months and years after the project is completed and released.

Talent Deferrals

Talent deferrals are common in the studio system, but they also have a place in the independent filmmaking world.

Suppose an actor normally charges £500,000 ($750,000) per picture. You offer him 10% of his normal fee, £50,000 ($75,000). The actor is looking to recoup the balance of their fee from the proceeds earned by the film.

There are two main ways to do this. Firstly, to give the actor a deferral of 90% by specifying that it will be paid from the proceeds of the film (assuming the film makes enough money) and secondly, is to give the actor a 'first dollar gross deal'.

First dollar gross deals

This deferral is structured like this: you make a 10% down payment, with the balance of the actor's payment secured by 10% of the gross from the first dollar. Once you have paid the actor the 10%down payment, you do not have to pay the actor anything else until the 90% is also paid – from the first proceeds of the film.

Thereafter, you must pay the actor a 10% bonus for everything that is earned by the film.

Assume a contract with an actor for £1 million. You make the advance payment of 10% (£100,000) and now you owe them £900,000. The film grosses its first £900,000, and straight away you pay this to the actor. Now you owe them nothing. Happily the film earns another £1 million at the box office. This time you get paid. But you only get £900,000 because you have agreed a 10% bonus to the talent for any profit the film makes, so you hand over another £100,000.

Gross participations and deferrals are difficult to negotiate. Often other producing partners and investors will not agree to giving the actor priority – as they too would like to be paid first.

Hint Talent deferrals are an essential element of independent filmmaking today and often is the only way that top directors and actors can be attracted to a project.

Producer Deferrals

In many an independent film production, the producer gets no money whatsoever until the film is in profit.

Producer fee deferrals work the same way as talent deferrals with the important exception that the producer never gets paid until everyone else has recouped.

Hint Some producers defer part of their fee and treat it as part of the contingency budget.

Other Sources of Funding

Soundtrack Album

It is a myth that soundtrack albums generate substantial income. In Hollywood the strategy is to get an advance against soundtrack royalties from a record company and use this cash to bump up the music budget. To get a substantial soundtrack advance you need either class A artists performing on the album or a major US/European distribution deal, or both. However, every year some independent filmmaker succeeds in making a film, usually with up and coming rappers, and secures financing for the film from the record companies or from the artists themselves.

Music Publishing

Music rights pre-sales will generate thousands, not hundreds of thousands

European producers can often relinquish all rights to their film music in exchange for cash and the rights to use the soundtrack in the film. Music pre-sales are almost unheard of in the US, because that, unlike in Europe, music publishers and record companies are separate entities.

Gaming Rights

If your project has the right kind of story, you may be able to sell the gaming rights for a substantial sum. This is usually difficult for independent films, but not unheard of.

Product Placement

Product placement is a deal whereby a manufacturer gives free product, or even pays for the privilege of having its product in a film.

Studio pictures with their accompanying huge marketing budgets, can raise substantial money from product placement, which the manufacturers are willing to pay, safe in the knowledge that their products will reach a large audience. With an independent film, you are more likely to get free product only.

The deal making process will boil down to a simple agreement detailing what products the company is giving/lending you, and your responsibilities to display the product for several time-specific intervals in the film.

Strategies for Raising Finance

There are a host of ways to finance your film. Successful producers seem to be able to blend and mix various financial elements together and when things are looking bleak, they somehow solve financial black holes using their resourcefulness and creativity.

Hint Over a thousand independent films get financed and made every year in English speaking territories. There is no reason why your film will not be one of these. You will not finance your film until you totally believe in it.

Summary

1. Money can be found everywhere – learn where to look for it.

2. Government tax structures change constantly. Seek advice.

3. Make sure the budget you raise suits the story you are trying to tell.

Knowledge is power. Information gives you knowledge. Turn the page for resources to kick-start your career.

Seven Essential Steps for Becoming Rich and Famous by Making a Low Budget Film

Step 7 Talent

If you don't have talent, you can still make it in the film industry. There are many filmmakers and film producers who are very good at the other six essentials skills for becoming rich and famous in the film industry, but who have little or no talent.

- They are good at raising money
- They know how to identify a great script
- They have excellent interpersonal communication skills
- They understand the principles of business and marketing
- They have unlimited resources of energy
- They know their limitations and resolutely know how to say no

But talent is not one of their fortes, and they still make hugely rewarding careers as filmmakers.

What does the film industry really call talent? And what do they mean by 'a talented newcomer'?

Essentially it is someone who can take a stage play, add a few cheaply produced elements that give it a cinematic feel, and from a stage play create cinema. That is what the industry calls talent. If you can do that you will earn a sinfully decadent amount of money, and from the industry executive's point of view, you will be worth every penny.

And if you really think about it, to take a limited budget, and go into production with a small shooting ratio like 4:1 or 5:1, with a limited crew over a short period of time, and make sure the script is good, and then add the editing, post-production, sound and music to the process does take talent.

If you can combine steps one to six with talent, then you truly are an amazing filmmaker, and even I believe you are worth every penny and every second of the outrageously huge amounts of fortune and publicity you will earn.

25

Resources

Pre-Production

Nextwave
Nextwave was a production branch of IFC before it closed in 2001. The website is still up and running and features case studies of some of the most successful low budget films like *El Mariachi* and *Clerks*.
www.nextwavefilms.com

Infinite Monkeys
A personal webpage that contains an impressive amount of information on film financing, particularly in the UK. The author explains key terms, demystifies the structure of the industry, and offers information on grants and financiers.
www.ironworks.demon.co.uk

Film People
Has an excellent indie producer's guide which lays out the options for financing and gives tips on keeping budgets low.
www.film-people.net

Indie Films
Online network to help filmmakers find investors, grants, funds, and distributors. There's a fee for membership, but has thousands of contacts.
www.indiefilms.com

UK Film Council
Established by the government in 2000 the UK Film Council is committed to fostering a competitive and vibrant film industry in the UK and has £20 million to allocate in training, production, and development funds annually. This website contains all the details on getting a piece of the pie for your production.
www.ukfilmcouncil.org.uk

Morrie Warshawski Consultancy
An excellent bibliography with many links to resources and publications

about fundraising as well as to funding sources compiled by fundraising consultant Morrie Warshawski.
www.warshawski.com

Writing Treatments
Explains in simple terms how to write a treatment with several examples from major films.
www.writingtreatments.com

DV Handbook
Features a series of essays outlining the basics of writing, developing, purchasing, protecting, and breaking down a script.
www.dvhandbook.com

Writers Guild of America
A series of colourful essays which target specific issues in writing and developing scripts.
www.wga.org/craft

Wordplay
Many excellent essays by industry professionals about various elements of screenwriting and the screenwriting trade.
www.wordplayer.com

Done Deal
All inclusive resources for the screenwriter: contacts for production companies, agencies, managers and lawyers; information on contests; examples of all necessary documents; and latest news in script sales.
www.scriptsales.com

Simply Scripts
The best way to write better screenplays is to read the ones that work. This website provides thousands of classic and contemporary film and TV scripts a mouseclick away.
www.simplyscripts.com

Script Shop
Provides reading and story consultancy for reasonable fees and offers the possibility of showcasing your polished script on the website for producers to buy.
www.scriptshop.com

Production

Pre-production Studio
Small site with downloadable pre-production documents.
www.preproduction-studio-advice.com

The Columbus Film Consortium

Offers word and pdf templates for essential production paperwork. The site includes forms including location releases, call sheets, set safety and insurance paperwork, as well as other writer, actor, and director specific paperwork.

www.thecfc.org

Arri Crew

From clapper loaders to steadicam operators, this website offers profiles, references, and CVs of thousands of crew members for hire.

www.arricrew.org

KFTV

An invaluable portal for searching out full crews or specialised technicians with the right experience across the entire globe.

www.kftv.com

Movie Services Guide

Features an impressive cache of contact information for companies and individuals that specialise in anything that you might not. Including wardrobe, special effects, make-up, and more.

www.movieservicesguide.com

Crew List

This site provides a searchable database of crew member CVs with direct email contact between client and professional. The search can be specifically categorised by skill, location, title, etc.

www.crew-list.com

Video University

Articles on how to improve DIY no-budget production from building your own steadicam to making video look more like film.

www.videouniversity.com

DV Central

Features the lowdown on all products DV. Specs, product reviews, and explanations for the not-so-savvy.

www.dvcentral.org

Cinematography

Resouces and information on handling film, plus a directory of crews.

www.cinematography.com

HD

Highly detailed guides to High Definition digital video production. Comprehensive technical information unlocking the mysteries of the world of DV and HD. Also includes equipment specifications and a directory of rental services.

www.hd-cinema.com

Location Sound
Maintained by a Californian sound production company, this website lots of the information on how to record location sound yourself. Tips on mic selection and placement for in the field shooting.
www.locationsound.com/proaudio/ls/techtips.html

Zero Budget Films
Guides, articles, and clips with a specific emphasis on DV tools, electronic cinematography, and comprehensive digital cinema information.
www.zerobudgetfilms.com/

DV Creators
Brilliant guide to making a film in DV. Advice on preproduction, production, post-production, and delivery. Includes offers on various software and DV products.
www.dvcreators.net

DV Links
Links galore to infomation and resources on all aspects of technical DV making. Includes reviews and comparisons on DV products.
www.adamwilt.com/DV.html

DV
Hub for news, reviews, and features on DV cameras, hardware, software, and all other things digital. Features articles on current artists doing significant work with DV and a community forum for tips and discussion on indie filmmaking.
www.dv.com

Post-production

Hardware Central
Step-by-step explanations of the technology required to effectively edit professionally on a desktop system.
www.hardwarecentral.com

Creative Mac
Specifically oriented towards those using Final Cut and After Effects, this website offers tips and tutorials to make the editing process faster and more sucessful.
www. creativemac.com

Computer Video
Website of a magazine by the same name offers reviews of new and classic desktop editing programs and a wealth of basic information that will help you turn your computer into a fully equipped editing suite.
www.computervideo.net

Evan Evans
Website of the famous composer Evan Evans contains a how to section focusing on film scoring theory and creative devices.
www.evanevans.org/filmscoring101.asp

Shop JT3
Articles and how tos on the technical side of scoring. Information on makes and models of recording equipment, synths, and midi devices.
www.shopjt3.com

Film Festival

Withoutabox
New international exchange that makes the process of submitting work to film festivals easy and efficient for filmmakers. Includes extensive information on film festivals around the world.
www.withoutabox.com

Film Festivals
International film festival site with links to submit. Information and news on film festivals and festival films, and links to watch festival films online.
www.filmfestivals.com

Movie Maker
Extensive database of links to information on film festivals.
www.moviemaker.com/festivals.html

Exposure
Listings of festivals, awards, and grants.
www.exposure.co.uk

Publicity

Fair Investment
Contains links to various PR companies in the UK.
www.fairinvestment.co.uk/compare.aspx/Public_Relations/

101 Public Relations
Comprehensive and highly informative PR site with links to resources which advise filmmakers of the dos and don'ts of public relations.
www.101PublicRelations.com/homeb.html

Indie Films
Short but very helpful advice on publicising independent films.
www.indiefilms.com/bag/pub.htm

General

So You Wanna...
Overview tips from pre- to post-production on a low-budget film project.
www.soyouwanna.com/site/syws/makemovie/makemovie.html

Web Film School
Part of Dov S-S Simens website for his renowned teaching methods which provide a crash course for writing, producing, and directing independent feature films. The resources section of his web film school site contains an exhaustive list of industry specific links from A to Z.
www.webfilmschool.com

Indiewire
Unbeatable source for news, buzz, and gossip on independent productions, festivals, and personalities. The site also contains a variety of well-kept message boards which harbour a community atmosphere and key contact information for companies you won't find anywhere else.
www.indiewire.com

Filmmaking.net
Large site that contains links for various aspects of the UK film industry from production information to film festivals to film reviews.
www.filmmaking.net

Filmmaking.com
An attractive site containing an abundance of great information on a mammoth scale of filmmaking topics.
www.filmmaking.com

Film Underground
Dedicated to helping independent filmmakers do what they love by offering links and information on current projects that are underway and on fellow filmmakers in your area.
www.filmunderground.com/

Indie Talk
Online community for independent filmmakers with a forum for communication, free ad posting, and a screening room to post your film for discussion and feedback. The discussion board is also browseable, providing a substantial resource for general filmmaking information.
www.indietalk.com

Shooting People
Massive newsgroup site that provides up-to-date bulletins to filmmakers regarding production, screenwriting, casting, animation, documentary filmmaking, and much more. The subscriber community is over 30,000 strong.
www.shootingpeople.org

Appendix 1: High Definition

In Conversation with Guy Moore

What is HD?

Guy Moore works for film and HD equipment hire specialists VMI. See www.vmi.co.uk

HD is the latest greatest digital format on the market! It's significantly better than the DigiBeta and with 11 stops of latitude (compared to 7 for DigiBeta) and compares easily to film in terms of look, latitude and picture quality. In fact, according to world class cinematographer James Cameron (*Ghosts of the Abyss*, *Titanic*), HDCAM is actually better than 35mm and in his opinion compares with 70mm. For the incredible quality, it is also fantastically good value with full production kits available from around £2,500 per week which avoids the prohibitive stock and processing cost of film. The BBC Modernisation Department conducted independent research and found that shooting on the HDW-750P Camcorder represented a cost saving of more than 30% compared with film. Comparisons are always dodgy but shooting HD can save you heaps compared with film whilst keeping the same high production values.

How would you define its characteristics?

HD offers very sharp picture quality (five times the resolution of DigiBeta), film gamma (the colour treatment of the camera makes it look like different film stocks), can have the shuttered look of film (25P) or have a TV look and can operate in extraordinarily low light levels. You have to bear in mind that it's not film, it is a format all of its own. I would recommend very strongly anyone using it to use crew familiar with the format or to receive training on using it prior to the shoot. In doing so, you can be assured of achieving the look that you want, because it does, in many ways, confound many traditional filmmaking values and you can shoot pretty much in the middle of the night and end up with a very good product.

In what ways does it confound traditional values?

You can shoot HD programmes and see the end result without having to wait for processing. Although you should still use the same level of crew as with film to ensure great images, you can also shoot HD with very compact kits. Finally you can save so much money on production, that the producer can now spend more money in front of the lens, which after all makes good programmes. Film still does have a very valid place in the market and is still better for high speed slo-mo work but HD is giving cinematographers a real alternative which can make their budgets go further.

Is the process of shooting on HD similar to shooting on film?

You need to look at an HD crew as you would for film. There are different approaches to lighting – you can get away with much, much less light. I'm not saying you should always work with low light but you can do things with HD that you can't on film. However, in spite of the lower lighting needs, I would still recommend a gaffer on a film set. You will need to use a DoP who is familiar with the format. You are going to have real problems if you think 'I can use film therefore I can use HD, and off I go' – make sure that you understand the format fully before you start shooting. Finally, go and test with a camera. You will get a much sharper image than you will with film and there are certain techniques you will need to be aware of in order to get the best out of it. You may well find yourself having to soften the image. If someone 30ft away steps away, they will be out of focus – and there are ways of dealing with that. It is strongly recommended that you use a damn good monitor because the picture quality is so sharp that if you want to be using that sharpness of image and maintain consistency in your end product, a traditional video nine inch monitor can let you down sometimes – a finger print on the lens will show up crystal clear.

What type of filmmaking is HD not good for?

High speed photography. The cameras on the market at the moment that can take high speed shots do not operate quite with the resolution that other HD cameras do. Sony are making some really good bits of kit now, but in terms of frame rate, you have got to go to some of the other HD formats from the other manufacturers – Panasonic Vari-cam shoots at a high frame rate, but it's another form of HD, it's only got half the resolution of the Sony.

Can you explain the difference between 50i and 24/25P?

It's the way the camera actually scans the picture. Interlaced mode actually takes two shots of half the picture, side to side, whereas progressive scan takes the picture top to bottom and gives the effect of a 'shutter' on a film camera. It's simply the way the camera views and plays back the images. Basically, in the European world of PAL, you have only one decision to make, whether to make your programme look like film – in which case you shoot at 25P mode, or whether to make your programme look like TV in which case you should shoot at 50i – editing systems for off-line are all fully compatible and if you want to shoot it for TV – even your normal on-line facility is compatible – all you need is an HD deck with SD (standard definition) output and you can edit all footage without hassle whether it is shot at 50i for a TV look or at 25P for a film look.

Is 'progressive scan' (25P) a convincing alternative to film?

HD is different to film and it always will be – it's visibly different; you get a sharper image, you get none of the grain you get in film. Shooting in progressive scan mode will give the same 'shuttered' effect as film as the camera shoots the same number of images as film with the same shutter speeds so it has to look the same.

Can HD match the various textures of different film stocks?

With film you have a choice of using lots of different sorts of film stock, with HD, you programme the look to match equivalent film stock types or create a unique one of your own. You have so much control over your look on HD, that the possibilities if you have an experienced DP or engineer are virtually endless.

Can you tell me what the differences between frame rates are?

There is 50i, 25P, 30P, 24P, 60i with 1080 vertical lines, 720 lines and several flavours using combinations of these – although there are some seventeen or more flavours of these, in reality for UK production you have only the one decision to make – to shoot at 25P for a film look, or 50i for a TV look. There is little justification for shooting at 24P unless you have serious budget (£6 million plus) as editing is all the more expensive.

The audio pitch change for shooting at 25fps and slowing down to 24fps (4.13%) can be corrected digitally and the programme converted to 30P using a procedure known as 3:2 pull-down without compromise. In fact this process is so good, that Discovery HD showcased the Oil Rig Programme (Pioneer Productions) on a Discovery HD event and showed the HD pictures as an example of the kind of programme to produce. In fact, this programme was shot at 25P and later converted to 30P and nobody ever noticed because you can't see the difference!

What is this new interface for transferring signals, HD SDI?

HD SDI is a new protocol of signal which carries more than five times the data to SDI. It uses a conventional BNC cable and is used to transfer uncompressed HD footage from deck to deck etc.

Do you lose quality if you transfer to SD?

Yes, DigiBeta is five times lower quality than HD, but the performance of the cameras is better, so the overall pictures look nicer. However editing on DigiBeta does not preclude you from re-conforming your programme in HD at a later date with all that lovely quality!

HD costs less. Why?

Significantly less. You are saving simply on the cost of your film stock and your film transfer – a very expensive process. And also you are saving on the turnaround time, you can just get straight on with things. This takes into account the more expensive rental costs of hiring HD kits instead of film kits.

How important are lenses when using HD?

Lenses in HD are supremely important – in the film world, DoPs are used to using primes and primes do exist in the HD world though they are supremely expensive. 35mm lenses can be converted using a Pro35 adapter, though images are prone to flare. In the video world, DoPs are quite used to using zooms and both Canon and Fuji make good HD zooms which have far better image quality and lack of focus zoom (zoom effect whilst focusing) than conventional zooms. Conventional broadcast zooms can be used with HD cameras but these tend to have three times the zoom effect whilst focusing (focus zoom) than HD lenses. Also the barrel distortion and chromatic aberrations are vastly improved on HD lenses.

SD lenses can be used very successfully on HD – our first HD feature used SD lenses and the results were stunning but HD lenses will always improve the overall result. Best of all are the Panavision lenses but at £80,000 each, they are also supremely expensive and are so large and heavy that they also create back focus problems with the HDW-750P HDCAM camcorders. A mount to fit large lenses onto the lightweight bars is currently in development and should help with this problem. Our experience is that once DoPs and directors have used the Canon HD lenses which we supply as standard with our HD kits, they are very happy with the performance and generally do not hire additional primes for their productions.

What are the considerations you must take when editing HD format ?

HD editing is significantly more expensive than SD editing – normally at least twice as much to reflect the higher purchase cost; £300 an hour is a fairly good estimate of edit rate to budget for. There is a bit of a fight going on in the media world as to which format is going to have supremacy with Quantel, Sony and AVID having HD post solutions. If you can stretch your budget to edit HD, then not only will you future-proof your programme but you can also increase the international marketability too. Foreign stations are much more likely to buy your programme if it is HD mastered than on DigiBeta and this is a trend set to continue in the future.

So what would you say are the disadvantages of HD?

A lot of filmmakers aren't familiar with it yet. Technically speaking, it is still a growing world. You can achieve the same look as lots of available film stocks, but it takes preparation time and the right crew and at the moment, many experienced cinematographers are still quite suspicious of it. High speed photography is a problem and high speed film photography for slo-mo beats HD hands down.

Appendix 2: Film Festivals

Major Festivals

Cannes Film Festival
3 rue Amélie
75007 Paris France
Tel +33 1 53 59 61 71
Fax +33 1 53 59 61 70
www.festival-cannes.org

Internationale Filmfestspiele Berlin
Potsdamer Strasse 5
D-10785 Berlin
Tel +49 30 25 920 +ext.
Fax +49 30 25 920 299
info@berlinale.de
www.berlinale.de

International Film Festival Rotterdam
PO Box 21696
3001 AR Rotterdam
The Netherlands
T +31 10 8909090
F +31 10 8909091
tiger@filmfestivalrotterdam.com
www.filmfestivalrotterdam.com

Karlovy Vary Film Festival
Film Servis Festival, a.s.
Panska 1
110 00 Praha 1
Czech Republic
Tel +420 2 24 23 54 12
Fax +420 2 24 23 34 08
festival@kviff.com
www.iffkv.cz

Sundance Film Festival
PO Box 3630
84101 Salt Lake City
Utah United States
Tel +1 801 328 3456
Fax +1 801 575 5175
www.sundance.org

Toronto International Film Festival
2 Carlton Street
Suite 1600
M5B 1J3 Toronto, Ontario
Canada
Tel +1 416-967-7371
Fax +1 416-967-9477

Telluride Film Festival
National Film Preserve, Ltd
379 State Street Number 3
Portsmouth, New Hampshire 03801
Tel +603 433 9202
Fax +603 433 9206
tellufilm@aol.com
www.telluridefilmfestival.com

Venice International Film Festival
Ca' Giustinian, San Marco 1364/A
30124 Venice, Italy
Tel +39 41 521 8711
Fax +39 41 522 7539

Mini-Major Film Festivals

Los Angeles International Film Festival
6712 Hollywood Blvd (Egyptian Theatre)
Hollywood, California 90028
Tel +1 323 856 7707
Fax +1 323 462 4049
afifest@afionline.org
www.afifest.com

Montreal Film Festival
1432, de Bleury Street
Montreal, Quebec, Canada, H3A 2J1
Tel +1 514 848 3883
Fax +1 514 848 3886
info@ffm-montreal.org

Palm Springs

1700 E.Tahquitz Canyon Way, Suite 3
Palm Springs, California 92262
Tel +760 322 2930
Fax +760 322 4087
info@psfilmfest.org

Raindance Film Festival

81 Berwick Street
London W1F 8TW
Tel +44 20 7287 3833
Fax +44 20 7438 2243
info@raindance.co.uk
www.raindance.co.uk

San Fransisco International Film Festival

39 Mesa Street, Suite 110
The Presidio
San Francisco, CA 94129
Tel +1 415 561 5000
Fax +1 415 561 5099
info@sffs.org

Slamdance Film Festival

5634 Melrose Avenue
Los Angeles, California 90068
Tel +1 323 466 1786
Fax +1 323 466 1784
mail@slamdance.com
www.slamdance.com

Tribeca Film Festival

www.tribecafilmfestival.org

Horror Film Festivals

Film Threat

5042 Wilshire Blvd P.M.B. 1500
Los Angeles, CA 90036 USA
Tel +1 818 248 4549
Fax +1 818 248 4533

Screamfest

13547 Ventura Blvd, #420
Sherman Oaks, CA 91423
Tel +1 323 656 4727
screamfestla@aol.com

Documentary Film Festivals

Festival Dei Popoli
fespopol@dada.it
www.festivalpopoli.org

Hot Docs
www.hotdocs.ca

New York International Documentary Festival
www.docfest.org

Sheffield International Documentary Festival
shefdoc@fdgroup.co.uk
www.sidf.co.uk

Yamagata
yidff@bekkoame.or.jp
www.city.yamagata.yamagata.jp/yidff/en/home.html

Underground Film Festivals

Chicago Underground Film Festival
info@cuff.org
www.cuff.org

New York Underground Film Festival
festival@nyuff.com
www.nyuff.com

Short Film Festivals

Brief Encounters
festival@brief-encounters.org.uk
www.brief-encounters.org.uk

Tampere Film Festival
office@tamperefilmfestival.fi
www.tamperefilmfestival.fi

Toronto
shortfilmfest@cdnfilmcentre.com
www.worldwideshortfest.com

Index

Join Raindance

Join Now and Receive

A subscription to Raindance Film Magazine, the quarterly journal for independent filmmakers, with interviews, features, tutorials and guest feature writers

Discounts and exclusive member offers on all film training courses

Reductions at Offstage Books in Camden and special offers on selected products at the Screenwriter's Store

Priority booking for the Raindance Film Festival

Concessionary tickets at the Genesis Mile End and the Everyman Hampstead

Reduced price tickets to the British Independent Film Awards

Free pass to Live!Ammunition!, the legendary pitching panel

Filmmaker services including script registration, reader's reports and script consultancy

Membership rates
UK £25 / Europe £35 / Rest of World £50 [cheques UK sterling only]

Detach the form and mail to
Raindance Film Festival Ltd
81 Berwick Street
London W1F 8TW

I enclose a cheque payable to 'Raindance Film Festival Ltd' for / charge my credit card the sum of £ _____

Mastercard ☐   Visa ☐   Switch ☐

Card No ☐☐☐☐☐☐☐☐☐☐☐☐☐☐   Exp Date ☐☐ / ☐☐

Issue No ☐☐ [Switch only]   Valid from ☐☐ / ☐☐ [Switch only]

Signature _____   Date _____

VAT REG NO 795 4763 70

About Raindance

Raindance was established in 1992 by filmmakers seeking to provide information and advice to the then struggling British independent film community. Dedicated to fostering and promoting independent film in both the UK and around the world, Raindance is unique, combining film training courses with the UK's only truly independent film festival, specialising in first time filmmakers.

Raindance film courses have launched the careers of many writers, directors and producers. We provide courses in writing, directing, producing and all aspects of filmmaking, attended by the likes of Matthew Vaughn (producer, *Lock, Stock and Two Smoking Barrels, Snatch*; director, *Layer Cake*), Stel Pavlou (writer, *51st State*), Christopher Nolan (director, *Memento*) and taught by respected professionals such as Mike Figgis, Roger Corman, William C. Martell, John Truby and Christopher Vogler.

The Raindance Film Festival was founded in 1993 to provide a public platform for independent filmmakers, allowing them to reach the many international sales agents in London at the time of the festival. Last year more than 9000 independent film lovers saw over 100 features and 200 shorts.

Raindance Feedback

Your comments are important to us. If you read and enjoyed this book, Raindance offers you the chance to participate in spreading the word!

Simply post a review to any website, like Amazon or Barnes and Noble and when the review appears we will send you a copy of the Raindance Film Festival Shorts DVD. We compile a DVD every year of the best shorts from the festival, so we'll send you the most recent edition. We normally sell these for £15 ($23).

How to Claim Your Free DVD

To prove that you have written a review that has been published on the Internet or in print, send a link to the page where your review appears or a cutting to info@raindance.co.uk or to 81 Berwick Street, London W1F 8TW along with your street address and we will send your free gift. We won't use your details for any other purpose.

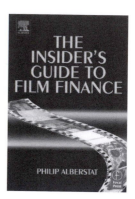